A Practical Guide to

VAT

for Charities and Voluntary Organisations

**Kate Sayer and
Alastair Hardman**

3rd edition

DIRECTORY OF SOCIAL CHANGE

Published by
Directory of Social Change
24 Stephenson Way
London NW1 2DP
Tel: 08450 77 77 07; Fax: 020 7391 4804
email: publications@dsc.org.uk
www.dsc.org.uk
from whom further copies and a full publications catalogue are available.

In association with Sayer Vincent
8 Angel Gate, City Road, London EC1V 2SJ Tel: 020 7841 6360
email: svinfo@sayervincent.co.uk
www.sayervincent.co.uk

Directory of Social Change Northern Office
Federation House, Hope Street, Liverpool L1 9BW
Policy & Research 0151 708 0136; email: research@dsc.org.uk

Directory of Social Change is a Registered Charity no. 800517

First published 1998
Second edition 2002
Third edition 2008
Reprinted 2011

ISBN 978 1 903991 91 6

British Library Cataloguing in Publication Data
A catalogue record for this book is available from the British Library

Cover design by Kate Bass
Text design by Kate Bass
Typeset by Keystroke, Wolverhampton
Printed and bound by CPI Group (UK) Ltd, Croydon, CRO 4YY

The information and commentary in this publication cover the law up to 31 March 2008 and is intended as guidance only, and is not a full or definitive statement of the law. Reasonable efforts have been made to ensure that the information and commentary is accurate at the time of going to press, but no responsibility for its accuracy and correctness, or for any consequences of relying on it, is assumed by the Directory of Social Change or the authors. The information and commentary do not, and are not intended to, amount to legal advice to any person or organisation on a specific case or matter and are not intended as a substitute for professional advice.

FSC
www.fsc.org
MIX
Paper from
responsible sources
FSC® C013604

Contents

Acknowledgements

The genesis of this book goes back a long way – to simple one-day courses at the Directory of Social Change that sought to explain VAT to charity staff and trustees. Based on those courses, Kate wrote the first edition of *A Practical Guide to VAT for Charities* in response to a huge demand for something that would simplify VAT for charities.

This is the third edition and a lot has changed in the meantime. VAT has become a significant issue for charities – mainly due to the additional cost burden it represents. So we have completely re-written the book and expanded the contents considerably to reflect the wide variety of activities undertaken by charities.

So we had a bigger team working on the content, but need to acknowledge the huge contribution by Helen Elliott who read, contributed and re-read every word of this book. She also contributed lots of ideas on how charities can manage their affairs better to cope with VAT and take advantage of the rules where possible. Her practical knowledge of doing this day to day helped both authors a great deal.

We are grateful to the Directory of Social Change for its support and patience, needed more than ever for this edition, as trying to make sure this was as up to date as possible was more difficult than ever.

About the authors

Kate Sayer is a partner with Sayer Vincent and has been working with charities for more than 25 years. She advises them on a range of finance, tax, governance and management issues, as well as auditing them. Her work involves consultancy and training in the largest charities as well as support for new and much smaller charities and social enterprises.

She is a member of the SORP Committee, established by the Charity Commission to review the charity SORP. She regularly leads seminars and writes articles on accounting and VAT, as well as other topics. A new edition of *A Practical Guide to Financial Management by Charities* was published recently, and *A Practical Guide to Charity Accounting* is forthcoming.

She participates in consultations and working parties on issues affecting the sector and is actively involved in Charity Finance Directors' Group and Charity Tax Group trying to get a better deal for charities on VAT.

Alastair Hardman writes about and advises on charity taxation and accounting. Previously Alastair worked in the voluntary sector and then for Sayer Vincent. Alastair is now an independent consultant and Sayer Vincent associate based in Cornwall.

Sayer Vincent is a specialist firm of consultants and auditors for the charity sector. With five partners and over 35 professional staff we are one of the largest teams of charity specialists. Our work focuses on making charities more effective through improved infrastructure, reporting and governance. We help charities with mergers, systems implementations and training. Charities appoint us as consultants, internal auditors or external auditors. Sayer Vincent also undertakes practical research to enhance the efficiency and effectiveness of not-for-profit organisations, for example through the Adaptive Performance Management Forum.

www.sayervincent.co.uk
svinfo@sayervincent.co.uk

About the Directory of Social Change

DSC has a vision of an independent voluntary sector at the heart of social change. The activities of independent charities, voluntary organisations and community groups are fundamental to achieve social change. We exist to help these organisations and the people who support them to achieve their goals.

We do this by:

- providing practical tools that organisations and activists need, including online and printed publications, training courses, and conferences on a huge range of topics

- acting as a 'concerned citizen' in public policy debates, often on behalf of smaller charities, voluntary organisations and community groups

- leading campaigns and stimulating debate on key policy issues that affect those groups

- carrying out research and providing information to influence policymakers.

DSC is the leading provider of information and training for the voluntary sector and publishes an extensive range of guides and handbooks covering subjects such as fundraising, management, communication, finance and law. We have a range of subscription-based websites containing a wealth of information on funding from trusts, companies and government sources. We run more than 300 training courses each year, including bespoke in-house training provided at the client's location. DSC conferences, many of which run on an annual basis, include the Charity Management Conference, the Charity Accountants' Conference and the Charity Law Conference. DSC's major annual event is Charityfair, which provides low-cost training on a wide variety of subjects.

For details of all our activities, and to order publications and book courses, go to www.dsc.org.uk, call 08450 777707 or email publications@dsc.org.uk

Introduction

This is the third edition of *A Practical Guide to VAT*. It has been updated to cover changes in VAT law and case law developments to the end of March 2008.

The book is specifically targeted at the VAT needs of voluntary organisations, that is: non-profit making entities such as charities, registered social landlords, tenant management organisations, campaign groups, voluntary clubs and associations. Some voluntary organisations have commercial arms such as trading subsidiaries, so the book also covers topics of relevance to these.

It is a fairly common misconception that VAT does not apply to charities and other voluntary organisations. This is not the case. There are some specific VAT rules for voluntary organisations and in particular for charities. Many activities of voluntary organisations will also be excluded from the VAT regime because they are 'non-business' or 'exempt'. However, this does not mean that all activities of voluntary organisations and charities are invariably excluded. As a very rough rule of thumb, if your organisation undertakes an activity that is also undertaken by a commercial business, and that commercial business charges VAT, your activity will be subject to VAT.

There are three key points you should bear in mind when dealing with VAT:

- You do not have to be registered for VAT to benefit from some of the VAT rules. Charities in particular are able to tell suppliers to 'zero rate' or add no VAT when making some types of supplies to the charity. This includes, in certain situations, the construction of a new building and the renovation of a building, so the VAT savings can be very significant. The special zero-rating rules are covered in Chapters 6 and 8.

- You should be aware of the fact that VAT guidance provided by HM Revenue & Customs (HMRC) is not the same as the law. VAT notices and leaflets are HMRC's interpretation of the law. Some published guidance may be out of date, wrong or just sets out HMRC's view of an uncertain situation. So you should not necessarily be put off by some of the guidance, but be prepared to seek further advice on the legal position. Some of the key risk areas for multiple interpretations of the law are highlighted in this book.

- VAT law is subject to constant change. New VAT laws are passed all the time and court cases regularly change long-established interpretations of the legislation or introduce new twists. This book explains the position as commonly understood in January 2008. You should always check to see if new VAT laws or court cases have changed that position since then. See Chapter 14: *Further information* for how to check for changes.

Background: VAT and the voluntary sector

VAT is a relatively new tax. It was first introduced in France in 1954 and was adopted as an EC-wide measure in 1972. The UK was required to implement VAT on joining the EC in 1973 and in 1993 the EC implemented legislation requiring harmonisation of the VAT rules in the different member states. This effectively gave the EC control over each member state's legislation.

As VAT is a young tax, there are many grey areas where the position still has to be ironed out or where further legislation is required in order to bring clarity. Two of these grey areas are of major importance to many voluntary organisations:

- VAT is designed to cover the activities of businesses but not the personal activities of individuals. However, the distinction between 'business' and 'non-business' activities can be unclear. Many activities of voluntary organisations sit in the grey area between the two.

- VAT law specifies that certain activities carried out in the public interest are 'exempt' from VAT. Many activities of voluntary organisations are carried out in the public interest and are potentially exempt. However, the distinction between what is exempt and what is not is again unclear and this uncertainty affects many voluntary organisations.

VAT is also an administratively burdensome tax. VAT-registered organisations have to issue invoices in the correct format, keep copies of VAT invoices received, monitor VAT charged and VAT paid on a transaction-by-transaction basis and submit VAT returns and pay any VAT due to HMRC within tight deadlines.

All VAT-registered organisations face these administrative burdens. However, many voluntary organisations have to deal with extra administrative burdens. Most commercial businesses simply charge VAT on everything they sell and reclaim all the VAT on the purchases they make. For many voluntary organisations the situation is not so straightforward. If there is a mix of non-business, exempt and normal 'taxable' activities, the VAT on purchases must be split. Only the VAT that is 'attributable' to the taxable activities can be reclaimed from HMRC. This splitting of the VAT on purchases can be a real challenge and may add considerably to the administrative burden.

Voluntary organisations are not the only ones that have to deal with these grey areas and extra administrative burdens. For example, most insurance companies and banks have a mix of taxable and exempt activities. However, they are usually large and can afford to employ VAT specialists to deal with these issues. Most voluntary organisations are not in such a fortunate position and cannot afford the high salaries that VAT specialists command. A few may be lucky and have a trustee or management committee member with VAT expertise, but most will not.

This is where this guide is useful. It is targeted at the voluntary sector and aims to provide a comprehensive first point of reference for most of the VAT queries that will arise in voluntary-sector organisations.

Layout of the book

The first three chapters provide an overview of VAT for people new to the subject and also serve as a general introduction to the VAT issues affecting voluntary organisations:

- **Chapter 1 – Overview**: provides an overview of how VAT works and the differences between non-business, exempt and taxable activities.

- **Chapter 2 – Registration and deregistration**: explains when you must register for VAT and when you may register for VAT voluntarily. It also explains when you must deregister for VAT, when you may deregister voluntarily and the consequences of deregistration.

- **Chapter 3 – Recovering VAT**: explains when the VAT incurred on purchases can be reclaimed from HMRC and how you calculate the amount you can reclaim when you have a mix of taxable, exempt or non-business activities. In particular, it explains the rules governing VAT 'methods' – the 'partial exemption method' and the 'non-business method' – and how these interact.

The next three chapters provide an overview of the three categories of activity for VAT purposes:

- **Chapter 4 – Business and non-business**: explains what the term 'supply' means and how to determine if an activity is 'business' or 'non-business'. The chapter considers some typical non-business activities encountered in voluntary organisations and also outlines the special rules that apply to 'non-business assets'.

- **Chapter 5 – Exempt activities**: explains which activities are exempt from VAT. There are many VAT-exempt activities, but only a few of these are commonly undertaken by voluntary organisations. The exempt activities covered in this section are education, health and welfare services, cultural services, sports and recreation and insurance services. The section also covers the exemption for

3

subscriptions paid to professional associations, learned societies, trade bodies and other organisations with objects in the public domain and that are of a political, religious, patriotic, philosophical, philanthropic or civic nature.

- **Chapter 6 – Zero- and reduced-rate activities**: the third VAT category of activity is 'taxable'. However, all taxable activities are 'standard-rated' if they do not qualify for 'zero rating' or 'reduced rating'. This chapter looks at which activities qualify for zero rating or reduced rating. In particular, it covers what supplies are zero-rated when made *to* a charity and when made *by* a charity.

The next six chapters provide a more in-depth look at particular topics:

- **Chapter 7 – Fundraising**: this chapter looks at the VAT implications of various fundraising activities commonly undertaken by voluntary organisations. The chapter includes commentary on auctions, challenge events, marathons, the rules on one-off fundraising events, selling donated goods, sponsorship and commercial participator arrangements, and many more.

- **Chapter 8 – Property**: this chapter looks at the VAT rules that apply to property – that is, land, buildings and civil engineering works such as playgrounds and outdoor sports facilities. The chapter also covers the special VAT property rules for charities and registered social landlords and also examines common property-related activities such as letting out rooms and sporting facilities and providing accommodation in hostels.

- **Chapter 9 – International aspects of VAT**: different VAT rules apply if you make purchases from a non-UK supplier or if you sell goods or services to a non-UK customer. For VAT purposes the UK comprises England, Wales, Scotland, Northern Ireland and the Isle of Man but excludes the Channel Islands. This chapter provides an overview of these rules and also the special international rules that apply to charities and other non-profit organisations.

- **Chapter 10 – VAT special schemes**: there are many special 'schemes' in VAT. Some are compulsory and some are optional, usually designed to simplify VAT administration for small organisations. This chapter covers the following VAT schemes: capital goods scheme; tour operators' margin scheme; reverse charge scheme; cash accounting scheme; annual accounting scheme; margin scheme; the retail schemes; the flat rate schemes; and the refund schemes for listed places of worship, memorials, galleries and museums. The chapter also considers the tax avoidance rules for schemes that reduce an organisation's VAT burden and the reporting requirements for certain 'listed' or 'hallmarked' schemes.

- **Chapter 11 – Other topics**: this chapter considers various miscellaneous topics: how to determine if you are making a 'single' or 'multiple' supply; the VAT rules for principals and agents; the rules for VAT groups, branches and joint ventures; the special issues relating to supplies of staff and supplies between connected organisations; the rules on transfer of a going concern and the VAT planning opportunities available to voluntary organisations.

- **Chapter 12 – Operational aspects**: covers the practical aspects of VAT, including: the VAT invoice rules; how to determine the time of supply; how to complete the VAT return; advice on dealing with HMRC; the 'blocking rules' on motor vehicles and business entertaining; and how to set up the tax codes in Sage Line 50 to deal with exempt and non-business activities.

The final three chapters provide useful reference material:

- **Chapter 13 – VAT cases**: summaries of some key VAT cases for voluntary organisations.

- **Chapter 14 – Further information**: HMRC contact details and how to locate information on the HMRC website. Other useful websites and other sources of information about VAT.

- **Chapter 15 – Glossary**: VAT makes use of many terms with very particular meanings. The glossary explains the technical terms used throughout the book.

Words in the text that are written in bold are terms that are explained in the glossary at the end of the book.

For a supplementary update on VAT please visit: www.sayervincent.co.uk/publications/practicalVAT

---

1 Overview of VAT

This chapter provides an overview of how VAT works and the differences between non-business exempt and taxable activities.

How VAT works

Value Added Tax (VAT) is a tax on sales. It is calculated as a percentage of the sale price and added to the price charged to the customer. The added VAT is called **output VAT**. The standard rate of VAT in the UK is currently 17½ per cent.

The price before VAT is added is called the **net price** and the price after output VAT is added is called the **gross price**.

Businesses do not get to keep the output VAT they charge to their customers. It must be paid to HM Revenue & Customs (HMRC).

Example: Woodwork Ltd

Woodwork Ltd manufactures and sells chairs. It sells a chair for £100 plus VAT. The price charged to the customer is:

Net selling price	£100.00
Plus output VAT: 17½% x £100	£17.50
Gross selling price	£117.50

Woodwork Ltd must pay the £17.50 output VAT to HMRC.

Businesses also incur VAT on the purchases they make. This is called **input VAT**.

Businesses are allowed to **recover** any input VAT they incur on making purchases that relate to the taxed sales.

They do this by deducting the input VAT from the output VAT and paying only the balance over to HMRC.

To make a chair, Woodwork Ltd purchases goods for £10 net. The gross cost to Woodwork Ltd is:

Net purchase price	£10.00
Plus input VAT : £10 x 17½%	£1.75
Gross purchase price	£11.75

Woodwork Ltd can recover this input VAT by deducting it from the output VAT it must pay to HMRC:

Output VAT	£17.50
Less input VAT	(£1.75)
VAT payable to HMRC	£15.75

If the input VAT is more than the output VAT, the balance is paid to the business by HMRC.

We can now see why the tax is called 'Value Added Tax'.

The amount of VAT payable to HMRC is the tax due on the value added.

The value added to the goods purchased for a chair by Woodwork Ltd is:

Selling price	£100.00
Less purchase price	(£10.00)
Value added	£90.00
VAT on value added: £90 x 17½%	£15.75

For Woodwork Ltd, VAT simply passes through the organisation. The VAT it incurs can be recovered from HMRC, so it is not a cost to Woodwork Ltd. The VAT it charges must be paid to HMRC, so it is not income for Woodwork Ltd. Woodwork Ltd is simply collecting tax on behalf of the Government.

However, if the person purchasing the chair cannot recover the VAT they incur on purchases, the VAT charged on the chair is a cost to them. Private individuals and unregistered businesses cannot recover the VAT they incur on purchases. The cost of

7

the chairs to a private individual is £117.50 whereas the effective cost to a VAT-registered business is £100, as it can recover the £17.50 VAT charged by Woodwork Ltd.

Types of activity

Not all types of activity are subject to VAT. For VAT to be due, there must first be a supply. **Supplies** are goods and services that are provided for consideration. **Consideration** is usually in the form of cash but it can also include barter transactions and other arrangements where no cash changes hands.

If you do something for someone and receive consideration in return, you are probably making a supply. If you do something for free then, with a few special exceptions, there is no consideration and hence no supply. If you receive a payment but do nothing in return, then, again with a few special exceptions, there is no supply and so no VAT is chargeable. Supply is considered in more detail in Chapter 4.

For a supply to be subject to VAT it must be made in the course or furtherance of a **business activity**. Business activities include commercially motivated activities but also many activities undertaken by voluntary organisations where commercial considerations are not the primary motivation. The distinction between business and non-business activities is considered in more detail in Chapter 4.

For VAT purposes, activities are divided into the following categories or types:

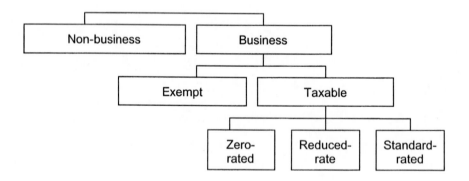

Non-business activities comprise activities where there is no supply and activities where there is a supply but which are not conducted in the course or furtherance of a business. Non-business activities are said to be **outside the scope of VAT**. VAT is not charged to any customers but VAT on purchases related to non-business activities cannot be recovered. Activities funded entirely by grants or donations are usually non-business.

All other types of activity are referred to as **business**. Certain types of business supply are specifically exempted from VAT by law. These are referred to as **exempt supplies**. Numerous activities of voluntary organisations are exempt and include many educational, welfare and cultural services. VAT is not charged on exempt supplies and generally VAT incurred in making exempt supplies cannot be recovered. Exempt supplies are considered in detail in Chapter 5.

If a business supply is not specifically exempted then it is **taxable**. If the total turnover from all taxable supplies exceeds a certain level (the 'VAT registration threshold') then an organisation must register for VAT and start charging VAT on the taxable supplies. The requirement to register for VAT is explained in Chapter 2.

Three different rates of VAT are currently used in the UK:

The standard rate	17½%	The standard rate applies to most taxable supplies of goods and services
The reduced rate	5%	The reduced and zero rates apply only to certain supplies specified in the Value Added Tax Ac 1994. Reduced-rate and zero-rate
The zero rate	0%	supplies are considered in Chapter 6.

VAT is charged on the taxable supplies but any VAT incurred in making the taxable supplies is recoverable.

If there is a mix of non-business, exempt and taxable supplies in an organisation then all VAT on purchases must be attributed to the different types of activity. Attribution involves directly allocating VAT wherever possible, then apportioning the remaining VAT between the different types of activity.

*   The VAT on purchases that is attributed to the taxable supplies is recoverable.

*   The VAT on purchases that is attributed to the exempt supplies is not recoverable unless it is below a certain level (the '*de minimis*' level). See Chapter 3 for details of how this level is calculated.

*   The VAT on purchases attributable to the non-business activities is not recoverable.

Example: The Advice Network has three projects:

A. Project A is a non-business activity entirely funded by a grant. No VAT is charged to the grant provider. The total VAT attributable to Project A is £30,000. This VAT cannot be recovered and represents an expense for The Advice Network.

B. Project B is an exempt educational service funded through a contract. No VAT is charged on the contract. The total VAT attributable to Project B is £20,000. This VAT cannot be recovered and represents an expense for The Advice Network.

C. Project C is a standard-rated contract for providing consultancy services. The net contract value is £100,000 per year. Output VAT charged on the contract is 17½% x £100,000 = £17,500. The total VAT attributable to Project C is £10,000. This can be recovered and does not represent an expense for The Advice Network.

Total output VAT	£17,500
Total recoverable input VAT	£10,000
The net amount payable to HMRC	£7,500

Total irrecoverable VAT is £30,000 + £20,000 = £50,000. This is an expense for The Advice Network.

Zero-rated and exempt activities

Zero rating means that an activity is taxable, but at a zero rate of VAT. The effect is to add no output VAT to the sale price but any input VAT attributable to the activity can be recovered. Zero rating applies to only a limited range of activities. These include the sale of books, children's clothing, some basic foodstuffs and the sale of donated goods by a charity (or by a trading subsidiary that donates its profits to the charity).

Zero rating is in many ways the ideal situation if your customers are private individuals or unregistered organisations and cannot recover the VAT they incur on purchases. The price charged to customers is not increased by VAT but all VAT incurred in making the zero-rated supplies can be recovered. If your customers can recover the VAT they incur on purchases then being able to zero rate your supplies is less important. The net cost to the customer will be the same whether or not the supply is zero-rated or standard-rated.

It is important to appreciate the difference between exempt and zero-rated supplies. For both of these, no VAT is actually charged to customers. However, with zero-rated supplies, the VAT incurred on associated purchases can be recovered, while for exempt supplies the VAT incurred on associated purchases cannot be recovered, except under very limited circumstances.

The limited circumstances in which VAT incurred in making exempt supplies can be recovered are explained in Chapter 3. Exempt supplies are considered in Chapter 5 and zero-rated supplies in Chapter 6.

Practicalities

An organisation making taxable supplies above the VAT registration threshold must register for VAT with HMRC. Zero-rated supplies count towards this limit. Organisations making taxable supplies below the VAT registration threshold may also register voluntarily. Registering for VAT is explained in Chapter 2.

Once registered, an organisation must charge VAT on its standard-rated and reduced-rate supplies at the appropriate rate. For all such sales, it must issue VAT sales invoices containing specified information. To be able to recover any input VAT, it must keep the associated VAT purchase invoices. It must keep detailed records of the amounts of output VAT charged and of input VAT recovered.

Periodically, usually every quarter, it must complete a VAT return showing the amount of output VAT charged in the period, the amount of input VAT that can be recovered in the period and the net amount due to or from HMRC. The VAT return must be sent to HMRC, together with any payment due, within a set time after the period end. There are penalties for submitting late returns and payments. If there is a net recovery of VAT from HMRC, they will send this to you.

If you cease to make taxable supplies, you must deregister, and if your level of taxable supplies drops below the 'deregistration threshold' then you can deregister voluntarily. You no longer charge VAT on your taxable supplies but cannot recover the VAT you incur in making those supplies. You may have to repay any input VAT you recovered on assets that are still on hand at deregistration.

Deregistration is explained in Chapter 2. The practical and administrative aspects of VAT are explained in Chapter 12.

2 Registration and deregistration

This chapter explains when you must register for VAT and when you may register for VAT voluntarily. It also explains when you must deregister for VAT, when you may deregister voluntarily and the consequences of deregistration.

Compulsory registration

You must register for VAT if the total value of your taxable supplies exceeds the VAT registration threshold. It is only the value of taxable supplies that counts towards the registration threshold. Income from exempt and non-business activities is ignored.

The VAT registration threshold at the time of writing (2007/08) is £64,000. The threshold changes each year and you can check the latest threshold on the HMRC website (see Chapter 14: *Further information*).

You are required to register for VAT if any of the following conditions are met:

a) **The 'past turnover' test**: at the end of any calendar month, the value of taxable supplies in the past 12 months has exceeded the VAT registration threshold. You must notify HMRC within 30 days of the end of the month in which the test is met and will be registered from the first day of the second month.

b) **The 'future turnover' test**: at any time, there are reasonable grounds for believing that the value of taxable supplies in the next 30 days will exceed the VAT registration threshold. You must notify HMRC within 30 days of becoming aware that the registration threshold will be exceeded in the following 30 days. The registration is effective from the date you became aware that the registration threshold would be exceeded.

c) **International supplies**: you must also register in the UK if you make distance sales from outside the UK to the UK over the distance sales threshold, or are based in the UK and make acquisitions of goods from other EC states over the registration threshold. If you supply goods or services from the UK to customers in another EC state, you may have to register for VAT in that EC state. For more details, see Chapter 9: *International aspects*.

Example: (a) 'Past turnover' test

A starts a new business on 15 May. The VAT registration threshold is £64,000. A's taxable turnover in the first few months of operation is:

	Turnover in month (£)	Cumulative turnover (£)
May	5,000	5,000
June	10,000	15,000
July	15,000	30,000
August	30,000	60,000
September	20,000	80,000

At the end of September A has exceeded the registration threshold. A must inform HMRC by 30 October and will be registered from 1 November.

This means that A starts to charge VAT on supplies made after 1 November – registration has no retrospective effect.

Example: (b) 'Future turnover' test

B has been running a business for several years, generating regular taxable sales of £4,000 per month.

On 10 September, B signed a contract for £200,000. Under the terms of the contract an invoice for £80,000 will be issued on 11 October and one for £120,000 six months later.

B knew on 10 September that its taxable turnover would be £84,000 in the next 30 days. B must notify HMRC by 10 October and will be registered from 10 September.

Applying for registration

You apply for registration by submitting a completed registration form (form VAT 1: for contact details, see Chapter 14). When HMRC have checked the registration they will send a registration certificate showing the VAT registration number, effective date of registration and the return periods to be used. From the point of registration onwards, you must provide proper VAT invoices and keep detailed VAT records. Quarterly returns will be sent automatically and must be completed and returned within one month of the end of the quarter.

If you do not receive your VAT registration details by your effective date of registration, you cannot issue valid VAT invoices even though you are registered for VAT and must charge VAT on your sales. You must issue invoices for the VAT-inclusive amount but without showing the VAT as a separate item on the invoice. You must explain the situation to VAT-registered customers and tell them that you will send them a valid VAT invoice when your registration details are confirmed.

What counts towards your taxable turnover?

Your taxable turnover comprises the following:

- Income from standard-rated, reduced-rate and zero-rated supplies, net of any VAT that may be due. Income is recognised at the tax point of the supply. See Chapter 12: *Operational aspects* for an explanation of how the tax point is determined.

- However, income generated from the sale of tangible and intangible fixed assets is ignored unless it was a standard-rated supply of land or buildings (see Chapter 8: *Property*).

- If you receive certain services from abroad ('reverse charge services'), the value of these services also counts towards your registration threshold. For details, see Chapter 9: *International aspects of VAT.*

- If you make certain purchases of 'reverse charge goods', the value of these purchases also counts towards your registration threshold. For details, see Chapter 10: *VAT schemes.*

Example: Calculating your taxable turnover

Charity C has received the following income in the last 12 months. The registration threshold is £64,000:

Donations	30,000
Grants	18,000
Sale of donated goods	24,000
Flag day	20,000
Christmas cards	12,000
Publications	15,000
Advertising in magazine	8,000
Sale of equipment	5,000

Bank interest	4,500
Total income	136,500

The sale of equipment can be ignored. Taxable income arises from the sale of donated goods (zero-rated), Christmas cards (standard-rated), publications and advertising (zero- or standard-rated). Taxable income is thus:

Sale of donated goods	24,000
Christmas cards	12,000
Publications	15,000
Advertising in magazine	8,000
Total taxable income	59,000 ✓

C does not need to register, as its taxable income is less than the registration threshold.

However, it should monitor the situation on a monthly basis, as it is near to the registration threshold.

Exemption from compulsory registration

You may be exempted from compulsory registration if:

a) you meet the 'past turnover' test but can satisfy HMRC that your taxable turnover in the following 12 months will be less than the deregistration threshold. The VAT deregistration threshold at the time of writing (2007/08) is £62,000. The threshold changes each year and you can check the latest threshold on the HMRC website (see Chapter 14: *Further information*), or

b) the majority of your taxable supplies are zero-rated and your recoverable input VAT will normally be more than your output VAT, so you would be a net recoverer of VAT.

You must apply for exemption from registration and must monitor your activities and notify HMRC as soon as there is any material change in your circumstances.

If you are exempted from registration on the basis of being a net recoverer of VAT, then a material change is considered to include total output VAT exceeding recoverable input VAT in any 12-month period.

Example: Exemption from compulsory registration

The Legal Advice Trust (LAT) publishes books and sends a newsletter to subscribers. It derives all its income from these activities. At the start of the tax year 2007/08 it estimates that its income from these sources will reach £70,000. The registration threshold for 2007/08 is £64,000.

Income from publishing books and newsletters is zero-rated and therefore LAT will have taxable supplies in excess of £64,000. It should monitor its monthly income and should plan to register. Alternatively, it could submit a VAT registration form explaining that its only turnover is zero-rated and that it wishes to be exempted from registration.

While avoidance of registration in this way keeps the bookkeeping simple, it does mean that LAT is unable to recover input VAT on costs such as telephone and stationery. Recovery of this input VAT is possible only if you register for VAT.

LAT should therefore compare the costs of registration (bookkeeping and administration costs) with the likely savings through being able to recover input VAT to decide whether or not to apply for exemption.

Late registration

If you register late, or fail to register when you should have done so, then you will have to account for the VAT which should have been charged. The VAT has to be calculated and paid over as if you had registered on time. This VAT may not be recoverable from your customers. There are two options:

- customers who are registered for VAT may be happy to receive and pay a VAT-only invoice for the VAT you should have charged (treating the amount originally billed as the net amount) as they will be able to offset it against their next VAT payment. Where this is possible you will not have to pay over the VAT out of existing sales income;

- for unregistered customers and VAT-registered customers who will not accept a late VAT-only invoice, you will have to assume that the amount you received included VAT at the appropriate rate. You then have to calculate the output VAT due using the formula (for standard-rated supplies at 17.5 per cent):

$$\text{Amount actually charged} \times \frac{17.5}{117.5}$$

You will also have to pay a penalty unless you can demonstrate that you have a reasonable excuse. Reasonable excuses include compassionate circumstances and situations in which there is genuine doubt over the liability of supplies. The penalty will depend on how late the registration is:

9 months or less	5% of tax payable
More than 9 months but less than 18 months	10% of tax payable
Over 18 months	15% of tax payable

Where the above amounts are small, or you are in fact due a repayment from HMRC as a result of registering, a minimum penalty of £50 applies. For more on penalties and reasonable excuses, see Chapter 12: *Operational aspects*.

You will be able to recover the VAT on purchases that are attributable to the taxable activity, so this will offset the amount finally due to the VAT office.

Example: Late registration

The Health Promotion Trust (HPT) received £100,000 from a company to fund research and the publication of the results.

It treated this as a donation but later discovered that it should have been treated as advertising, since the company received considerable promotion from the deal. HPT's registration was six months late. This is its only taxable supply in the year.

This income on its own exceeds the registration threshold and VAT must be accounted for. The company has refused to accept a late invoice adding the VAT, so HPT will have to treat the amount received as the VAT-inclusive amount. The output VAT due on this income is:

£100,000 x (17.5 /117.5) = £14,893.61

The amount is rounded down to the nearest penny on an invoice-by-invoice basis.

HPT goes through its purchase invoices and establishes that input VAT of £2,580 is attributable to the research and can be claimed. The net amount due to HMRC is:

Output VAT due	£14,893.61
Less input VAT	£(2,580.00)
Due to HMRC	£12,313.61

If HPT is unable to establish that it had a reasonable excuse for late registration then a penalty may be due. This would be:

5% x £12,313.61 = £615.68

This example also underlines the need for careful wording in contracts. Had there been a clause in the contract (or exchange of letters) stating that all fees payable would be subject to VAT where applicable, then HPT would have been able to issue a late invoice. However, the omission of such a clause means that the company was allowed to insist that the amount paid included VAT.

Voluntary registration

You can register for VAT voluntarily if:

- you make taxable supplies

- you intend to make taxable supplies

- you make or intend to make supplies outside the UK that would be taxable if made in the UK (see Chapter 9: *International aspects of VAT*).

The advantages of voluntary registration are that you may be able to recover some VAT on costs, and that you can operate one bookkeeping system right from the beginning of a new business where you anticipate that registration will be necessary at some future date. This can be especially advantageous if you must make significant capital investment well before taxable income is generated.

You have to write a letter with your completed registration form, explaining the nature of your business, why you want to be registered and from what date.

If you apply for registration on the basis of future intent, HMRC will need to be sure that you are in business and do genuinely intend making taxable supplies. HMRC may require evidence such as contracts, copy invoices showing investment for new activity or other appropriate evidence. Any repayment of VAT on purchases in the first year is provisional; you may have to make a payment to HMRC if you do not make any taxable supplies.

Example: Voluntary registration

The Dickens Charity (DC) provides free meals to the homeless. It receives grants and donations of approximately £200,000 per year for this work. It plans to provide consultancy and advice to local authorities in other areas on ways in which such schemes can be established. It estimates that it will earn about £30,000 from this source.

DC can apply for voluntary registration, once it is clear that the consultancy service will go ahead.

VAT would have to be charged on the invoices for the consultancy services only. DC would have to keep detailed records of its costs as well, and ensure that it identified which related to the consultancy activity.

The input VAT on purchases which related to the consultancy could be reclaimed, but not any of the VAT on the other activities. VAT incurred on overheads will have to be apportioned between the consultancy and other services.

Recovering pre-registration VAT on purchases

It is possible to recover VAT that has been incurred prior to the date of registration by making a claim on the first VAT return. HMRC must give permission for a claim to be made on a later return and no pre-registration input VAT may be recovered on a claim made more than three years after the date the first claim was due.

Goods that have been purchased for the purpose of the business and are still 'on-hand' at the date of registration, as either fixed assets or stock, are eligible for the VAT recovery, providing they were not purchased more than three years prior to registration.

Services supplied up to six months prior to the date of registration are eligible for the recovery. The services must have been used for the business and not re-supplied at the date of registration.

Compulsory deregistration

A VAT-registered organisation must deregister in the following circumstances:

* The organisation stops making taxable supplies.

* The organisation was registered on the basis of its intention to make taxable supplies but no longer intends making taxable supplies.

* The taxable activity is sold or transferred to another entity.

* The legal status of the organisation changes. For example, if the organisation becomes incorporated, the incorporated organisation will have its own VAT registration.

- The organisation becomes part of a VAT group. For more details, see Chapter 11: *Other topics*.

Voluntary deregistration

A VAT-registered organisation may also deregister voluntarily if it can satisfy HMRC that:

- its taxable turnover in the next 12 months will fall below the deregistration threshold. The VAT deregistration threshold at the time of writing (2007/08) is £62,000. The threshold changes each year and you can check the latest threshold on the HMRC website (see Chapter 14: *Further information*), or

- its input VAT will normally exceed its output VAT and so it will be a net recoverer of VAT. The conditions are the same as those for exemption from registration (explained above).

Repaying VAT on deregistration

If, at the point of deregistration, you have any stock or fixed assets on hand on which you recovered input VAT then you may have to repay part of this VAT to HMRC.

Relevant stock and assets should be valued at the price you would expect to pay for them in their present condition. If this cannot be determined, they should be valued at the price you would expect to pay for similar items.

If any of the items were acquired partly for non-business or exempt purposes then only the portion of VAT used for taxable activities is repayable. It may be necessary to reach agreement with HMRC as to how this is calculated.

If the total VAT due on the assets is £1,000 or less, then it can be ignored and no VAT is repayable.

Example: Repaying VAT on deregistration

At deregistration, charity D had the following assets on hand. All assets were used in D's taxable activities and associated input VAT recovered:

Assets	Value (net)
Zero-rated stock	5,000
Standard-rated stock	6,000
Fixed assets (standard-rated)	7,000

No VAT is due on the zero-rated stock. The total value of standard-rated assets is £13,000, so the VAT due is:

£13,000 x 17½% = £2,275

3 Recovering VAT

When you are registered for VAT you must charge VAT on your taxable supplies. The VAT you charge must be paid over to HMRC periodically. However, you can deduct from this payment any VAT you incur on purchases that relate to the taxable supplies. This chapter explains the rules for determining how much VAT you can deduct.

Chapter 1 explained that, for VAT purposes, activities are divided into three types. These are:

*   **Non-business activities**: these include activities where there is no supply (for example, an activity entirely funded by a grant); and activities where there is a supply but the supply is non-business (for example, premises let at a peppercorn rent). See Chapter 4 for an explanation of the terms 'supply', 'business' and 'non-business' and for more examples of non-business activities.

*   **Exempt activities**: these are activities that generate exempt supplies, for example a welfare service provided under contract to a health authority or the letting of premises. See Chapter 5 for more examples of exempt activities.

*   **Taxable activities**: these are activities that generate taxable supplies, for example a shop selling goods, or the sale of publications. Taxable activities are subject to VAT, though some attract a reduced or zero rate. See Chapter 6 for examples of zero-rated and reduced-rate activities.

Taxable and exempt activities are both business activities for VAT purposes.

If you are registered for VAT, you can recover the VAT you incur on purchases that are **attributable** to your taxable activities. The VAT incurred on purchases that are attributable to your exempt or non-business activities cannot be recovered, except in a few special situations. A purchase is attributable to a type of activity if it is used or is going to be used in that type of activity.

The VAT on purchases that are attributable to your business activities (taxable and exempt) is called **input VAT**.

Only UK input VAT can be recovered on the UK VAT return. UK input VAT is VAT charged under the UK's VAT rules. VAT incurred in other EC states may be recoverable, but because it is not UK VAT it cannot be recovered through the UK VAT return. Instead, if you are registered for VAT in the EC state where you incurred non-UK VAT, you may be able to claim it on that state's VAT return. If you are not VAT-registered in that state you may be able to make a claim to that state's tax authorities. There are special procedures for submitting a claim to another EC state, and these are explained in Chapter 9.

Blocked input VAT

The VAT on certain types of purchase is 'blocked'. This means that it is not recoverable under any circumstances, even if it is attributable to a taxable activity. Blocked input VAT includes VAT attributable to:

* The **purchase of a car**, unless the car is to be used exclusively for business purposes and will not be available for private use. If a car will be available for private use then the input VAT on the car cannot be recovered. See Chapter 12 for more details.

* **Business entertaining**: VAT incurred in certain types of business entertaining cannot be recovered. See Chapter 12 for more details.

Attributing VAT to activities

If all your activities are taxable then you can recover all the VAT you incur in making purchases, unless it is specifically blocked. Your accounting system will need to be able to identify all the VAT you incur in making purchases and any blocked VAT.

If you have a mix of different types of activity (taxable, exempt or non-business) your accounting systems will also have to be able to attribute the VAT you incur on purchases to one of the activity types.

The process of attributing VAT to the activity types will be familiar to anyone used to the principles of absorption costing or of full cost recovery. VAT is directly attributed to the activity types as far as possible, then the remaining VAT is apportioned across the activity types.

VAT is directly attributable to an activity type if the associated purchase is used or to be used exclusively in that type of activity. For example, a purchase is directly attributable to taxable activities if it is used or to be used exclusively in taxable activities. If a purchase cannot be directly attributed to a particular type of activity, it is said to be residual. This is an important distinction, and for VAT purposes you must differentiate between:

- **Directly attributable purchases**. These are ones that are used exclusively in making a particular type of supply: taxable, exempt or non-business. Directly attributable VAT is recoverable if the related supply is taxable, but irrecoverable if the associated supply is exempt or non-business (subject to the exceptions as explained below).

- **Residual purchases**. These are purchases that cannot be directly attributed to a particular type of activity. Often this will include an organisation's core costs or overheads that cannot be directly attributed to any type of activity, but it will also include, for example, a purchase that is used in making taxable and exempt supplies. The VAT incurred in making residual purchases is called **residual VAT**. The residual VAT must be apportioned between the taxable, exempt and non-business activities. The part apportioned to the taxable activities is recoverable, but the parts apportioned to non-business or exempt activities are irrecoverable (subject to the exceptions as explained below).

Your accounting systems will have to, as far as possible, link VAT on purchases to the type of activity incurring the expense – taxable, exempt, non-business or residual. With a manual, ledger-based system, this could be achieved by using separate columns to subdivide VAT on purchases into the different types. With a computerised accounting system you may be able to use the system's tax-coding structure to achieve this (as illustrated in Chapter 12 for Sage 50 Accounts) or link all expenditure and the associated VAT to the activity generating it and thereby be able to attribute VAT on purchases to individual activities.

Example: Attributing VAT

Local Advice Organisation (LAO) receives a grant to fund a free advice service (a non-business activity), rents out premises to other organisations (an exempt activity) and charges for consultancy services (a taxable activity). LAO's accounting systems allow it to allocate costs and the associated VAT to activities. In quarter 1, LAO's expenditure was as follows (note that not all purchases incur VAT):

Incurred on	Net	VAT	Gross
Consultancy service	£3,500	£500	£4,000
Premises rental	£2,000	£200	£2,200
Advice service	£2,000	£100	£2,100
Overheads	£2,500	£200	£2,700
Totals	£10,000	£1,000	£11,000

The attribution of VAT on purchases for quarter 1 is:

Directly attributable to taxable activities (consultancy services)	£500
Directly attributable to exempt activities (premises rental)	£200
Directly attributable to non-business activities (advice service)	£100
Residual (overheads)	£200

Apportioning residual VAT

Every organisation that has a mix of taxable, exempt and non–business activities must decide how residual VAT is to be apportioned between the different types of activity. This apportionment must be carried out in a specific order:

- **The business/non-business apportionment**: If there are non-business activities the residual VAT must first be apportioned between business and non-business activities. Any VAT apportioned to the non-business activities is irrecoverable, subject to the exceptions as explained below. This apportionment is commonly known as the organisation's **non–business method**. The residual VAT apportioned to the business activities is referred to as **residual input** VAT.

- **The taxable/exempt apportionment**: If there are exempt activities, any remaining residual VAT (after discarding any apportioned to non-business activities) must be apportioned between exempt and taxable activities. Any VAT apportioned to the exempt activities is irrecoverable unless exempt activities are *de minimis*, in which case it is recoverable. The *de minimis* rules are explained below. Any VAT apportioned to taxable activities is recoverable. This apportionment is known as the organisation's **partial exemption method**.

Example: Apportionment

Local Advice Organisation (LAO) has agreed non-business and partial exemption methods with HMRC under which 50 per cent of all residual VAT is apportioned to non-business activities and the remaining residual VAT is split 60/40 between taxable and exempt activities. LAO incurred VAT of £1,000 in VAT quarter 1. This broke down as follows:

Directly attributable to taxable activities	£500
Directly attributable to exempt activities	£200
Directly attributable to non-business activities	£100
Residual	£200
Total	£1,000

The VAT is attributed to the activity types as follows:

	Taxable activities	Exempt activities	Non-business activities
Directly attributable	£500	£200	£100
Residual: apportion 50% of residual VAT to non-business			£100
Split the remaining residual VAT 60% taxable & 40% exempt	£60	£40	
Total VAT attributed	£560	£240	£200

In quarter 1 LAO attributes VAT on purchases as: £560 to taxable activities, £240 to exempt activities and £200 to non-business activities.

The exceptions

There are some situations in which VAT attributed to non-business or exempt activities is recoverable. The main ones are:

- **Exempt activity is *de minimis*:** If the total VAT attributed to exempt activities is *de minimis* it is recoverable. The total VAT attributed to exempt activities includes any VAT that is directly attributable to exempt activities and any residual VAT that is apportioned to exempt activities. The *de minimis* test is explained below.

- **The level of non-business activity is insignificant:** There is no statutory *de minimis* level for non-business activity, however HMRC officers are allowed discretion in deciding that non-business activity is too small to be worth bothering about.

- **Out-of-country supplies**: If a supply takes place outside the UK, it is outside the scope of UK VAT and so the related activity falls into the 'non-business' type. Such supplies are called 'out-of-country supplies'. However, if the supply would have been taxable had it taken place in the UK, any UK VAT incurred in making the supply is recoverable. The rules for recovering VAT that is attributable to out-of-country supplies are explained below.

- **Outside the scope activities**: Sometimes VAT that is directly attributable to non-business activities is residual. This means that part of this VAT can be recovered. See the comments on the Children's Society case in Chapter 4 and see the further comments below.

- **Non-business use of assets**: Where an asset is purchased, acquired or constructed and the asset will be used for mixed business and non-business purposes, an organisation can opt to treat the asset as acquired wholly for business purposes and then charge itself output VAT on any non-business use. The VAT incurred in purchasing the asset that is attributable to the taxable and non-business use can be recovered. This is known as the 'Lennartz mechanism', following a case of that name. See Chapter 4 for more information on the Lennartz mechanism.

The *de minimis* test

If the total of the VAT directly attributed and apportioned to exempt activities is:

- less than £625 in a month or £1,875 in a VAT quarter or £7,500 in a VAT year, and

- less than 50 per cent of the total input VAT (the total input VAT is the total of the VAT directly attributed and apportioned to taxable and exempt activities)

then it is said to be *de minimis* and it is recoverable. If it is not *de minimis* it is irrecoverable. Both conditions must be fulfilled – if one condition fails or if both conditions fail, the test is not met and the VAT attributed to exempt activities is not recoverable.

Example: The *de minimis* test

Using the figures from the above example for Local Advice Organisation, the VAT on purchases in quarter 1 was attributed to activities as follows:

Taxable activities	£560
Exempt activities	£240
Non-business activities	£200
Total	£1,000

Applying the *de minimis* test:

- the VAT attributed to exempt activities (£240) is less than £1,875, and

- the VAT attributed to exempt activities (£240) is less than 50% of the VAT attributed to business activities (£560 + £240 = £800).

So the VAT attributed to exempt activities is *de minimis* and therefore recoverable. LAO claims £560 (taxable) + £240 (exempt) = £800 VAT in its quarter 1 VAT return.

The *de minimis* test must be applied to each VAT return and again in the annual adjustment (explained below). If you make quarterly returns, the figure to use in the first test is £1,875. In the annual adjustment, the figure to use in the first test is £7,500.

Insignificant non-business activity

Where non-business activity is regarded as insignificant, HMRC officers may use their discretion to allow a waiver of the non-business apportionment. There is no statutory *de minimis* level as with exempt activity, and it is left to HMRC officers to determine whether the benefit in terms of revenue is outweighed by the cost to the organisation in administration and to HMRC in checking that the correct apportionment has been carried out. Any waiver of apportionment will be conditional on the level of non-business activity remaining minimal, and if the level of non-business activity increases the organisation will need to apply a non-business apportionment.

The waiver is commonly applied to small levels of non-business income such as bank interest and investment income received by charities. Note that, even if the overall level of non-business activity is significant, it may be possible to reach agreement with HMRC that some types of non-business income such as bank interest may be excluded from the non-business method on the ground that the level of VAT-bearing residual cost incurred in generating the income is insignificant – see the section on incidental and distortive activities below.

The annual adjustment

The non-business and partial exemption methods and *de minimis* test must be applied to each VAT return and then again after the end of the VAT year using figures for the whole VAT year. This is to eliminate, as far as possible, any seasonal distortions or distortions caused by purchases being made in one quarter but used in another.

The VAT year normally runs to the VAT return ending on 31 March, 30 April or 31 May, though you may change this with the approval of HMRC.

The amounts for the annual adjustment are derived by adding together the amounts used in all the VAT returns for the year – but excluding any annual adjustment from the previous VAT year.

Any resulting adjustment is included in the first VAT return of the following VAT year. For an organisation making quarterly returns, this will be the return for the quarter ending 30 June, 31 July or 31 August. You should submit your annual adjustment calculations with the VAT return. Any annual adjustment is made by increasing or decreasing the quarter's figure for box 4 on the VAT return. See Chapter 12 for information on completing the VAT return.

Note that the annual adjustment is not an error or mistake and does not give rise to any penalties.

Example: The annual adjustment

Local Advice Organisation has agreed non-business and partial exemption methods with HMRC under which 50% of all residual VAT is apportioned to non-business activities and the remaining residual VAT is split 60/40 between taxable and exempt activities. VAT on purchases and VAT reclaimed in quarters 1 to 4 was:

Attributable to	Quarter 1	Quarter 2	Quarter 3	Quarter 4	Totals
Taxable activities	£500	£300	£400	£300	£1,500
Exempt activities	£200	£450	£450	£500	£1,600
Non-business activities	£100	£150	£250	£200	£700
Residual	£200	£250	£100	£200	£750

Totals	£1,000	£1,150	£1,200	£1,200	£4,550
VAT claimed in each quarter	£800	£375	£430	£360	£1,965

The annual adjustment is based on the totals for all four quarters (the last column above):

	Taxable activities	Exempt activities	Non-business activities
Directly attributable	£1,500	£1,600	£700
Apportion 50% of the residual VAT to non-business activities			£375
Split the remaining residual VAT 60% taxable & 40% exempt	£225	£150	
Total VAT attributed	£1,725	£1,750	£1,075

The VAT attributed to exempt activities (£1,750) is not *de minimis* – it is less than the annual *de minimis* limit (£7,500) but it is more than 50% of the VAT attributed to business activities (£1,725 + £1,750 = £3,475).

The annual adjustment shows the VAT recoverable for the year is £1,725 – the VAT attributed to taxable activities only. This is less than the VAT already claimed in the four VAT returns (£1,965) and so £1,965 - £1,725 = £240 must be repaid to HMRC. An adjustment for £240 is made in the first VAT return of the following year.

Methods

VAT law makes a distinction between non-business and partial exemption methods. If there is a mix of non-business, exempt and taxable activities, the non-business method must first be used to split residual VAT between business and non-business activities and then the partial exemption method must be used to split the remaining residual VAT between taxable and exempt activities.

The non-business method

The non-business method is used to apportion residual VAT between business and non-business activities. If you do not have any non-business activities, there is no need for a non-business method.

There is no 'standard' non-business method and there is no need to obtain the prior approval of HMRC for the method you use or for any change in the method used. However, it must be 'fair and reasonable' and you must be able to justify it to HMRC if asked. 'Fair and reasonable' means that it results in residual VAT being attributed to business activities to the extent that the associated purchases are used in making business supplies. HMRC may only reject a non-business method on the grounds that it does not provide a fair and reasonable result. However, it is possible to agree a non-business method in writing with HMRC and it is usually possible to get an agreement that includes the non-business and partial exemption methods in a single document.

Non-business methods are commonly based on the levels of income generated by business and non-business activities, the number of staff or cost of staff working in the different activities, or the floor areas occupied by the different activities. Many of the considerations applicable to non-business and 'special' partial exemption methods are similar, and these are examined below.

The partial exemption method

The partial exemption method apportions residual VAT between taxable and exempt activities. If you also have non-business activities, you must first use a non-business method to apportion residual VAT to the non-business activities and then apply the partial exemption method to the residual VAT apportioned to business activities.

There are two types of partial exemption method:

- **The standard method.** All VAT-registered organisations with a mix of taxable and exempt activities must use the 'standard' partial exemption method unless they have agreement from HMRC that they can use a 'special method'. The standard method uses the value of taxable and exempt supplies (income net of any VAT) to apportion residual VAT.

- **A special method**. Any partial exemption method that is not the standard method is called a 'special method'. You must obtain the agreement of HMRC to use a special partial exemption method and it must produce a fair and reasonable result. This means that it must result in residual input VAT being apportioned to taxable activities to the extent that the associated purchases are used in making taxable supplies.

The standard partial exemption method

The standard method calculates the percentage of residual input VAT that can be recovered as:

$$\text{Percentage of residual input VAT apportioned to taxable activities} = \frac{\text{Value of taxable supplies in the period (net of any VAT)}}{\text{Value of all business supplies in the period (net of any VAT)}} \times 100\%$$

The percentage is rounded up to the nearest whole number, unless the amount of residual input VAT apportioned to business activities is more than £400,000 per month on average, in which case it is rounded to two decimal places.

Example: The standard partial exemption method

Children's Help Centre (CHC) is registered for VAT and has a mix of taxable and exempt activities. It uses the standard partial exemption method. In VAT quarter 4 its residual input VAT is £2,000 and its sales were:

	Taxable	Exempt	Total
Sales – net	200,000	170,000	370,000

The apportionment of residual VAT is as follows:

	Taxable	Exempt
Business income	200,000	170,000
Percentage of total business income	200,000 / 370,000 = 54.05%	170,000 / 370,000 = 45.95%
Rounded up / down	55%	45%
Apportioned residual VAT	£2,000 x 55% = £1,100	£2,000 x 45% = £900

The standard method apportions the £2,000 residual input VAT as £1,100 to taxable activities and £900 to exempt activities.

Special partial exemption methods

You cannot start to use, change or cease using a special partial exemption method without the consent of HMRC. Any partial exemption method that does not strictly use the value of taxable and exempt supplies to apportion residual VAT is a special method and therefore requires approval. This is so even if it differs in only minor ways from the standard method.

From 1 April 2005 all new or revised special methods must be approved under a formal written agreement with HMRC and, from 1 April 2007, you must make a written declaration that, to the best of your knowledge and belief, the method will result in a fair and reasonable attribution of VAT to taxable supplies. HMRC can serve a notice to recover any over-claimed VAT in the previous three years (but not earlier than the start of the method) in the event that:

- the method is found to be unfair or unreasonable, and

- the method results in an over-recovery of VAT, and

- the person making the declaration knew or ought to have known this when making the declaration.

An application for a new special method or for a change to a special method or to stop using a special method should be made to your local VAT Business Centre. If applying for a new special method, you should provide full details of the proposed method and explain why it is fair and reasonable. HMRC will also usually require you to provide a worked example of the method using actual figures.

A special method should result in a fair and reasonable apportionment of input VAT. Here, 'fair and reasonable' means that it results in input VAT being recovered to the extent it is used in making taxable supplies. The method must also avoid ambiguities and situations in which interpretation is unclear and it must be capable of being verified by HMRC without undue difficulty.

Some special methods may require you to keep specific records. For example, if your method is based on staff time spent on different activities, you will have to keep records of how much time staff spend on different activities. HMRC will generally refuse methods that use records that are kept only for the purposes of the method. However, if records are kept for other purposes as well, they should be acceptable.

When a special partial exemption method is appropriate

Usually, organisations implement special partial exemption methods when:

- the standard method does not produce a fair and reasonable apportionment, or

- there is a special method that is administratively easier to use and that also provides a fair and reasonable apportionment.

Choosing a special method because it ties in with how you manage your organisation or how you cost projects is a perfectly reasonable and valid approach – so long as it also provides a fair and reasonable attribution of VAT.

There are many situations in which the standard method does not provide a fair and reasonable result. The standard method assumes that each pound of taxable sale and each pound of exempt sale incur the same levels of VAT-bearing residual expense. Situations in which this might not be the case include:

- One type of activity produces high-value sales but these incur, on a transaction-by-transaction basis, no more VAT-bearing residual costs than do low-value sales generated by a different type of activity.

- One type of activity makes heavy use of volunteers and so requires a lower level of income than another type which makes little use of volunteers. However, both types of activity consume similar levels of VAT-bearing residual cost.

- There is a significant timing difference between the receipt of supplies and the associated sales, for example where sales are made in one tax year but the associated costs were incurred in a different tax year.

Basis for non-business and special partial exemption methods

The most important consideration in determining an appropriate non-business or special partial exemption method is determining what drives the residual costs. If you use cost drivers to apportion overheads to projects in your management or statutory accounts then these may provide a suitable basis for a non-business or special partial exemption method, and one that, in the case of special partial exemption methods, will be acceptable to HMRC.

Non-business and special partial exemption methods are commonly based on:

- **The number of full-time equivalent staff employed in the different areas of activity.** When used as a non-business method the proportion of residual VAT attributed to business activities is the number of staff working in business activities divided by the number of staff working in business and non-business activities. When used as a partial exemption method the recoverable proportion is the number of staff working in taxable activities divided by the number of staff working in business activities. You will have to agree with HMRC how core staff are dealt with. Logically, core staff should be excluded from the calculations, however HMRC sometimes insist that they are included. HMRC view the aim of any method as being the production of a fair and reasonable result, and if this requires a method that conflicts with mathematical logic, then so be it. The staff numbers method assumes that core staff are a small proportion of all staff, that VAT-bearing residual costs comprise mainly the cost of supporting staff, and each member of staff incurs roughly the same amount of VAT-bearing residual cost.

- **The staff cost of different areas of activity.** This is broadly the same as using the number of staff but may be easier to implement as figures for staff costs are likely to be more readily available. It assumes that higher-paid staff incur more VAT-bearing residual cost than lower-paid staff.

- **The staff time spent in different areas of activity.** This is again broadly equivalent to using the number of staff but allows for staff working flexibly across different activities. It will be necessary to keep records of how much time staff spend working in different activities, for example staff timesheets, and HMRC may reject the method if the only reason the staff time records are kept are for VAT purposes.

- **The staff and volunteer time spent in different areas of activity.** If volunteers make a significant contribution and incur roughly the same level of residual VAT-bearing cost as employed staff per hour worked, this method allows you to include volunteers in the calculation. As with the staff time method, you will have to keep verifiable records of the amount of staff and volunteer time spent on each activity and HMRC may reject a special method if such records are only kept for VAT purposes.

- **The floor area occupied by different activities.** If VAT-bearing premises costs form a major part of residual costs and if activities occupy clearly defined areas, using the floor area occupied by different activities may be appropriate. See the comments above for whether or not areas occupied by core functions are excluded from the calculations. HMRC generally reject floor area based methods where there are significant areas under shared use, for example an area used by taxable and exempt activities, unless there is a clearly defined pattern to the shared use, for example the taxable and exempt activities occupy the area at specific times.

- **The levels of expenditure incurred in different areas of activity.** This method assumes that VAT-bearing residual costs are incurred in proportion to the level of direct expenditure on a project. Though superficially attractive this method can be complicated to operate in practice.

The percentages derived by non-business and special partial exemption methods should be rounded to two decimal places. Before 1 April 2005 it was permissible to round the percentages generated by output-based special partial exemption methods up to the nearest whole percentage (as described above for the standard method). Any such methods agreed before 1 April 2005 are still valid, though as soon as the method is modified this advantage is lost.

Example: Special method

Specialist Learning Services (SLS) uses staff costs to apportion residual VAT in both its non-business and partial exemption methods. In quarter 1 the staff costs incurred by the different areas of activity were:

Taxable activities	£7,500
Exempt activities	£6,200
Non-business activities	£28,450
Core staff	£6,340

The core staff cost is ignored. Total activity staff costs are: £7,500 + £6,200 + £28,450 = £42,150. The apportionment of residual VAT is as follows:

Taxable activities	£7,500 / £42,150 = 17.79%
Exempt activities	£6,200 / £42,150 = 14.71%
Non-business activities	£28,450 / £42,150 = 67.50%

Note that all percentages are rounded to two decimal places.

Sectorised methods

Where a single method does not result in a fair and reasonable attribution of residual VAT, it may be appropriate to split the residual costs into different sectors and then apply different methods to each sector. Sectorised methods are commonly used in large organisations and often reflect the organisation's internal costing structure.

Example: Sectorised method

National Rescue Services (NRS) has a mix of taxable and exempt activities. It uses a sectorised method in which residual costs are split into:

- Management and administration costs – residual VAT is split on the basis of staff cost.

- Premises costs – residual VAT is apportioned on the basis of floor area.

In quarter 1 the residual VAT relating to management and administration costs was £4 million and the residual VAT relating to premises costs was £3 million. The split of staff costs and floor area was:

Activity type	Staff cost (£m)	Staff costs (%)	Floor area (m²)	Floor area (%)
Taxable activities	24	24/56 = 42.86%	300	37.5%

Exempt activities	32	32/56 = 57.14%	500	62.5%
Totals	56	100%	800	100%

The apportionment of residual VAT for quarter 1 is:

Activity type	Management & admin	Premises	Total
Taxable activities	£4m x 42.86% = £1,714,400	£3m x 37.5% = £1,125,000	£2,839,400
Exempt activities	£4m x 57.14% = £2,285,600	£3m x 62.5% = £1,875,000	£4,160,600

Incidental and one-off transactions

In calculating the value of supplies under any partial exemption method, certain incidental supplies must be excluded, as their inclusion would otherwise distort the apportionment of residual VAT. These include:

- **Income from one-off transactions.** This includes income from the sale of capital goods such as the sale of cars, equipment and property; income from one-off financial transactions such as a sale of investments; and income from one-off real estate transactions such as the grant or assignment of a lease.

- **Passive income** where no real effort is made to generate the income, and the VAT-bearing costs incurred in generating such income are insignificant. However, if your organisation incurs significant VAT in generating such income, the income will not be passive.

Bank interest and investment income received passively is non-business and so will not enter the partial exemption method. However, the principle can also be applied to the non-business method. Where the VAT-bearing residual cost incurred in generating a type of non-business income is insignificant, inclusion of the income in any non-business method is likely to be distortive and therefore will not produce a fair and reasonable result.

Legacy income

For many charities, legacy income will also be received passively. Legacy income is usually highly variable but sometimes significant. If the effort put into generating legacy income is insignificant, for example restricted to periodic reminders put into publicity material, the inclusion of legacy income in an income-based non-business method may result in the method being unfair. In such a situation, legacy income should be excluded from the non-business method, though it would usually be wise to seek the prior agreement of HMRC to this approach.

Provisional recovery rates

As it can be a lengthy process to calculate the amount of VAT recoverable each quarter, HMRC may be prepared to agree a provisional rate of recovery. This would probably be agreed after a period of registration – say, one year. The first annual adjustment would calculate the recovery rate for the past year. This rate could then be used on a provisional basis for the coming year. The annual adjustment calculation would ensure that the correct amount of VAT is recovered overall for the year and then provide the new figure for the provisional basis of recovery calculations on VAT returns in the coming year. A change in the provisional recovery rate does not represent a change in the partial exemption method.

Income-based non-business methods

Many organisations use income-based non-business methods, especially if they also use the standard partial exemption method. A typical income-based non-business method is:

$$\text{Percentage of residual VAT apportioned to business activities} = \frac{\text{Business income in the period}}{\text{Business income plus non-business income in the period}} \times 100\%$$

However, there are dangers with this method that may result in an unfair attribution of residual VAT:

• Some passive non-business income such as deposit interest and legacies may incur little or no VAT-bearing costs to generate, so its inclusion in the denominator would be distortive. Passive non-business income may therefore need to be removed from the denominator.

• Some activities may be taxable but receive grants and other non-business income in support of the activity – see Chapter 4 for more about this scenario. If this non-business income is excluded from the numerator it may result in an under-apportionment of residual VAT to the activity.

- Recent case law (see the Children's Society case in Chapter 4) suggests that the costs incurred in generating certain types of non-business income are residual. The affected income is income that is unrestricted, outside the scope of VAT because it is not a supply and used to support the business activities. This may include such income as unrestricted grants, donations and legacies. The 'standard' non-business may need to be adjusted for this type of income.

Gaps in special partial exemption methods

Sometimes a special method may not cover a situation – for example, if it fails to deal with a new activity or a new type of residual expense. The special method is said to have a gap. When there is a gap in a special method it does not mean that any associated VAT is irrecoverable. The affected residual VAT must be recovered according to its use in taxable activities.

The presence of a gap may indicate that the special method will need to be revised. If there is a gap in a special partial exemption method, you will have to agree with HMRC how the gap is to be dealt with in the interim and in future periods. However, it is important to appreciate that the primary motivation of many HMRC officers is the maximisation of tax yield to the Exchequer. HMRC may therefore see this as an opportunity to completely revise, to your detriment, a method that is fundamentally sound but just requires minor modifications. You should therefore propose a solution to HMRC and show how this produces a fair and reasonable result, rather than relying on HMRC to provide a solution. If in doubt, it may be wise to seek independent advice before contacting HMRC.

Retrospective changes to methods

Retrospective changes to special partial exemption methods are not normally allowed, though methods may be approved with effect from the start of the VAT year in which an application is received. Without this, the annual adjustment may be problematic.

Requests for retrospective changes beyond this are only allowed in exceptional circumstances, for example where HMRC has been at fault, the method is inoperable, where the method of calculation produces a nonsensical result or where there has been an exceptional natural disaster necessitating a temporary change of working practices.

Non-business methods can be changed retrospectively if the existing method does not produce a fair and reasonable result, but the proposed method does. However, if the existing method does produce a fair and reasonable result, it cannot be changed retrospectively.

Methods and VAT groups

Where different organisations are members of the same VAT group (see Chapter 11 for information on VAT groups) there is a single entity for VAT purposes, and therefore a single non-business method and a single partial exemption method must be applied across the group. The *de minimis* test is also applied across the group, but when determining whether any supplies are incidental (and should therefore be excluded from any method calculations) the group entities must be considered separately. For example, the incidental sale of a building by a company does not have to be included even if the organisation is in the same VAT group as a business that trades in property.

Partial exemption method overrides

If a partial exemption method does not produce a fair and reasonable result it may be overridden. There are different override rules for the standard and special partial exemption methods.

The standard method override

The standard partial exemption method is automatically overridden if:

1. it does not provide an attribution of residual VAT that reflects the actual use of residual purchases, and

2. total residual input VAT (i.e. residual VAT excluding any attributed to non-business activities) is more than £50,000 per year or £25,000 per year for group undertakings that are not members of the same VAT group, and

3. the difference between the results produced by the standard method and one based on actual use is more than £50,000 or more than £25,000 and 50 per cent of the residual input VAT (excluding any attributed to non-business activities).

The standard method override will only affect large organisations. Where residual input VAT exceeds £50,000 per year, HMRC advise that the organisation should carry out a parallel partial exemption calculation based on actual use at the end of the tax year. Any special method that produces a fair and reasonable apportionment will be acceptable. If the difference between the standard method and the use-based method exceeds the above limits, the resulting adjustment should be included with the annual adjustment. There is no need to submit the parallel computations with your annual adjustment, unless they result in a standard method override.

The special method override notice

If HMRC consider that a special partial exemption method is not fair and reasonable, they can serve a special method override notice. The notice allows HMRC to impose an immediate override on the results of the special method until a replacement method is implemented. A notice served by HMRC will usually specify how the partial exemption calculation should be performed in the period until a new method is agreed.

The organisation can also serve a special method override notice on HMRC. This has the same effect but must be approved by HMRC before the organisation can implement it. See VAT Notice 706 for details of how to serve a special method override notice. See Chapter 14 for how to access the VAT Notices from the HMRC website.

Changes in intention or use

If you purchase goods or services with the intention of using them in making taxable supplies, you can recover any associated input VAT at the time of the purchase. However, if your intention is not fulfilled, for example if goods originally intended for use in a taxable activity are actually used in an exempt activity, you may have to correct the original recovery. This also works the other way around – if you originally intended to use purchases in exempt or non-business activities but your intention or use changes, you may be able to recover some of the VAT that was irrecoverable at the time of the purchase.

There are specific rules that allow for changes in use of:

- land and buildings or civil engineering works costing more than £250,000 or computer equipment costing more than £50,000 that are used for mixed taxable and exempt activities: see the Capital Goods Scheme in Chapter 10

- business assets that are put to non-business or private use: see the section on Lennartz assets in Chapter 4

- non-business assets that are put to business use and zero rating was claimed on the original transaction, for example the construction of a building that is intended for a relevant charitable purpose. See Chapter 8 for details.

For other changes in intention or use, an adjustment must be made in the VAT return for the period when the intention or use changed.

- If the change of intention or use occurs in the same tax year as the original purchase, the amendment is made in the annual adjustment.

- If the change of intention or use occurs after the end of the tax year of the original purchase, but before six years after the first day of the VAT period of the purchase, the annual adjustment for the year of purchase must be reworked and an

41

adjustment made in the VAT return for the period when the change of intention or use occurred.

- If the change of intention or use occurs more than six years after the first day of the VAT period of purchase, no adjustment can be made.

Abortive purchases

Where a purchase is made with the intention of being used in an activity, but the activity is aborted, the initial attribution of any VAT incurred on the abortive purchases stands and no adjustment is possible if the purchase is not used to make any supply. However, if the purchases are instead put to use in a different type of activity then there is a change of use and an adjustment must be made under the change of intention or use rules, as explained above.

Out-of-country supplies

Out-of-country supplies are supplies made by a UK-registered organisation where the place of supply is outside the UK. See Chapter 9 for details of how to determine the place of supply. UK VAT incurred in making out-of-country supplies is:

- recoverable if the supply would have been taxable had it been made in the UK;

- irrecoverable if the supply would have been exempt had it been made in the UK (with the exception of certain out-of-country supplies of financial and insurance services which carry the right of recovery).

If there are out-of-country supplies with the right of recovery then an additional step is required in the partial exemption calculations. First, residual input VAT (i.e. residual VAT after discarding any attributable to non-business activities) must be apportioned to the out-of-country supplies with a right of recovery on the basis of use. This residual input VAT is recoverable, and the normal partial exemption calculation is performed. This should include any out-of-country supplies without a right of recovery. Since 1 April 2007 it has been possible to agree a 'combined method' with HMRC that combines the out-of-country apportionment and the standard or special partial exemption method.

4 Business and non-business

This chapter explains the terms 'supply', 'consideration', 'business' and 'non-business' and explains how to determine whether your activities are business or non-business. The first part of this chapter explains the basic principles, then the second part examines some typical non-business activities encountered in voluntary organisations.

Basic principles

The scope of VAT

If an activity is subject to VAT it is said to be 'within the scope' of VAT. To be within the scope of VAT, an activity:

1. must involve making a **supply** for **consideration**, and

2. the supply must be of **goods** or **services**, and

3. the supply must take place in the course or furtherance of a **business activity**.

If any of these conditions is not met, then the activity is said to be outside the scope of VAT. This means that no VAT is due on any sales or outputs from the activity and that no VAT incurred on purchases attributable to the activity can normally be recovered.

The three conditions amount to a series of tests that must be applied to an activity to determine if it is within the scope of VAT. If any of the tests fail, the activity is **outside the scope of VAT**. If all succeed, it is a business activity and within the scope of VAT.

In addition to the three conditions above, there are in fact two further conditions that must be satisfied before an activity is subject to VAT:

4. it must take place in the UK (to be subject to UK VAT) or another EC state (to be subject to that state's VAT), and

5. It must be made by a person or organisation that is either registered for VAT or required to be registered for VAT.

For details of how to determine where a supply takes place, see Chapter 9. For details of when you should be registered for VAT, see Chapter 2. In this chapter we examine the first three conditions.

Supply

You must first decide if your activity involves making a supply for consideration. A supply for consideration usually takes place where someone agrees to do something in return for a fee or payment in some form.

In a few exceptional situations a supply is deemed to have been made even where there is no consideration. Examples of these situations include:

- the temporary use of business assets for non-business purposes

- the retention of business assets on deregistration

- the non-business use of services supplied to a business

- the permanent transfer or disposal of business assets.

However, for a supply to be within the scope of VAT consideration must normally be paid in return for the supply.

Consideration

Consideration is what is given in return for the supply. Consideration does not have to be monetary; it includes barter transactions, part-exchange, the granting of rights and the acceptance of constraints or limitations. The consideration also does not have to be paid by the recipient of the supply: it can be paid by a third party and it can be by way of public subsidy. However:

- the consideration must be directly linked to the supply

- the consideration must be capable of being valued monetarily

- there must be some form of consensual agreement that the consideration is provided in return for the supply.

Though there must be a direct link between the value of the supply and the amount of consideration paid, the fact that people pay the same amount for varying benefits or pay differing amounts for the same benefit does not stop the payment from being consideration.

Though the supply and consideration do not have to arise under the terms of a contract, there must be some form of consensual agreement that the consideration is provided in return for the supply. If the payer has no choice but to pay the consideration or if the payer has no control over the service provided this may indicate that the payment is not consideration. If the values of the supply and purported payment for the supply are clearly very different this may indicate that not all of the payment is consideration for the supply.

Case law on supply

'Supply' and 'consideration' are poorly defined in the legislation and we must turn to case law for an understanding of these terms. Three old decisions of the European Court of Justice (ECJ) were important in setting boundaries to what constitute supply and consideration:

In the case of *Coöperatieve Aardappelenbewaarplaats* (commonly referred to as the 'Dutch potato case') a Dutch agricultural co-operative provided potato storage facilities for its members. The members normally paid a fee to use the facilities, but one year the co-operative provided the storage free. The Dutch tax authorities claimed that the consequent reduction in the value of the members' shares in the co-operative was consideration for the supply of storage. The ECJ decided that any reduction in the value of the shares as a result of the free storage was unquantifiable and insufficiently directly connected to constitute consideration.

In a case involving the Apple and Pear Development Council the Council charged a statutory levy to apple and pear growers, based on the acreage under cultivation. UK Customs claimed the levy was consideration for the supply of promotional services to the growers by the Council. The ECJ decided there was no direct link between the levy and promotional services. The growers had to pay the levy whether or not they received any promotional services and, even if they did, there was no direct link between the size of the levy and level of promotional services received.

In the case of RJ Tolsma, Mr Tolsma solicited donations by playing a barrel organ on the streets of Leeuwarden in the Netherlands. The Dutch tax authorities claimed that the donations from passers-by were consideration for the supply of musical entertainment. The ECJ decided that there was no link between the supply of musical entertainment and donation. Passers-by received musical entertainment whether or not they paid a donation and gave differing amounts despite receiving the same supply.

Supply of goods or services

If you determine that you are making a supply, you must then decide if the supply is of goods or services. If it is neither a supply of goods nor one of services then it is outside the scope of VAT. In fact, almost all supplies are either a supply of goods or a supply of services.

Goods are tangible property. A supply of goods is the transfer of the right to dispose of tangible property as owner. Usually it is obvious when you are supplying goods. The law defines a 'supply of services' as any supply which is not a supply of goods. See

Chapter 9 for further information on the distinction between a supply of goods and a supply of services.

At first sight this suggests that all supplies are supplies of goods or services. However, the law deems certain supplies to be neither a supply of goods nor of services. The key example is the transfer of a going concern. Some supplies are also disregarded – for example, supplies between members of a VAT group. See Chapter 11 for more information on VAT groups and transfers of a going concern.

In the course or furtherance of a business activity

Once you have decided that you are making a supply of goods or services you must then decide if the supply is made in the course or furtherance of a business activity. Only supplies made in the course or furtherance of a business activity are within the scope of VAT.

The term 'business' is a feature of UK legislation. It does not figure in the EC legislation, even though the UK VAT legislation derives from it. EC legislation uses the term 'economic activity' instead. If there is a supply but the associated activity is not business, then the supply is said to be 'non-business' or to 'lack economic content' and it is outside the scope of VAT. If a supply is made in the course of a business then the activity of making the supply is said to be business activity and its inherent nature is said to be economic.

As with supply, the terms 'business' and 'economic activity' are poorly defined by the legislation and we must rely on case law for guidance. The case law understanding of what constitutes a non-business activity, especially when undertaken by a charity, has developed in recent years and some of the earlier UK case law concepts, such as the 'business tests', are now being overtaken by the EC concept of 'economic activity'.

Deemed business activities

Section 94 of the VAT Act 1994 deems that certain supplies are always made in the course or furtherance of a business activity. These include:

*   The provision by a club, association or organisation, for a subscription or other consideration, of the facilities or advantages available to its members (though there are some concessions for charities – see Chapter 5).

*   The admission, for a consideration, of persons to any premises.

*   Anything done in connection with the termination or intended termination of a business is treated as being done in the course or furtherance of that business.

*   The disposal of a business is normally a supply made in the course or furtherance of the business, though if the disposal meets the rules for a transfer of a going

concern, it is outside the scope of VAT. See Chapter 11 for information on the transfer of a going concern rules.

If a supply meets one of these descriptions then it will always be a business supply and thus within the scope of VAT.

The business tests and economic activity

UK case law in the 1980s and 1990s established six tests to determine whether or not an activity was business. The tests were:

1. Is the activity a serious undertaking earnestly pursued?

2. Is the activity an occupation or function, which is actively pursued with reasonable or recognisable continuity?

3. Does the activity have a certain measure of substance in terms of the quarterly or annual value of taxable supplies made?

4. Is the activity conducted in a regular manner and on sound and recognised business principles?

5. Is the activity predominantly concerned with the making of taxable supplies for a consideration?

6. Are the taxable supplies that are being made of a kind which, subject to differences of detail, are commonly made by those who seek to profit from them?

The tests were not intended as a checklist – but more as a series of questions to ask about an activity in order to gain a general impression of its nature. The fifth test was considered the most important. If this test failed then the activity was non-business. Many cases revolved around deciding what the predominant concern of the activity was.

The concept of 'predominant concern' has now been overtaken by the concept of 'intrinsic nature'. Recent case law suggests that what really matters is the intrinsic nature of the activity – is it economic or is it something else? In the recent Sheiling Trust case (2006, VAT Tribunal 19472), the tribunal reviewed recent case law and suggested the following approach for deciding whether or not an activity is business or non-business:

(1) A wide-ranging enquiry must be made with the objective of discovering the intrinsic nature of the activity: that enquiry should extend to the features of the activity, and the manner and context in which it is carried out, including the relationship between all the parties.

(2) To comprise a 'business', the activity must have 'economic content' – its intrinsic nature must be economic (and not, for example, social or charitable).

(3) The fact that in the carrying out of the activity a supply is made for a consideration is not in itself sufficient to give the activity such 'economic content'.

(4) The fact that in the carrying out of the activity no profit is made (or there is no intention to make a profit) is not in itself sufficient to enable the activity to be characterised as having no such 'economic content': in particular, an activity may have 'economic content' where it is carried out by way of making supplies which are of a kind that are made commercially, even if they are made for no profit.

(5) The motive of the person carrying out the activity does not dictate its tax treatment (and in particular, whether or not it is a business for VAT purposes): that treatment must be ascertained from the nature of the activity rather than its purpose.

(6) If the activity is undertaken by a charity, then the fact that the activity is a means whereby the charity carries out its charitable objects is not in itself sufficient to enable the activity to be characterised as having no 'economic content': but that fact is relevant to the intrinsic nature of the activity and therefore to the question of whether or not the activity has 'economic content'.

(7) The six 'business tests' are useful tools which can be employed in the analysis of an activity to determine whether it is a business, but they are no more than tools and should not be applied as a comprehensive and rigid code.

Though the profit motive does not have to be present for an activity to be business, its presence or absence is often an important factor. Where a 'supply' is made by a voluntary organisation at undervalue or so as to just cover costs this may indicate that there is in fact no supply or the supply is non-business. However, this feature is unlikely to be decisive in itself. If, in addition, the activity clearly has a charitable or social objective and possesses other features that would be unusual in a commercial profit-oriented environment, then it may well be non-business.

Case law on business activity

Some recent cases illustrate these points:

In a case involving the Yarburgh Trust, the trust let premises at a nominal rent to a charitable playgroup. The playgroup charged fees but set them so as to just cover costs in order to remain as affordable as possible to parents on low incomes. The playgroup involved the parents in its running and also provided support services to the parents and families of the children above and beyond those that would normally be provided by a commercial playgroup. The judge decided that the trust rented the premises to the group on a concessionary basis and so it was not a business activity, nor was the activity of the playgroup itself. The intrinsic nature of the playgroup's activity was charitable and not economic and so it was not a business activity.

In a case involving St Paul's Playgroup, the playgroup charged fees of £85–95 per place per week. The cost of providing a place was £130 and fees were subsidised by a grant. The admission policy was skewed towards disadvantaged children and fees were set as low as possible to be affordable. Fees were less than commercial alternatives, despite the playgroup providing higher staff-to-child ratios and more highly qualified staff than most commercial alternatives. The judge decided that this too, like Yarburgh, lacked economic content and that the intrinsic nature of the activity was social or charitable and not economic.

HMRC announced their position on the St Paul's case in Business Brief 02/05 (see Chapter 14 for how to access Business Briefs). They stated that they considered both Yarburgh and St Paul's to be wrongly decided but that they would not appeal the cases and that they will accept that the provision of nursery and crèche facilities by charities, along the same lines as those in Yarburgh and St Paul's, is not a business activity. However, the impact of these cases is clearly wider than nurseries and crèches, and recent tribunal decisions illustrate this.

In a case involving Donaldson's College, an Edinburgh-based college provided education for deaf children. Substantial fees were charged by the college, the fees being met partly by the Scottish Executive and partly by each child's local authority. The tribunal decided that the provision of education by the college was a non-business activity. There was no intention to make a profit and fees were set to cover costs. The payment by the Scottish Executive was a grant but did not constitute third-party consideration. The Scottish Executive decided the split between itself and the local authorities. There was thus insufficient connection between the service received by the local authority and the payment it made for education to constitute consideration for a supply. Therefore there was no supply to the local authorities and no supply by the college.

The Children's Society case

Until fairly recently it was widely assumed that all VAT on purchases made by non-business activities was attributable to those activities and therefore irrecoverable. However, the Church of England Children's Society case suggests that where the activity with which a purchase is most closely linked is outside the scope of VAT because it is not a supply, that linkage is irrelevant for the purposes of determining deductibility. What matters is the link, if any, with taxable supplies. Where the income generated by such an activity is unrestricted and used for the general purposes of the organisation, the related VAT is residual.

In the Children's Society case the society employed professional fundraisers to recruit committed givers. The funds raised from the committed givers were used partly to support the taxable activities of the society. The court decided that the VAT incurred on the professional fundraisers was residual as it was linked to the business activities of the society.

In practice this means that the costs of generating donations are residual if the donations are used for the general purposes of the organisation. In addition to the cost of professional fundraisers, this may apply to such costs as investment management costs, general appeal costs and the costs of generating legacies. As with other residual VAT, the VAT on such expenses must be put through any non-business and partial exemption methods to determine the recoverable part.

The decision may also impact on non-business methods. Note that you do not have to obtain prior approval from HMRC for a change to your non-business method, and you may backdate a revised non-business method up to three years if the previous method was unfair or unreasonable.

Non-business assets

Non-business assets are the assets that are used to support the non-business activities of an organisation. Usually the VAT incurred in purchasing non-business assets cannot be recovered. If an asset is purchased for mixed business and non-business use then there are several ways of dealing with it.

- You can treat the asset as a **non-business asset**. This means that VAT incurred in purchasing the asset cannot be recovered. If the asset is in fact also used for business activities then any VAT incurred in the use and maintenance of the asset is recoverable to the extent it can be attributed to the making of taxable supplies, and recovery of this VAT does not automatically indicate that the asset is in fact a business asset. If the asset is later sold and it has remained a non-business asset then no output VAT is chargeable on the sale.

- You can treat the asset as a **business asset**. This means that VAT incurred in purchasing the asset is recoverable (subject to the normal recovery rules) and that output VAT may be due if the asset is later sold. If any VAT incurred in purchasing the asset was recovered then any non-business use of the asset is a deemed supply of services and output VAT must be accounted for on the non-business use. This is known as the Lennartz mechanism. The rules for 'Lennartz assets' are explained below.

- You can treat the asset as a mixed business/non-business asset. The VAT incurred on the business part of the asset is recoverable (subject to the partial exemption rules (see Chapter 3) and the capital goods scheme rules (see Chapter 10)), while the VAT relating to the non-business part of the asset is irrecoverable. If the asset is later sold, no output VAT is due on the non-business use part.

Lennartz assets NB.

If you put a business asset on which you recovered input VAT (even if only partly) to temporary non-business or private use, then there is a deemed supply and output VAT is due on the non-business or private use. Where you purchase an asset that will be put to mixed business and non-business use, you have the option of treating it as a business asset and accounting for output VAT on any non-business use of the asset.

This process of treating an asset as acquired for business purposes then accounting for output VAT on any non-business (or private) use is commonly called the 'Lennartz mechanism' or 'Lennartz accounting', and such assets are referred to as 'Lennartz assets'. The Lennartz treatment is sometimes adopted by voluntary organisations as it gives a cash flow advantage – input VAT is recovered up front while output VAT is paid when the non-business use occurs. However, the Lennartz treatment is not always advantageous – it is possible to pay more output VAT than was gained in input VAT recovery.

The Lennartz approach is only relevant where there is to be some business use of the asset and where VAT is incurred in the purchase, acquisition or construction of the asset. If the asset is purchased entirely for non-business or exempt purposes, no VAT can be recovered on the purchase and so there is no need to account for output VAT on any non-business use. Similarly, if the asset is zero-rated, there is no VAT to be recovered and so the Lennartz mechanism is not relevant.

In 2003 the UK legislated to prevent the Lennartz approach from being used for land and buildings. However, a 2005 ECJ decision made it clear that EC VAT law does not permit member states to block the Lennartz approach for land and buildings, and the legislation was replaced in 2007. It should be noted that at the time of writing (2007) there is a proposal before the EC to block the Lennartz approach permanently with effect from July 2008.

The Lennartz approach is available for the purchase, acquisition or construction of tangible assets, including land and buildings. It is not available for intangible assets such as intellectual property rights, and VAT incurred in the purchase or creation of such assets must be apportioned between business and non-business use.

The 2007 UK legislation sets out how the output VAT on the deemed supply arising from any non-business (or private) use is to be calculated from 1 November 2007. The value of the deemed supply in a period (for example, a VAT quarter) is the depreciation on the goods in the period multiplied by the proportion that non-business use forms of total use in the period. Land and buildings are taken to have an economic life of 120 months and other goods are taken to have an economic life of 60 months, unless the interest in the asset lasts for less. The economic life commences when the goods are first put to use. The value of the deemed supply is net and the output VAT charge is calculated at the standard rate on this.

Example: Lennartz asset

IN VAT quarter 1 an organisation buys a new commercial building costing £2m + VAT of £350,000 that will be put to mixed taxable and non-business use. The building is first put to use on 3 June and the organisation's VAT quarter 1 runs to 30 June. Non-business use in the period 3 to 30 June is 65%.

The deemed economic life of the building is 120 months.

During quarter 1 the building is used for 27/30 of a month, i.e. 0.9 months.

The deemed depreciation on the building in the period is (0.9 months / 120 months) x £2m = £15,000.

The depreciation that relates to the non-business use is £15,000 x 65% = £9,750.

The output VAT charge is therefore £9,750 x 17.5% = £1,706.25.

In the VAT return for quarter 1 the organisation reclaims the £350,000 input VAT in full and pays an output VAT charge of £1,706.25 for the non-business use.

Note that if the organisation was a charity it might have been able to zero rate the portion of the purchase cost that relates to non-business use – see Chapter 8.

The non-business use of a Lennartz asset constitutes a taxable supply by the organisation. This is therefore likely to affect any non-business or partial exemption methods in place, and if the introduction of a Lennartz asset results in existing methods becoming unfair, they will need to be modified.

If the Lennartz asset is also used for exempt purposes and falls within the capital goods scheme (see Chapter 10 for details of the capital goods scheme) then the capital goods scheme will restrict initial VAT recovery on the asset but, for the purposes of the capital goods scheme, the non-business use counts as taxable use. The interaction between the Lennartz and capital goods schemes can be very complicated. HMRC provide some guidance on this in VAT Information Sheet 14/07. See Chapter 14 for how to access the VAT Information Sheets.

If a Lennartz asset is already in use at 1 November 2007, its economic life is deemed to commence on 1 November 2007 but its duration is reduced to take account of any output VAT charged on non-business use up to that point. See VAT Information Sheet 14/07 for details of the calculation.

Non-business activities of voluntary organisations

In this section we examine activities of voluntary organisations that are often non-business or have non-business components.

Grants and donations

Most grants and donations (including legacies) received by charities are outside the scope of VAT. The donor gives funds to the charity in the form of a donation but there is no supply by the charity to the donor.

A grant-making charitable trust may achieve its objects through the work funded by its grant. However, this does not turn the grant into a supply. Service-level agreements and administrative conditions attached to grants, such as the need to meet specific service standards or to complete returns or provide details of how the grant was spent, do not constitute a supply by the recipient charity to the grant-maker.

However, if the funder (or someone connected to the funder) receives some direct benefit as a result of its funding of the recipient charity's activities, there may be a supply by the recipient charity, bringing the transaction within the scope of VAT. Note that even if the activity amounts to a supply by the recipient charity, the supply must still be made in the course or furtherance of a business activity for it to be within the scope of VAT.

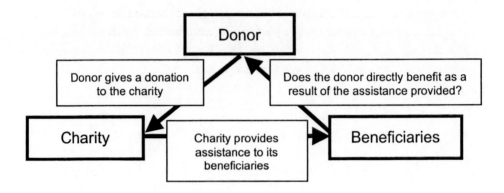

Grant versus contract

It can sometimes be difficult to ascertain the VAT status of funding agreements. Funding agreements may variously describe themselves as 'grants', 'service-level agreements', 'contracts', or sometimes several of these in the same document. Even where a funding agreement specifically states that it is outside the scope of VAT or exempt from VAT, this cannot necessarily be relied upon. The basic principles outlined in the first part of this chapter must be used to determine if the agreement amounts to a business supply. If it does, you should then consider if it is exempt (see Chapter 5) or zero-rated (see Chapters 6 and 8).

In cases of doubt, it is advisable to obtain a written ruling from HMRC. Where a voluntary organisation has incorrectly treated a funding agreement as outside the scope of VAT, or exempt based on terms in the funding agreement or on advice from the funder, then HMRC may be prepared to waive penalties and interest if they consider the voluntary organisation made reasonable efforts to establish the status of the agreement but was effectively misled by the funder. HMRC will consider the resources and expertise available to the organisation, so large organisations may be less likely to benefit from this concession than small organisations.

Funding from statutory bodies

Difficulties sometimes arise with funding from statutory agencies and from local and central government departments. These bodies often use template agreements designed to cope with a wide range of situations.

- If a voluntary organisation applies for financial support and the statutory body does not have a statutory duty to provide the service funded, then any funding is likely to be outside the scope of VAT.

- If the voluntary organisation provides goods or services directly to the statutory body (for example training for its staff) on commercial terms then this is likely to be a business supply and within the scope of VAT, however the funding is described.

- If the voluntary organisation is providing goods or services to a third party and the statutory body has a statutory duty to provide the third party with those goods or services (so that the statutory body is effectively contracting out the activity) then the voluntary organisation may be making a supply to the statutory body. If the supply also amounts to a business activity of the voluntary organisation, then it will be within the scope of VAT, though potentially exempt, for example, if welfare services are being provided.

Contracted out local authority leisure services

In a Scottish case (*Edinburgh, South Lanarkshire & Renfrewshire Leisure Services, 2004, VAT Tribunal 18784*) the VAT Tribunal found that funding provided by Scottish local authorities to non-profit organisations set up to run their leisure services were not grants, but consideration for a VATable supply by the leisure service organisations to the local authorities. This was because the local authorities had a statutory duty to provide leisure services that was not satisfied by commercial providers. The local authorities had effectively sub-contracted this obligation to the leisure service organisations and they derived a benefit as a result of the arrangement.

Revenue and Customs Brief 28/07 sets out HMRC's position on the treatment of contracted out local authority leisure services. Where these were developed and owned independently and the owner is merely seeking financial support from the local authority, any local authority funding is likely to be an outside the scope grant. Where management of the facilities has been contracted out, any local authority funding received is more likely to be seen as consideration for a supply of services to the local authority.

However, the contractor may be acting as principal or agent for the local authority. The contractor will be acting as principal if the leisure facilities are provided in the contractor's own name and the contractor accepts responsibility for the services. In this situation, charges to users will belong to the contractor and the fee charged to the local authority will be, however calculated, a standard-rated supply. The contractor will act as agent if the facilities are provided in the local authority's name and the contractor merely collects charges on the local authority's behalf. The customer charges handed over to the local authority will be outside the scope as far as the contractor is concerned, but the contractor's management fee to the local authority will be standard-rated.

Grants in support of business activities

If an activity is business or economic then receipt of a grant as subsidy for the activity will not necessarily stop the activity from being a business activity or block full recovery of VAT on purchases attributable to the activity.

A fairly common example is a start-up grant, where a grant is received to get the activity going but the activity will clearly be a taxable business activity once it is up and running. The grant may be outside the scope of VAT but the funded activity is taxable so all inputs are recoverable, including those on start-up costs and the costs of applying for the grant. Even if the start-up is a failure and the only funding was a grant, this need not block VAT recovery.

The key requirement is that the activity is or will be a taxable business activity. If there will be no fees charged (so there is no consideration) or if the fees are set below cost and other 'un-commercial' features are present (as in the *Yarburgh* or *St Paul's* cases) then it may not be a business activity.

Consideration paid by a third party

Voluntary organisations sometimes receive a grant towards the costs of providing a supply to a specified third party. The supply helps achieve the organisation's objects but is also of direct benefit to the third party. The third party may or may not contribute towards the costs.

EC VAT legislation provides that, with certain specific exceptions, the consideration for a supply includes everything which has been or is to be obtained by the supplier from the recipient or a third party for the supply, including subsidies directly linked to the price of the supply.

Consideration for a supply therefore does not have to be paid by the recipient of the supply – it can be paid by an independent third party. However, the consideration must still be directly linked to the supply.

This is illustrated by the ECJ case Keeping Newcastle Warm (2002, EUECJ C-353/00). Keeping Newcastle Warm was a business providing energy efficiency advice to local residents. It received a government grant of £10 for every piece of energy-saving advice it gave. This was held to be part of the consideration for the supply of energy advice. The Advocate General in the case drew a distinction between subsidies that were directly linked to a supply (as in this case), which could be consideration for a supply, and global subsidies which would generally not constitute consideration for a supply. So if Keeping Newcastle Warm had received a block grant and used it to subsidise its prices this would probably not have been VATable.

HMRC guidance quotes the example of a charity that receives a grant to build a wall around an unsightly factory. The factory owner must pay all costs not covered by the grant. The objective for the charity is to improve the environment for the local community but the factory owner also receives a supply (the new wall).

In HMRC's view, the value of the supply by the charity to the factory owner is the full cost of the wall, and VAT is due on this amount. Even though the factory owner must only pay the charity the difference between the cost of the wall and grant subsidy, the VAT element of the invoice to the factory owner is based on the full cost of the wall and not the amount actually paid. The HMRC guidance does not explain what happens if the VAT component is greater than the actual amount paid.

Donor benefits

Many charities offer donors small benefits to encourage donations. The gift aid rules allow charities and community amateur sports clubs to give fairly substantial benefits to donors without affecting gift aid recovery. However, there is no similar concession for VAT.

HMRC accept that small tokens given in acknowledgement of donations are not supplies as long as a minimum donation is not specified. Examples include flags, poppies, badges and stickers.

Where a minimum donation is specified, the minimum donation is likely to be deemed consideration for the benefits offered, with any donation above the minimum a genuine outside the scope donation. If a minimum donation is suggested but not required, then the entire amount can be treated as an outside the scope donation.

Where more substantial benefits are given then, provided no minimum donation is required to obtain the benefit, there is still unlikely to be a supply of the benefit. However, giving away substantial benefits to donors for no guaranteed return may be a questionable use of resources for a charity.

Goods and services provided at or below cost

The provision of goods or services at or below cost can be either a business or a non-business activity. The absence of a profit motive does not automatically imply that an activity is non-business, but it is sometimes indicative of the fact that no supply is being made or that the activity is non-business.

At one extreme, a commercial organisation running a loss-leader campaign will be providing goods or services at undervalue, but with a clear commercial purpose. At the other extreme, a charity providing a welfare service for a nominal or token charge is unlikely to be considered to be making a business supply.

Where an activity is subsidised by a grant, then the grant may constitute consideration if it is directly linked to a supply made by the activity. For example, see the case of Keeping Newcastle Warm above. However, if the grant is a global subsidy for the activity then it is unlikely to constitute consideration.

Where a charity subsidises fees from its own resources or from grants, and the activity has a clear charitable or social objective and also possesses significant features that would be unusual in a commercial environment, then the activity is likely to be non-business. For examples of the recent case law on this, see the above section: Case law on business activity.

HMRC, by concession, allow charities that provide welfare services at significantly below cost to distressed persons for the relief of their distress, to be treated as non-business. 'Significantly below cost' means subsidised by at least 15 per cent, and the subsidy must be available to everyone. 'Distressed' means someone who is suffering from pain, grief, anguish, severe poverty and so on. The charity must be providing the service to the distressed individual, and not a local authority. The subsidy can come from the charity's own resources or from grants and donations. When calculating the subsidy, HMRC exclude capital expenditure on buildings and notional costs such as depreciation, contingencies, and the time donated by volunteers.

Goods and services provided free of charge

Goods and services provided genuinely free of charge are unlikely to be considered supplies and so are outside the scope of VAT. Examples include rescue at sea, first aid, religious ceremonies, free education and free admission to a museum or gallery. Note that national museums and galleries may be eligible for a refund of the VAT incurred on providing free admission to collections. See Chapter 10 for details of the scheme.

Where a charity provides goods free of charge to a destination outside the EC, for example as aid or disaster relief, it is deemed to be a zero-rated business activity. This allows the charity to recover all associated input VAT. The goods must qualify as exports for VAT purposes. See Chapter 6 for more details.

Where a beneficiary gives a donation in return for any service provided for free this is outside the scope as long as it does not amount to a mandatory charge. If the free goods or services are part of an arrangement in which consideration is received in another form or from another party connected to the beneficiary or are part of a business activity they may be considered a supply.

The gift or loan of business assets

Small gifts made as part of a business activity are the subject of a special exemption. If the total value of gifts in a year to any individual or organisation is £50 or less, the gifts are not considered to be a supply and so are outside the scope of VAT. However, input VAT recovery is not restricted. The gifts must be made as part of a business activity to qualify for this treatment.

If the value of a business gift exceeds the £50 limit then there is a deemed supply and output tax is due on the gift.

Where business assets are loaned for free to another organisation, for use in that organisation's business activities, the loan is outside the scope of VAT. Examples include vehicles and equipment loaned by suppliers. However, if the assets will be put to non-business use by the acquiring organisation, there is a deemed supply by the lender and output VAT must be accounted for.

Investment income

Several court cases have established that the management and generation of investment income is a non-business activity if the investor does not play an active role in the management of the entity invested in. If the investment income is unrestricted, the Children's Society case (see above) suggests that any VAT incurred in generating or managing the investments is residual.

The leading case on the VAT status of investment income in the hands of a charity is the ECJ Wellcome Trust case. The trust was prohibited by its constitution from trading in investments. It decided to sell 288 million shares in the Wellcome Foundation and sought to recover the VAT it incurred on professional fees on the basis that a sale of this scale must be business (as suggested by the business tests). The ECJ rejected this and said that as the trust was prohibited from trading in investments, and as the sale of investments could only be incidental to the achievement of the trust's charitable objects, it was more akin to a sale by a private investor and therefore a non-business activity.

Dividend income is always outside the scope of VAT, irrespective of the status of the recipient. This is because it is a profit share and there is no supply by the dividend payer.

Secondment of staff

HMRC state that in some circumstances they will accept that income from the hire or loan of staff from one voluntary organisation to another can be treated as non-business. Here a 'voluntary organisation' is a body which operates otherwise than for profit, but does not include any public or local authority. This is subject to the following conditions:

- the employee has been engaged only in the non-business activities of the lending charity/organisation and is being seconded to assist in the non-business activities of the borrowing charity/organisation;

- the payment for the supply of the employee's services does not exceed the employee's normal remuneration. 'Normal remuneration' means the total costs incurred by the lending charity/organisation in employing the member of staff including National Insurance and pension scheme contributions etc.

See Chapter 11 for more on supplies of staff between organisations.

Non-returnable deposits

The VAT status of non-returnable deposits depends on whether or not they count towards payment for an ultimate supply. If the deposit counts towards the final consideration for any supply, then the VAT status of the deposit follows that of the supply. If a non-returnable deposit is taken and the customer defaults, so there is no supply, then the forfeited deposit is not consideration for any supply and is therefore outside the scope of VAT. In the ECJ case *Société Thermale d'Eugénie-les-Bains* (2007, EUECJ C-277/05) the French tax authorities tried to claim that forfeited deposits held by a hotel were consideration for the supply of a reservation service. The ECJ saw no direct link between the deposit and reservation service and considered that the fact that under normal circumstances the deposit formed part of the consideration for the hotel accommodation meant that it could not also be for an independent supply.

Insurance claims and compensation payments

Claim payments by insurance companies are compensation for the loss suffered and are outside the scope of VAT. If the loss was suffered on non-business or exempt activities, on which VAT is irrecoverable, the irrecoverable VAT should form part of the claim.

Most other compensation payments amount to a financial settlement of losses caused by the breach of an agreement or the infringement of rights. As such, there is no supply and so the compensation payment is outside the scope of VAT. However, compensation agreements can sometimes include the granting of rights by one party to the other, in which case any settlement may comprise partly or wholly consideration for the supply of the rights.

5 Exempt activities

This chapter explains which activities are exempt from VAT. There are many VAT-exempt activities, but only a few of these are commonly undertaken by voluntary organisations. The exempt activities covered in this chapter are education, health and welfare services, cultural services, sports and recreation and insurance services. This chapter also covers exemptions available for certain membership subscriptions.

There are certain business activities which are exempt from VAT in all situations; there are also certain activities which are exempt when undertaken by a charity. If the activities are exempt, then no VAT should be charged, nor may VAT on related purchases be recovered, unless theses activities are minimal (see Chapter 3: *Recovering VAT*).

The main exemptions are listed in Schedule 9 to the VAT Act 1994, as updated and amended from time to time. The groups to Schedule 9 are listed below:

1. Land

2. Insurance

3. Postal services

4. Betting, gaming and lotteries

5. Finance

6. Education

7. Health and welfare

8. Burial and cremation

9. Subscriptions to trade unions, professional and other public interest bodies

10. Sport, sports competitions and physical education

11. Works of art etc.

12. Fundraising events by charities and other qualifying bodies

13. Cultural services etc.

14. Supplies of goods where input tax cannot be recovered

15. Investment gold

In this chapter we will look at the following in more detail:

- Education

- Health and welfare

- Cultural services

- Sports and recreation

- Subscriptions

- Insurance services.

Land is covered in Chapter 8: *Property*; charity lotteries and fundraising events are covered in Chapter 7: *Fundraising*.

Education

While 'education' has a broad meaning for the purposes of charitable status, this is not the case for VAT. 'Education' is not actually defined in law, but regarded by HMRC as meaning:

> 'a course, class or lesson of instruction or study in any subject, whether or not normally taught in schools, colleges or universities and regardless of where and when it takes place. Education includes lectures, educational seminars, conferences and symposia, together with holiday, sporting and recreational courses. It also includes distance teaching and associated materials, if the student is subject to assessment by the teaching institution.' (VAT Notice 701/30)

The provision of education by an **eligible body** is exempt from VAT, as provided for in the VAT Act 1994, Schedule 9, Group 6. The provision of education by public authorities is usually **non-business** rather than exempt because they make no charge, though where a charge is made (e.g. for music lessons) the provision is exempt.

An 'eligible body' can be:

- a recognised school (including LEA schools, independent, grant maintained, community, foundation and voluntary schools)

- a UK college or university

- a further education institution (including the Workers' Educational Association and any other bodies that have been designated as such under various education acts)

- an organisation providing teaching of English as a foreign language (but the exemption only applies to the tuition in EFL)

- a not-for-profit body, providing its constitution prohibits the distribution of profits and it does not in fact distribute any profits. In addition, any profits made from exempt educational supplies, including research and vocational training, must be applied to the continuance or improvement of those activities.

Clearly, most charities would qualify as eligible bodies, and education and training services they provide will therefore qualify for exemption, providing they use any profit to further the educational activities. Consequently, most independent schools and training centres will be making exempt supplies of education, although there have been two cases, Donaldson's College and Sheiling Trust, where tribunals agreed that the activities were in fact non-business rather than exempt.

Charities will operate a number of different activities falling within the education exemption, which are clarified below. Note that the overall provision that the supply must be made by an eligible body applies in all cases.

Vocational training

'Vocational training' means training, re-training or the provision of work experience for any trade, profession or employment, or for any voluntary work of a charitable nature (including education, health, safety or welfare). The net is cast widely and vocational training will apply to courses, conferences, lectures, workshops and seminars for these purposes. The training can be for those already in work, where the intention is to improve their knowledge, to improve their performance at work, or to prepare people for future work. So, for example, a conference organised by a charity for employees and voluntary workers (including trustees) to provide information and discuss current topics will be vocational training and therefore exempt.

It does not include consultancy designed to improve the efficiency or smooth running of the whole organisation, which should be standard-rated. Individual counselling is also excluded from this category, although it may be exempt if it is part of a training package.

Note that if you do not want the activity to be exempt, then training by a for-profit body is standard-rated, as is training by a charity when the profits are applied to another activity.

Government-approved training schemes

There are various schemes for vocational training that are Government-sponsored, and while the actual schemes have changed over the years, they have always been specifically exempt from VAT. All contracts or sub-contracts are covered if the scheme is ultimately funded by the Government or education funding councils in the UK. The management and administration of the contract is exempt if this is included in the overall supply, but would be standard-rated if the contract allowed for a separate supply of management services.

New Deal

The various elements of New Deal can be identified as either:

- vocational training (and therefore exempt)

- subsidy of wages (and therefore outside the scope)

- one-to-one counselling or awareness training (usually a standard-rated supply to the Employment Service).

Detailed guidance on the VAT liability of various elements of New Deal is available from HMRC in VAT Information Sheet 3/99 on their website.

Research

For VAT purposes the term 'research' means:

> 'original investigation undertaken in order to gain, advance or expand knowledge and understanding'.

The intention at the beginning of a project determines whether a supply qualifies as research, and the intention should be to advance knowledge and understanding. Merely confirming existing knowledge is not research, nor is consultancy, market research, writing software or testing components. In practice, HMRC would expect the research to be academic in nature and of a type that usually takes place in universities etc. The fact that the research may have a commercial application does not in itself exclude it from the exemption. However, the supply of research services to a commercial body is standard-rated, whereas supplies between eligible bodies are exempt (even if the recipient is not involved in the field of education).

Examination fees

Examination services provided by eligible bodies to individuals or other eligible bodies are exempt. This includes assessment and setting training standards. The full list includes:

- setting and marking examinations

- setting educational or training standards

- making assessments

- other services provided with a view to ensuring that educational and training standards are maintained.

Even if you are not an eligible body, the examination services you supply are exempt if the person receiving your services is either:

- an eligible body, or

- an individual receiving education or vocational training that itself is not liable to VAT.

Ancillary supplies

Schools and other bodies often sell additional goods and services to pupils and trainees. Some of these will not fall within the exemption, but some are closely related to the main supply of education and are exempt. Examples of closely related supplies are accommodation, catering, transport and school trips. They have to be for the direct use of the student and necessary for the delivery of education to that student. Sales from vending machines, shops, bars, uniform sales and other separately charged services will not be closely related to the supply of education, and VAT will apply as normal. To qualify for the exemption, the goods or services should be for the direct use of the pupil or student, or the exemption can apply where the school (or other eligible body) is buying in related services from another eligible body.

If the school or educational institution supplies teaching staff to another educational institution, then this may qualify as an ancillary supply, but not a supply of education. The case of Horizon College in ECJ established that a supply of teachers may be a supply closely related to the supply of education and is therefore exempt on that basis. Both bodies must be eligible bodies for this to apply.

Youth clubs

Subscriptions to youth clubs are exempt, as are any other payment by members for the ordinary activities of the youth club. A youth club is a club established to promote the social, physical, educational or spiritual development of its members run by a charity or other not-for-profit organisation fulfilling the criteria of an eligible body. The members of the club should be mainly under 21, which means that at least 51 per cent of the members should be 20 or younger. Youth clubs should be separately constituted, and the youth sections of sports clubs and the like are not regarded as youth clubs. Other activities organised by the youth club will not necessarily be exempt, such as holidays and sales of food and drink.

Further information on some detailed aspects of education are covered in VAT Notice 701/30.

Health and welfare

There is a general exemption for health and medical services provided by registered health professionals. The profession has to be statutorily registered, so practitioners such as acupuncturists and reflexologists are excluded, whereas osteopaths are included in the exemption. So services from opticians, nurses and dentists are all exempt. Note that the exemption does not extend to all supplies, so, for example, spectacles are standard-rated, unless supplied in hospital or as low-vision aids for the severely visually impaired. Note the rules were tightened up and clarified in a new Notice 701/57, issued in January 2007.

Health professionals are:

- medical practitioners

- ophthalmic and dispensing opticians

- professionals registered under the Health Professions Order 2001. These professionals are: arts therapists, biomedical scientists, chiropodists/podiatrists, clinical scientists, dieticians, occupational therapists, operating department practitioners, orthoptists, paramedics, physiotherapists, prosthetists and orthotists, radiographers, and speech and language therapists, but will also include medical care professionals added in future

- osteopaths

- chiropractors

- nurses, midwives and health visitors

- hearing aid dispensers

- dentists, dental hygienists, dental therapists, dental nurses, clinical dental technicians, dental technicians, orthodontic therapists

- pharmacists.

If you are a health professional, your services are exempt when both of the following conditions are met:

- The services are within the profession in which you are registered to practise.

- The primary purpose of the services is the protection, maintenance or restoration of the health of the person concerned.

Examples of services which are for the primary purpose of protecting, maintaining or restoring a person's health include:

- sight testing and prescribing by opticians

- hearing tests

- treatment provided by osteopaths and chiropractors

- nursing care provided in a patient's own home

- pharmaceutical advice.

Some medical reports and certificates may be exempt or standard-rated, depending on their principal purpose. Where the service is principally aimed at the protection, maintenance or restoration of health of the person concerned, the supply is exempt. However, where the principal purpose of the service is to provide a third party with a necessary element for taking a decision, for example in connection with a compensation claim, the supply is taxable at the standard rate. Detailed guidance on this aspect is given in VAT Notice *Health Professionals* 701/57.

The following services are not covered by the exemption and so are taxable at the standard rate:

- Health services not performed by an appropriately qualified and registered health professional, except when either directly supervised by such a person or provided within a hospital or similar institution. This is explained further below under 'Supervised services'.

- Services not aimed at the prevention, diagnosis, treatment or cure of a disease or health disorder, such as paternity testing and the writing of articles for journals.

- Services directly supervised by a pharmacist.

- General administrative services such as countersigning passport applications and providing character references.

If you provide medical treatment that is exempt from VAT, any charge that you make for bandages, drugs, medicines or prostheses, administered or applied to your patient in the course of the treatment is also exempt.

Any items that are separable from the treatment (such as privately dispensed drugs supplied for self-administration by a patient, for example for overseas travel purposes) are not exempt from VAT, and will usually be standard-rated.

Supervised services

Care services performed by a person not enrolled on a statutory medical register can be exempt when the service is health or nursing care provided in a hospital or nursing home or similar institutions such as nursing homes and hospices that are state regulated. The conditions for this are not onerous, but the unregistered staff must be providing care that is directly connected with the welfare of the recipient. This would normally involve the provision of personal care services, but not services such as catering or hairdressing.

Other care services provided in the community (e.g. in the individual's home) will be exempt if they are provided under the 'direct supervision' of a health professional (other than a pharmacist) who monitors the services through regular checks.

'Directly supervised' in this context is when **all** of the following conditions are met:

- The services are supervised by health professionals, and the supervisor is professionally qualified to perform and supervise the service.

- The service requires supervision by a health professional, and is provided predominantly to meet the medical needs of a client.

- The supervisor has a direct relationship with the staff performing the service, and is contractually responsible for supervising their services.

- A qualified supervisor is available for the whole time that the care service is provided.

- No more than 2,000 hours per week of staff time are supervised by a single health professional.

- A supervisor has a say in the level of care to be provided to the client, and will usually see the client prior to the commencement of the care service.

- The supervisor must be able to demonstrate that they monitor the work of the unregistered staff.

Where the above conditions are not met, your services are standard-rated, even when performed to meet the medical or healthcare needs of a client.

Note that these arrangements apply to for-profit businesses as well as charities, so exemptions will apply if the supervision is within the rules.

Welfare services

Welfare services are directly connected with:

- the provision of care, treatment or instruction designed to promote the physical or mental wellbeing of an elderly person, a sick person, a distressed person or a disabled person

- the provision of care or protection designed to promote the physical or mental wellbeing of children and young people

- the provision of spiritual welfare by a religious institution as part of a course of instruction or a retreat.

Welfare services must be provided to individuals rather than promoting the interests of a class of persons and must not be designed primarily to provide recreation or a holiday. The precedent for a wide definition of welfare was established by the Yoga for Health (1984) case. This case looked at the application of the Sixth Directive, and in particular Article 13A(1)(g) relating to welfare services. The charity provided therapeutic services to clients, most of whom suffered from ill health, who paid fees and made donations to support the work of the charity. HMRC argued that it was a taxable service. The charity won its appeal against the tribunal decision. The word 'welfare' connoted general physical and mental wellbeing and was not confined to material benefits. The language of Article 13A went beyond mere material benefit and standard of living. Neither was paragraph (g) restricted to services providing for the relief of poverty to the exclusion of services providing healthcare.

Directly connected with the provision of care, treatment or instruction

Care, treatment and instruction includes the protection, control or guidance of an individual when this is provided to meet medical, physical, personal or domestic needs.

Examples include:

- personal or nursing care (including assistance with bathing, dressing, toileting and other personal hygiene)

- general assistance and support with everyday tasks such as form filling, letter reading/writing or bill paying

- certain routine domestic tasks

- counselling

- looking after or supervising vulnerable people

- support or instruction designed to develop or sustain a person's capacity to live independently in the community

- protection, control, guidance or companionship that is required to meet an individual's personal or domestic needs

- residential care, including accommodation, board and other services provided to residents as part of a care package.

Routine domestic tasks (such as housework, simple odd jobs, shopping and collecting a prescription or pension) that are performed by a 'welfare provider' are exempt when all of the following conditions are met:

- the recipient of the service is an elderly, sick, distressed or disabled person

- an assessment of the recipient's health condition, medical needs and ability to perform each task has been carried out by an appropriately trained person – such as a medical or health professional or any person with relevant training or experience in social work or social care

- this assessment has shown that the recipient is unable to carry out the tasks safely or adequately or without significant pain or discomfort and that this inability presents a risk to their health or welfare

- a record of each assessment is maintained by the supplier of the service

- the service provided is a routine domestic task that the majority of the population would expect to carry out for themselves and which is required to keep a household going. This excludes specialist services such as non-essential gardening, decorating and other house maintenance, including re-roofing, plumbing and electrical services.

A person is considered to be unable to carry out a routine domestic task safely when their performance of the task involves a likelihood of physical harm or injury. For example, a person who has a poor sense of balance may be unable to dust high-up areas safely if this dusting would involve standing on a chair or ladder.

A person may be unable to carry out a task adequately when they are unable to perform tasks properly or effectively. For example, an elderly or disabled person who has mobility problems may be unable to shop regularly enough to meet their nutritional needs.

The word 'significant' is used to exclude the low levels of pain or discomfort experienced by many people in carrying out routine domestic tasks. Assessments of a service recipient's needs should distinguish between low levels of pain or discomfort, and a significant level of pain or discomfort that restricts ability to carry out routine tasks. Examples of when tasks cannot be carried out without significant pain or discomfort include a person suffering from a debilitating condition who finds carrying out routine domestic tasks physically exhausting, and so suffers significant discomfort.

Care or protection of children and young persons

Exemption applies to services supplied by welfare providers which are directly connected with the care and protection of specific children, rather than children in general. Examples include:

- care provided in a children's home

- daycare services such as those provided by a nursery, playgroup or after-school club (but not activity-based clubs such as dance classes etc.), though note that nurseries and playgroups run along similar lines to St Paul's Playgroup (see Chapter 4 and Chapter 13) are likely to be non-business

- the placement of a child with foster carers by a fostering agency

- the care, support and protection of looked-after children.

In addition, the training and assessment of prospective adopters by an adoption agency is exempt.

After-school clubs and other providers of non-residential care for children are only required to register under the appropriate social legislation if they provide a designated number of hours of care to children under the age of eight. If you are a qualifying institution that:

- provides care on a commercial basis to children who are younger than eight years old, as well as to older children

- operates identical hours of opening for all age groups

- provides activities for over-eights that are comparable with those provided for younger children,

you may, if you wish, choose to regard the care you provide to over-eights as VAT-exempt, in addition to the care you provide to younger children.

Some welfare providers, such as independent fostering agencies, receive fees for services that, although concerned with the overall welfare of one or more child, are not primarily and directly connected with the care or protection of a specific child. Examples include fees received for:

- training of carers, or potential carers, where this is not linked to the needs of a specific child

- assessment of a potential foster carer's suitability to look after children, where this is not linked to the needs of a specific child

- activity-based clubs not required to be registered with the Office for Standards in Education (OFSTED), such as football clubs and dancing lessons

- consultancy or research services

- education of children.

These services are not usually exempt unless they are provided as part of a single supply of exempt care and protection. However, education and training services provided by certain 'eligible bodies' are exempt from VAT under separate provisions. You can find out more about the exemption for education and training in Notice 701/30 *Education*.

Welfare providers

These include the following types of organisations:

- **charities** – bodies that have been established to advance education or religion; relieve poverty, sickness or infirmity; or carry out certain other activities beneficial to the community, that cannot distribute profits. You can assume that you fall into this category if you are a registered charity or recognised as charitable by HMRC

- **public bodies** – government departments, local authorities and bodies that perform functions similar to those carried out by government departments or local authorities, and which act under any enactment or instrument for public purposes rather than for their own profit

- **state-regulated private welfare institutions or agencies** – establishments or other providers that are registered with, and/or regulated by, one of the following regulatory bodies:

  - Commission for Social Care Inspection (CSCI)

  - Scottish Commission for the Regulation of Care

  - Care Standards Inspectorate for Wales

  - Northern Ireland Health and Personal Social Services Regulation and Improvement Authority

  - Office for Standards in Education (OFSTED) or any other similar regulatory body.

  State-regulated private welfare agencies include domiciliary care agencies, independent fostering agencies, voluntary adoption agencies and nurses agencies. Suppliers that have a reasonable expectation that in due course they will become state-regulated private welfare agencies may (but are not required to) exempt the welfare services they provide under an extra-statutory concession.

The inclusion of for-profit bodies in the scope of the welfare exemption is relatively new and followed the Kingscrest case (see Chapter 13) which had to go to the ECJ for a decision. This removed the requirement for welfare services to be provided by a not-for-profit entity in order to be exempt and introduced the concept of state-regulated private welfare agencies.

Goods provided as part of, or in connection with, an exempt supply of welfare services are usually also exempt. Examples include:

- meals and refreshments provided to beneficiaries of welfare services in the course of care or spiritual welfare services for which no additional charge is made

- bandages, plasters or ointments supplied in the course of a supply of care and treatment in the recipient's home

- items provided to children by playgroups or nurseries, such as picture books, crayons and toys, when these are provided in connection with the care.

However, any goods that are separable from an exempt welfare service, or are not provided in connection with such a service, are not exempt.

Welfare advice is advice or information that directly relates to the care or protection of children or young people or physical or mental welfare of elderly, sick, distressed or disabled people. This can be supplied at a reduced rate of VAT (5 per cent) – more detail on this is given in Chapter 6. However, any advice that directly relates to a specific child or to an individual is a supply of welfare services and is exempt from VAT.

Welfare services and related goods, supplied consistently below cost by charities to distressed people for the relief of their distress, are not business (see Chapter 4).

Spiritual welfare

The provision of spiritual welfare as part of a retreat is exempt when provided by a religious institution. This may include:

- spiritual counselling of an individual

- guided exploration of spiritual needs and development

- discussion, meditation and prayer or worship sessions.

Supplies that are **not** exempt from VAT include:

- any supply made by a body other than a religious institution or community

- any supply that is not made as part of an organised retreat or course of instruction provided by a religious institution

- conferences or retreats when the predominant purpose is not spiritual welfare

- educational courses in theology, or similar subjects, where the predominant purpose is to expand knowledge of spiritual matters rather than to provide spiritual welfare services

- meetings to discuss theology or aspects of Church doctrine.

The course or retreat cannot be designed primarily to provide recreation or a holiday.

Additionally, the supply by a religious community (for example, a nunnery or monastery) of goods and services incidental to the provision of spiritual welfare, such as accommodation and food, are exempt. The supplies must be made otherwise than for profit and made to a resident member of that community in return for a subscription or any other payment made as a condition of membership.

Cultural services

Under certain circumstances admission charges to museums, galleries, art exhibitions and zoos and theatrical, musical or choreographic performances of a cultural nature are exempted from VAT when provided by a public authority or eligible body.

To qualify as an eligible body, an organisation must satisfy three tests:

1. It must be a non-profit making organisation.

2. It must apply any profits made from exempt admission fees to the continuance or improvement of the facilities made available by means of the supplies.

3. It must be managed and administered on an essentially voluntary basis by people who have no direct or indirect financial interest in the activities of the body.

Non-profit making

This means an organisation that does not systematically aim to make a profit and which, if profits nevertheless arise, must not distribute them. A body whose constitution or articles of association preclude it from distributing surpluses of income over expenditure to its members, shareholders or any other party (other than in the event of a liquidation or cessation of activities), and which as a matter of fact does not distribute any profit, will normally be accepted as having satisfied this condition.

Any profits are applied towards the cultural services

All profits arising from exempt admission fees must be used:

• for the continuance or improvement of the facilities made available to the fee-paying public by payment of the exempt admission fees

• applied in connection with the making of related cultural supplies (such as research or conservation projects).

If profits are applied to any other activities of the body than those above, the body is not eligible for exemption.

Managed and administered on an essentially voluntary basis

This is the key test and the one that is the source of much dispute. This test was the subject of an ECJ referral in a case involving the Zoological Society of London. Before this case, HMRC insisted this meant that there must be no paid administrators or managers, so any reasonably sized organisation would fail the conditions for exemption. The ECJ rejected this line of reasoning, stating that it should be the persons who take the decisions of last resort concerning policy who are voluntary. This will normally be the trustees of a charity, though if shadow directors exist or if paid staff routinely take decisions that would be considered the preserve of the trustees then they would be included for consideration.

There have been several cases since Zoological Society of London which have further examined this test.

Zoological Society of Wales

Here, one of the trustees had made a secured loan to the charity, charged rent for the use of some of her garages and received a pension for service that she had supplied to a predecessor organisation. This trustee resigned and HMRC agreed that the admission charges to the zoo were exempt from this date onwards but not before. The tribunal decided that the presence of this trustee did not impair the conditions for cultural exemption as:

- the trustee was elderly, had not attended meetings of the board for several years and took no part in decision making

- the payments made by the charity for the loan, garages and pension were on normal commercial terms. The trustee provided matching services and these services did therefore not constitute the extraction of profits and so could not be considered to constitute a financial interest. Even if they did then the fact that the trustee took no part in decision making was enough.

Bournemouth Symphony Orchestra

Here, the managing director and the musical director were paid employees and voting members of the board. The court of appeal did not consider that the managing director's salary gave him a financial interest in the results of BSO's activities as it was not performance related, and was not a disguised way of removing profits. However, it found that the BSO was not managed and administered on an essentially voluntary basis because the managing director's job involved his carrying out managerial functions as a board member. His membership of the board was not incidental to another function. As a board member he had real input and was centrally involved in all important discussions. This contrasted with the musical director whose participation on the board was essentially voluntary.

Longborough Festival Opera

Mr Graham built a large barn which he decided to use as an opera house. He added a 'Palladian-style' front, a stage, an orchestra pit and seating. At first the opera performances were produced and managed by Longborough Developments Ltd (LDL), of which Mr Graham and his wife were the directors. LDL produced the operas on a commercial basis with a view to profit. By 1999 Mr Graham considered that the opera at Longborough had reached a stage at which it would benefit from the support of patrons. To this end, in 2000 Mr Graham incorporated LFO, a company limited by guarantee and a registered charity.

LFO has four trustees, of whom two were Mr and Mrs Graham. Mr Graham was the Chairman. In 2002 Mr Graham provided two 'letters of comfort' to the Trustees, confirming that he or LDL would make good any financial deficiency arising from the 2002 season of performances and operations. In 2003 LDL stated that it intended to charge a rent of £20,000 – £30,000 in respect of the use of the opera house in 2002. HMRC took the view that Mr Graham, as guarantor of potential losses, was a person with a financial interest in the LFO in that he personally stood to lose money. If LDL charged a rent Mr and Mrs Graham would have a further financial interest.

The VAT Tribunal decided that Mr Graham had a financial interest in LFO. The High Court rejected this: 'interest', in this context, meant such an interest as might lead to the enrichment of the person with the interest, and there was no such interest in this case. Furthermore, Mr Graham was excluded from any participation in the decision whether the LFO should enter into a contract with him or with LDL.

As a consequence of these cases, it has become clear that there are two separate tests both of which must be satisfied for the cultural exemption to apply.

- **Managed on an essentially voluntary basis** – if someone is paid for their role as a board member, and this is not a nominal, token or one-off payment and the person genuinely plays an active role on the board and takes part in important decisions, then this will preclude management on an essentially voluntary basis. Note that the Zoological Society of London case established that this extends to shadow directors.

- **By people who have no direct or indirect financial interest in the activities of the body** – this requires some ability to profit from the success of the organisation (e.g. by bonuses) or an ability to extract profits (e.g. by being paid an excessive salary). However, a market rate salary does not constitute financial interest. An interest in this context means a beneficial interest. A trustee underwriting a potential loss does not have a financial interest – the financial interest has to be potentially beneficial in a positive sense (i.e. not that the trustee could avoid making a loss but stands to gain in some way).

The relevant VAT Notice (701/47 *Culture*) was updated in April 2007 to reflect these changes.

Sports and recreation

Certain sporting and physical education services supplied by eligible bodies are exempt, as are entry fees to certain competitions in sport or physical recreation.

An eligible body is a not-for-profit organisation:

- with a prohibition in its constitution on the distribution of profits, other than transfer to another not-for-profit organisation on winding-up

- spending any surplus it does generate from the exempt sporting activity on the maintenance and improvement of facilities, or on the objects of the organisation

- which is not subject to 'commercial influence'. This term refers to any transactions with the committee members, such as purchasing services or renting premises from them or their companies. Payments to committee members and performance-related bonuses would also amount to commercial influence. Specifically, management and administration services and property transactions supplied by a committee member would create commercial influence. A supply of other goods and services under normal terms should not create commercial influence, but it would be advisable to agree this with your VAT office. Transactions with other charities and local authorities will not be caught under the definition of 'commercial influence', even if representatives from those bodies are on the management committee. This is a complex area of anti-avoidance legislation, and so if you think you may be caught by it, check the guidance issued by HMRC in VAT Notice 701/45 on this point. (See Chapter 14 for how to access the VAT Notices). For most charities providing sporting facilities, it is unlikely that there will be problems and you should be able to treat charges as exempt.

- an eligible body cannot be a public body such as a local authority or government body.

The sections below explain what the exemption does and does not cover.

- Services closely linked with and essential to sport or physical recreation supplied to individuals taking part in the activity provided by an eligible body. The term 'individuals' includes families, but spectators are excluded as they are not taking part.

- Entry fees and admission fees to sporting facilities run by an eligible body such as swimming pools and sports centres are exempt.

- Ancillary services such as use of changing rooms, showers and playing equipment, as well as umpiring services, coaching, training and physical education.

- Membership subscriptions and joining fees for participating in sporting activities. Access to the club bar is a benefit, but seen as integral to the membership and therefore it can be included in the exemption. However, if a significant element of the membership subscription related to other benefits, then it may be necessary to apportion the subscription and standard rate certain elements. If you wish to zero rate elements that relate to printed matter, then it will be necessary to review the whole subscription for apportionment, including the social element.

- Exemption does not extend to catering, accommodation or transport services, nor to admission charges for spectators.

- Subscriptions to sports governing bodies are exempt in so far as they can be attributed to 'services closely linked and essential to sport' supplied to individuals or sports clubs. Affiliation fees are frequently calculated on the basis of head count of the members in the club, so this would still qualify for the exemption. Additional services provided such as priority booking for international matches and similar benefits are not exempt and should be standard-rated.

Sports competitions

Entry fees to competitions in sport or physical recreation organised by anyone are exempt, providing the entry fee is entirely used to provide the prizes. In addition, eligible bodies established for the purposes of sport or physical recreation can exempt the entry fees to competitions. The sports that can be included are extended in this case to include dancing, darts and pigeon racing. Note that local authorities are not within this definition as they are not established for the purposes of sport or physical recreation.

Renting out sports facilities

Short-term lets are standard-rated, but letting out facilities for more than 24 hours or a series of lettings to the same person may be exempt. This will apply to letting out a village hall for badminton as well as letting out facilities in a purpose-built sports centre. This area is covered in more detail in Chapter 8: *Property*.

Subscriptions

The VAT treatment of subscriptions paid by members to an organisation depends on the nature of the organisation and the benefits received by the members in return for the subscription.

- There are special rules for subscriptions paid to trade unions, professional associations, learned societies, representative trade associations and bodies which have objects in the public domain and are of a political, religious, patriotic, philosophical, philanthropic or civic nature. See below for details.

- If the members receive no significant benefits in return for their subscription then the subscription will effectively be a donation and so outside the scope of VAT. The right to attend and vote at an AGM or to receive statutory accounts and the annual report is not usually regarded as a significant benefit.

- If there is a single type of benefit (standard-rated, zero-rated or exempt) for the whole cost then the VAT status of the subscription will follow that of the benefit. For example, if the only benefit of membership is receipt of zero-rated printed magazines then the entire subscription will be zero-rated.

- If members receive several benefits with mixture of VAT statuses (standard-rated, zero-rated or exempt) then the single/multiple supply tests (see Chapter 11) must be applied to see if there is a single or multiple supply. If there is a single supply the whole subscription follows the status of the principal supply. If there is a multiple supply the subscription must be apportioned between the different types of supply. Apportionment of membership subscriptions is considered below.

- By extra-statutory concession, non-profit-making organisations may treat the subscription as a multiple supply even when, under the single/multiple supply test, it would be regarded as a single supply. Apportionment of membership subscriptions is considered below. A body will usually be accepted as non-profit-making if its governing documents bar it from distributing surpluses of income over expenditure to its members, shareholders or any other party, other than in the event of a liquidation or cessation of activities.

- If a subscription amounts to a statutory levy imposed on an entire class of individuals or organisations then it may be outside the scope of VAT. See, for example, the case of the Apple and Pear Development Council in Chapters 4 and 13.

- Member benefits can include benefits provided by unconnected third parties. For example, it is fairly common for commercial retailers to provide discounts to members of particular voluntary organisations on production of a membership card. If these benefits have effectively been purchased by the membership body, typically as part of a wider sponsorship or licensing agreement, then they will count as member benefits. However where benefits are provided by an unconnected third party entirely at the third party's volition and without any contra-flow of benefit to the third party apart from the members' custom, there is unlikely to be a membership benefit for VAT purposes.

Subscriptions to trade unions, professional and other public interest bodies

Subscriptions to the following bodies are exempt:

- **Trade unions** and other organisations whose main objective is to defend the collective interests of its members. The members may be workers, employees, independent professionals or traders carrying out a particular economic activity.

- **Professional associations** the membership of which is wholly or mainly restricted to individuals who have or are seeking a qualification appropriate to the practice of the profession concerned. HMRC regard 'wholly or mainly' as meaning 75 per cent or more.

- **Learned societies**. A learned society is a body whose primary purpose is the advancement of a particular branch of knowledge or the fostering of professional expertise. Membership of the society must be restricted wholly or mainly to those whose employment is, or has been, directly connected with its aims. Again, HMRC interpret 'wholly or mainly' as meaning 75 per cent or more. A branch of knowledge is usually interpreted as relating to academic knowledge of a scientific, artistic, historic or similar nature.

- **Representational trade associations**. These are bodies whose primary purpose is to make representations to Government on legislation or other public matters, which affect the business or professional interests of its members. A representational trade association must restrict its membership 'wholly or mainly' to individuals or organisations whose business or professional interests are directly connected with the purposes of the association. Again, HMRC interpret 'wholly or mainly' as meaning 75 per cent or more.

- **Political etc. bodies**. These are bodies with objects in the public domain and that are of a political, religious, patriotic, philosophical, philanthropic or civic nature. Objects are in the public domain if they are directed outside the particular organisation and beyond the members themselves to the general community. Bodies which are not registered charities may qualify – major political or religious bodies will also often satisfy this requirement because the public will have a general interest in their activities.

  - A political body campaigns for or against legislative and constitutional changes or campaigns in local and central government elections.

  - 'Religious body' includes all denominations and creeds, old and new, that command a following.

  - A patriotic body does good work for the benefit of a nation state or for those who have served their country and their dependants.

- A philosophical body's primary purpose is the advancement of a particular way of thinking but is not of a political or religious nature. They are very similar to learned societies.

- A philanthropic body does good work for the direct benefit of the general community or a particular section of the community or promotes the wellbeing of mankind.

- A civic body has objects which promote the rights and duties of citizens in matters of public interest and public affairs, and whose objects do not solely or mainly benefit its members.

The exemption also extends to subscriptions paid by these types of organisation to an umbrella body, provided the umbrella body's objects fall into the same category as the members or are purely to support the members.

Where a membership organisation falls into one of the above categories, the supply of benefits to members is exempt provided:

- The benefits are provided in return for the subscription and without payment of a further fee. If a benefit is only obtainable on payment of an additional fee then the VAT status of that fee follows that of the benefit it obtains.

- Any benefit that comprises a right of admission to any premises, event or performance for which non-members have to pay or to which non-members are not admitted is specifically excluded from the exemption. If the package of benefits includes such admission rights the subscription must be apportioned and the admission rights treated separately. However, in many situations the admission rights will be exempt themselves, for example admission to a cultural or sporting event or to an educational or training event.

- The benefits are referable to the aims of the organisation. Benefits that are not referable to the aims of the organisation are taxed according to the normal subscription rules. You must first decide if the benefit is ancillary to another supply, is inseparable from another supply or constitutes a separate supply. If the organisation is non-profit-making it may use the extra statutory concession to treat the benefit as a separate supply.

Other subscriptions

Subscriptions and membership can take many forms, so it important to look at what the subscriber receives for their subscription.

- Where nothing is received in return for the subscription then this is substantially a donation and is outside the scope of VAT. This is still the case where minimal benefits are given, such as an annual report and the right to vote at the AGM. This would apply in situations where charities are basically using the subscription as a means of attracting supporters.

• Where more substantial benefits are given in return for the subscription, then the whole subscription will be standard-rated, unless another exemption applies or the extra statutory concession for non-profit organisations is used to zero rate or exempt some of the benefits.

• Membership of sports clubs and centres will usually be exempt – see the section on 'Sports and recreation' above.

• Membership of arts organisations may be exempt if the subscription entitles the member to admission to a museum, gallery, art exhibition, zoo or performance and the organisation qualifies as an eligible body – see 'Cultural services' under 'Exempt activities' above.

Apportioning membership benefits

Values need to be attributed to the various membership benefits, usually by reference to cost. Then the VAT category applicable to the goods and services provided as membership benefits determines the VAT rate to apply. This must be agreed with the local VAT office in advance.

Example: Membership subscriptions

Membership benefits amount to a free magazine four times a year (cost to the charity £2.50 each) and a discount on tickets for performances worth approximately £2 per ticket. The overall discounts given last year per the accounting records totalled £24,000. Since there are 3,000 members, this is the equivalent of each member benefiting from discounts of £8 each in a year. The membership subscription is £35 per year. The apportionment could be calculated as follows:

Magazine	£10	Zero-rated benefit
Discount on tickets	£ 8	Exempt benefit (cultural services)
Balance = donation	£17	Outside the scope

When apportioning subscriptions only benefits provided to members in return for the subscription should be taken into account. Benefits that are available to non-members and members alike do not come into the apportionment, likewise items that are free to both members and non-members. The apportionment will not be agreed if the amount of zero-rated or exempt supplies is trivial compared with the benefits provided as a whole.

The value of each element can be just its direct cost or basic cost plus a share of overheads and other indirect costs. You should look at both options to see which provides a fair and reasonable apportionment. The costs may be shown as a percentage of total costs of providing membership or of the subscription value.

Life subscriptions will have to be apportioned on a basis that is reasonable. A proposal for the basis should be sent to the VAT office for agreement.

Similarly, different rates of membership will have to be reflected in the apportionment agreed.

Overseas subscriptions will normally follow the same rules, and VAT should be charged on the same basis as UK subscriptions. However, where the benefits are principally the provision of information and advice then the subscription may be outside the scope of UK VAT. This will be the case where the subscription is from a business based in the EC or anyone based outside the EC. UK VAT applies to membership subscriptions for individuals in the EC.

Remember that any apportionment should be agreed with HMRC *before* it is used as a basis to recover VAT. The costs for each element will need to be updated each year. In addition, if membership benefits change, the apportionment will need to be recalculated and agreed again with HMRC. For example, you may start to provide a members-only area on your charity's website, and this is a standard-rated benefit.

Insurance services

Generally, insurance premiums are exempt from VAT and instead insurance premium tax is added to the basic cost of insurance and included in the premiums customers pay. Insurers have to be registered with the Financial Services Authority (FSA) as it is a regulated industry. Charities may supply insurance services in two ways:

- membership bodies may hold a block insurance and sell the insurance to their members. This is treated as a sale of insurance for VAT purposes and is exempt, even though the charity is not itself the insurer. The charity is acting as principal in this arrangement

- charities may act as agents, arranging insurance for individuals. The charity may receive a commission from the insurance company, which is income to the charity. This is subject to VAT at standard rate if the charity is merely a sales agent. If, on the other hand, the charity provides help to the individual in choosing an appropriate policy, completing and submitting forms on the individual's behalf, then this is an insurance introductory service and exempt from VAT.

Charities that sell travel insurance in connection with fundraising events will be able to treat the charges they make for arranging the insurance as exempt if the insurance is supplied:

- in isolation of any travel

- in relation to a supply of a travel service on which no UK VAT is payable

- in relation to the sale of a travel service which bears UK VAT, provided that you notify the traveller, in writing, of the price of the insurance as due under the contract of insurance and any fee related to that insurance charged over and above the premium.

6 Zero and reduced rates

This chapter looks at which activities qualify for zero rating or reduced rating. In particular it covers what supplies are zero-rated when made to a charity and when made by a charity.

Zero-rated and reduced-rate supplies

Supplies that are made in the course of a business activity (see Chapter 4 for the meaning of 'business activity') and that are not specifically exempted (see Chapter 5 for 'exempt supplies') are referred to as 'taxable supplies'. This means they are subject to VAT. Output VAT is added to the selling price and input VAT on purchases that are attributable to taxable supplies can be recovered.

Most taxable supplies are standard-rated. This means that VAT is charged at the standard rate of VAT, currently 17½ per cent. However, certain supplies attract lower rates of VAT. There are currently two lower rates of VAT: the zero rate and the reduced rate.

- VAT is charged on zero-rated supplies at a rate of 0 per cent. This means that no VAT is actually added to the selling price. However, unlike exempt supplies, input VAT attributable to the zero-rated supply is recoverable.

- VAT is charged on reduced-rate supplies at 5 per cent.

Zero rating is normally considered to be very desirable, especially if sales are made to individuals or organisations that cannot recover all the VAT they incur in making purchases. The price charged to the customer is not increased by VAT, but the costs of making the sale are reduced by being able to recover associated input VAT. As a result there are detailed rules on when supplies can be zero-rated.

Supplies that are always zero-rated are explained in the section 'General zero-rated supplies' below.

However, for charities there are two additional aspects to zero rating:

- Certain goods and services that are normally standard-rated are zero-rated when supplied *to* a charity and any qualifying conditions are met. This applies even if the charity is not registered for VAT. See the section 'Zero-rated supplies to charities'.

- Certain goods are zero-rated when supplied *by* a charity. Goods that would normally attract a different VAT treatment become a zero-rated business supply when made by a charity and under specific circumstances. See the section 'Zero-rated supplies by charities'.

Sometimes a supply can qualify as both zero-rated and reduced rate or exempt. Zero rating takes precedence over other possible treatments and you can choose to zero-rate the supply if you wish.

Most of the special zero-rating reliefs are restricted to purchases or sales made by charities. HMRC will accept that an organisation is a charity if it is registered with the Charity Commission (or equivalent in Scotland or Northern Ireland), or if it is accepted as charitable by HMRC for income or corporation tax purposes. However, there are charities that will fall into neither of these categories, such as very small charities, charities based outside the UK and organisations that are in the process of registration. In such circumstances you may need to persuade HMRC that you are charitable. Note that a Community Amateur Sports Club is not considered charitable for zero-rating purposes unless it is also a charity.

Zero-rated supplies to charities

Certain goods and services are zero-rated when supplied to a charity and any qualifying conditions are met. It does not matter whether the charity is VAT-registered or not. If the qualifying conditions are met, the supplier must zero rate their supply. This represents a saving to the charity if it is not registered or if it will be using the supply partly or wholly for non-business or exempt purposes, as no VAT is added to the purchase price.

If the goods are purchased from a UK supplier, the supplier must obtain evidence that the customer is a charity and that any qualifying conditions are met. Where the supplier cannot independently verify any qualifying conditions and must rely on representations by the charity, they must obtain a declaration of eligibility from the charity and the charity must supply this if asked. There are standard declaration forms for certain types of supply, and these are explained below.

If the supplier incorrectly charges VAT, the supplier should be asked to issue a VAT-only credit note and refund the VAT. HMRC will not make refunds of VAT.

If qualifying goods are imported from outside the EC then the import is also zero-rated, though a declaration of eligibility must be provided to HMRC at the point of importation. If qualifying goods are acquired from another EC state by a VAT-registered charity then the charity may zero rate the acquisition provided proof of eligibility is retained. No proof of eligibility need be provided to the overseas supplier. If the charity is not registered then the EC supplier may charge VAT in the EC state of supply if there are no similar reliefs available in that state. This VAT cannot be recovered from HMRC. See Chapter 9: *International aspects of VAT* for information on the VAT implications of purchasing goods and services from suppliers outside the UK.

The goods and services that can be zero-rated when supplied to a charity are:

- advertising services
- aids for disabled people
- ambulances
- boats and lifeboats
- goods connected with collecting donations
- construction of new buildings
- disabled access
- hearing aids
- emergency alarm systems

- medical goods and services
- medicines
- Motability scheme
- motor vehicles
- rescue equipment
- talking books for the blind
- visual aids for the partially sighted
- wireless sets for the blind.

Each of these is considered below. Note that in some situations (for example, medical goods and services) the relief applies to other organisations besides charities.

Advertising services

Advertising and closely related services are zero-rated when supplied to a charity. This includes supplies of advertising services by one charity to another. Initially the scope of this relief was restricted to newspaper advertising, but zero rating has since been extended. To qualify, the advert must be placed in purchased or donated advertising time or space and not targeted at selected individuals. So advertising on a charity's own website or in its own publications does not qualify.

The zero rating applies to all types of advertising by charities, including recruitment advertisements, attracting new members, pupils or students, advertising events, raising awareness or fundraising.

All forms of media are allowed, including billboards, cinema, TV, radio, newspapers, magazines, the sides of vehicles and internet advertising (except for adverts on the charity's own website) and advertising on goods such as badges, balloons, banners, carrier bags, business cards, calendars, clothing, flags, car parking tickets, diaries, greetings cards, lottery tickets, posters and stationery.

Services of design and production of the adverts are zero-rated, along with any closely related goods such as photographs.

In order to zero rate the invoice, the supplier must be satisfied that it is a supply of advertising to a charity. HMRC recommends that charities give suppliers a declaration that the conditions for zero rating have been met. HMRC provide a template declaration in VAT Notice 701/58.

Zero rating is not available in the following situations:

- where the advertising is targeted at identified individuals, for example personally addressed letters, direct marketing and telesales. However, it may be possible for individual items of the promotional material used to be zero-rated. (see 'Books and printed matter' below)

- where the advertisement appears in a charity's own magazine, notice board, calendar or other publication or on the charity's own website, as these are not placed on someone else's time or space

- where the charity prepares its own advertisements in-house

- where the supply is not directly to a charity, for example where the supply is to a trading subsidiary or to a recruitment agency placing the advertisement on behalf of a charity. See the comments in the 'Principal and agent' section in Chapter 11 for agency supplies of advertising to a charity.

Aids for disabled people

Certain specialised goods and services needed by disabled people are zero-rated. A 'disabled person' means a chronically sick or disabled person, including people who are blind, deaf or dumb or substantially and permanently handicapped by illness, injury or congenital deformity, but excludes people who are only temporarily disabled. Being elderly is not sufficient alone. The zero rating in this section relates to goods and services for use by a specific disabled person, whether purchased by the disabled person or by a charity on their behalf. It does not extend to goods and services used for business purposes.

A separate piece of legislation also permits non-profit-making hospitals and research institutions and charities caring for the disabled to obtain the same relief if the aids are bought from charitable funds or are being donated.

The following goods are covered:

- Medical or surgical appliances designed solely for the relief of a severe abnormality or severe injury. The appliances included are special clothing, footwear and wigs, renal haemodialysis units, oxygen concentrators, artificial respirators, TENS machines and other similar apparatus (see VAT Notice 701/7 for further details).

- Electrically or mechanically adjustable beds designed for invalids.

- Commode chairs and stools, devices incorporating a bidet jet and warm air drier and frames, and other devices for sitting over or rising from sanitary appliances.

- Chair or stair lifts designed for use in connection with invalid wheelchairs, even if the invalid is not in a wheelchair when using them.

- Hoists and lifters designed for use by invalids.

- Certain adapted motor vehicles: see the section on 'Motor vehicles' below.

- Other equipment and appliances designed solely for use by a disabled person, including wheelchairs. General-purpose goods are not eligible, even if they are being used by a disabled person. HMRC will consider the intention of the supplier in designing and marketing the product in assessing whether the goods were designed solely for use by a disabled person. However, the fact that such an item may be used by able-bodied persons does not mean that it does not qualify for zero rating.

- Adaptations of general-purpose goods (excluding motor vehicles) so that those goods suit the condition of a disabled person are zero-rated, though it is only the service of adaptation that is zero-rated and not the purchase of the general-purpose goods.

Some goods will not qualify for zero rating, even if the supply is to a disabled person. An example of this would be the provision of shoes to someone whose disability does not mean that they need special surgical footwear. Since spectacles, hearing aids and dentures are normally standard-rated, there can be situations where VAT is being paid on these goods for disabled people. Goods that will always be standard-rated include:

- air-conditioning units

- asthma, hay fever and allergy products, including special filters for vacuum cleaners and the like

- carpets

- computers – only specialist items may be zero-rated, even when the computer is sold as a package

- golf buggies

- hearing aids

If an item qualifies for zero rating, then parts and accessories necessary for the item are included in the zero rating, as is the hire or the repair and maintenance of the item.

See VAT Notice 701/7 for model eligibility declarations by a charity purchasing or importing qualifying goods or services.

Ambulances

An ambulance is an emergency vehicle used for transporting sick and injured people or animals. This includes specially equipped air ambulances or watercraft. To qualify for zero rating as an ambulance, the vehicle must have the following features:

- The front and both sides must bear permanently fitted signs indicating that the vehicle is an ambulance.

- In the case of an ambulance for transporting human patients, adequate door space for the loading of a patient on a stretcher.

- Seating to the rear of the driver (or pilot) for at least one attendant.

- One or more stretchers that, with handles extended, measure at least 1.95 metres, together with permanent fittings to hold this stretcher in position. This size specification applies only to ambulances that transport human patients. For ambulances that transport animals, any reasonable lifting or carrying equipment is acceptable.

If the ambulance is purchased by an eligible body that is not a charity, the eligible body must use wholly charitable funds or wholly voluntary contributions for its purchase.

Boats and lifeboats

Boats that have been designed or substantially and permanently adapted for use by disabled people will qualify for zero rating. To qualify, the boat should allow for the embarkation of disabled people in wheelchairs and their movement about the boat, as well as wheelchair clamps. It should have special toilet and washing facilities and may have sleeping, galley and steering facilities for use by disabled people.

The supply, repair and maintenance of any vessel made direct to a charity providing rescue or assistance at sea is zero-rated. Also included is the supply of tractors, winching equipment and the construction and repair of slipways. In addition repairs, maintenance, spares and accessories are zero-rated.

Goods connected with collecting donations

Various goods connected with collecting donations are zero-rated if supplied to a charity:

- Collecting boxes, providing they are tamper-proof (capable of being sealed) and specifically designed for collecting money for charity. They should bear the charity name in indelible printing, embossing or raised letters, or allow for the charity name to be added later.

- Collecting envelopes used for house-to-house collections or in church collections.

- Pre-printed letters appealing solely for money for the charity.

- Envelopes used with appeal letters for sending in a donation, providing they are overprinted with an appeal request related to that contained in the letter.

- Lapel stickers and badges given free as an acknowledgement to donors which have a nominal value. Badges or other tokens given in return for an anticipated donation of £1 or less are considered to be of nominal value as long as the cost to the charity is considerably less than £1 and the item is not sold for a fixed price. Included are small items such as paper stickers, ribbons, artificial flowers where these are an emblem of the charity, and metal badges, subject to the minimal cost criteria.

Excluded are:

- Elaborate boxes which have an additional purpose, such as a game or a quiz machine, though HMRC state that receptacles where, for example, a simple balance mechanism moves the money from one level to another or the weight of a coin causes it to roll helter-skelter fashion into the collecting area are included in the relief.

- General-purpose buckets, although special lids designed to seal standard buckets may qualify for the zero rating.

- Appeal letters that incorporate a survey or questionnaire.

Construction of new buildings

Costs of constructing new buildings can be zero-rated when:

- the building is intended for use solely for a relevant charitable purpose, or

- the building is intended for use solely for a relevant residential purpose, or

- the building is designed as one or more dwellings.

'Relevant charitable purpose' means use by a charity for non-business activities or as a village hall or similar in providing social or recreational facilities for a local community. 'Use for a relevant residential purpose' means use as a children's home, care home, hospice, student accommodation or similar. However, zero rating does not extend to the services of professionals such as architects and surveyors unless supplied as part of a design and build contract. For more details, see Chapter 8: *Property*.

Disabled access

Certain access works are zero-rated when carried out on the private residence of a disabled person or to a charity building, and if the purpose is to improve disabled access. The zero rating includes:

- The supply of building services and of associated goods and materials, though goods and materials purchased by a charity undertaking the work itself do not quality.

- Any necessary preparatory work, restoration or making good.

Qualifying disabled access works include:

- The construction of ramps.

- The widening of doorways and passages, though the construction of new doorways and passages is excluded.

- Services of providing, extending or adapting a bathroom, washroom or lavatory. If the services are carried out in a charity building the building must comprise residential accommodation or a day centre where at least 20 per cent of the individuals using the centre are disabled persons.

- Services to a charity of providing, extending or adapting a washroom or lavatory provided the work is carried out in a building, or part of a building used principally by a charity for charitable purposes.

- Services of installing, repairing and maintaining an ordinary vertical lift in a charity building used as a day centre or as a temporary or permanent residence for disabled people.

Emergency alarm systems

The alarm system must be capable of operation by a disabled person and be set up to enable him or her to alert directly a specified person, such as a warden, or a control centre. The zero rating is available on purchases by a disabled person or by a charity for onward supply to a disabled person. The zero rating is extended to the supply of services necessarily performed by a control centre in receiving and responding to calls.

Hearing aids and induction loop systems

Generally hearing aids are not within the zero-rating relief and the majority of people have to pay standard-rate VAT on the purchases of hearing aids. However, specialist devices designed for the auditory training of deaf children are zero-rated, as are special harnesses designed solely for use by deaf children when using the training device. Other specialised aids designed for people with severely defective hearing but which are not hearing aids as such are zero-rated. Such aids include TV hearing aids, induction loop systems and tinnitus maskers.

Such supplies are zero-rated when made directly to a disabled person or to a charity or other eligible body which will make them available to a disabled person for their personal or domestic use. 'Personal or domestic use' precludes business use and it also precludes making the items available for the general use of any disabled person. So the installation of an induction loop system in a room that is hired out commercially will not qualify for zero rating. However, HMRC may accept that induction loop systems can be zero-rated when installed in non-business premises such as village halls and community centres.

Medical goods and services

The purchase of certain medical goods and services by an eligible body is zero-rated when purchased mainly for use in medical or veterinary research, training, diagnosis or treatment. Eligible bodies comprise:

- health authorities, health trusts and not-for-profit hospitals

- not-for-profit research institutions

- charities providing care or medical or surgical treatment for disabled people either in a hospice, residential care home, day centre (not one providing primarily social or recreational activities) or in their own homes. To qualify, over time 50 per cent or more of service users must be disabled or chronically sick

- charities providing rescue or first aid services for humans or animals

- charities that provide transport services mainly to disabled people

- charities that have as their sole purpose and function the provision of a range of services for, or on behalf of, chronically sick or disabled people

- any person or body purchasing qualifying goods for donation to one of the above.

See VAT Notice 701/6 for detailed guidance on eligible bodies.

Where the goods or services are being purchased by an eligible body that is not a charity, they must be wholly funded from charitable or voluntary donations.

Qualifying goods include:

- Medical equipment: equipment having characteristics that identify it as having been designed for a medical or dental purpose.

- Scientific equipment: equipment designed to perform a scientific function. This includes precision measuring equipment and analytical equipment such as thermometers, weighing machines and spectrometers.

- Computer equipment and certain software: computer hardware, peripherals and software.

- Video equipment: video cameras, recorders and playback equipment.

- Sterilising equipment such as autoclaves and other specialised equipment using steam or other high-temperature processes. Standard microwave ovens and other cooking appliances are not sterilising equipment, even if they can be used to sterilise. Sterilising fluid is not 'equipment'.

- Laboratory equipment: equipment that is designed for use in a laboratory, such as laboratory glassware, Bunsen burners, fume cupboards, laboratory benches and specialised sinks. It does not include ordinary cupboards, lockers, seats and other furniture and consumables.

- Refrigeration equipment: includes all cooling and freezing equipment, whether designed for industrial, domestic or any other purpose.

The hire or installation, repair and maintenance of qualifying goods is also zero-rated provided, for a non-charitable eligible body, it is funded from charitable or voluntary funds.

Medicines

Medicines are zero-rated when supplied to a charity looking after humans or animals or undertaking medical research. This applies to all substances used in the treatment or diagnosis of illness or for the prevention of illness. It includes anaesthetics, vaccines, contraception and the ingredients for making medicines. Any substances used directly in medical research are also zero-rated, although this relief only applies to charities actually engaged in medical research. This applies equally to veterinary research.

Motability scheme

The lease of vehicles, whether or not specially adapted for use by a disabled person, are zero-rated when let under the Motability scheme. The subsequent sale of vehicles at the end of the lease is also zero-rated.

Motor vehicles

There are a variety of circumstances in which motor vehicles can be zero-rated:

a) The purchase of an adapted vehicle for the personal use of a disabled person.

b) Adaptations to an unadapted vehicle to suit a disabled person's needs.

c) The purchase of certain vehicles by eligible bodies.

Each of these is considered below.

a) The purchase of an adapted vehicle is zero-rated provided:

- the vehicle is supplied to a disabled person who normally uses a wheelchair or stretcher to be mobile

- the vehicle seats no more than 12 people (including driver)

- it is designed, or substantially and permanently adapted for, the carriage of a disabled wheelchair or stretcher user.

Zero rating also extends to the hire and maintenance of such vehicles and to a supply to a charity where the charity is making the vehicle available to a qualifying disabled person for their personal use.

b) Adaptations to a vehicle are zero-rated when they adapt a vehicle to suit a disabled person's condition. The adaptations are zero-rated; however, the initial purchase of the unadapted vehicle is not. The adaptations can be supplied directly to a disabled person or to a charity carrying out the work on a qualifying vehicle.

c) The purchase of certain vehicles by an eligible body is zero-rated. See the section 'Medical equipment' above for the definition of an 'eligible body'. Eligible bodies which are not charities must use wholly charitable funds or wholly voluntary contributions for the purchase of the eligible vehicle in order to obtain VAT relief. An eligible vehicle is:

- a motor vehicle that is capable of carrying up to 12 people (including driver), and has been designed or substantially and permanently adapted for the carriage of a person in a wheelchair or on a stretcher

- an unadapted motor vehicle that has between 7 and 50 seats (including driver's seat), and is purchased or hired for use by an eligible body mainly for the transportation of blind, deaf, mentally handicapped or terminally ill people

- a vehicle that has been substantially and permanently adapted to carry at least one disabled person in a wheelchair. The number of wheelchair spaces and access facilities depend on the seating capacity of the vehicle (including driver's seat), as follows:

- 1–16 seats: one or more wheelchair spaces and a fitted ramp or electric or hydraulic lift;

- 17–26 seats: two or more wheelchair spaces and an electric or hydraulic lift;

- 27–36 seats: three or more wheelchair spaces and an electric or hydraulic lift;

- 37–46 seats: four or more wheelchair spaces and an electric or hydraulic lift;

- 47–50 seats: five or more wheelchair spaces and an electric or hydraulic lift.

- an ambulance. See section above on 'Ambulances'.

Rescue equipment

Specialist equipment needed by search and rescue teams such as heat-detecting equipment, image intensifiers and other equipment. Such equipment will be zero-rated only when supplied to a charity providing rescue or first aid services. General items such as mobile phones and binoculars are not eligible for the zero rating.

Talking books for the blind

Charities working with the blind may buy certain supplies at zero-rate VAT. These include sound recording equipment, parts and accessories for making tape recordings for use by the visually impaired. Radios and cassette recorders supplied to charities for free loan or rental to blind people are also included in the relief provisions and may be zero-rated. Evidence must be given to the supplier that the goods are to be used in accordance with the conditions above. A declaration should be given to the supplier confirming this, which the supplier must retain for their records.

Visual aids for the partially sighted

Spectacles and contact lenses cannot be zero-rated. However, special low-vision aids will qualify for zero rating. Included are custom-made spectacle-mounted low-vision aids and closed-circuit video magnification systems capable of magnifying text and images.

Wireless sets for blind people

Radios and tape players bought by a charity for free loan or rental to blind people will be zero-rated.

Zero-rated supplies by charities

The following supplies are zero-rated when made by a charity or other type of organisation as indicated. Note that the supplies described in the section 'General zero-rated supplies' will also be zero-rated when made by any type of organisation.

Sale of donated goods

The sale or hire of donated goods is zero-rated when made by a charity or a person who has agreed in writing to give all profits from the sale of the goods to a charity (normally a charity's trading subsidiary). The goods may be new or second-hand, but must be donated for the purpose of a sale or hire and should be available for purchase or hire by the general public. Sales through charity shops are zero-rated, but also sales at fundraising events, including auctions, providing they are open to the general public. By concession, HMRC also allows zero rating of the sale of donated goods that are in a poor condition and unwanted donated goods such as electrical items to scrap merchants and similar.

Charities or their subsidiaries may also restrict sales to the disabled and those on means-tested benefits, for example in schemes whereby recycled furniture is sold at low prices to those in need and still zero rate them.

This is a valuable relief, but there are conditions and anti-avoidance rules:

- The relief only applies to goods, not services. In particular, it cannot apply to land and buildings.

- It does not apply to donated raffle prizes, though it does apply to donated auction items.

- The goods must be donated for the purpose of a sale or hire, not for the charity's own use. The charity may not use them while they are waiting to sell or hire them.

- The goods can be cleaned or repaired as long as this does not alter their structure or original use. However, if the donated goods are converted or used to make other goods for sale the derived goods do not qualify, for example, if a painting is donated and used to make prints for resale.

- Pre-arranged sales will not be eligible for zero-rating. Likewise, an arrangement by the donor of the goods with the charity or a purchaser will exclude the sale from the scheme. Thus zero rating will not apply to schemes where the charity collects used goods such as toner cartridges from businesses and then sells them on to one pre-arranged purchaser.

Export of goods

The export of goods by a charity is a deemed business activity and zero-rated. Goods are exported when they are sent to a destination outside the EC. It does not matter if the goods were purchased or donated. If the goods are sold commercially then they can be zero-rated under the normal export rules (see Chapter 9: *International aspects of VAT*). However, under this provision the donation of goods to a destination outside the EC will be considered a zero-rated business activity. This allows recovery of all associated input VAT, and even if a charity has no other business activities it can register on the basis of its export of goods.

Proof of export must be obtained – see Chapter 9 for what HMRC consider to be acceptable proof of export.

However, the following are not covered:

- the export of services, for example the services of engineers and doctors

- goods sent to destinations inside the EC, including the UK.

General zero-rated supplies

The following types of supply are zero-rated when made by any type of organisation, including commercial businesses and charities:

- books and printed matter

- passenger transport

- clothing and footwear

- certain types of food and animal feed.

Books and printed matter

The supply of printed matter such as books and magazines is generally zero-rated. Zero rating extends to the sale, hire or loan of qualifying matter. Potentially zero-rated printed matter includes:

- books and booklets

- brochures and pamphlets

- leaflets

- newspapers and magazines

- journals and periodicals

- children's picture and painting books

- music (printed, duplicated or manuscript)

- maps, charts and topographical plans.

To qualify for zero rating, an item must pass two tests:

1. Its physical description must meet one of the above categories. It is the nature of the item, not the method of production which determines whether it is zero-rated. For example, a newsletter produced by photocopying would still qualify for zero rating.

2. Its function is primarily that of the ordinary understanding of a book, booklet, brochure etc., so, for example, a book of carpet samples physically resembles a book but its function is not that ordinarily understood of a book, that is, to convey information by words or images.

Publishing by electronic means does not fall within the zero rating. This includes publishing by CD, the internet or e-mail, cassette or video, though talking books for the blind are the subject of a separate zero-rating allowance.

Items that contain significant areas for completion are not considered to be zero-rated printed matter but standard-rated stationery. Examples include blank diaries and address books, postcards and greeting cards. Where printed matter contains areas for completion or areas to be detached and returned, HMRC allow the document to be zero-rated if the areas for completion or detachment make up less than 25 per cent of the area of the entire document, though if the entire document is intended to be returned HMRC consider the document to be standard-rated. The 25 per cent rule is however merely a guide and has no basis in law.

A leaflet is considered to be either ephemeral in nature or designed to accompany some other product or service. It should be a single sheet not larger than A4 primarily intended to be held in the hand for reading by individuals (rather than for hanging up for general display). It has to convey information and be complete in itself. It should contain a significant proportion of text, and at least 50 copies should be produced so that it can be generally distributed. A leaflet may also be up to A2 in size provided it is printed on both sides, folded down to A4 size or smaller and meets all the other conditions.

The following items will usually not qualify for zero rating as printed materials:

*   posters

*   diaries and calendars

*   stationery

*   postcards and greeting cards

*   commercial plans or drawings

*   globes and similar

*   badges

- bingo cards

- book covers supplied separately

- bookmarks

- business cards

- calendars

- certificates

- folders

- invitation cards

- tickets

- membership cards

- photographs and printed pictures

- questionnaires

- waste paper

- wrapping paper.

However, these items may qualify for zero rating if supplied as part of a package of advertising services or as goods connected with collecting donations and supplied to a charity. See the section on the 'package test' below.

Supplies connected with producing zero-rated printed matter

Services involved in producing zero-rated printed matter are themselves zero-rated if they result in the production of new zero-rated goods.

A printer with a contract to supply zero-rated goods may zero rate any preparation work, such as design and typesetting, and any post-production work, such as folding, inserting into envelopes and wrapping. This applies even if the printer sub-contracts parts of the work and even if the printer charges separately for the various processes. It can therefore be advantageous to arrange for all services to be provided by the printer and then invoiced as one zero-rated supply.

However, if an organisation purchases component supplies separately, only those that result in the production of zero-rated goods may be zero-rated. For example, if layout and design services are purchased separately, they will be standard-rated.

If zero-rated printed matter is packed and delivered or posted, see Chapter 11: *Other topics*, 'Postage and packing'.

Zero-rated printed matter supplied with standard-rated items

Where minor items such as covers, binders and bookmarks are supplied with zero-rated matter for a single charge, they are zero-rated. For more substantial items such as CDs the single/multiple supply tests must be used to determine if there is a single or multiple supply. See Chapter 11 for details of the single/multiple supply tests.

THE 'PACKAGE TEST' Where there is a multiple supply of zero-rated and standard-rated printed matter, by concession the 'package test' may be used. The package test only applies when all items in the package comprise items of printed paper or card. Under the package test, if there are more zero-rated than standard-rated items then the whole package is zero-rated and vice versa. If there are equal numbers then the VAT status follows the higher of the costs of the zero-rated and standard-rated items. For package test purposes the outer envelope is ignored.

Where a mixed package of printed matter is supplied to a charity for use in collecting monetary donations, then for the purposes of the package test the following items are considered to be zero-rated items: appeal letters, printed envelopes for use with the appeal letters, money-collecting envelopes and collecting boxes made of card.

Printed matter supplied with other services

If the supply of printed matter is incidental to another supply then its VAT treatment will follow that of the other supply. Examples include translation services and reports by consultants, though if extra copies are provided and charged as such then these may be zero-rated.

Where printed matter is supplied as part of a package of education for a single fee then the single/multiple supply tests (see Chapter 11) must be used to determine whether there is a single supply of education or a mixed supply of education and printed matter.

If zero-rated printed matter is the only supply received in return for a subscription then the whole subscription will be zero-rated. Where other supplies are received in return for a subscription to certain non-profit-making bodies the subscription may be apportioned between the various supplies involved, with the part relating to the zero-rated supply of printed matter being zero rated. See Chapter 5.

See VAT Notice 701/10 for more information on the zero rating of books and other printed matter.

Passenger transport

There is a supply of passenger transport where a vehicle is supplied, in return for consideration, together with driver for the carriage of passengers. 'Vehicles' include road transport, rail transport, ships and aeroplanes. You must either employ or take on legal responsibility for the driver or pilot, for example by having responsibility in law for ensuring the driver of a road vehicle adheres to the driving hours regulations. There are broadly three scenarios:

1. You supply transport for passengers from your own resources. You own or hire the vehicle without driver/pilot and you employ or take on legal responsibility for the driver or pilot. You do not supply the passenger transport as part of a package together with other bought-in supplies of transport or accommodation. There is a supply of passenger transport.

2. You supply passenger transport from your own resources but as part of a package with other bought-in supplies of transport or accommodation. The supply comes under the Tour Operators' Margin Scheme – see Chapter 10.

3. You buy in and resell passenger transport. You do not own or hire the vehicle on its own and you do not take on legal responsibility for the driver. The supply comes under the Tour Operators' Margin Scheme – see Chapter 10.

Under certain conditions a supply of passenger transport is zero-rated. If these conditions are not met, it is standard-rated.

Many voluntary organisations organise occasional outings where participants contribute towards meeting the cost of transport hire. If the outings are occasional and there is no intention to make a profit then this is likely to be considered a non-business activity, even if the organisation collects the payments and pays the transport company.

Organisations making exempt supplies of education (see Chapter 5: *Exempt supplies*) may treat a supply of passenger transport to students as exempt if it is supplied to the students and necessary for the supply of education. However, if the transport would also qualify for zero rating, it can be zero-rated in preference. If the organisation is VAT-registered, this allows it to recover input VAT on costs attributable to the supply of passenger transport.

A supply of passenger transport by a welfare or health institution that is part of a broader non-business activity or exempt supply will also be exempt if it forms an integral part of the wider non-business or exempt activity. However, if the passenger transport also qualifies as zero-rated, it may be treated as such in preference.

If the supply involves travel outside the UK, for example in another EC state or outside the EC, then only the part of the journey taking place within the UK is subject to UK VAT. Journeys taking place partly or wholly in another EC state may be subject to VAT in that EC state. For further details, see Chapter 9: *International aspects of VAT*.

A supply of passenger transport is zero-rated, subject to the exceptions listed below, to the extent that it takes place in the UK and any of the following applies:

a) the vehicle is adapted to carry ten or more persons, including passengers, drivers and any crew. If the vehicle has been adapted to cater for the special needs of people with disabilities, for example to carry wheelchairs, then the number of persons that could have been carried but for that adaptation is used. If the vehicle has been adapted for another reason, for example to carry luggage, then the spaces lost are not ignored

b) the journey involves taking passengers from the UK to a place outside the UK or vice versa. It is the part of the journey taking place in the UK that is zero-rated. If the journey also takes place partly in another EC state, it may be liable to VAT in that EC state. If you merely take passengers to the departure point for the international part of their journey this does not count

c) the journey is on a scheduled air flight. A scheduled air flight is one that operates to a published or regular timetable

d) it is provided by the Post Office company or one of its subsidiaries.

If the supply of passenger transport is zero-rated then incidental supplies may also be zero-rated, even if there is a separate charge. 'Incidental supplies' include the transport of accompanied luggage and pets, seat reservations and airport charges. If meals are provided for no extra charge then they can be zero-rated, but if there is a separate charge they are standard-rated as a supply of catering. Charges for car parking, cycle storage and left luggage are always standard-rated.

Even if the zero-rating conditions are met, the following supplies of passenger transport cannot be zero-rated:

• The transport of passengers to or from a place of entertainment or of cultural, historic or scientific interest, by the person supplying the right of admission or by a person connected to the person supplying the right of admission, unless the destination is accessible for free or operated by an unconnected person.

• Pleasure flights such as hot balloon rides where the flight is publicised as being for entertainment, recreation or amusement or for the experience of flying. However, pleasure cruises and excursions by coach or train can be zero-rated.

• Donkey rides and novelty rides on miniature railways, fairground equipment and similar.

Clothing and footwear

Most supplies of clothing and footwear are standard-rated, however the following are zero-rated:

- The supply of clothing or footwear designed for children under 14 and not suitable for use by older children or adults. HMRC generally accept that items below specified garment or foot sizes are designed for children under 14 and not suitable for older persons. HMRC publish tables of acceptable sizes in VAT Notice 714. If a garment is designed to stretch, its maximum stretch size must not exceed specified limits. In addition, there are restrictions on garments containing fur. Garments supplied to schools or clubs that cater exclusively for under-14s can be zero-rated irrespective of garment or foot size.

- The supply of protective boots and helmets: the item must conform to British, EC or equivalent safety standards. Qualifying items include motorbike and cycling helmets and the hire or loan of such items. However, protective boots and helmets are standard-rated when supplied to an organisation for use by its employees.

- The sale of donated clothing or footwear made by a charity or its subsidiary. See the section on sale of donated goods.

- The export of clothing and footwear of all types by a charity. 'Export' means sending to a destination outside the EC. See the section on the export of goods by a charity.

The hire or loan of a zero-rated item of clothing or footwear is also zero-rated, as is the hire of roller skates, ice skates and similar items if the foot size criteria are met.

Food

The VAT status of food is one of the most complex and bizarre areas of VAT law. The supply of most foodstuffs of a kind used for human consumption or as animal feed are zero-rated, though there are many exceptions and exceptions to the exceptions.

- Supplies made in the course of **catering** are generally standard-rated. See below.

- Supplies of **ice cream, frozen yoghurt and similar frozen products** are standard-rated if the product is designed to be consumed frozen. However, this does not include products which are sold frozen but designed to be thawed before consumption.

- Supplies of **confectionery** are standard-rated. 'Confectionery' includes sweets, chocolates, biscuits partly or wholly covered in chocolate and any item of sweetened prepared food normally eaten with the fingers. However, biscuits without external chocolate, and cakes, whether or not covered in chocolate, are zero-rated.

- **Alcoholic drinks** are standard-rated.

- **Non-alcoholic beverages** are standard-rated except for tea, herbal teas and similar, coffee and coffee substitutes, milk and milk-based drinks such as milkshakes which are zero-rated. A beverage is a product that is consumed to slake thirst, for pleasure, or to fortify or enhance energy. Carbonated drinks, fruit and vegetable juices, mineral water, non-alcoholic beer and wine are all standard-rated if they are beverages.

- **Potato crisps and similar products derived from potatoes, savoury snacks made by swelling cereals to produce an expanded or aerated product and de-shelled and salted or roasted nuts** are all standard-rated. However, products derived from cereals that have not been aerated are zero-rated, for example tortilla chips.

- The sale of **animal feed** is zero-rated unless it is canned, packaged or prepared pet food or food which is packaged and sold as feed for wild birds which are standard-rated. Pets are animals kept as objects of affection or for ornamental purposes and exclude animals on farms and working animals such as sheepdogs.

- **Plants** grown as foods for human consumption or animal feed are zero-rated, as are seeds and other means of propagating such plants. Plants and seeds produced for ornament are standard-rated. Crops grown for producing industrial products such as lubricating oils and biofuels are standard-rated.

- The supply of **live animals** of a kind generally used to produce food for human consumption is zero-rated.

Where there is a multiple supply of both zero-rated and standard-rated products for a single price, an apportionment must be made to calculate the VAT due, though where the value of standard-rated items is less than £1 and less than 20 per cent of the entire package price, the whole package may be zero-rated.

Further processing of a product is zero-rated if it results in a zero-rated product. If it results in a standard-rated product, the processing is standard-rated.

See VAT Notice 701/14 for further information.

Catering

Catering is the supply of prepared food and drink and is characterised by the inclusion of a significant element of service. Catering occurs when prepared food and drink are provided:

- as part of a contract to supply food and drink

- in connection with an event or function such as a conference or social event

- together with delivery, service, cutlery, crockery, catering staff or similar

- for consumption on the premises from which they are provided, for example in a restaurant or café

- for consumption off the premises as hot takeaway food.

However, if the customer must carry out further preparation before the food can be consumed, it is not a supply of catering but of food. 'Further preparation' includes cooking, reheating and arranging the food on serving plates.

If the catering is provided free or at significantly below cost as part of a welfare-related activity, then it is a non-business activity. HMRC consider 'significantly below cost' to mean subsidised by at least 15 per cent. Examples include meals provided to the homeless, and subsidised lunch clubs where the primary aim is to provide social or welfare facilities for the members.

If catering is provided as part of a broader activity then there may be a single supply with the catering assuming the VAT status of the broader activity. Examples include catering provided to students in an educational establishment, to patients in a health institution and to recipients of welfare services.

Where an educational institution makes a non-business or exempt supply of education to its students, a supply of catering that is closely related to the supply of education is also non-business or exempt, though supplies to staff and non-students will be standard-rated. A supply of catering is 'closely related' if it is for the students and necessary for the delivery of education to the students. By concession, this treatment also extends to supplies by student unions made at higher education institutions on behalf of and with the agreement of the parent institution, though the concession does not extend to food and drink provided from shops or bars.

Supplies of catering in health institutions that are provided to relatives staying with a sick child are exempt. However, supplies of catering to staff and to other visitors are standard-rated.

Catering supplied as part of an exempt one-off fundraising event will also be exempt, even if supplied for a separate charge. Catering supplied as an incidental part of a zero-rated supply of passenger transport is zero-rated if it is not supplied for a separate charge, though where catering forms a major part of the supply, for example on a wedding cruise, the whole supply may be standard-rated.

If a business supply of catering is not part of a broader supply then it is standard-rated.

It can sometimes be difficult to distinguish between a standard-rated supply of catering and a zero-rated supply of food and drink. Common areas of difficulty are:

- Establishing the **boundaries** of any premises involved. Supplies of unheated food for consumption off the premises may qualify as zero-rated if the underlying food or drink is zero-rated. 'Premises' extend to any facilities provided to enable customers to consume the food, such as outdoor seating areas.

- The definition of **'hot food'**. 'Hot food' is food which has been heated for the purposes of enabling it to be consumed at a temperature above the ambient air temperature. If the food is merely hot because it has just been made or has just been heated to comply with health and safety regulations, then it may be able to qualify as zero-rated. Examples include fresh bread and frozen products such as pies that have been heated in order to defrost and cook and that must be maintained at a certain temperature in order to comply with health and safety requirements.

- **Delivered cold takeaway food** such as sandwich platters. The case law is complex and the VAT status may depend on the nature of the food provided, the event (if any) being catered for and the extent of any attendant supplies and services. Indicators of catering are: the supply of catering staff, the supply of a complete meal, the provision of crockery and cutlery which is later returned and further processing of the food by the supplier at the customer's premises, such as laying it out. Indicators of a supply of food are: the supply is limited to snacks such as sandwiches, the supplied items are similar in substance and appearance to those commonly purchased in shops and any items supplied with the food such as knives forks and plates are disposable.

Dispensing of medicines and medical goods

The dispensing of qualifying goods by a registered pharmacist against a prescription issued by a registered medical practitioner, dentist or nurse is zero-rated if the goods are for the personal use of an individual. Dispensing by GPs qualified to provide pharmacy services is also zero-rated though private dispensing by a GP is standard-rated. Note that standard NHS prescription charges are not payment for a supply but a statutory fee that is outside the scope of VAT.

Qualifying goods are any goods designed or adapted for use in connection with medical or surgical treatment except for hearing aids, dentures, spectacles and contact lenses. HMRC will accept that medicines on the Drug Tariff are qualifying goods.

Zero rating does not cover goods provided when a person is being treated in a health institution such as a hospital, hospice or nursing home, though by concession HMRC accept that goods dispensed under an NHS prescription by a GP to patients in a health

107

institution can be zero-rated. Where medicines are administered at the time of treatment then this forms a single supply of exempt medical care.

Reduced-rate supplies

Reduced-rate supplies are taxable business activities that attract a reduced rate of 5 per cent. Reduced-rate supplies include:

- supplies of fuel and power

- installation of energy-saving materials

- the grant-funded installation of heating equipment or security goods

- supplies of welfare advice and information

- mobility aids for the elderly

- residential conversions

- renovation or alteration of empty residential property

- contraceptive products.

Each of these is considered below.

Fuel and power

Supplies of fuel and power for qualifying use are reduced rate. Supplies of fuel and power include mains gas and electricity, solid fuels such as coal, wood logs and peat, cylinder gas and fuel oils such as kerosene, but not petrol or diesel. Batteries are excluded but electricity from a mobile generator is included if the supplier operates the equipment and charges for the power supplied.

Qualifying use is domestic use or use for a relevant residential purpose (see Chapter 15: *Glossary*) or use by a charity for its non-business activities or use for any purpose that is below certain *de minimis* limits. If a supply of fuel or power is partly qualifying, then provided that 60 per cent or more of the supply is for qualifying purposes, the whole supply can be considered qualifying.

De minimis limits are: mains electricity − 1,000 kWh per month: mains gas − 4,397 kWh per month. See VAT Notice 701/19 for details of other *de minimis* limits.

Note that fuel supplied to a charity providing rescue at sea that is used in a lifeboat is zero-rated.

Installation of energy-saving materials

The supply and installation of certain energy-saving materials in a qualifying building is reduced rate if the materials are supplied by the person who installs them. If the materials are purchased and installed separately neither the materials nor installation services qualify, and if the installation is incidental to other building or construction work it will follow the VAT treatment of that work.

A qualifying building is a dwelling, a building used for a relevant residential purpose (see Chapter 15: *Glossary*) or a building used for a relevant charitable purpose (see Chapter 15: *Glossary*). Qualifying energy-saving materials are: insulation and lagging, draught strips, central heating and hot water controls, solar panels, wind and water turbines, ground and air source heat pumps, micro CHP units and boilers designed to be fuelled solely by wood, straw or similar.

Any incidental work such as minor building work is also reduced rate. Note that if the materials are installed as part of a zero-rated construction, they may be zero-rated.

The grant-funded installation of heating equipment or security goods

The supply and installation of certain goods in a qualifying person's residence is reduced rate to the extent the work is funded by a relevant scheme.

Qualifying supplies are:

- The supply and installation of thermostatically controlled gas-fired room heaters, electric storage heaters, closed solid-fuel fire cassettes, electric dual immersion heaters with factory-insulated hot water tanks, gas- and oil-fired boilers and radiators.

- Services of connecting or reconnecting a mains gas supply.

- The installation, maintenance or repair of a central heating system including the lease of such a system.

- The installation, maintenance or repair of a renewable-source heating system.

- The supply and installation of window locks, window bolts, door locks, door bolts, door security chains, spy holes and smoke alarms.

In all cases the reduced rate is only available when the goods are supplied and installed by the same person. A qualifying person is someone over 60 at the time of supply or someone who is in receipt of one or more of the following benefits: child tax credit (other than the family element), council tax benefit, disability living allowance, disablement pension, housing benefit, income-based job seeker's allowance, income support, war disablement pension or working tax credit. A relevant scheme is one that has an objective of funding the installation of energy-efficiency measures in the homes of less well-off people.

See VAT Notice 708/6.

Residential conversions

Certain supplies are reduced rate when connected with the conversion of premises into one or more single household dwellings, a multiple-occupancy dwelling such as bedsits, or premises intended for use solely for a relevant residential purpose (see Chapter 15: *Glossary* for definition of 'relevant residential purpose').

For conversions into a relevant residential property, the last use of the property must not have been for a relevant residential purpose. It does not include the remodelling of an existing relevant residential-purpose building, such as a care home, and any conversion where a new qualifying residential institution is not created in its entirety, such as the conversion of outbuildings into additional bedrooms for an existing care home.

The reduced rate covers the supply and installation of building materials and any works of repair, maintenance (such as redecoration), or improvement (such as the construction of an extension or the installation of double glazing) carried out to the fabric of the building.

See VAT Notice 708.

Renovation or alteration of empty residential property

The renovation or alteration of qualifying residential premises is reduced rate if the premises have not been lived in for two years or more at the time the work starts. Until 31 December 2007, the minimum period was three years.

Qualifying residential premises are single-household dwellings, multiple-occupancy dwellings, such as bedsits, a building (or part of a building) which, when last lived in, was used for a relevant residential purpose and after the renovation or alteration will be used solely for such a purpose, or a building (or part of a building) which, when last lived in, was one of a number of buildings on the same site that were used together as a unit for a relevant residential purpose, and after the renovation or alteration will be used solely for such a purpose.

The reduced rate covers the supply and installation of building materials and any works of repair, maintenance (such as redecoration), or improvement (such as the construction of an extension or the installation of double glazing) carried out to the fabric of the building.

See VAT Notice 708.

Contraceptive products

From 1 July 2006 supplies of contraceptive products are reduced rate. Supplies of contraceptives on prescription remain zero-rated, and where contraceptive products are fitted, injected or implanted by a health professional there is a single supply of exempt medical care.

Supplies of welfare advice and information

From 1 July 2006 the reduced rate applies to supplies of welfare advice and information made by certain organisations. Welfare advice is advice or information that directly relates to the care or protection of children or young people or physical or mental welfare of elderly, sick, distressed or disabled people. However, any advice that directly relates to a specific child or to an individual is a supply of welfare services and is exempt from VAT.

Only supplies of welfare advice made for a charge by charities and state-regulated private welfare institutions or agencies qualifies for the reduced rate (see Chapter 15: *Glossary* for definition of a 'state-regulated private welfare institution'). Supplies of welfare advice by a trading subsidiary of a charitable body are not covered by the reduced rate.

The reduced rate covers supplies of goods when the purpose of the goods is the giving of welfare advice. Examples include a video advising the elderly on safety in the home, or a DVD featuring advice for children on dealing with bullying. The inclusion on such goods of incidental information, for example an appeal for donations or information on the charity's objects will not affect the reduced rate. Goods that have an independent use and also carry incidental welfare advice, such as a mug or T-shirt bearing a slogan, are not covered by the reduced rate. 90–95 per cent of the purpose of any goods used must be the conveying of the welfare advice.

Mobility aids for the elderly

From 1 July 2007, the supply and installation of certain mobility aids is reduced rate when installed in domestic accommodation occupied by a person aged 60 or over at the time of the supply. It will not apply to installations in residential care homes or similar establishments.

The reduced rate applies to the supply and installation of grab rails, ramps, stair lifts, bath lifts, built-in shower seats or showers containing built-in shower seats and walk-in baths with sealable doors. The reduced rate will not apply to any repairs or replacements of those goods once installed. The reduced rate does not apply to the supply of goods alone but does apply to a supply of installation services alone. Customers should give suppliers a written statement of eligibility. If the elderly person cannot complete a declaration personally a declaration by a relative, partner or other responsible person is acceptable.

7 Fundraising

This chapter looks at the VAT implications of various fundraising activities commonly undertaken by voluntary organisations. The chapter includes commentary on auctions, challenge events, marathons, the rules on one-off fundraising events, selling donated goods, sponsorship and commercial participator arrangements, and many more.

This chapter looks at the VAT categories that apply to the activities of charities aimed specifically at raising funds for the work of the charity. For example, collecting donations will be outside the scope of VAT and does not count as a business activity (see Chapter 4). However, charities may use several methods to obtain donations, alongside selling goods and inviting members of the public to participate in events. Hence the VAT position may be fairly complex for a fundraising activity. It is important that the VAT status is established at the outset and it may be possible to arrange the transactions so that the VAT treatment is beneficial to the charity.

The specific areas of fundraising activity examined in more detail below are:

*   admission fees

*   advertising space

*   affinity credit cards

*   bingo

*   cause-related marketing

*   challenge events

*   charity auctions

*   Christmas cards

*   collecting donations

*   corporate events

*   fundraising events

- gifts in kind from companies and barter arrangements

- London Marathon and similar participative events

- lotteries including raffles

- merchandising

- recycled goods

- sale of donated goods

- services to other charities

- shops

- sponsorship

- supporter schemes.

Raising income from renting out premises is covered in Chapter 8: *Property*.

Fundraising is constantly changing and new ideas come forward all the time. It is therefore important to grasp the underlying principles to use in all situations even if the particular situation is not covered here.

- VAT only applies to business transactions, so donations and grants are outside the scope of VAT. So are other donated goods and services, providing they are given without any expectation of a benefit in return.

- In general, the sale of goods or services will be subject to VAT, unless covered by a specific zero rating or exemption. A considerable amount of charitable activity is exempt, and certain fundraising activities will be exempt or zero-rated. However, the closer you get to straightforward commercial arrangements, the more likely it is that you should be charging VAT.

- Underlying all VAT law is a consideration that the tax rules should not distort competition. If a charity has an unfair advantage because of its charitable status yet is competing with commercial traders, then it is likely that the charity is on the edge of what is permitted by law and there may be a challenge to the treatment by HMRC.

- The VAT treatment needs to be sorted out *before* you start the activity, as it will be too late afterwards to change the wording on the leaflet, advertisement or other documentation.

Admission fees

Charities organising events will usually be covered by the exemption for fundraising events, and so admission fees in this situation will be exempt. Admission fees to theatres, galleries and any performance and most visitor centres will be covered by the cultural services exemption (see Chapter 5).

However, some situations may arise where a charity is not organising the event so that it does not qualify for exemption. Admission fees are then liable to VAT at the standard rate. However, if you only suggest an amount that may be given, this can be treated as a donation, but you would have to allow free admission to anyone who asked for it. You may also charge an admission fee that is simply enough to cover the direct costs of the event and then invite donations in addition. VAT then has to be accounted for on the admission fees only. Again you would have to admit someone who only paid the admission fee.

Advertising space

Generally, the sale of advertising is standard-rated, with a few exceptions.

- Advertising in the programme or brochure for a fundraising event will be seen as part of the income from the event and will therefore be exempt.

- Advertising from private individuals in a charity publication can mean that the income is treated as a donation. This will apply if at least 50 per cent of the advertisements are clearly from private individuals where there is no promotion of commercial objectives. Advertisements from businesses are not from private individuals even if there is no specific reference to a particular trade or service. If the 50 per cent rule is broken then standard rating applies to all the advertisements.

- Selling advertising space to another charity will be zero-rated, providing the conditions are met (see Chapter 6).

Affinity credit cards

These are credit cards carrying a charity name and logo. The credit card company has the use of the charity's mailing list and some assistance in the recruitment of the charity's members and supporters to become subscribers to the card. The charity usually receives a fixed payment on first use of the card and an agreed percentage of all retail spending thereafter. There should be a proper written agreement which will allow for the use of the charity's name and logo and mailing list. In practice, there are usually two agreements. The first of these is between the credit card company and the charity's trading subsidiary for the assistance in recruiting members, which is a standard-rated supply. The second agreement is between the charity and credit card company allowing use of the logo. It may be possible to set these agreements up as one tripartite agreement.

HMRC have agreed that it is appropriate to treat a proportion of the initial payment to the charity, usually 20 per cent, as a fee, subject to VAT, for use of the charity name and mailing list. All the rest is treated as a donation and is outside the scope of VAT.

Bingo

Generally, the total amount charged to play bingo is exempt. For the organiser, the value of the exempt supply is the net proceeds after deducting the VAT-inclusive cost of goods given as prizes. Generally, charities will be involved in small-scale bingo in clubs or as part of a fundraising activity.

- Small-scale cash bingo in clubs does not require a licence under the Gambling Act 2005. Only members and their bona fide guests may participate.

- Fundraising bingo at a function may be open to the public. The proceeds must be applied to a charitable or not-for-profit purpose.

In both these cases, the amounts paid are exempt. Commercial bingo houses charge an admission fee and sometimes charge a membership fee, both of which are standard-rated. The stake money is, however, exempt.

Cause-related marketing

Cause-related marketing is really sponsorship in reverse – companies value charity brands and may wish to pay the charity a fee (usually under a licence agreement for the right to use your charity name and logo for a certain period of time). This is a commercial arrangement and is standard-rated for VAT. It may be structured as a royalty; this is still standard-rated for VAT.

The charity may receive donations in addition to the licence fee. The donations will be outside the scope of VAT, but the arrangement must make it quite clear that the donations are quite separate. These arrangements should be documented in an agreement, as the company is a commercial participator under the fundraising regulations of the Charities Act 1993. In such an agreement it is necessary to set out clearly what is a fee and what is a donation.

Challenge events

Challenge events usually involve participants undertaking some activity for which they have raised sponsorship from friends and relatives, for example cycling across a desert or undertaking the Three Peaks Challenge.

Frequently, challenge events will not be covered by the fundraising event exemption because accommodation and other travel services are provided. Bought-in accommodation disqualifies an event from being a fundraising event. In addition, more than two nights' accommodation provided by the charity itself (if the charity has its own property, for example) would disqualify the event from being a fundraising event. Overseas events are caught where a package of travel and accommodation is provided.

There are two ways in which charities might structure these events; the charity may be acting as agent for a tour organiser, or the charity may be organising the whole event itself. The main way that you would determine that the charity is acting as agent is if the travel company or tour organiser is taking the financial risk and organising the event so that the charity does not have financial risk. In addition, you should see the name of the tour organiser on event information and tickets, and the contract between charity and tour organiser would specify that the charity will be acting as agent.

A charity would be acting as principal (or undisclosed agent) if it takes the financial risk, for example setting up the tour and committing to various suppliers for minimum numbers of participants. The charity may, in fact, still be using a tour organiser, but the difference is that the charity is taking a financial risk – they have a contract with the tour organiser that commits the charity to a certain fee or a minimum number of participants. If the tour organiser is not named in literature about the event, then the charity may be operating as an undisclosed agent and the rules for being a principal apply.

If the charity is acting as agent, then it would normally collect fees from participants to pass on to the tour organiser, but keep additional sums raised as donations. The charity would usually retain some of the fees to cover its costs – this element will be treated as an agent's commission and VAT will be payable at standard rate on this.

Example: Charity as agent

A tour organiser puts together the package of travel, accommodation etc. which they say will cost £1,500 to participants. This amount has to be paid in two instalments: a non-returnable booking fee of £250, then the balance eight weeks before departure. The charity sets a minimum sponsorship target for participants of £2,500 which must be raised eight weeks before they go, of which £1,500 will have to go to the tour organiser, so the charity will get £1,000 extra from each participant, plus any higher amounts raised in sponsorship. The contract between the tour organiser and the charity states that the charity will only have to pay for the places it fills. So the charity does not have any risk and is acting as agent. The charity also collects a registration fee from participants of £350, which the agreement allows the charity to retain to cover its costs of recruiting participants. This is in effect a commission paid to the charity by the tour organiser. So the actual transactions would be:

1. the participant pays £350 registration fee to the charity

2. the charity pays £250 booking fee to the tour organiser

3. the participant raises enough sponsorship before the event and pays it over to the charity over the weeks preceding, so their place is confirmed eight weeks before the departure date

4. eight weeks before departure date, the charity pays £1,250 for each participant to the tour organiser

5. the charity issues an invoice to the tour organiser for £297.87 + VAT = £350, which is the commission earned by the charity for its services in recruiting participants to the event, as set out in the agreement.

If the charity is acting as principal, then it must use the Tour Operators' Margin Scheme (TOMS) for VAT. What this means in practice is that you have to calculate the 'margin' and remit VAT to HMRC at the appropriate rate. The margin is calculated by deducting the direct costs of buying in the travel and accommodation etc. from the selling price for the tour. In the context of a charity challenge event, the selling price will be the registration fee plus the minimum sponsorship a participant has to remit before they are allowed to go on the event. Where the event takes place outside the EU, the rate of VAT to apply to the margin is zero; where the event takes place within the EU, the rate of VAT is standard. The VAT is calculated on an inclusive basis, so the margin should be multiplied by the VAT fraction $\frac{7}{47}$ to arrive at the amount of VAT to be remitted to HMRC. In either case, the VAT on overhead costs such as advertising can be recovered.

If you operate the TOMS, then the margin is the equivalent of turnover (or income) for the purposes of calculating recovery rates on residual input VAT for the charity as a whole.

Example: Charity as principal

A charity commissions a tour organiser to put together a package of travel, accommodation etc. which costs the charity £1,500 per participant to buy in. This amount has to be paid in two instalments: a non-returnable booking fee of £250, then the balance eight weeks before departure. The charity asks participants to raise sponsorship of at least £2,500, which must be raised eight weeks before departure. The contract between the tour organiser and the charity states that the charity will have to pay for a minimum of 30 places, so the charity is carrying the risk. The charity also charges a registration fee to participants of £350 to cover its administration costs. So the actual transactions would be:

1. the participant pays £350 registration fee to the charity

2. the charity pays £250 booking fee to tour the organiser

3. the participant raises enough sponsorship before the event and pays it over to the charity over the weeks preceding, so their place is confirmed eight weeks before the departure date

4. eight weeks before departure date, the charity pays £1,250 for each participant to the tour organiser

5. the charity calculates the margin as £1,350 and has to remit VAT of £201.06 per participant to HMRC if the event is in the EU, or zero if outside the EU. Margin was calculated as above.

The charity can recover VAT on overheads such as advertising, and the margin counts as taxable income in overall recovery rate calculations.

The costs of advertising for participants may well fall within the special relief for charities and therefore be at zero rate. Note that the advertisement has to be placed by a charity. The relief does not apply to the travel company advertising for participants.

Thus if events are outside the EU the charity will be able to keep all the proceeds raised if it is principal, although this is offset by it taking risks on the event, but the VAT is complicated and you could have unforeseen liabilities if you have not charged VAT when you should have done. Revised guidance from HMRC is expected and charities should check that they are operating in line with this.

Charity auctions

Charity auctions at a fundraising event will be covered by the overall exemption for all income at the event, unless the goods being sold in the auction are donated, in which case they can be zero-rated if the auction is open to the general public. An auction can itself be a fundraising event, although again if the goods for the auction have been donated then the proceeds from the sale are zero-rated if the auction is open to the general public.

Christmas cards

The sale of greeting cards is standard-rated.

Collecting donations

Charities may use several methods for collecting donations, including shaking tins, regular envelope collections in churches, telephone fundraising, direct mail, house-to-house collections and many more. The basic principle here is that money freely given to a charity with no expectation of goods or services in return is outside the scope of VAT as it is not a business activity. If the charity provides any service then it is not freely given and you need to consider whether VAT should apply.

Flag days and similar collections are usually still donations. Lapel stickers, emblems and badges may be given free as an acknowledgement to donors providing they have no intrinsic value. The types of badges included are small items designed to be worn on clothing such as paper stickers, ribbons, artificial flowers (if these are used as a symbol of the charity) and metal pins and badges. They must be given in return for a non-specified donation or a suggested donation of up to £1. If lapel emblems or attachments are offered for a fixed price, even if this is only £1 or less, they are not given away freely and so fall within the scope of VAT, which is then chargeable at standard rate. To remain a donation, the charity should only *suggest* an amount.

Purchases directly relating to collecting donations may be residual (see comments on the Children's Society case in Chapter 4), but a charity can reduce its VAT burden still further by purchasing goods at zero rates of VAT. Collecting tins, lapel badges and fundraising advertisements and literature will qualify for zero rating. See Chapter 6 for more information about the goods that qualify for zero-rate relief in this way.

Corporate events

Companies may organise an event in order to raise funds for charity, or a charity may organise an event for a company. These are often race days or events at major sporting events.

If the company organises an event and states that it intends to donate money raised to a charity, then the charity is not responsible for the financial arrangements. The charity merely receives a donation after the event, which is outside the scope of VAT.

If the charity organises the event it is likely to be a fundraising event and therefore exempt. However, you do need to fulfil the criteria of fundraising events. So, for example it should be clear that the event is for raising funds for your charity. Corporate events that are sold as a team-building exercise may fall outside the scope of the fundraising event definition and may be standard-rated supplies.

Fundraising events

A supply of goods and services made in connection with a fundraising event is exempt when the event is put on by a qualifying body. Qualifying bodies are:

- A charity

- The wholly owned subsidiary of a charity, provided the subsidiary's profits are payable to a charity

- A non-profit making trade union, professional association or other public interest body (see chapter 6 for the full list and eligibility conditions)

- An eligible sporting or recreational body (see chapter 6 for the full eligibility conditions).

Fundraising events do not have to be one-off: qualifying bodies may have up to 15 events of the same kind in the same location in one financial year, but the limit of 15 applies to a charity and its wholly owned subsidiary jointly.

Events can be widely interpreted, so that it can include an event on the internet and they do include participatory events such as golf days and charges to spectators at events. Events can include gala dinners, premiere nights, dinner dances and any other events organised for a fundraising purpose. They can include performances that run for several nights, but the limit is 15 and each performance is treated as a single fundraising event. If the charity exceeds the limit and organises 16 similar events in one location, then the exemption would be lost for all 16 events. Excluded would be regular or continuous activities, such as weekly parachute jumps or sales of Christmas cards.

Adventure or challenge events such as parachute and bungee jumps can also be included in the exemption as long as any accommodation provided does not exceed two nights and the event does not fall within the Tour Operators' Margin Scheme (see 'Challenge events' above).

Events do have to be organised with a clear fundraising purpose, which should be made known to the public. Any events which create a distortion of competition and place a commercial enterprise at a disadvantage will not be exempt fundraising events.

Small-scale events can be ignored, as long as the aggregate gross takings from events of that type in that location do not exceed £1,000 in a week. This means that jumble sales and coffee mornings are not included when counting up the number of events and are exempt from VAT.

All income at the fundraising event will be covered by the exemption, including entry fees, sponsorship, advertising space, sale of brochures and commemorative items, unless they would normally be zero-rated, in which case the zero rating prevails.

As the income from the event is exempt, the VAT on directly related purchases cannot be recovered, unless it is *de minimis*, in which case it must be taken into account when budgeting the costs for the event.

Gifts in kind from companies and barter arrangements

Companies donating goods to a charity for sale, hire or export are making a zero-rated supply. If the charity sells or hires the donated goods, then this will be zero-rated provided the conditions are met (see 'Sales of donated goods' below). The export of the donated goods will also be a zero-rated supply by the charity. If the goods are used for the charity's own activities then there are no VAT consequences for the charity, but the company donating the goods has to account for the VAT under the self-supply rules.

If the company provides goods or services in return for advertising or promotion of its name, then this amounts to a barter arrangement and is subject to VAT under the normal rules.

Example: barter arrangement

A company offers to print the charity's annual report free of charge. The company does, however, want its logo in a prominent position on the annual report.

The charity is providing advertising space to the company in return for the printing of the annual report. There are, in fact, two transactions. VAT has to be accounted for on the advertising service. The deemed value of this will be the cost to the company of printing the annual report. The charity can either issue an invoice to the company for the VAT amount or treat the value received as inclusive of VAT and remit the appropriate amount to HMRC. The company in this situation has no VAT to remit, as the printing of an annual report is zero-rated.

It might have been simpler to avoid this situation by:

- simply acknowledging the donation of the free printing in the text of the annual report in plain type without prominent display of the logo

- alternatively, charging the company a fee for advertising in the annual report. The company could charge for printing the annual report, perhaps offering a discount.

London Marathon and similar participative events

Participative events will qualify as fundraising events providing they do not provide any accommodation. These events usually involve the payment of an entry fee or registration fee. This amount is not subject to VAT if the event qualifies as a fundraising event. Note that the event must be organised by a charity or its subsidiary to qualify for the exemption. The amounts raised as 'sponsorship' are covered by the exemption from VAT and are generally donations from third parties to the charity.

Problems have arisen with the London Marathon because it is an event organised by a for-profit company rather than a charity, even though so much fundraising takes place through the marathon. Thus it cannot qualify as a fundraising event. If a charity charges a registration fee or entry fee to a participant, then this is subject to VAT. If the charity goes further and insists that the participant raises a minimum amount of sponsorship, then this too will be subject to VAT. However, HMRC have clarified that they will accept that these amounts can be outside the scope of VAT and treated as donations if the charity only asks the participant to *pledge* an amount of sponsorship. In addition, charities can charge a registration fee, which can be as little as £1.

Charities usually buy 'gold-bond' places in the London Marathon – and these are subject to VAT. Charging VAT on the registration fee enables the charity to recover this VAT in full. Similar arrangements may apply for other marathons or events organised on a similar basis, i.e. by a commercial body.

In addition, the charity should not provide substantial benefits. In relation to events such as marathons, charities may provide the following which will not count as substantial benefits:

- free training and health advice

- free T-shirt, running vest or similar that clearly portrays the charity the individual is supporting

- free massages and support for physical wellbeing during the event

- free pre-event meeting, which may include free professional advice or support, a simple meal, energy drinks and encouragement from the charity and other participants

- free post-event meeting, which may include medical treatment or advice, changing facilities and light refreshments, and which gives the charity the opportunity to thank participants.

If, however, significant items such as free travel or gifts such as bikes or watches are provided, this may change the nature of the arrangement, and amounts raised by the individual as well as the registration fee may be taxable at the standard rate.

Lotteries

The sale of lottery or raffle tickets is exempt from VAT. While there is no statutory definition of a lottery, it has been defined in a case as 'the distribution of prizes by chance where the persons taking part in the operation, or a substantial number of them, make a payment or consideration in return for obtaining their chance of a prize'. Where any merit or skill plays a part in determining the outcome, then it is a competition not a lottery. Competition entry fees are generally standard-rated.

For the organiser, the value of the exempt supply is the net proceeds after deducting the VAT-inclusive cost of goods given as prizes. If you receive donated raffle prizes, then you cannot make the sale of the raffle tickets zero-rated as a sale of donated goods. (see Chapter 6 and below for the conditions that apply to the sale of donated goods for the sale to be zero-rated.)

Many charities organise fundraising that amounts to a lottery or raffle, because there is a prize distributed on the basis of chance. For example, 'guess the name of the teddy bear' is considered a lottery as there is more chance than skill in guessing the correct name and winning the prize.

Note that lotteries are covered by the Gambling Act 2005 and may have to be registered with the Gambling Commission. If you use the services of a lottery management company, then the charge for the service however made is subject to VAT at the standard rate.

Merchandising

Generally, goods sold by a charity to raise funds will be standard-rated, unless covered by a zero rating. So mugs, T-shirts and other items will be standard-rated, even if they have the charity's name and logo on them. Goods sold at a fundraising event will be covered by the exemption for the event, unless the goods are zero-rated, such as books or children's T-shirts.

Recycled goods

Quite a number of schemes exist whereby charities can collect used printer cartridges, used mobile telephones or other equipment and then sell these to companies which will recycle the goods. Even though the charity is collecting donated goods, these arrangements are not sales of donated goods as there is a contract to sell to one purchaser. These supplies are taxable at the standard rate.

Similar arrangements may exist for the collection of old clothes, shoes, books and so on. If the charity is collecting the goods to be sold on to a third party, then the sale is a taxable supply at the standard rate. The charity may only have to allow the company to establish collection points and is really allowing the use of the charity name and logo. This arrangement is more like cause-related marketing, and the charity should consider licensing the use of its logo and a commercial participation agreement.

Sale of donated goods

The sale of donated goods is zero-rated, whether the sale is through a shop or not, and the sales may be through a charity's trading subsidiary. The goods may be new or second-hand, but must be donated for the purpose of a sale or hire and should be available for purchase by the general public. So sales through charity shops are zero-rated, but also sales at fundraising events open to the public, such as auctions.

Charities or their subsidiaries may also sell donated goods to the disabled and those on means-tested benefits. This will help the schemes whereby recycled furniture is sold at low prices to those in need, as now no VAT has to be charged.

See also Chapter 6 on this topic.

Services to other charities

The sale of services to other charities will normally be standard-rated. An educational charity may exempt the provision of educational services to another charity, such as letting out conference facilities. It may also be possible to treat the secondment of staff as outside the scope where one charity is seconding the member of staff to another to work on non-business activities (see Chapter 11).

Shops

Donated goods sold in a shop are zero-rated, but bought in goods are standard-rated, unless they are covered by another zero rating, such as books.

Sponsorship

Corporate donations may in fact be sponsorship, and great care is needed in this area. The same principle described above under 'Gifts in kind from companies and barter arrangements' applies – you need to check to see that the company is not receiving a service in return for its 'donation'. It is often the case that the company is receiving advertising or promotional services in return for its funding. If the company's logo is being reproduced on publications, leaflets, posters or even a vehicle, then this is likely to be interpreted as promotional services by HMRC. This service is standard-rated for VAT. A simple acknowledgement will not create a taxable supply, so mentioning the company's name in the annual report or in small print on the back of a publication will not change a donation into a promotional service. Generally it is the use of the company's logo, together with a consideration of the size and prominence of its position, that will create a sale of advertising rather than a donation.

Frequently the amount being given by the company is in excess of the value of the service being provided. It is possible to split the amount into an element which is a payment for promotional services, which should be invoiced and VAT applied if you are registered for VAT, and a donation. However, you do need to make this explicit from the outset and document appropriately. It is unlikely that you could obtain a retrospective agreement from HMRC to a split. It would be normal to expect VAT on the full amount paid, as demonstrated by the Tron Theatre case.

However, note that sponsorship income for a fundraising event is exempt, because all supplies of the event are exempt. (see 'Fundraising events' above).

Sponsorship of the type where an individual undertakes an activity and friends and relatives support the effort by giving an amount to the nominated charity will be outside the scope of VAT. This is effectively donated income and no service is being provided in return for the monies given.

Supporter schemes

Many charities run supporter schemes as a means of raising funds. If no benefits are given in return other than the right to attend the AGM and receive the annual report, then the sums received under the supporter scheme are substantially donations and are outside the scope of VAT.

However, the charity may wish to attract supporters by offering benefits such as free admission to exhibitions or visitor centres, the right to receive regular publications, discounts on shop purchases and so on. If benefits are offered in return for a minimum payment, then the minimum payment is standard-rated or may be apportioned between zero-rated and standard-rated benefits. If a supporter pays more than the minimum amount you can treat the excess as a donation and outside the scope of VAT as long as it is made voluntarily. This is explained further under 'subscriptions' in Chapter 5.

8 Property

This chapter examines the VAT implications of selling, leasing or licensing land, buildings and civil engineering works – collectively referred to as 'property'. The VAT rules on property are complex, particularly for charities and voluntary organisations. Property transactions are often high value and so of particular interest, as the amount of VAT involved can be significant. Property transactions should therefore be planned with care. VAT cannot always be avoided, but every charity and voluntary organisation should consider the VAT options available before embarking on high value property transactions.

Introduction

In this chapter 'property' means immoveable property: land, buildings and civil engineering works such as playgrounds and outdoor sports facilities. Property transactions include the sale or purchase of a freehold or leasehold interest in property; the construction, refurbishment or extension of built property; and the letting of property on long-term or short-term leases or licences.

Major interest

VAT law makes a distinction between two broad types of property transaction:

- the sale of the freehold or a long lease or licence of property – this is referred to as the sale of a **major interest**

- the sale of a short lease or licence of property.

A long lease or licence is one that lasts for a definite term of more than 21 years in England, Wales and Northern Ireland or 20 years or more in Scotland. If a lease or licence is terminable at will or after a short notice period it is a short lease or licence. However, a break clause before 21 or 20 years does not necessarily prevent a lease from being a major interest.

Basic VAT rule for property

Generally, property transactions are exempt, but there are many exceptions. Exceptions considered in this chapter are:

- **The option to tax**: in certain circumstances someone with an interest in a property can 'elect to waive the exemption' or 'opt to tax' that property. This means that most property transactions that would have been exempt become taxable. This is usually done to avoid irrecoverable VAT. The option to tax is examined in the section 'The option to tax' below.

- **Qualifying buildings**: some property transactions are zero-rated when the property is a 'qualifying building'. A qualifying building is a building that is:

  - designed as a dwelling or number of dwellings

  - intended for use solely for a relevant residential purpose

  - intended for use solely for a relevant charitable purpose.

  These terms have particular meanings that are explained in the section 'Qualifying buildings'.

- **Specific situations**: there are a number of specific situations in which property transactions are standard-rated. These include the supply of:

  - accommodation in hotels, inns, boarding houses and similar

  - holiday accommodation

  - sporting facilities

  - parking facilities.

  Each of these situations is considered in the section 'Letting property' below.

- **The letting of property at significantly below market rent**: where property is let out at a peppercorn rent or at significantly below market rates there may not be any supply at all, or if there is, it is not made in the course or furtherance of a business activity. In such situations the letting will be outside the scope of VAT. See Chapter 4 for details of how to decide if a property transaction is outside the scope of VAT.

Organisation of the chapter

This chapter first explains the option to tax rules and how to determine if a building is qualifying. The sections are then organised to reflect the different types of property transaction that voluntary organisations commonly encounter:

- **Construction services**: in VAT terms, construction services are only supplied in the creation of a new building. Building services used for extensions, refurbishments, alterations etc. are not 'construction services'. Normally, construction services are standard-rated. However, if the building is 'qualifying', the construction services can be zero-rated. This section examines the meaning of 'construction services' and when they are zero-rated.

- **Buying and selling property**: this section examines the VAT implications of buying or selling a major interest in property – that is, the freehold or a long lease. This may be standard-rated, zero-rated, exempt or outside the scope of VAT, depending on the circumstances.

- **Refurbishing and extending buildings**: normally, supplies made in the course of refurbishing or extending a building are standard-rated. However, in some situations they qualify for zero or reduced rating. This section examines those circumstances.

- **Short-term lets**: this section examines the VAT implications of letting out property on short-term leases or licences, including the supply of hotel and holiday accommodation, sporting facilities and parking facilities.

This chapter considers the UK VAT rules on property. The place of supply of a transaction related to immoveable property is where the property is located. So if the property is in the UK, its place of supply is the UK and it is subject to the UK VAT rules. If it is situated in another EC state, it is outside the scope of UK VAT but subject to that state's VAT rules. If it is situated outside the EC, it is outside the scope of UK VAT and EC VAT, but may be subject to that state's equivalent of VAT. If property is situated outside the UK, see Chapter 9 for information about supplies that take place outside the UK.

The option to tax

An organisation can, under certain circumstances, 'opt to tax' transactions related to a particular property. This means that property transactions that would otherwise be exempt become taxable. The option to tax is sometimes referred to as a 'waiver of exemption'.

For example, if an organisation opts to tax a building and lets it out, it must charge VAT on the rent. If it then sells the building, it must charge VAT on the sale. However, it can recover any input VAT that is attributable to the rental activity or the sale, as these are now taxable activities.

If a landlord opts to tax a building that is rented out, the tenant will be charged VAT on the rent. If the tenant is registered for VAT and can recover all the VAT it incurs, this will not be a problem for the tenant. However, if the tenant is unregistered or cannot recover all the VAT it incurs, then this may increase the tenant's costs. In addition, stamp duty land tax is charged on the VAT-inclusive price of a property, so opting to tax may increase a purchaser's stamp duty land tax charge.

However, an option to tax can be 'disapplied' in certain situations. This means that, even though a property is opted, a landlord cannot add VAT to the rent and a vendor cannot add VAT to the selling price. The situations include use for a relevant residential or relevant charitable purpose. The situations in which an option is disapplied are examined below.

Organisations undertaking exempt activities are particularly at risk from landlords deciding to opt let property. It is sometimes possible to agree that any rent specified in an agreement is gross of any VAT or that the landlord must obtain the tenant's consent before applying an option. However many landlords will not agree to such terms and this risk must therefore be factored in to your decision making.

At the time of writing, the Government is proposing to change some of the 'option to tax' rules with effect from 1 June 2008, though full details of the changes are not yet available. The anticipated changes are outlined below. You should check the HMRC website to see if the rules outlined below have changed – see VAT Notice 742A and look in the Revenue & Customs Briefs.

The option to tax rules are complicated and a potential minefield for the unwary. Because options last for a minimum of 20 years and large sums are usually involved, we strongly recommend that any organisation contemplating opting property or taking on opted property should seek professional advice if it is not available in house.

Scope of the option to tax

The option to tax applies to a specific organisation in respect of a specific piece of land or a specific building:

- The option to tax only affects the transactions of the organisation that has opted to tax. So, if a landlord opts to tax a building and lets it out to a tenant, the rental charges to the tenant will be standard-rated (assuming the tenant cannot disapply the landlord's option). If the tenant sub-lets the property, the tenant's charges to the sub-tenant are not affected by the landlord's option. They will be exempt, unless the tenant has also opted to tax the property or is in the same VAT group as the landlord.

- An option that applies to one member of a VAT group applies to all members of the group. See Chapter 11 for more information on VAT groups. If a company opts to tax a property and later joins a VAT group, the other members of the group are bound by the option. If a company leaves a VAT group, it is still bound by any options that applied to it as a member of the group.

- If you opt to tax a piece of land the option covers any buildings or civil engineering works already on that land. If you later construct a building or civil engineering work on the land, it is not covered by the option and you must issue a separate option to cover it if you wish it to be VATable.

- If you opt to tax a part of a building, the option covers the whole of your interest in the building and any land within its curtilage, including any interests in the building you purchase in future. However, if the building is demolished or destroyed the option will not apply to the land on which the building stood, and if you later construct another building on that land it will not be covered by the option.

- If you opt to tax a building then any buildings that are 'linked' to that building are considered to be part of the same building and are covered by the option. A link is an internal access or a covered walkway between buildings the purpose of which is to allow movement of goods and people, but it does not include: a car park, either above or below ground, a public thoroughfare, or a statutory requirement such as a fire escape. A complex consisting of a number of units grouped around a fully enclosed concourse is considered to be a single building, for example a shopping mall. If in doubt you can submit plans and photographs to HMRC and ask them to advise you on what will be covered by an option.

- If you have opted a building and you later extend it, the option will apply to the whole of the extended building. However, if you have opted a building and later decide to link it to another building, the option will not flow through with the link unless you are creating a single building.

- If you have opted property and deregister, for example because your taxable supplies fall below the deregistration threshold, the option remains in place and you may have to account for output tax on the opted property at deregistration. See Chapter 3 for information on output charges at deregistration.

Disapplication of the option to tax

The option to tax is suspended or disapplied in certain situations, and transactions related to the property remain exempt. Note that affected property remains opted, however the option simply has no effect while the property is put to a disapplying use. Situations in which an option is disapplied include where the property is:

- A dwelling or number of dwellings or a supply of property where the recipient informs the supplier they intend to use it as a dwelling or convert it into a dwelling.

- To be used for a relevant residential purpose. See the section 'Qualifying buildings' for the definition of 'relevant residential purpose'. Before the option can be disapplied, the recipient must give the supplier a certificate confirming the intended use.

- To be used for a relevant charitable purpose other than as an office for general administration. Use for a 'relevant charitable purpose' means use for non-business activities or use as a village hall or similar. See the section 'Qualifying buildings' for the definition of 'relevant charitable purpose'. The option is only disapplied when the recipient has given the supplier a certificate confirming the intended use. Use as an office for general administration refers to office accommodation that is used for the general administrative functions of the organisation. An office used to provide free advice would qualify as a relevant charitable purpose. However, an office used for general administration will not qualify even if all the charity's activities are non-business.

- Land supplied to a registered housing association which certifies that, after any necessary demolition work, they will be constructing a dwelling, dwellings or a relevant residential building on it. Note that if the vendor starts to construct any dwellings or relevant residential buildings, it may be possible to zero rate the sale as the first grant of a major interest in a partially completed building. See below.

- Land supplied to a DIY house builder who will build a dwelling on it for their own use, but not for use in any business activity.

There is no prescribed format for any certificate that must be provided. To be effective, the certificate must be received by the supplier before the supply takes place. Where property is rented, a certificate only disapplies rental periods after the certificate is delivered, and where property is sold (freehold or leasehold) the certificate must be delivered before completion. If you are purchasing opted property and intend disapplying the option, you should discuss this with your conveyancing solicitor at an early stage.

Landlords may be reluctant to let property to an organisation that will disapply the option as this may affect the landlord's ability to recover input VAT. Some landlords may refuse to let property under such circumstances and some may require a higher rent to cover the extra costs to the landlord. If you disapply a landlord's option part-way through a lease the landlord may have no choice in the matter, though you should examine the lease as the lease agreement may contain a clause permitting the landlord to increase the rent in the event of disapplication.

Landlords may by concession ignore minor non-qualifying charitable use (under 10 per cent) when deciding if the option is disapplied, though they can choose to disregard this concession. Where non-qualifying use is more than 10 per cent, the entire use must be apportioned between qualifying and non-qualifying use and VAT charged on the non-qualifying part.

Making the option

An option takes effect from the date you formally decide to opt to tax. HMRC recommend that you keep a written record of the decision, for example, the minutes of the board meeting where the option was approved. You must notify HMRC within 30 days of this decision by writing to the HMRC Option to Tax Unit in Glasgow (see Chapter 14 for contact details). HMRC provide form VAT 1614 on their website which can be used to help ensure that all the information required is provided, though use of the form is not mandatory. HMRC will accept late notifications if there is evidence of the decision genuinely being made and VAT being charged from then on, however you cannot backdate an option to before the decision was made. See Business Brief 13/05 for HMRC's policy on late notification of an option to tax.

Note that there are special notification rules where a purchaser is opting a building that is part of a transfer of a going concern. If the supplier has opted the building then the purchaser must opt the building before the supply takes place for the building to be included under the VAT transfer rules. See Chapter 11 for information on transfers of a going concern.

Once an option has been made you can ask HMRC for permission to revoke the option within the first three months (the 'cooling-off period'). HMRC will normally grant this if no rent has been charged or VAT recovered under the option. After this, you cannot ask for the option to be revoked until 20 years or more after it took effect. At the time of writing this has not yet happened (options will first become eligible for revocation under the 20-year rule from 1 August 2009) and the rules for 20-year revocations have yet to be finalised. HMRC outlined their planned 20-year revocation rules in Business Brief 23/05.

Permission to opt

If you have not made an exempt supply of the property before the option takes effect you do not need HMRC's permission to opt to tax the property. If you have previously made an exempt supply of the property, for example by letting it out, you need HMRC's permission unless the conditions for 'automatic permission' are met. These conditions are set out in VAT Notice 742A and have the force of law. There are four conditions: if you meet any of them, you have automatic permission. If you meet none of them, you must obtain permission. The conditions for automatic permission are set out in the box opposite.

The option to tax: Conditions for automatic permission

1. It is a mixed-use development and the only exempt supplies have been in relation to the dwellings.

2. You do not wish to recover any input tax in relation to the land or building incurred before your option to tax has effect; and

   - The consideration for your exempt supplies has, up to the date when your option to tax is to take effect, been solely by way of rents or service charges and excludes any premiums or payments in respect of occupation after the date on which the option takes effect. Regular rental and/or service charge payments can be ignored for the purposes of this condition. Payments are considered regular where the intervals between them are no more than a year and where each represents a commercial or genuine arm's-length value; and

   - The only input tax relating to the land or building that you expect to recover after the option to tax takes effect will be on overheads, such as regular rental payments, service charges, repairs and maintenance costs. If you expect to claim input tax in relation to refurbishment or redevelopment of the building you will not meet this condition. When deciding whether you meet this condition you should disregard:

     - VAT refundable to local authorities and other bodies under section 33(2)(b) of the Value Added Tax Act 1994
     - any input tax you can otherwise recover by virtue of the partial exemption *de minimis* rules
     - any input tax you are entitled to recover on general business overheads not specifically related to the land or building, such as audit fees.

3. The only input tax you wish to recover in relation to the land or building incurred before your option to tax takes effect relates solely to tax charged by your tenant or tenants upon surrender of a lease; and

   - The building or relevant part of the building has been unoccupied between the date of the surrender and the date the option to tax is to take effect; and

   - There will be no further exempt supplies of the land or building; and

   - You do not intend or expect that you will occupy the land or building other than for taxable purposes.

4. The exempt supplies have been incidental to the main use of the land or building. For example, where you have occupied a building for taxable

purposes the following would be seen as incidental to the main use and the condition would be met:

- allowing an advertising hoarding to be displayed
- granting space for the erection of a radio mast
- receiving income from an electricity sub-station.

The letting of space to an occupying tenant, however minor, is not incidental.

If you must obtain permission to opt, paragraph 5.5 of VAT Notice 742A sets out the information you should send with your application. In urgent situations it may be possible to fast-track applications – ring the HMRC option to tax unit (see Chapter 14 for contact details).

Recovering pre-option input VAT

Once you have opted a property, you may be able to recover input VAT incurred on pre-option purchases if those purchases relate to taxable supplies made after the option takes effect, for example renovation work. If you made a pre-option exempt supply of the property then you will have to obtain permission to opt and HMRC will want to know how much of the pre-option input VAT you intend recovering before they grant permission to opt.

Opting a building that has previously been used to make exempt supplies may bring it within the capital goods scheme (see Chapter 10), in which case the scheme will allow you to make adjustments to the recovery of pre-option input VAT during the capital goods scheme adjustment period. If the property does not fall within the capital goods scheme, then by concession HMRC may allow recovery on a similar basis. You should contact HMRC to agree an appropriate method of recovery.

You may also be able to recover pre-option input VAT before the option is made, on the basis of evidence of the intention to opt and then make taxable supplies. There must be a clear and demonstrable intention to opt and make taxable supplies. If you opt but the supply is then disapplied you will not be able to recover the associated VAT.

If you become registered for VAT as a result of making an option, the normal limits on recovering pre-registration inputs (see Chapter 3) can be overridden if this results in inequitable treatment compared with a business carrying out similar activities, but which was already VAT-registered when the tax was incurred. If you consider you have suffered because of this you should write to your local VAT office and explain the circumstances.

Option to tax anti-avoidance rules

There are a number of anti-avoidance measures designed to block schemes based around the option to tax. In particular, the rules block the use of an opted subsidiary company to undertake construction or refurbishment work with the subsidiary then renting the property back to the parent entity for use in an exempt or non-business activity. The rules are as follows:

If, at the time of the grant of land or buildings (the development):

- it is the intention or expectation of the grantor, or the person responsible for financing the grantor's development, or anybody connected to either of them, to occupy the development, and

- the person occupying the development will be doing so, or will expect to do so, for other than eligible purposes, and

- the development is, or is expected to become, a capital item for the purposes of the capital goods scheme (see Chapter 10 for details of the capital goods scheme)

then the option to tax will not have effect in respect of supplies that arise from that particular grant.

'Occupation for eligible purposes' means occupation for the purpose of making mainly supplies which entitle the occupier to credit for their input tax. HMRC state that 'mainly' means substantially more than half. However, occupation by a local authority or other public authority (a 'section 33' body) for non-business purposes, or occupation by a government department, is eligible.

Example: Option to tax anti-avoidance rules

An exempt education charity wishes to construct a new building costing £2 million for use in its educational activities. If it decides to construct the building itself, the VAT incurred on construction costs will be irrecoverable.

If the charity uses a subsidiary to construct the building, opts to tax the building then lets it back to the school, this would in theory allow the subsidiary to recover the input VAT on construction immediately then spread the irrecoverable VAT cost to the school over many years through the rental charges.

However, this is caught by the anti-avoidance rules. The school is connected to the subsidiary, the school will be occupying the building for other than eligible purposes (exempt education) and the development is within the capital goods scheme, so the subsidiary's option to tax is blocked.

Proposed changes to the option to tax rules

At the time of writing the option to tax rules are being rewritten with some minor changes. It is expected that the changes will take effect from 1 June 2008. It looks as if the following changes will be made (please do check for the actual changes made):

- A buyer intending to display a vendor's option will have to provide the vendor with a certificate. This will include organisations purchasing opted property for conversion to relevant residential use or use as a dwelling

- Relaxation of the revocation rules (the 'cooling off period'). You will be able to revoke an option within six months (currently three months) and even if input VAT has been claimed – provided it is repaid

- A business's option will automatically lapse six years after the business's interest in the property ceases

- The rules on when options on land apply to buildings on that land and vice versa will be changed. An option on a building will apply to the associated land, and an option on land will apply to any building later constructed on it. However, where new buildings are constructed on opted land it will be possible to disapply the option subject to various conditions

- The rules on when permission to opt is required will be relaxed slightly. It will only be necessary to consider any exempt supplies of the land or property made in the last 10 years when considering if the conditions for automatic permission are met.

- HMRC will be able to treat an option as valid if it has been notified but prior permission was not obtained.

- Where prior permission is required, it will be possible to backdate the option to the date of application.

Qualifying buildings

Certain property transactions are zero-rated when the building is 'qualifying'. A building is qualifying if it is:

1. designed as a dwelling or as a number of dwellings, or

2. intended for use solely for a relevant residential purpose, or

3. intended for use solely for a relevant charitable purpose.

The meaning of each of these qualifications is explored below.

Zero-rating certificates

In cases 2 and 3 above, the recipient of the supply must provide the supplier with a certificate confirming the intended use of the property – a 'zero-rating certificate'. There are penalties for incorrectly issuing a certificate. The supplier cannot zero rate the transaction without the certificate. There is no statutory format for the certificate but HMRC provide a sample certificate in VAT Notice 708. See Chapter 14 for HMRC website links.

- If you are purchasing an interest in property, the certificate should be given to the vendor.

- If you are dealing with a main supplier on a building contract then you should only issue a zero-rating certificate to the main contractor. The sub-contractors of the main contractor are not issued with zero-rating certificates and they must treat their supplies to the main contractor as normal.

- If you are undertaking the zero-rated work yourself see the section on the DIY builders' scheme below.

- For a building designed as a dwelling or a number of dwellings there is no need for a zero-rating certificate. Both the main contractor and sub-contractors must zero rate their supplies.

Intended use

In 2 and 3 above, the building must be intended for a qualifying use at the time a transaction takes place in order for the transaction to qualify for zero rating. This means that, for example, if a new building was not intended for a qualifying use at the time of its construction, but was later put to a qualifying use, the construction cannot be zero-rated.

If the building was intended for relevant residential or charitable use at the time of the transaction but that use later changed, the 'change of use' rules may apply and a VAT repayment may have to be made. The change of use rules are explained below.

Apportionment for part-qualifying buildings

If only part of a building will be used solely for a qualifying purpose, you must apportion transaction costs between those relating to the qualifying use and those relating to the non-qualifying use. Only the costs that are apportioned to qualifying use can be zero-rated. Any method of apportionment can be used as long as it produces a fair and reasonable result.

If part of a building will be put to qualifying and non-qualifying use, for example an area which is put to qualifying use on some days of the week and non-qualifying use on other days, then it will not be used solely for a qualifying purpose, so it is a non-qualifying part of the building. However, there is a concession which allows minor non-qualifying use to be ignored in the case of a relevant charitable purpose building. If the non-qualifying use of a whole building or part of a building will be less than 10 per cent of its overall use, the non-qualifying use can be ignored and the whole building or part of a building treated as qualifying. This concession is explained below.

If the balance of qualifying and non-qualifying use changes within 10 years the 'change of use' rules may apply. The change of use rules are explained below.

Designed as a dwelling or a number of dwellings

A building is designed as a dwelling or a number of dwellings where it is or will be a dwelling or dwellings and all the following conditions are satisfied:

1. each dwelling consists of self-contained living accommodation

2. there is no provision for direct internal access from the dwelling to any other dwelling or part of a dwelling, although internal fire doors for use in an emergency are allowed

3. the separate use or disposal of the dwelling is not prohibited by the terms of any covenant, statutory planning consent or similar provision, and

4. statutory planning consent has been granted in respect of that dwelling, and its construction or conversion has been carried out in accordance with that consent.

A dwelling is where someone lives or can live and treat it as their home. To be self-contained, the accommodation must contain all the facilities that are normally associated with a dwelling, such as access to a public highway, sleeping, washing, toilet and cooking facilities. Where essential facilities are shared with another dwelling or lacking, this will prevent it from being self-contained.

The meaning of 'self-contained' was explored in the tribunal case *Agudas Israel Housing Association* (2004, VAT Tribunal 18798) where the association constructed flats on top of an existing care home. The flats had their own front doors and also en-suite bathing facilities, but cooking facilities were limited to the provision of points for a microwave, kettle and fridge, and in practice many tenants ate their meals in the care home below. The tribunal decided that though basic, the cooking facilities were sufficient to allow the flats to be considered self-contained.

The requirement that there is no prohibition on the separate use or disposal of the dwelling will preclude most annexes, self-contained extensions and accommo-dation attached to property such as caretakers' flats. However, the condition does not preclude restriction on the type of occupant, for example by age, disability or occupation.

The requirement for statutory planning consent to have been given for use as a dwelling is dropped in the case of the zero-rating provisions for protected buildings, as in many cases the building will have been constructed before statutory planning consent was introduced.

Relevant residential purpose

'Relevant residential purpose' means use as in any of the categories listed below. However, use is excluded if it is use as a hospital or similar, prison or similar, or use as a hotel, inn or similar. The relevant residential purpose categories are:

- **a home or other institution** providing residential accommodation for children: for example, a children's home

- **a home or other institution** providing residential accommodation with personal care for persons in need of personal care by reason of old age, disablement, past or present dependence on alcohol or drugs or past or present mental disorder. Care homes providing treatment or nursing beyond personal care may fall within the exclusion for hospitals or similar establishments

- **a hospice:** a hospice is an institution providing care for the terminally ill

- **residential accommodation** for students or school pupils, for example halls of residence at a university, polytechnic or college, pupils' living accommodation at a boarding school and residential accommodation in field study centres

- **residential accommodation** for members of any of the armed forces: for example, barrack blocks and unaccompanied officers' mess quarters (married quarters may qualify as dwellings)

- **a monastery, nunnery or similar** establishment: this includes any establishment where followers of a recognised faith or religious order live and worship

- **an institution** which is the sole or main residence of at least 90 per cent of its residents: for example, a nurses' home, a police section house, almshouses or ex-offenders' hostel. Note that many hostels qualify as similar to a hotel, inn etc, and so are blocked from qualifying here.

The above categories of relevant residential purpose fall into three broad groups:

- **Residential accommodation**: here, any relief is restricted to the residential element, which must include some form of sleeping accommodation. Residential accommodation need not provide all the facilities required of a qualifying dwelling (see above) and shared facilities are acceptable. When provided with sleeping accommodation other residential areas such as kitchens, bathrooms, dining halls and sitting areas will qualify as residential accommodation if they are for the exclusive use of the residents. However, such areas do not qualify if they are provided without sleeping accommodation or for use by non-residents as well. Where there is a small amount of use by non-residents it may be possible to agree with HMRC that it is *de minimis* and can be ignored. A building, annexe or extension must qualify in its own right as residential accommodation. So, for example, the addition of a dining hall to a building or the construction of a separate dining hall does not qualify. However, if a dining hall is constructed at the same time as other buildings and together they will constitute residential accommodation, they all qualify.

- **Homes or other institutions**: here, the whole of a building can be qualifying, including areas that do not directly relate to residential use such as recreational areas and offices. A building, annexe or extension must qualify in its own right as a home or institution so, for example, the addition of an occupational therapy unit to a care home will not qualify as the unit is not an institution in itself. However, where several buildings are built at the same time and together they comprise a home or other institution, they all qualify.

- **Hospices**: if a hospice provides both residential and day-care facilities, use must be apportioned to determine the relevant residential element. However many hospices are charities, and so day-care facilities may also qualify under the relevant charitable purpose conditions set out below.

- **Monasteries, nunneries or similar**: here, areas for residential use and areas set aside for worship qualify.

By concession, universities and higher education institutions may ignore the commercial letting of student accommodation during vacations when considering if student accommodation is used solely for a relevant residential purpose. In a judicial review, the High Court (in a case involving Greenwich Properties Ltd, 2001 EWHC Ch 230) held that the concession also extends to the wholly-owned subsidiary of a higher education institution.

Difficulties can arise in determining if a care institution is similar to a hospital. The distinction is between an institution that aims to make life more comfortable for people by providing for their personal needs and an institution that diagnoses and treats illness by the exercise of professional skill. Where a situation is borderline you must decide if any supply of medical diagnosis or treatment is incidental to a supply of care or vice versa. Relevant factors include the proportion of staff that are professionally qualified doctors or nurses, the extent of any diagnosis or treatment undertaken, the level of medical facilities, the physical appearance and layout of the building, the statutory registration of the institution and any links to other medical or care institutions.

Relevant charitable purpose

Use for a 'relevant charitable purpose' means use by a charity:

- for non-business activities, or

- as a village hall or similar in providing social or recreational facilities for a local community.

The way in which the work is funded is not the relevant fact here; it is the use to which the building will be put which is pertinent. The type of building also makes no difference – any type of building may qualify. This includes offices, warehouses, churches, daycentres, scout or guide huts, lifeboat stations and so on. The crucial point is the use to which the building will be put.

Non-business activities

Non-business activities of charities are covered in Chapter 4. It is important to note that, besides activities wholly funded by grants and donations, non-business activities can include activities for which a fee is charged. See, for example, the cases of St Paul's Playgroup (where the playgroup was held to be a non-business activity despite significant fees being charged) and Donaldson's College (where substantial fees were charged to local authorities for the education of deaf children but the activity was considered non-business).

Village halls and similar

'Village halls and similar' broadly refers to traditional village halls, community centres, church halls, scout or guide huts and pavilions attached to charitable playing fields and recreation grounds. To qualify as 'use as a village hall or similar in providing social or recreational facilities for a local community', case law suggests that several conditions must be met:

- There must be a high degree of community and voluntary involvement in the running of the building, a desire to promote the use of the facilities by members of the community, a great emphasis on the needs of and benefits to the local community, and any charges should not be set 'commercially' – that is, with the intention of making a 'commercial' profit.

- The facilities provided must be social, recreational or sporting. The majority of the activities undertaken must be social, recreational or sporting and the building must be capable of use for a variety of such activities.

- The facilities must be provided for a local community. This requires the provision to be of benefit to members of the community and the community should be local. The persons who are able to benefit must not be too narrow a section of that community and the members of the local community must benefit as members of the community and not in some other capacity. In the St Dunstan's Educational Foundation case (1999, Court of Appeal STC 381) a fee-paying school built a sports hall and allowed public access. The court decided that the pupils, though from the local community, were there as members of the school and not as members of the local community. This was the primary purpose of the sports centre and so its use could not be said to be intended for use solely for a relevant charitable purpose.

• The members of the local community must not inhabit or work in an area too large and populous to be sensibly described as a local community. Case law suggests that a radius of six miles is acceptable, though 23 miles is too much. However, it is acceptable for a minority of users come from outside this area. In addition the nature of the area must be considered. In the case Jubilee Hall Recreation Centre Ltd (1999, Court of Appeal STC 381, heard together with St Dunstan's, above) the area of Covent Garden in London was considered to be too large and have too many non-residents working in the area to be sensibly described as a 'local community'.

Minor non-qualifying use of a relevant charitable building

Where a building or part of a building will be used primarily for a relevant charitable purpose there is a concession (ESC 3.29) which allows you to ignore minor non-qualifying use. A building or part of a building can be treated as being used solely for a relevant charitable purpose when, at the time of first use and for the ten years following the zero-rated transaction it is intended that:

1. the whole building will be used solely for qualifying use for 90 per cent or more of the time it is available for use, or

2. in respect of an identifiable part of the building, that part will be used solely for qualifying use for 90 per cent or more of the time it is available for use, or

3. 90 per cent or more of the floor space of the whole building will be used solely for qualifying use, or

4. 90 per cent or more of the people using the whole building will be engaged solely on qualifying activity.

When calculating usage you can select any representative period of use. The first method can be used without permission from HMRC. Permission must be obtained to use any of the other methods and you cannot mix methods. However, you are usually allowed to use the method that gives the best result – so if you fail on the time-based methods and floor area but succeed on headcount, you can use the headcount method.

The first method can only be applied to a whole building. Any time when any part of the building is being used for a non-qualifying activity counts as non-qualifying use.

The second method is the same as the first, but applied to an identifiable part of the building such as a floor or room.

The third method can only be applied to a whole building. Areas such as lobbies, staircases, cloakrooms and toilets count as non-qualifying unless their use is limited in some way. However, if a non-qualifying area can only be accessed through a qualifying area this does not render the qualifying area non-qualifying, for example a business activity café in a museum that must be accessed through a non-business gallery does not stop the non-business gallery qualifying.

The fourth method is based on headcount and must be applied to all users of the entire building. You will need to be able to label building users as qualifying or non-qualifying. HMRC state that an individual is non-qualifying if they are involved in any level of non-qualifying activity and no apportionment can be made for users involved in qualifying and non-qualifying activities. HMRC also state that you cannot make an apportionment to allow for the fact that some staff or volunteers are part-time staff – a part-time member of staff or volunteer has the same effect on headcount as a full-time member of staff or volunteer. However, you can omit incidental building users such as visitors (unless visitors are a part of the building's purpose) and staff who make an incidental contribution to activities, such as cleaners.

If you anticipate that non-qualifying use will exceed 10 per cent at any point within 10 years of the transaction under all methods, then you cannot use the concession and you must apportion use between qualifying and non-qualifying.

Before 21 March 2007, HMRC imposed a self-supply charge (i.e. output VAT must be accounted for) where this concession was applied but non-qualifying use actually exceeded 10 per cent within 10 years of the zero-rated transaction. However, with effect from 21 March 2007, HMRC announced that they will not enforce this if there has been a change of use that was not anticipated at the time that zero rating was obtained under the concession. As the concession should not be used if it is anticipated that non-qualifying use will exceed 10 per cent within 10 years, this effectively means that any change of use can be ignored for the purpose of the concession. Any charity that paid a 'change of use charge' under the 10 per cent concession may be entitled to a refund, subject to the standard three-year limitation on claims.

Change of use of a relevant residential or charitable building

If the use of a relevant residential or relevant charitable-purpose building (or part of a building) changes within 10 years of zero rating, there may have to be a VAT adjustment under the 'change of use' rules. The change of use rules apply when:

- one of the following has been zero-rated: (i) the construction of a new building; (ii) the first grant of a major interest in a building; or (iii) the conversion of a non-residential building for a registered housing association, and

- the concession for minor non-qualifying charitable use has not been applied – see above for an explanation of the concession. If you relied on the concession for minor non-qualifying use but the non-qualifying use exceeded 10 per cent unexpectedly, then the change of use can be ignored.

The change of use rules do not apply to: (i) approved alterations to a protected building; (ii) the first grant of a major interest in a substantially reconstructed protected building; (iii) supplies under the DIY builders' scheme; or (iv) any reduced-rate allowances.

A change of use may happen because:

a) the property is disposed of (sold or leased), or

b) the interest in the property is retained but the balance of qualifying and non-qualifying activities undertaken in the building changes.

(a) If the interest in the building is disposed of then the VAT treatment of the disposal consideration is as follows:

- If the interest is no longer intended for use solely for a relevant residential or charitable purpose, VAT must be charged on the disposal consideration at the standard rate. If the building was only partly zero-rated then an apportionment must be made. If you are not registered for VAT, this may cause you to have to register.

- If the interest is still intended for use solely for a relevant residential or charitable purpose, then you must first consider if the transfer of a going concern rules are met – see Chapter 11. If they are not met, you must next consider if the conditions for zero rating the disposal are met – see below. If not, the disposal is exempt.

(b) If there is a change of use without disposal then the increase in non-qualifying use is a deemed standard-rated self-supply and output VAT must be accounted for. This output VAT is however deductible to the extent that the change of use is attributable to taxable supplies.

However, there is a concession that allows the switching of areas of qualifying and non-qualifying use within the 10-year adjustment period without incurring the self-supply. This concession can only be used with the written agreement of HMRC. When a change of use takes place so that one part of the building ceases to be qualifying but another part starts to be qualifying the change of use can be ignored. The concession states:

(i) Following the change of use, the part of the building used for qualifying use must be at least 80 per cent of the floor area of the original zero-rated part and the taxpayer must expect that this condition will be satisfied until 10 years after the building was completed.

(ii) If the building has been refurbished in the last three years, areas switched must have been refurbished to a similar standard.

The meaning of the second point is ambiguous. HMRC say 'the standard of refurbishment need not be identical between the two areas but it should be clear that the switch is not being made to gain an unfair advantage'.

If the concession does not apply, the formula for calculating the value of the deemed supply is:

$$\text{Output VAT due} = \frac{A \times (10 - B)}{10}$$

where A is the VAT that would originally have been due on the change of use part and B is the number of whole years since the day the building was completed for which the building or part concerned has been used for a relevant residential purpose or a relevant charitable purpose.

Example: Change of use without disposal

A charity paid £1 million net for a new building that was agreed as 50% zero-rated and 50% standard-rated at 17.5%. After four years' use the qualifying use drops to 40%. The change of use concession does not apply.

The VAT that would originally have been due on the 10% change is 10% x £1m x 17.5% = £17,500

The output VAT due is £17,500 x (10 – 4) / 10 = £10,500

This is recoverable as input VAT if the change of use relates to taxable activity. If the change of use relates to residual activity it is residual VAT.

Note that:

•   The change of use rules use the original VAT recovery and building value – there is no adjustment for any change in the rate of VAT or change in the value of the building.

- The adjustment is one way – if qualifying use increases there is no recovery of the original VAT paid as the changed use was never intended for use solely for a relevant purpose.

- If the change of use relates to exempt activity it may bring the building within the scope of the capital goods scheme. See Chapter 10 for the capital goods scheme.

- HMRC state (in Revenue & Customs Brief 29/07) that the concession permitting any change of use of a relevant charitable-purpose building that was not anticipated at the time that zero rating was obtained to be ignored for the purposes of the minor non-qualifying use concession (see above) 'may' also apply to changes of use under these rules. In such situations the charity is advised to contact HMRC for advice.

Supplies eligible for zero rating

Where a building contractor holds a zero-rating certificate, it can zero rate most of its supplies to the person issuing the zero-rating certificate. However, there are some restrictions on the goods that can be zero-rated. The supply of services in installing ineligible goods may, however, still be zero-rated. To be zero-rated, any goods that are supplied:

- must be building materials. Building materials are goods ordinarily incorporated by builders in a building of similar description – but with certain specified exceptions, as explained below

- must be supplied in the course of supplying zero-rated services

- the zero-rated services must include the 'incorporation' of the building materials in the building or its site. Goods are incorporated in a building when they are fixed in such a way that the fixing or removal would either require the use of tools or result in either the need for remedial work to the fabric of the building or substantial damage to the goods themselves.

Building materials include:

- materials used in the fabric of the building: steel, bricks, blocks, cement, slates, plumbing, electrical goods, doors, window frames and so on

- built-in or fitted kitchen furniture, but generally not other types of fitted furniture unless ordinarily incorporated into a building of that type. For example, the following are usually accepted as building materials, in schools: fixed blackboards and gymnasium wall bars; in churches: altars, church bells, fonts, lecterns, pipe organs and pulpits

- built-in, wired-in or plumbed-in appliances such as appliances designed to heat space or water or designed to provide ventilation, air cooling, air purification, or dust extraction; door entry systems, waste disposal units, or machines for compacting waste; burglar alarms (but not safes), fire alarms, fire safety equipment, or devices for summoning aid in an emergency (but not phones or electric gates and barriers); lifts or hoists

- TV aerials and satellite dishes, fixed bathroom mirrors, solar panels that form part of a heating system and in-line water softeners

- the provision of soft landscaping within the site of a building to the extent that it is detailed on a landscaping scheme approved by a planning authority under the terms of a planning consent condition

- floor coverings such as linoleum, ceramic tiles, parquet and wooden floor systems, but not carpets and carpet underlay.

Where any of the prohibited goods are supplied by a developer as part of an overall zero-rated supply, the developer cannot recover the input VAT incurred on those goods.

Certain supplies connected with the construction cannot be zero-rated. These include:

- the separate supply of architectural, surveying, supervisory and building consultancy services. However, it is possible to zero rate these services – see the section below on design and build contracts

- the hire of goods without an operator, such as site fencing, plant hire and scaffolding without erection and dismantling.

See VAT Notice 708 for detailed guidance on what goods and services HMRC consider can and cannot be zero-rated.

Construction services

The supply of construction services used in the creation of a new building is:

- zero-rated if the building is qualifying. See the section 'Qualifying buildings' above for the meaning of 'qualifying'

- standard-rated otherwise.

New buildings

To qualify for zero-rating, 'construction services' must be provided in the construction of a new building. Services provided in the conversion, reconstruction, enlargement, extension or alteration of an existing building are not construction services unless:

- an enlargement or extension creates an additional dwelling or dwellings. The additional dwelling(s) must be entirely contained in the new part of the building

- an annexe to an existing building is constructed where the annexe is intended for use solely for a relevant charitable purpose and the annexe is capable of functioning independently and has a separate entrance – see the section 'Charitable annexes' below.

Supplies made in the course of conversion, reconstruction, enlargement, extension or alteration of an existing building are usually standard-rated but can be zero-rated or reduced-rated in certain situations, as explained below.

To qualify as a new building, any existing building must be demolished completely to ground level. The retention of cellars, basements and the slab at ground floor level is allowed. The retention of a façade (or if on a corner, a double façade) is permitted if this is required for planning consent. For terraced properties, the retention of a party wall is permitted if it forms part of a neighbouring property that is not being developed.

Design and build contracts

Normally the separate supply of architectural, surveying, supervisory and consultancy services associated with a construction project cannot be zero-rated. However, if these are provided as part of a single supply of design and build services they can be zero-rated. There must be a single contract for the supply of design and construction services for a lump sum.

Organisations may wish to consider whether this is an effective way for them to buy in construction services for a qualifying building and thereby save VAT on the professional fees. Usually a separate company is established in order to buy in the professional services and undertake the construction work. The company then makes one charge to the organisation for the supply of construction services, which is all zero-rated. Design and build contracts are usually accepted by HMRC as being a legitimate way of arranging building contracts, and indeed the VAT Notice on construction services (Notice 708) explains how to arrange a design and build contract in paragraph 3.4.

DIY builders' scheme

The DIY builders' refund scheme puts DIY builders and converters in a broadly similar position to a developer selling a zero-rated property, by refunding them the VAT on their main construction or conversion costs. The scheme is available for:

- goods used in the construction of a qualifying building – see the section 'Qualifying buildings'

- goods and services used in a non-residential conversion. A non-residential conversion is the conversion of a non-residential building into a residential building. See the section 'First grants of a major interest' below for more on non-residential conversions.

The developed building must not be used for business purposes, so, for example, VAT cannot be recovered on the purchase of building materials used to construct a care home that will be undertaking a business activity. If the building will be used for business and non-business purposes, costs should be apportioned on a fair and reasonable basis and a corresponding portion of the VAT claimed.

Qualifying goods are those that could be zero-rated if provided by a developer – see the section 'Qualifying buildings'. They are, broadly, building materials that are incorporated into the building, and exclude carpets, free-standing furniture etc. For non-residential conversions, services supplied by sub-contractors are also eligible for VAT refund, though the services of architects, surveyors, supervisors and consultants are excluded. Note that the services of sub-contractors used to create a building designed as a dwelling or a number of dwellings should be zero-rated by any sub-contractors.

Claims can include foreign VAT incurred in purchasing building materials from other EC states and any import VAT incurred in importing building materials from outside the EC.

VAT claims should be made on form VAT 431, which can be downloaded from the HMRC website. You can only make a single claim in respect of any one building and the claim should be made when the building is complete. No claim can be made for VAT incurred after completion.

Self-supply of construction services

If, for the purpose of your business (or your VAT group's business), you use your own labour to:

- construct a building

- extend, alter or construct an annexe to a building such that the works increase the floor area by 10 per cent or more

- construct any civil engineering work

and

- the open-market value of the work is £100,000 or more

then you are deemed to be making a self-supply, and you must account for VAT on those services in your VAT return for the period in which you complete the work. But you do not have to account for a self-supply charge if the work would have been zero-rated.

The output VAT charged on the self-supply is recoverable as input VAT to the extent that the building works will be used in taxable activities. If the value of the self-supply exceeds £250,000 and the building is used partly for exempt purposes, this may bring it within the capital goods scheme – see Chapter 10.

Buying and selling property

This section considers the purchase or sale of a 'major interest' in property, that is, the freehold or a long lease. See the above section 'Major interest' for the definition of this term. The purchase or sale of a short lease or licence is considered in the section 'Letting property'.

Normally the purchase or sale of a major interest in land or buildings is exempt, unless the land or buildings are opted to tax (see above) or the transaction takes place as part of the transfer of a going concern (see Chapter 11). In addition, there are three key situations in which a purchase or sale is taxable:

1. It is zero-rated if it is the first grant of a major interest in:

    - a new building that will be put to qualifying use

    - a non-residential conversion. A non-residential conversion is a non-residential building that is converted into a residential building

    - a substantially reconstructed protected building that will be put to qualifying use after reconstruction.

    In each case the grant must be made by the person undertaking the development, and in each case the building must be intended for a particular qualifying use when the sale occurs.

2. It is standard-rated if it is the sale of the freehold of a building that is non-qualifying and new or incomplete. New means the transaction takes place within three years of completion. Completion is the earlier of the issuing of a certificate of practical completion and full occupation.

3. It is standard-rated if it is the grant of a major interest in a new dwelling but the purchaser is prohibited from residing there throughout the year or using it as their principal private residence. 'New' means the transaction takes place within three years of completion. These conditions are most commonly attached to holiday homes.

Each of these exceptions is examined below.

First grants of a major interest

As explained above, there are three situations in which the first grant of a major interest in a building can qualify for zero rating. They all have various features in common:

- **First grant of a major interest:** The zero-rated transaction must constitute the first grant of a major interest in property. This means that it is a major interest (freehold or long lease) and it is the first time after the relevant work that a major interest has been granted in respect of that property or part of the property. Zero rating is not affected if the building is let on short leases or licences between the development work and the first grant of a major interest, however long the gap is.

- **What is zero-rated?** For a freehold sale, it is the sale price that is zero-rated. For a long lease, it is the lease premium or, if no lease premium is paid, the first instalment of rent. Subsequent payments under a lease are exempt or standard-rated if the property is opted and the option is not disapplied.

- **Person developing status**: In each zero-rating situation substantial development work is undertaken, and it is the first grant of a major interest made after the development that is zero-rated. The grant of the major interest must be made by the person carrying out the development work – the 'person developing'. This is the person who makes the grant and physically undertakes the work or contracts with another person to physically undertake the work.

A person can be, for example, an individual, partnership, company, trust or un-incorporated association. For companies within a VAT group, 'person developing' status is restricted to the company actually undertaking the development and is not transferable to the other companies in the group. However, major interest transfers within a VAT group can be ignored when determining if the grant of a major interest to an entity outside the VAT group is the first.

Note: where a zero-rated building is being constructed, the person developing is usually referred to as the 'person constructing'.

Residence restrictions: A dwelling does not qualify for zero rating if the person purchasing the interest is not entitled to reside there throughout the year, or is prevented from residing in the accommodation throughout the year by the terms of a covenant, statutory planning consent or similar. See the section 'Holiday homes' below.

Qualifying goods and works: The restrictions on the goods and services that can be zero-rated are explained in the section 'Qualifying buildings'. Where the person developing supplies goods that are not incorporated into the building (such as furniture) these do not qualify for zero rating and must be standard-rated. Where goods are incorporated into the building but those goods would not qualify for zero rating if the purchaser was carrying out the work themselves, the person developing is blocked from recovering input VAT on those goods.

Zero-rating certificates: Where the result of the development is a building that is intended solely for relevant residential or charitable purposes, the purchaser must give the person developing a zero-rating certificate. See the section 'Qualifying buildings' for information on zero-rating certificates.

Part-qualifying buildings: Where only a part of the building granted qualifies for zero rating or the grant includes qualifying and non-qualifying buildings, you must apportion the work and zero rate a corresponding part of the cost of the grant. See the section 'Qualifying buildings'.

First grant of a major interest in a new building

The first grant of a major interest in a new building or part of a building is zero-rated if the following conditions are met:

1) The grant must be the first grant of a major interest in the building after its construction. A building is only 'constructed' if any existing building is demolished completely to ground level, though retention of external walls is possible in some situations. See the section 'Construction services'.

2) The grant must be made by the person who constructed the building. See above for an explanation of 'person developing' status.

3) The building or part of a building must be qualifying. See the section 'Qualifying buildings' for an explanation of the term. Dwellings or sites for dwellings where there is a residence restriction are specifically excluded from zero rating. See the section 'Holiday homes'.

4) If the building or part of the building will be used for a relevant residential or charitable purpose, the purchaser must give the person developing a certificate to this effect. See the section 'Qualifying buildings' for information on zero-rating certificates

The effect is to put a qualifying purchaser in the same position as they would have been had they undertaken the construction work themselves. If the developer zero rates goods or services that would have been ineligible for zero rating had the purchaser constructed the building, the developer cannot recover the VAT incurred in purchasing those goods and services.

First grant of a major interest in a non-residential conversion

The first grant of a major interest in a non-residential conversion can be zero-rated if all the following conditions are met:

1) The sale is the first grant of the major interest after the conversion work.

2) The building or part of a building is a non-residential conversion. See below for the definition of a 'non-residential conversion'.

3) The grant is made by the person undertaking the development. See above for an explanation of 'person developing' status.

4) If the result of the conversion is a building intended for a relevant residential use, the purchaser gives the developer a zero-rating certificate to this effect.

A non-residential conversion is the conversion of a non-residential building or part of a building into a residential building or part of a building. The building before conversion must either:

a) not have been designed or adapted for use as a dwelling or number of dwellings or for a relevant residential purpose, or

b) have been designed or adapted for such use but was constructed more than 10 years before the grant and no part of it has, in the 10 years immediately preceding the grant, been used as a dwelling or for a relevant residential purpose.

Following conversion, the building must be either:

c) designed as a dwelling or number of dwellings, or

d) intended for use solely for a relevant residential purpose.

See the section 'Qualifying buildings' for the meaning of the terms 'designed as a dwelling or number of dwellings' and 'Intended for use solely for a relevant residential purpose'.

Tribunals take the view that that the dwelling test on the building before conversion in a) is weaker than the test that is applied after conversion in c). In particular the requirement that the dwellings are self contained is not applied. This means that, for example, bedsits with shared facilities converted into studio flats do not qualify unless the 10-year rule in b) is met. See, for example, the cases of Amicus Group (2002, VAT Tribunal 17693) and Belvedere Properties (2004, VAT Tribunal 18851). In cases of doubt the burden of proof rests with the person claiming zero rating.

Where part of a building is being converted into a dwelling or number of dwellings and the building already contains a residential part then the conversion cannot be zero-rated if the conversion covers any of the pre-existing residential area. However if the conversion results in a new dwelling or new dwellings contained entirely within the previously non-residential area, those areas can be zero-rated subject to the other conditions being met. This condition does not apply if the building or part of the building is being converted to relevant residential use.

First grant of a major interest in a substantially reconstructed protected building

The first grant of a major interest in a substantially reconstructed protected building is zero-rated if the building will be put to a qualifying use after reconstruction. There are five conditions that must all be satisfied for zero rating to apply:

1) The grant must be the first grant of a major interest following the substantial reconstruction.

2) The grant must be made by the 'person developing'. See above for an explanation of 'person developing' status.

3) The building must be protected. A building is protected if it is listed or is a scheduled monument. Buildings within the curtilage of a listed building, such as outhouses or garages which, although not fixed to the building, form part of the land and have done so since before 1 July 1948, are treated for planning purposes as part of the listed building. However, such buildings must meet the other conditions for zero rating to apply. Unlisted buildings in conservation areas, or buildings included in a local authority's non-statutory list of buildings of local interest (Grade III buildings) are not protected buildings for the purposes of VAT.

4) The building must be substantially reconstructed. A reconstruction is substantial if it involves major work to the building's fabric, including the replacement of much of the internal or external structure and either:

   • at least 60 per cent of the total cost of the reconstruction could be zero-rated as 'approved alterations' (see the section 'Approved alterations'). When applying the 60 per cent test it is the entire reconstruction costs that are used in the denominator but excluding the services of an architect, surveyor or other person acting as consultant or in a supervisory capacity, or

   • the reconstruction involves gutting the building. This means no more of the original building is retained than an external wall or walls, or external walls together with other external features of architectural or historic interest.

5) After the substantial reconstruction the building must be:

   • designed to remain as or become a dwelling or number of dwellings, or

   • intended for use solely for a relevant residential purpose, or

   • intended for use solely for a relevant charitable purpose

The relevant residential and charitable purpose conditions are the same as for a qualifying building (see the section 'Qualifying buildings'), however the dwelling condition is slightly different. As with a building that is 'designed as a dwelling or number of dwellings', it must be a self-contained dwelling with no direct internal access to another dwelling and no restriction on separate use or disposal. However, there is no requirement that statutory planning consent was obtained for use as a dwelling. This is because most protected buildings will have been constructed before statutory planning consent for new properties was introduced.

Buying or selling the freehold of a new non-qualifying building

The sale of the freehold of a new, or partly completed, non-qualifying building is standard-rated. Non-qualifying buildings are buildings that are not designed as a dwelling or a number of dwellings nor intended for use solely for a relevant residential or charitable purpose. Non-qualifying building commonly include commercial buildings such as offices, warehouses, retail premises and factories.

A building is new for three years from the date that it is completed. The date of completion is the date the certificate of practical completion is issued, or the date the building is fully occupied – whichever happens first. Freehold sales that take place within the three-year period are standard-rated and freehold sales that take place after three years are exempt unless the building is opted.

Bare land and civil engineering works

Civil engineering works include drains, roads, street lighting, bridges, playgrounds, football pitches, running tracks and hard landscaping.

'Bare land' is land without any buildings or civil engineering works. The sale of bare land cannot be zero-rated and is exempt unless the land is opted. If a landowner sells bare land and enters into a separate construction contract there will be two supplies – one of bare land and one of construction services. However, if there is a single contract there is a single supply of a constructed building. This will still apply even if the building is only partly constructed, provided construction has progressed beyond the foundation stages. It may therefore be possible effectively to standard rate or zero rate a sale of bare land if the vendor commences construction work before the sale and effectively sells a partly completed building.

The VAT status of a sale of land together with civil engineering works depends on the principal element of the supply:

- Where the principal element is the civil engineering work: the sale of the freehold in a new or incomplete civil engineering work is standard-rated. 'New' means the sale takes place within three years of completion. After three years, the sale is exempt. The rules are as for new non-qualifying buildings, as explained above.

155

- Where the principal element is the land, the sale is exempt unless the land is opted.

A serviced building plot is a plot of land together with access to essential services such as gas, electricity, water, main drainage, street lighting and sewerage. The sale of a serviced building plot by the landowner is a single exempt supply (or standard-rated if the plot is opted). The supply of civil engineering works to the landowner to provide access to essential services is standard-rated unless the landowner can demonstrate that these services were received in the course of construction of a qualifying building, in which case the civil engineering works are zero-rated. HMRC state that they would normally expect all the following to be met to demonstrate that zero rating is appropriate:

- the landowner holds sufficient planning consent to demonstrate that the civil engineering works were received in the course of construction of a qualifying building

- the civil engineering is closely connected with or facilitates the construction of a qualifying building

- the construction of the qualifying building will follow on closely after the completion of the civil engineering works.

Holiday homes

Purpose-built or converted holiday accommodation frequently contains some form of restriction preventing permanent occupation or use as a principal private residence. If there is no such restriction and any major interest is sold as the sale of a normal dwelling, the normal property rules will apply.

Where the major interest in a dwelling is sold but there is a restriction on permanent residence in either the lease, a covenant or under planning permission, the building does not qualify as 'designed as a dwelling' and the sale is standard-rated when the property
is new.

After three years the sale of the freehold or a premium for a lease or licence is exempt, unless the property is opted to tax. However, any periodic payments such as rent or service charges are standard-rated, though there are exceptions. See the section 'Holiday accommodation' below.

Where a lease or licence in a plot of land is sold with the right to construct and occupy holiday accommodation, the sale of the plot is standard-rated. However, the sale of the freehold in bare land is exempt unless the land is opted.

Refurbishing and extending buildings

Generally, work done to an existing building, including any alteration, extension, reconstruction, enlargement or annexes are standard-rated. However, there are some exceptions:

- the construction of an annexe that will be used solely for a relevant charitable purpose is zero-rated – see below for more details

- services supplied in converting a non-residential building into a residential building for a housing association are zero-rated

- approved alterations to protected buildings that are used for qualifying purposes are zero-rated

- the renovation or alteration of empty residential properties and the conversion of premises to a different residential use is reduced rate. See Chapter 6 for details.

Construction, alteration or repair and maintenance?

It can be difficult to determine whether building work should be classified as construction, alteration or repair. The VAT differences can be significant. Under certain circumstances works of construction and alteration can be zero-rated. Works of repair and maintenance cannot be zero-rated, though in some circumstances the VAT incurred in carrying out repairs and maintenance on listed places of worship, national galleries and monuments can be reclaimed – see Chapter 10 for details.

Construction comprises demolishing any existing buildings to ground level and rebuilding. The retention of cellars, basements and the slab at ground floor level is allowed. The retention of a façade (or if on a corner, a double façade) is permitted if this is required for planning consent. For terraced properties, the retention of a party wall is permitted if it forms part of a neighbouring property that is not being developed. Extensions and enlargements can only constitute construction if:

- the enlargement or extension creates an additional dwelling or dwellings. The additional dwelling(s) must be entirely contained in the new part of the building; or

- an annexe to an existing building is constructed where the annexe is intended for use solely for a relevant charitable purpose and the annexe is capable of functioning independently and has a separate entrance.

Alterations are works which alter or change the fabric of a building, unless the change to the fabric is minimal. The fabric of a building comprises the elements that characterise the structure as a building, such as walls, roofs, internal surfaces, floors, stairs and landings and all doors and windows. The fabric of the building also includes plumbing and central heating systems, and mains wiring and lighting systems.

There is a great deal of case law on the sometimes confusing distinction between works of alteration and works of repair and maintenance. In the VAT Tribunal case Haresfield Court Tenants' Association (2007, VAT Tribunal 20133) the tribunal reviewed the case law and drew up eight principles for distinguishing between works of alterations and works or repair or maintenance:

1) 'Alteration' means any alteration to the building – not just a structural alteration.

2) 'Repair or maintenance' is a composite phrase to be construed in its ordinary sense; the words are not antithesis.

3) 'Maintenance', if one is to be permitted to consider it separately, reflects a task designed to minimise, for as long as possible, the need for and future timescale of further attention to the fabric of the building.

4) A radical and fundamental alteration to the building will not be repair or maintenance.

5) Because 'repair or maintenance' is an exclusion from 'alteration', works of repair or maintenance will always be works of alteration.

6) The effecting of a repair using modern building materials does not prevent the work from being repair and maintenance.

7) If an alteration is an integral part of wider works of repair and maintenance, it should be viewed as repair or maintenance. 'Integral' implies a measure of necessity.

8) An alteration which achieves some measure of repair and maintenance is not thereby necessarily constituted repairs or maintenance.

The chairman of the tribunal went on to say: 'almost any alteration of a building will give rise to some feature which will mean less future need of repair as a result of the work. The issue will be one of degree: a repair which is a consequence of a larger change will not turn the change into repair and maintenance; an alteration which is a necessary part of a repair does not prevent the works being repairs or maintenance. Between the two extremes lies a band of possibilities'.

Relevant charitable purpose annexes

The creation of an annexe to a building may be regarded as the construction of a separate building and qualify for zero rating if all the following conditions are met:

1) The structure can properly be regarded as an annexe. Here, 'annexe' connotes something that is adjoined to a building but is either not integrated with the

existing building or of tenuous integration. Extensions do not qualify as annexes, nor do enlargements to buildings.

2) The annexe or part of the annexe is intended solely for use for a relevant charitable purpose. It is the use to which the annexe will be put that matters, not the use to which the existing building is put or how the construction work is funded. If only part of the annexe qualifies, the construction costs must be apportioned.

3) The annexe is capable of functioning independently from the existing building. This means that activities can be undertaken in the annexe without reliance on the main building. You should ensure that it has its own toilets, at the very least. The sharing of building services such as electricity, water and sewerage is, however, allowed.

4) The only access (or main access where more than one) to the annexe is not via the existing building and vice versa. This does not preclude connection by a door or corridor to another building but the annexe should be capable of functioning as intended even if the door or corridor were closed off.

5) The main contractor is given a zero-rating certificate. See the section 'Qualifying buildings' for information on zero-rating certificates.

6) The limitations on the goods and services that can be zero-rated are the same as set out in the section 'Construction services'.

This does not mean that all extensions or enlargements to charity buildings will qualify for zero rating as annexes. Each case will need to be considered on its own merits. You should obtain agreement from the VAT office to the zero rating before construction commences, and you may need to submit plans or allow a site visit to obtain agreement.

Non-residential conversions for registered housing associations

Services supplied to a registered housing association in converting a non-residential building into a residential building are zero-rated. The conditions are similar to those applying to the zero rating of the first grant of a major interest in a non-residential conversion (see above):

1) The services must be supplied to a registered housing association. In England and Wales these are referred to as 'registered social landlords'.

2) The building (or part of a building) being converted must not have been designed or adapted for residential use or, if it was, not put to residential use in the 10 years before the work starts.

3) The conversion work must result in a new dwelling, new dwellings or a building (or part of a building) intended for use solely for a relevant residential purpose.

4) If the work results in a relevant residential building, the housing association must give the converter a zero-rating certificate, and only the supplies by the main contractor are zero-rated.

5) Where the conversion work will result in a partly qualifying building, the costs must be apportioned between qualifying and non-qualifying on a fair and reasonable basis.

6) Architectural, surveying, supervisory and consultancy services are excluded from zero rating if supplied separately.

Approved alterations to protected buildings

Approved alterations to protected buildings are zero-rated if the building is qualifying. There are four conditions that must be satisfied for zero rating to apply:

1) The building must be **protected**. A protected building is a listed building or a scheduled monument. For details, see the section 'First grants of a major interest'.

2) The building must be **qualifying**. See the section 'Qualifying buildings'.

3) The work must be **approved**. This means that consent must have to be obtained for the work, that consent was obtained before the work was undertaken and the work was carried out in accordance with that consent. Alterations to certain ecclesiastical buildings and Crown or Duchy buildings do not require listed building consent but, for VAT purposes, such alterations are treated as if they did: see VAT Notice 708 for details.

4) The work must constitute an **alteration**. See above for commentary on the distinction between works of alteration and works of repair or maintenance. Zero rating does not apply to works of repair and maintenance unless they are incidental to the alteration work. Repairs and maintenance carried out on the building at the same time as an alteration that are not covered by the listed building consent are standard-rated. Architects' fees and the fees of any other consultants, surveyors or supervisors are always standard-rated if charged for separately.

Fittings, furniture and carpets are standard-rated as for new construction work. If the owner of the building buys any goods and materials for inclusion in the approved alteration, then they cannot be zero-rated; all goods and services must be supplied by the main contractor who zero rates the contract sum. In the case of works to a relevant residential or charitable building, a zero-rating certificate must be supplied to the contractor by the purchaser in the same way as for new buildings.

See Chapter 10 for details of VAT refund schemes for works of repair to listed places of worship and for the construction, renovation and maintenance of memorial structures.

Letting property

This section examines the VAT implications of letting out property on short-term lets. A short-term let is one that is terminable at will or lasts for a term of 21 years or less in England and Wales or less than 20 years in Scotland. Long-term lets are considered in the section 'Buying and selling property'.

Rental income

Generally, rental income will be VAT-exempt unless the property is opted (see the section 'The option to tax' for the meaning of 'opted'). Even if the property is opted, rental charges cannot be standard-rated if the tenant will be using the property for a qualifying purpose. This means:

- use as a dwelling or number of dwellings

- use for a relevant residential purpose

- use for a relevant charitable purpose, other than as an office used for general administration.

See the section 'Qualifying buildings' for an explanation of these terms. If the tenant is to use the property for a relevant residential purpose or a relevant charitable purpose other than as an office they must give the landlord a certificate confirming this. The option is then disapplied in respect of any supplies made from that point on. See the above section 'The option to tax' for more information on disapplying an option and the problems this may cause.

The VAT statuses of various payments closely connected to rental payments are as follows:

- **Lease premiums**: Where a tenant pays a lease premium to the landlord, the payment is exempt unless the property is opted, in which case it is standard-rated.

- **Lease inducements**: Where a landlord pays an inducement to the tenant to take up a lease, the payment will be outside the scope of VAT unless it is directly linked to a specific benefit supplied by the tenant to the landlord, in which case it will follow the VAT status of the supply provided by the tenant. Situations in which an inducement payment would be taxable include agreeing to undertake repair work or acting as an anchor tenant. An anchor tenant is a prestige business that will attract other tenants. For example the presence of a major supermarket in a shopping mall will attract shoppers and permit smaller businesses to enjoy their custom. This will enable the mall owner to charge higher rents. Lease inducements to anchor tenants frequently take the form of a rent-free period, for which see below.

- **Rent-free periods**: A rent-free period given by a landlord is outside the scope of VAT unless something is supplied by the tenant to the landlord in return, in which case its VAT status follows that of the supply by the tenant.

- **Payments to surrender a lease** given by a landlord to a tenant are generally exempt unless the tenant has opted to tax the property. Payments to surrender a lease made by a tenant to a landlord are generally exempt unless the landlord has opted to tax.

- **Dilapidation payments** may be charged by the landlord to the tenant at or near the end of a lease. Such payments are a claim for damages by the landlord and are not consideration for a supply. They are therefore outside the scope of VAT.

Service and other charges

As well as charging rent, landlords will recharge some costs and service charges for additional services supplied. Generally, charges that are really part of the supply of property will be treated as falling into the same VAT category as the rent. So if the rent is exempt, then the additional charges will be exempt. Additional services that are optional or are not closely linked to the supply of property are generally standard-rated. However, if the landlord is merely acting as agent in collecting money from tenants and paying bills on their behalf, then this is outside the scope of VAT. Some specific situations that commonly arise:

- **Insurance**: the landlord will often be the policyholder for the buildings insurance, but will recharge the cost to the tenant. This will normally be covered by a lease term and therefore fall into the same VAT category as the rent itself.

- **Rates** may be the responsibility of the landlord and recharged to tenants. Again, if this is in the lease, it will fall into the same VAT category as the rent. If the tenant is responsible for the rates, then the landlord may be acting as agent in collecting rates and paying them over on behalf of tenants, and the associated charge will be outside the scope of VAT.

- **Light and power** provided as part of an inclusive rental amount will not be subject to VAT where rent is exempt. A separate supply of light and power would be subject to VAT. A landlord collecting reimbursement from a tenant for a separately metered supply would be outside the scope as the landlord would be acting as an agent.

- **Telephone** lines in the name of the landlord which are then recharged to the tenants are a supply of standard-rated services.

- **Reception services** which are not discretionary and are part of the lease agreement will fall into the same VAT category as the rent, even when charged separately. If they are an optional additional service then they will be standard-rated.

- **Photocopying and other support services** will generally be standard-rated, as charges will usually be an optional extra and charges made based on usage. If an all-inclusive rental is charged, however, then the whole amount may be exempt, though you must apply the 'single/multiple supply tests' (see Chapter 11) to determine if there is a single exempt supply or a multiple supply of exempt property rental services and standard-rated support services.

- **Management charges** by the landlord for collecting service charges and managing the property are part of the main property supply and therefore follow the VAT category of the rent.

Letting rooms for events

Where an organisation lets out rooms for an event organised by a third party the room hire charge will usually follow the principles outlined above. It will be exempt (unless the building is opted) and supplies that are automatically included with the hire, such as the use of tables and chairs, projectors and whiteboards will follow the status of the main supply. Where these are optional extras they will be standard-rated unless they qualify for zero rating or exemption in their own right.

If the accommodation is provided primarily for a supply of catering and the catering is supplied by the person supplying the accommodation, then the whole supply is standard-rated. This will apply to events such as parties, wedding receptions and gala dinners. However if the customer arranges the catering themselves the room hire will be exempt unless the building is opted.

If the rooms are hired by an organisation that meets the definition of a hotel, inn, boarding house or similar (see the section below) special rules apply where charges are made on a 'per delegate basis'. Where rooms are supplied by hotels and similar, for meetings, conferences etc. (but not where the primary use is a supply of catering) and the charge to the organiser is based on the number of delegates or attendees requiring different facilities, the VAT status is:

- for the use of rooms only: exempt (unless the building is opted)

- for the use of rooms plus a meal or overnight accommodation: the supply must be apportioned. The room element is exempt (unless the building is opted), but the meal and accommodation elements are standard-rated

Before January 2006 HMRC saw the supply of rooms, meal and accommodation for an inclusive price (the '24-hour delegate rate') as a single taxable supply. HMRC announced their change of policy in Business Brief 01/06 with effect from 19 January 2006.

Accommodation in hotels, hostels and similar

The sale of a major interest in a hotel or similar is covered in the section 'Buying and selling property'. In many situations the sale of a major interest in a hotel or similar will qualify under the 'transfer of a going concern' rules. See Chapter 11 for details of these rules.

Accommodation in hotels, inns, boarding houses and similar establishments is standard-rated subject to the 'reduced value rule'. UK law defines a 'similar establishment' as 'premises in which there is provided furnished sleeping accommodation, whether with or without the provision of board or facilities for the preparation of food, which are used by or held out as being suitable for use by visitors or travellers'. Typically similar establishments include B&Bs, private clubs, hostels and halls of residence (under certain circumstances) and serviced houses or flats for use by travellers and visitors.

Where an individual stays in hotel accommodation or similar for more than 28 days consecutively, then, from the 29th day on, VAT should be charged on the non-accommodation element of the charge only, that is, the element that relates to meals, service charges and other facilities that are provided. This is known as the 'reduced value rule'. If an inclusive charge is made it must be apportioned between the supply of accommodation and the supply of other facilities and services. VAT is charged on the supply of other facilities and services but not on the accommodation element.

To do this, you must calculate the amount of the charge that is for meals, drinks and other services, and also treat at least 20 per cent of the remainder as being for facilities. However, if the true value of the facilities is more than this, you must charge VAT on the true amount.

Example: Reduced-value rule

The normal charge for one night's stay in a hotel is £100 + VAT, of which the meal element is £40 + VAT. The reduced-value charge is calculated as follows:

The charge for accommodation and facilities is £100 - £40 = £60 net.

At least 20% of this must be treated as being for the supply of facilities, i.e. 20% x £60 = £12 net.

The charge for accommodation is £60 - £12 = £48 net.

The reduced value charge is:	Net	VAT	Gross	
Accommodation	48.00	–	48.00	No VAT charge on accommodation
Facilities	12.00	2.10	14.10	VAT is charged on facilities and other
Meals etc.	40.00	7.00	47.00	supplies
Total	100.00	9.10	109.10	

The reduced-value charge is applied from the 29th day on.

The 'reduced-value rule' does not mean that the supply becomes partly exempt – it remains fully taxable but with a reduced VAT charge. Input VAT recovery is therefore not restricted by the reduced-value rule.

If you only provide accommodation and facilities and the value of the facilities is below 20 per cent then the effective rate of VAT on the whole supply will be 3.5 per cent (20 per cent x 17.5 per cent).

The supply does not have to be paid for by the guest. In a case involving the Afro Caribbean Housing Association (2006, VAT Tribunal 19450) the housing association provided hostel accommodation for asylum seekers under contract to the British Refugee Council. HMRC argued that, for the reduced-value rule to apply, the accommodation must be occupied by the recipient of the services. The tribunal found that there was no such requirement and so the reduced-value rule applied to the supply to the British Refugee Council.

Normally the departure and later return of a guest will break a period of stay. However, a guest's departure is not seen to end a period of continuous stay provided the guest:

- is a long-term resident and leaves for an occasional weekend or holiday

- is a student who leaves during the vacation but returns to the same accommodation for the following term. Note that where accommodation is provided by an eligible educational institution, the supply of accommodation is likely to be ancillary to the supply of education and therefore exempt. See Chapter 5

- pays a retaining fee.

In these cases the time away is ignored and you only have to charge VAT in full for the first 28 days of the overall stay. It does not matter whether the guest returns to the same room or not.

If accommodation is provided for the purpose of catering in a hotel, inn, boarding house or similar establishment (for example at a wedding reception), the supply is standard-rated whatever the length of let – the reduced-value rule does not apply.

Some voluntary organisations run hotels or other establishments that share some of the characteristics of a hotel, for example hostels for the homeless or for asylum seekers. The VAT treatment of such supplies is as follows:

* If the accommodation is provided free of charge and funded by grants or donations, it is likely to be a non-business activity. If a fee is charged for the accommodation but the fee is heavily subsidised, the activity may also be non-business. See Chapter 4.

* If the accommodation is only provided as an incidental or ancillary part of another activity, its VAT status will generally follow that of the other activity.

* If none of the supplies commonly found in hotels is provided, apart from furnished rooms and sleeping facilities, the supply may amount to a supply of furnished accommodation and will be exempt subject to the property being opted. This may be the case if, for example, there are no permanent on-site staff, no meals are provided (or provided only as supermarket vouchers or food parcels) and there is very limited or no cleaning of rooms etc.

* If the main purpose of the activity is to provide accommodation of a type similar to that supplied in a hotel, inn, boarding house or similar, then the supply will be standard-rated subject to the reduced-value rule.

Some recent cases illustrate some of the differences. In Dinaro Ltd (1999, VAT Tribunal 17148) a hostel for the homeless only accepted people with mental health problems for whom they provided a high degree of care and supervision. The tribunal found that the hostel was not similar to a hotel or inn, and there were three main elements in establishing the dissimilarity: the selectivity exercised over the choice of residents, the high degree of care and supervision for all the inhabitants and the emphasis on a family concept for all those who were residents.

In a case involving North East Direct Access (2003, VAT Tribunal 18267) the organisation provided accommodation, meals and supervised personal care for homeless men, many of whom had a high level of need and had lived at the hostel for many years. The tribunal nevertheless found that the main supply was of accommodation and food and the supply of care was ancillary. The case was distinguished from Dinaro by the fact that there was a lesser degree of selectivity exercised over the choice of residents, the care requirements of residents varied widely and there was no emphasis on a family concept or any other particular philosophy.

In a case involving the Macmillan Cancer Trust (1998, VAT Tribunal 15603) the trust provided short-term holiday accommodation for cancer patients and their carers in a former seaside hotel. Only cancer patients and their carers were admitted and nursing staff were employed to deal with emergencies and provide comfort and counselling. The tribunal decided that the premises were not run as a hotel but were instead ancillary to a supply of care.

Holiday accommodation

The sale of a major interest in holiday accommodation is covered in the section 'Holiday homes'. Holiday accommodation is accommodation in a building, hut (including a beach hut or chalet), caravan, houseboat or tent which is advertised or held out as holiday accommodation or as suitable for holiday or leisure use, but excludes any accommodation that qualifies as hotel accommodation or similar (for which see above). The supply of a short lease or let of holiday accommodation is standard-rated. There is no reduced-value rule as for hotels, inns, boarding houses and similar; however off-season letting can be exempted provided:

* it is let to a person as residential accommodation and not as holiday accommodation

* it is let for more than 28 days

* holiday trade in the area is clearly seasonal. HMRC state that the holiday season normally lasts from Easter to the end of September, though some areas, such as London, are not regarded as having a seasonal holiday trade.

When a let qualifies as off-season letting, the whole of the let is exempted, including the first 28 days.

The same considerations that apply to hotels, hostels and similar (see above) are relevant when deciding whether a supply is of holiday accommodation or of something else. If a supply of holiday accommodation is incidental to or ancillary to another activity its VAT status will generally follow that of the other activity. Note that a package of travel and accommodation will usually fall within the Tour Operators' Margin Scheme (see Chapter 10).

In a case involving The Evangelical Movement of Wales (2004, VAT Tribunal 18556) the charity ran camps for young people. The camps aimed to be a spiritual experience for the attendees and there was an extensive programme of recreational and spiritual activities. HMRC claimed the camps were a supply of holiday accommodation. The tribunal found that the camps were courses of instruction not designed primarily to provide recreation or a holiday, and therefore exempt as a supply of spiritual welfare.

Sports facilities

The letting of sports facilities is standard–rated, unless:

a)   the let lasts for a continual period of longer than 24 hours, or

b)   the hirer is a school, club, association or representative body, and it books a series of 10 or more sessions and various other conditions (see below) are met

in which case it is exempt.

Premises are sports facilities if they are designed, adapted or equipped for playing any sport or taking part in any physical recreation, such as swimming pools, football pitches, dance studios and skating rinks.

General-purpose facilities such as a village hall or school hall do not qualify as sporting facilities unless they are hired together with sports equipment. The let of a village hall is therefore exempt, unless hired together with sports equipment, in which case it is standard-rated unless it also meets either condition a) or condition b) above.

In condition b) the terms 'club' and 'association' have a broad meaning and can apply to a single team, incorporated association (i.e. a company), an unincorporated association, a members' club, a union or a social club. A school is an institution that provides statutory education (primary or secondary) required by the Education Acts. So a private dance school would not qualify for exemption under b), though it may under a).

The conditions in b) are that:

(i)   each period is in respect of the same activity carried on at the same place, and

(ii) the interval between each period is not less than one day and not more than 14 days, and

(iii) consideration is payable by reference to the whole series and is evidenced by written agreement, and

(iv) the grantee has exclusive use of the facilities.

Condition b)(ii) states that a series of 10 or more lets is:

•   exempt if the smallest interval between lets is one day or more and the largest interval is 14 days or less

•   standard-rated if the smallest interval between lets is less than one day or if the largest interval is more than 14 days.

In the case of Polo Farm Sports Club (2007, VAT Tribunal 20105), the tribunal decided that the interval refers to the gap between the end of one period of use and the beginning of the next. The tribunal was undecided on the meaning of a day – does it mean that the hires must be on separate days or that the gap must be at least 24 hours? The tribunal preferred the former interpretation but HMRC consider the latter to be the case. Whatever the interpretation of condition b)(ii) it can lead to some odd distinctions:

Example: Letting sports facilities

Assume condition b)(ii) refers to the number of hours between the end of one let and the start of the next (i.e. the HMRC interpretation). A sports centre lets out sports facilities to schools as follows:

School A: 9 am–10 am every weekday for a term: the smallest gap between hires is 23 hours. This is less than 24 hours, so the hire is standard-rated.

School B: 10 am–11 am every Monday, Wednesday and Friday for a term: the smallest gap between hires is 47 hours. This is at least one day. The largest gap is 11 am Friday to 10 am Monday which is less than 14 days, so the let is exempt.

School C: 11 am–12 am every Monday, Tuesday and Friday for a term: the smallest gap between hires is 23 hours. This is less than 24 hours, so the hire is standard-rated

School D: 1 pm–2 pm and 4 pm–5 pm every Monday for a term: the smallest gap between hires is two hours. This is less than 24 hours so the hire is standard-rated.

Parking facilities

Parking facilities are property that is either:

- designed or adapted for parking vehicles, or

- provided specifically for parking vehicles.

Parking facilities include garages, car parks and spaces in them, parking bays, taxi ranks and land that is let specifically for the construction of a garage or for parking vehicles.

The freehold sale of a new or partly completed parking facility is standard-rated unless the parking facility is provided in conjunction with a new dwelling. 'New' means within three years of completion. After three years the freehold sale of a parking facility is exempt unless the parking facility is opted.

The leasing or letting (long-term or short-term) of parking facilities is standard-rated, but with some exceptions.

If a parking facility is specifically designed or adapted for parking vehicles (for example a garage or car park) then its supply is standard-rated even if it is used for some other purpose such as storing goods, unless the lease or licence of the facility specifically excludes the parking of vehicles.

If land is specifically provided for the parking of vehicles, for example under a term in the planning consent, conveyance or contract, then the supply of land is standard-rated unless any supply of parking facilities is either incidental to the main use of the land or closely linked to it. Incidental uses include use for a market or car boot sale, the exhibition of vehicles, or a travelling circus or fair.

Where a supply of parking facilities is closely linked to another supply of property, it follows the VAT status of that supply. So the letting of a garage or parking space provided with a dwelling is exempt, and the letting of parking spaces provided with commercial premises follows the VAT status of the commercial premises. To be regarded as being closely linked to the supply of property the parking facility must be near to the property and supplied by the same landlord.

The rules on parking facilities can be a problem with right to buys. If a tenant exercises their right to buy and purchases the freehold of their property but continues to rent a garage, the supply of the garage is standard-rated because it is no longer closely linked to the supply of the property.

Sharing property

If you share a property with another charity, then care is needed when recharging services to them. If one charity is the 'lead tenant' and pays all the property bills such as rates, light, heat and so on and then charges the other charity or charities for their share, the lead tenant is supplying services to the other charities, which are standard-rated. If all charities are tenants or joint tenants, one charity can act as an agent on behalf of the others in paying the bills. Collecting reimbursements from the other tenants is then outside the scope of VAT.

9 International aspects of VAT

If your staff travel abroad and make purchases in other EC member states then any VAT incurred is foreign VAT and cannot be recovered through the UK VAT return. There are special rules and procedures for recovering foreign VAT.

In addition, if you make supplies to or receive supplies from a country outside the UK, there are special VAT rules for determining the VAT liability of the supply.

This section outlines these rules.

The UK

For VAT purposes, the territory of the UK comprises England, Scotland and Wales, Northern Ireland and the Isle of Man but excludes the Channel Islands and Gibraltar. The Channel Islands and Gibraltar are, for VAT purposes, outside the EC. Though the Isle of Man is not part of the UK, there is a Customs agreement between the UK and Isle of Man and the two territories are regarded as one for most VAT purposes.

The EC

The other EC states currently (2007) comprise:

EC state	What VAT is called in the EC state	
Austria	Mehrwertsteuer, Umsatzsteuer	Mwst, Ust
Belgium	French: Taxe sur la Valeur Ajoutée; Dutch: Belasting over de Toegevoegde Waarde	TVA BTW
Bulgaria	Данък върху добавената стойност	ДДС
Cyprus excluding Turkish-controlled areas	Arithmos Egrafis FPA, Φόρος Προστιθεμένης Αξίας	FPA, ΦΠΑ

Czech Republic	Daň z přidané hodnoty	DPH
Denmark excluding the Faroe Islands and Greenland	Omsaetningafgift, Merverdiavgift	MOMS
Estonia	Kaibemaksukohustuslasena, käibemaks	KM
Finland excluding the Aland Islands	Arvonlisavero	ALV
France including Monaco but excluding Martinique, French Guiana, Guadeloupe, Réunion and St Pierre and Miquelon	Taxe sur la Valeur Ajoutée	TVA
Germany excluding Busingen and Isle of Heligoland	Mehrwertsteuer, Umsatzsteuer	Mwst Ust
Greece excluding Mount Athos (Agion Poros)	Arithmos Forologikou Mitroou, Foros Prostithemenis Axias, Φόρος Προστιθεμένης Αξίας	FPA, ΦΠΑ
Hungary	általános forgalmi adó	AFA
Ireland	Value Added Tax, Cáin Bhreisluacha	VAT, CBL
Italy excluding the Communes of Livigno and Campione d'Italia, the Italian waters of Lake Lugano and Vatican City	Imposta sul Valore Aggiunto	IVA
Latvia	Pievienotās vērtības nodoklis	PVN
Lithuania	Pridėtinės vertės mokestis	PVM
Luxembourg	Taxe sur la Valeur Ajoutée	TVA
Malta	Value Added Tax, Taxxa tal-Valur Miżjud	VAT
Netherlands	Omzetbelasting, Belasting over de Toegevoegde Waarde	OB BTW
Poland	Value Added Tax, Podatek od towarów i uslug	VAT, PTU
Portugal including the Azores and Madeira	Imposto sobre o Valor Acrescentado	IVA
Romania	Taxa pe valoarea adăugată	TVA
Slovakia	Daň z pridanej hodnoty	DPH

Slovenia	Davek na dodano vrednost	DDV
Spain including the Balearic Islands but excluding the Canary Islands, Ceuta and Melilla	Impuesto sobre el Valor Anadido	IVA
Sweden	Mervardeskatt	MOMS

Recovering VAT incurred on purchases in another EC country

VAT incurred in another EC member state cannot be recovered through the UK VAT return. Instead, it must be claimed directly from the country concerned. If you are registered for VAT in that country, you reclaim it by completing a local VAT return. If you are not registered for VAT in that country then you may apply for the VAT to be refunded if the following conditions are met:

- you must be VAT-registered in another EC member state and supply a certificate of VAT status with your claim. In the UK a certificate of VAT status (VAT 66) is issued by HMRC on application

- you must not be registered or liable to be registered or have a place of business or residence in the other EC state and you must not make any supplies in that country other than transport services related to the international carriage of goods or reverse-charge supplies of services (see below)

- the VAT must be recoverable under the EC state's local rules. This means that, if you had been registered for VAT in the EC state, you would have been able to recover the input VAT. Many EC states apply different rules from the UK for commonly incurred types of expense such as accommodation, travel and subsistence costs, and you should check that your expenses qualify before making a claim. See Chapter 14: *Further information* for details of the EC websites where you can find this information.

Claims must be made on a special claim form, in the language of the country concerned, and sent with original invoices or receipts. Documentation sent with the claim is returned with payment of the claim. Each EC country sets a minimum amount that may be claimed for a period of less than one year, though if one claim is submitted for a whole year, any amount may be claimed.

Claims must be made within six months of the end of the claim year in which the VAT was incurred. EC countries set their own VAT claim years, most ending on either 30 June or 31 December. Countries are required under EC law to pay refunds within six months, however in some EC states it can take considerably longer for claims to be processed.

Am I supplying goods or services?

To determine the VAT status of international supplies you first need to decide whether you are supplying goods or services. There are different rules for each.

A supply of goods takes place where there is a transfer of both title to and possession of tangible objects. Any supply that is not a supply of goods is a supply of services.

If goods are sold under an agreement under which title will pass by the time the final instalment is paid, for example a hire purchase agreement, it is a supply of goods. However, operating lease-type agreements where no transfer of title is contemplated at the outset are supplies of services and not of goods.

Sometimes a contract may involve the supply of both goods and services, for example where work is undertaken by the supplier in installing or customising those goods. The 'single/multiple supply tests' (see Chapter 11) must be applied to determine whether there is a single supply of goods or services or a mixed supply of goods and of services. If there is a single supply and one component costs considerably more than the other, then the status will generally follow that of the major cost component.

The supply of computer software is a supply of goods when it comprises a standard product supplied on physical media such as a CD or DVD. However, where the software is sent electronically it is a supply of services. Software that is produced specifically for a customer or that is heavily customised is likely to be considered a single supply of services.

The supply of goods

VAT legislation uses particular terms to describe supplies of goods within and outside the EC:

- **exports** are goods sent to a destination outside the EC

- **imports** are goods received from a source outside the EC

- **acquisitions** are goods received from a source within the EC but outside the UK

- **removals** and **despatches** are goods sent to a destination within the EC but outside the UK.

Exports and imports

In VAT terminology, goods sent to a destination outside the EC are called 'exports' and goods brought into the UK from outside the EC called 'imports'. The administrative procedures associated with exports and imports can be complex and are beyond the scope of this book. Many organisations use agents to handle exports and imports and make the necessary Customs declarations on their behalf. However, if you do use an agent, you retain responsibility for making sure the administrative procedures are followed and that any VAT due is paid. If your agent makes a mistake, HMRC will hold you responsible and you will be liable for any fines and penalties due.

Most imports and exports must be declared to Customs, usually on a form called the Single Administrative Document (SAD or form C88). If you make a postal export, the postal company should be able to provide you with declaration forms. If you receive postal imports, most commercial suppliers will complete an International Customs Declaration on your behalf.

Goods sent as aid

The distribution of goods for free or at significantly below cost would normally be considered a non-business activity, meaning that associated input VAT cannot be recovered. However, UK law specifies that the export of goods by a charity in pursuit of its charitable objects is a deemed zero-rated business activity. This means that the charity is able to recover all related input VAT, including VAT on the costs of buying, storing and handling the goods.

The goods must qualify under the normal rules (see below) as exports. This broadly means that they are sent to a destination outside the EC and that adequate proof of export is held. Aid sent to a destination inside the EC does not qualify.

The charity may register for VAT on the basis of this deemed business activity even if this is the charity's only business activity. It will generally be beneficial to do so in order to recover associated input VAT, though the impact of having to charge VAT on any taxable supplies must be considered.

Transfer of goods abroad

The transfer of goods abroad without charge is outside the scope of UK VAT. If the goods are transferred to be used in a business activity abroad, then attributable UK input VAT is deductible if it would have been had the business activity been undertaken in the UK. If the goods are transferred for use in a non-business activity then, unless the organisation transferring the goods is a charity (see above), attributable UK input VAT is not deductible.

Even if the goods are to be used for a non-business activity, they may need to be declared to Customs and valid proof of export should be retained.

Returning purchased goods

If you return goods that you imported from a non-EC supplier then any import VAT you paid on the import may be refundable. If the goods are being returned because they are faulty and are returned within 12 months of import then you can reclaim any import VAT paid on the goods:

- for a VAT-registered organisation where the import was for taxable business purposes: by recovering the import VAT paid in the next VAT return. The import VAT certificate is used as evidence of payment of the import VAT and proof of return of the goods must be retained

- for an unregistered organisation or a registered organisation where the import was for non-business, exempt or partly taxable purposes: by making a refund claim to HMRC.

Selling goods

Where goods are sold commercially to a non-EC customer then, provided various conditions are met, the supply is zero-rated. If any of the conditions are not met VAT is chargeable by the supplier as if the goods had been supplied within the UK.

There are two types of commercial export:

- **Direct exports**: where the supplier or supplier's agent is responsible for delivering the goods to the non-EC customer. This includes postal deliveries where the delivery service is acting as agent for the supplier.

- **Indirect exports**: where the customer or an agent of the customer collects the goods from the UK supplier and then takes them outside the EC. This includes situations where the customer instructs a delivery service to collect the goods.

The conditions for the zero rating are:

- The goods are taken out of the UK within three months of the time of supply. The time of supply is the earlier of full payment by the customer or the goods being physically sent.

- Evidence of export is obtained within three months of the time of supply and retained for six years. See below for what constitutes acceptable evidence of export.

- For direct exports, the goods must be delivered to an address outside the EC.

- For indirect exports, the goods must be supplied to an overseas person and not used before export. An overseas person is an individual or organisation that is not UK resident, not registered for VAT in the UK, and does not have a business establishment in the UK from which taxable supplies are made

If any of these conditions are not met, then VAT must be charged as if the goods were supplied in the UK. The actual sale price is assumed to be the gross selling price inclusive of any VAT due. If evidence of export is not obtained within three months then you should account for any VAT due in the next VAT return, though if evidence of export is later obtained, you can then recover this.

Evidence of export

The most onerous requirement is the obligation to obtain proof of export. The documentation must clearly identify the exported goods, prove that those goods were exported and received by a non-EC customer and that the associated financial transaction actually occurred. To prove export you must retain a mix of documents including official HMRC export documentation, the customer's order, sales invoice, consignment note, packing list, insurance and transport documentation, evidence of payment and evidence of receipt by the customer. If you appoint an agent to handle the delivery it is still your responsibility to ensure that adequate documentation is provided by the agent.

For indirect exports obtaining adequate proof of export may be particularly difficult, and HMRC suggest that you take a deposit for any VAT that might be due in case the customer fails to provide appropriate evidence within three months. See also the comments below on the retail export scheme.

See VAT Notice 703 for detailed guidance on what HMRC consider to be acceptable proof of export.

Goods sent to branches of international organisations

There is no supply when a UK organisation sends goods to its own non-EC branch. UK input VAT on such goods can be deducted in the UK VAT return subject to the normal UK rules.

Goods sent to a non-EC branch of another UK VAT-registered organisation can be zero-rated if the supplier is responsible for delivery and all the other zero-rating conditions are met. This applies even if the UK office of the organisation pays for the goods. However they cannot be zero-rated as exports if the customer arranges the delivery.

Goods ordered by British Embassies, High Commissions and diplomats abroad which are delivered to the Foreign and Commonwealth Office (FCO) can be zero-rated provided a certificate of shipment is obtained from the FCO within three months of the supply and the other proof of export evidence is held. However goods supplied to other UK government departments can only be zero-rated if the supplier delivers them to a destination outside the EC.

Goods sent to overseas governments are zero-rated if the normal zero-rating conditions are met. In addition, goods supplied to overseas authorities which are ordered through their embassies, High Commissions or purchasing agents in the UK can be zero-rated if proof is obtained that the goods have been exported within three months and the goods are not used before export either for their normal purpose or for display, exhibition or copying.

Retail export scheme

The retail export scheme is a voluntary scheme that allows retailers to zero rate sales of certain goods to visitors from outside the EC. There is no need to use the scheme for zero-rated goods. Most standard-rated and reduced-rate goods qualify for the scheme, though exceptions include motor vehicles and certain boats, goods over £600 in value to be used for the customer's business purposes, goods that will be exported as freight or unaccompanied baggage, goods requiring an export licence and goods purchased by mail order or over the internet.

The customer must live outside the EC (as evidenced, for example, by producing a non-EC passport) or must demonstrate that, on departure from the EC, they will remain outside the EC for at least 12 months. The customer must intend to leave the UK for a destination outside the EC with the goods by the last day of the third month following the month of purchase and must produce the goods, purchase documentation and a VAT refund claim for certification by an HMRC (or equivalent) officer at the point of departure. Consumable goods must not have been wholly or partly consumed in the EC.

At the point of sale the retailer charges VAT as normal but provides the customer with a VAT refund claim. The retailer is responsible for checking that the customer meets the scheme conditions. Once the goods have been certified at the point of departure the customer then sends the certified refund form to the retailer who refunds the VAT paid after checking that the timing conditions are met. The certified refund document allows the retailer to treat the sale as zero-rated.

For full details of the scheme, see VAT Notice 704: *VAT Retail Exports.*

Imported goods

For VAT purposes goods are imported when they are brought into the UK from a destination outside the EC. VAT is generally payable on imported goods as if they had been purchased within the UK, though there are some exemptions and reliefs, as explained below. This import VAT is due when the goods arrive in the UK, though payment may deferred in certain situations. Import VAT is payable whatever the status of the UK customer – registered and unregistered customers are both liable. VAT-registered customers may treat the import VAT paid as input VAT and recover this subject to the normal rules.

All imported goods must be declared to and cleared by Customs at the point of arrival in the UK. Declaration may be done on paper documents accompanying the goods or electronically. All organisations making imports for business purposes require a Trader's Unique Reference Number (TURN), which can be obtained on application to HMRC. If you are not VAT-registered you will be issued with a 'Pseudo TURN', which must be shown on all import documentation.

Import VAT must be paid in order for the goods to be released by Customs, though there are ways in which this can be avoided:

- For postal consignments (other than International Datapost/EMS packages) valued at under £2,000, if the customer is VAT-registered and the goods are accompanied by a declaration to this effect, no import VAT is charged at the point of entry, but it must be accounted for in the customer's VAT return.

- For International Datapost/EMS packages valued at less than £2,000, import VAT will be charged by the deliverer when the package is delivered.

- A customer may apply for a deferment account. The customer must provide HMRC with security for the amount covered. All import VAT due at the point of entry is charged to the account and HMRC take payments from the account by direct debit at a later date. If the customer's credit limit is exceeded, goods are held by Customs until payment is received or the account is cleared.

After payment of import VAT, HMRC usually issue an Import VAT Certificate to the person holding the TURN shown on the import documentation. This certificate is required as evidence to support any associated input VAT recovery. For postal consignments under £2,000 where no import VAT was due at the point of entry, the stamped import documentation or Datapost receipt must be retained as evidence.

Import VAT exemptions

The following goods are exempt from import VAT.

- Certain goods imported by relevant organisations. A relevant organisation is a registered charity, a state organisation devoted to welfare, or certain other non-profit-making organisations whose objectives are the welfare of the needy. Goods covered are:

  - basic necessities required to meet a person's immediate needs obtained free of charge for distribution free of charge to the needy

  - goods donated by a person established outside the EC for use to raise funds at occasional charity events for the benefit of the needy. There must be no commercial intent on the part of the donor

- equipment and office materials donated by a person established outside the EC for meeting the relevant organisation's operational needs. There must be no commercial intent on the part of the donor

- goods imported for distribution or loan, free of charge, to victims of a disaster affecting the territory of one or more EC countries. The EC Commission must first make a decision authorising the import of the goods, though national governments may pre-empt this decision on condition that they recover any import VAT if the EC fails to make the decision. Goods for the operational needs of the relevant organisation in distributing to victims are also exempted; however materials and equipment intended for rebuilding disaster areas are excluded

- articles donated free of charge to a relevant organisation principally engaged in the education of or provision of assistance to physically disabled persons for loan, hire or transfer other than on a profit-making basis to such persons. The goods must be specifically designed for the education, employment or social advancement of the disabled persons and there must be no commercial intent by the donor. Spare parts, tools and accessories for the goods are also exempted.

These goods are also exempt from any Customs duties that may be due. If VAT and duties are paid, or if it is necessary to pay them in order to get the goods out of Customs quickly, the overpaid taxes can be reclaimed later on.

- Audiovisual materials produced by the UN.

- Capital goods and equipment on transfer of activities from abroad. Goods from a business that has ceased to be carried on outside the EC may be imported without import VAT if they will be used exclusively for a new taxable business activity in the UK. If they will be absorbed into an existing activity no exemption is available. The goods must usually have been imported within 12 months of the non-EC business ceasing and the non-EC business must generally have been carried on for at least 12 months, though these conditions may be waived in special circumstances.

- Goods used to promote trade, such as samples of negligible value, catalogues and other related printed matter, and goods imported solely for demonstration purposes.

- Goods imported for testing, examination or analysis and used for technical or research purposes.

- Any consignment of goods not exceeding £18 in value. Certain goods, such as alcohol and perfume, are excluded.

- Works of art and collectors' pieces imported by approved museums, galleries or other institutions other than for sale. The exhibits must either be supplied free of charge or if charges are made, not supplied in the course or furtherance of a business activity.

- Property acquired as an inheritance by a body incorporated in the UK or Isle of Man solely concerned with carrying on a non-profit-making activity. The incorporated body must have become entitled to the goods as legatee and the property must be imported within two years of the date of entitlement as legatee unless HMRC allow otherwise.

- Goods imported for sale to another EC country, provided the sale would be zero-rated and HMRC are provided with proof that the goods will be removed within one month of importation or a longer period as agreed with HMRC.

Acquisitions, removals and despatches

Goods are said to be acquired when they are brought from another EC state and removed or despatched when sent to another EC state. In addition to normal business supplies, supplies of goods between branches of an organisation in different EC states are deemed to be VATable supplies if the goods are transferred for business purposes.

The basic rules for supply of goods between organisations in different EC states are:

1. If the supply of goods is a business activity of the supplier and the supplier is VAT-registered and supplies them to a VAT-registered customer: the supplier may, subject to various conditions, zero rate the supply. The customer must account for 'acquisition VAT' under the local rules. This means that the customer charges themselves VAT on the supply and can recover this as input VAT subject to the local rules on recovery of input VAT. See 'Business supplies between VAT-registered organisations' below.

2. If an unregistered customer receives acquisitions from VAT-registered suppliers in excess of the acquisition threshold, then it may be required to register for VAT. See 'Registering for acquisitions' below.

3. If the supply of goods is a business activity of the supplier and the supplier is VAT-registered and supplies the goods to an unregistered customer, VAT is charged by the supplier according to the rules of the country of despatch. However, if the supplier is responsible for delivery and the total annual value of such sales to the destination EC country exceeds that country's distance selling threshold, then the supplier must register for VAT in the destination country. That country becomes the place of supply and VAT is charged locally according to the local rules, and the supplier must complete a local VAT return. See 'Distance sales' below.

4. Supplies to embassies, consulates, organisations established by international treaty and NATO forces in other EC states can be zero–rated under conditions similar to those for exports. The supplier must obtain evidence of removal within three months of the supply and the goods must be for the use of the specified body.

Business supplies between VAT-registered organisations

Where a VAT-registered supplier in one EC state supplies goods to a VAT-registered customer in another EC state, the supplier can zero rate the supply and the customer must account for 'acquisition VAT' as if the goods had been purchased from a local VAT-registered supplier. In order to be able to zero rate the supply:

- The supplier must obtain the customer's VAT registration number and show this on the invoice. The supplier must check that the customer's VAT registration number is valid and retain evidence of this check. See Chapter 14 for how to check a VAT registration number.

- The supplier must obtain evidence of removal of the goods. A UK supplier must have removed the goods from the UK within three months of the time of supply. The UK evidence requirements are similar to the evidence requirements for exports.

The effect is to remove distortions of competition presented by different VAT rates in EC member states. For the purchaser of the goods there is no VAT difference between goods purchased locally and goods purchased from other EC states.

Example: Acquisition VAT

Alpha Ltd is VAT-registered in Austria.

Beta Ltd is VAT-registered in Bulgaria. The standard rate of VAT in Bulgaria is 20%.

Alpha sells standard-rated goods to Beta for €100 net. Alpha zero rates its supply in Austria

Beta charges itself 20% x €100 = €20 acquisition VAT (or the Bulgarian equivalent). If this is incurred for taxable business activities it may be recovered in its Bulgarian VAT return as input VAT.

A UK VAT-registered customer must show acquisition VAT separately in box 2 on the VAT return and the net value of acquisitions (EC purchases) in box 9. If the acquisition VAT is recoverable, it is included with other recoverable input VAT in box

4 on the VAT return. A UK VAT-registered supplier must include the value of removals (EC sales) in box 8 on the VAT return. See Chapter 12 for information on how to complete the UK VAT return.

Registering for acquisitions

If an unregistered organisation makes relevant acquisitions above its country's acquisition threshold it must register for VAT. Relevant acquisitions are goods acquired for a business or non-business activity, but not for an exempt activity. The goods must be supplied by a VAT-registered business in another EC state in the course of that supplier's business.

If a UK organisation has made relevant acquisitions in excess of the UK threshold in the period from the last 1 January or expects to exceed the threshold in the next 30 days, it must register within 30 days. UK organisations can register voluntarily and can be exempted from the requirement to register if all acquisitions would be zero-rated. Once an organisation is registered it must charge VAT on all its taxable supplies as well as accounting for VAT on acquisitions.

The latest available acquisition thresholds are:

€10,000	Greece, Spain, France, Luxembourg, Netherlands, Portugal, Slovenia, Finland
Others	Belgium: €11,200; Bulgaria: 20,000 BGN; Czech Republic: 326,000 CZK; Denmark: 80,000 DDK; Germany: €12,500; Estonia: 160,000 EEK; Ireland: €41,000; Italy: €8,263; Cyprus: €10,308; Latvia: 7,000 LVL; Lithuania: 35,000 LTL, Hungary: 2.5m HUF, Austria: €11,000, Poland: 39,700 PLN; Romania: 33,800 RON; Slovakia: 420,000 SKK; Sweden: 90,000 SEK; UK: £64,000

The transfer of goods within a legal entity

If goods are transferred to another branch of the same legal entity located in another EC state and are to be used for the business purposes of that branch, they are removals and acquisitions for VAT purposes and liable for VAT as such. However, this does not include the temporary transfer of goods abroad, for example for use in an exhibition or in a supply of services.

- If both branches are registered for VAT in their respective states then, providing the zero-rating conditions are met, the supplying branch zero rates the removal and the acquiring branch charges itself acquisition VAT.

- If the foreign branch is not registered for VAT locally, but the supplying branch is VAT registered in its EC state, it must charge its country's VAT on the removal. This will be a business activity of the supplying branch, so any attributable input VAT is recoverable. However, any VAT incurred by the foreign branch cannot be recovered.

- If neither branch is registered for VAT no VAT is chargeable by either party, though the receiving branch may need to register locally if its acquisitions exceed that country's acquisition threshold.

Distance selling

Distance sales are sales of goods, made in the course of a business, to unregistered customers in other EC states where the supplier or an agent of the supplier is responsible for the delivery of the goods.

Where a UK supplier makes distance sales, UK VAT is charged at the rates that would apply if the sales had been made to customers in the UK. The sales are not included in box 8 (EC sales) on the VAT return, although they are included as part of UK sales on the return.

However, when the total annual VAT-exclusive value of sales to customers in any particular EC state reaches that state's distance-selling threshold the UK supplier must register for VAT in that state and then charge local VAT on those sales and complete a local VAT return. Businesses may also register voluntarily in the destination state before the distance-selling threshold is reached. The sales are then included in box 8 of the UK VAT return.

Current distance selling thresholds are:

€35,000	Belgium, Czech Republic, Finland, Greece, Hungary, Ireland, Malta, Poland, Romania, Slovakia, Slovenia, Spain
€100,000	Austria, France, Germany, Luxembourg, Netherlands
Others	Cyprus: €34,354; Denmark: 280,000 DKK; Estonia: 550,000 EEK; Italy: €27,889; Latvia: 24,000 LVL; Lithuania: 125,000 LTL; Portugal: €31,424; Sweden: 320,000 SEK; UK: £70,000

The EC sales list

All UK suppliers that supply goods to VAT-registered customers in the EC must complete and submit an EC sales list (ESL). This lists total sales to each customer in the period covered by the return. Normally the ESLs must be submitted quarterly, to arrive within 42 days of the end of the quarter. However there are two concessions:

- suppliers using the annual accounting scheme may submit an annual sales list if their total taxable turnover in the year does not exceed £145,000 and annual sales to other EC states do not exceed £11,000

- suppliers with total taxable sales in the year of less than the VAT registration threshold plus £25,500 and annual sales to other EC states below £11,000 may submit a simplified annual ESL which just lists customers' VAT registration numbers.

Where a UK supplier enters a figure into box 8 on their VAT return they will be automatically sent an EC Sales List (VAT 101). The ESL should:

- include all sales of goods made in the course of a business of the supplier to VAT-registered customers in other EC states

- include all goods removed to a branch in another EC state for business purposes

- exclude all sales of goods to unregistered customers. This includes distance sales

- exclude all supplies of services to EC customers, whether VAT-registered or not

- exclude any export of goods outside the EC.

If a supplier is using the cash accounting scheme, they must nevertheless declare transactions at the date of invoice rather than date of payment.

The Intrastat return

Intrastat is a system for gathering statistics on the trade in goods between EC states. Unregistered businesses and organisations moving goods for non-business purposes are exempt from the Intrastat requirements, as are businesses below the Intrastat assimilation threshold, currently £260,000. Where the level of despatches or arrivals exceeds the assimilation threshold then an Intrastat return must be submitted in respect of despatches or arrivals or both. The return requires a breakdown of despatches or arrivals by international commodity code, showing the nature of the transaction, mass, and destination/source country. See HMRC Notice 60 for further information on completing the Intrastat return.

The supply of services

International services are services supplied across national borders. The VAT liability of international services depends on the 'place of supply' of the services. If the place of supply is:

- **The UK**: then UK VAT is chargeable as if the service was supplied to a UK customer. Non-UK organisations will need to register for VAT in the UK if their total taxable supplies in the UK exceed the UK registration threshold.

- **Another EC state**: VAT may be chargeable in that state under that state's rules. It may be necessary to register for VAT in that state if your total taxable supplies in that state exceed its VAT registration threshold.

- **Outside the EC**: the service is outside the scope of VAT in any EC state and no VAT is chargeable. However, many countries operate tax systems similar to VAT and it may be necessary to register in that country under that country's equivalent system.

Place of supply

The following rules are used for determining the place of supply of services except for services covered by the Tour Operator's Margin Scheme (see Chapter 10) and some financial services.

It is first necessary to determine where the supplier and customer have establishments and where they belong. Establishments take two forms. A business establishment is the place from which the entire organisation is run, usually its head office. An organisation can have only one business establishment. A fixed establishment is an establishment which has the resources necessary for providing or receiving supplies on a permanent basis. Fixed establishments are typically local branches or offices. However, the definition is wider than this. A subsidiary may be a fixed establishment of its parent if it supplies services to the parent that are connected to the supply in question, and an organisation with only a registration address in the UK may have a fixed establishment there if it receives services there.

An organisation belongs in a country if:

- it has establishments in that country but no establishment in any other countries, or

- it has no establishment anywhere but the country is where the organisation is legally constituted, or

- it has an establishment in the country and in one or more other countries, but the establishment in the country is the one most directly connected with the supply. To determine which establishment is most directly connected with a supply the following factors should be considered: where the services are supplied from or used; where the people who entered into the contract are permanently based; where decisions are taken and controls exercised over the performance of the contract; and where invoices, contracts and correspondence are addressed to, though it is possible for services to be supplied to one branch and paid for by another.

The basic rule for the supply of services is: the place of supply is where the supplier belongs. This means that the supplier charges VAT in the state where it belongs. However there are many exceptions, and most services fall into one of the exceptions. The main exceptions are:

- services related to land

- services involving physical performance

- supplies of transport and ancillary services

- certain services specified in Schedule 5 to the VAT Act 1994 ('Schedule 5 services').

Each of these exceptions is examined below.

At the time of writing, it seems likely that the 'place of supply' rules will be modified from 2010 onwards – see the section below. The basic rule for the supply of business to business services will be modified. The default place of supply will be where the customer belongs. However, the basic rule for business to customer supplies will remain where the supplier belongs.

The reverse charge

In some situations the basic rule that the supplier charges VAT is reversed. This is known as the 'reverse charge':

- The supplier treats the supply as if it were zero-rated. No VAT is added to the invoice value and for recovery purposes the supplier can treat it like a supply to a local customer.

- The customer must charge themselves output VAT on the invoice value. The customer calculates the VAT according to the rules applicable in the customer's EC state. The customer adds this charge to the output VAT box on their VAT return. The effect is that, from the customer's perspective, the VAT cost of purchasing the supply from local or foreign suppliers is the same.

- The customer can then recover this output VAT charge as input VAT subject to their country's normal VAT deduction rules. Again the effect is to equalise the VAT treatment between supplies purchased from abroad and supplies purchased locally.

Example: The reverse charge

A VAT-registered UK organisation receives consultancy services for business purposes from a Greek consultancy firm. The Greek firm charges €1,000 net of any VAT.

The Greek firm's bill is for €1,000, and no VAT is added.

In the UK consultancy services are standard-rated and attract VAT at 17½%

The UK organisation must credit its UK VAT account with 17.5% x €1,000 = €175.

This may be treated as input VAT and can be recovered if it is attributable to the UK organisation's taxable activities.

The reverse charge never applies to exempt supplies. For some types of taxable supply the reverse charge is required under EC law and must be implemented by every EC state. For certain other supplies it is an option that can be implemented by EC states in particular situations if they so choose. The UK has opted to extend the reverse charge to all applicable situations, as explained in more detail below, but the situation varies across the EC.

Where a UK VAT-registered customer receives a reverse charge supply they should:

- account for any reverse charge VAT due on the supply in box 1 of the VAT return

- include any recoverable element of this in box 4 (input VAT)

- include the net value of the supply in box 6 (outputs) and in box 7 (inputs).

Reverse charge evidence requirements

In order to justify reversing a VAT charge the supplier must retain appropriate evidence that the qualifying conditions are met. Where the service is supplied to a VAT registered EC customer, this should include the customer's VAT registration number and this should also be included on the invoice. The supplier must take reasonable steps to check that the VAT registration is genuine, such as checking that the VAT number is in the correct format for the country concerned and is held at the customer's address. The validity of a VAT number can be checked using the EC's online VIES system, but to check if the number is associated with a particular address you must contact HMRC by phone. See Chapter 14 for information on checking VAT numbers.

For electronically supplied services a UK supplier must verify an unverified customer's VAT registration number if sales to that customer exceed £500 in a VAT quarter.

If there is any doubt as to whether the customer will put the supply to business or non-business purposes then the supplier should obtain written confirmation from the customer that they will be using the services for business purposes. There is likely to be doubt if the customer cannot provide a VAT registration number or is a charity, philanthropic organisation or government body.

Services related to land

Services related to land include hotel accommodation, property management services, property construction and maintenance services, legal services connected to land such as conveyancing and related engineering and professional services.

The basic rule for services related to land is that they are supplied where the land is located. This means that a UK business making taxable supplies of services related to land situated in another EC state does not charge UK VAT on the supply, but may have to register in the other EC state and charge local VAT if the total value of taxable supplies in that state exceeds its VAT registration threshold. If the land is outside the EC then the supply is outside the scope of both UK and EC VAT.

However, EC states have the option of allowing the reverse charge to apply to such transactions if the customer is registered for VAT and receiving the supply for business purposes.

The UK has implemented this option. So, if a foreign business makes a taxable supply of services related to land that is situated in the UK to a VAT-registered UK customer who is using the supply for business purposes, the UK customer must account for VAT under the reverse charge. If the foreign business makes the supply to an unregistered customer or a UK-registered customer using the supply for non-business purposes, it does not charge any VAT but must register for VAT in the UK if the total value of such supplies, together with any other taxable supplies made in the UK, exceeds the UK VAT registration threshold.

The position in other EC states varies. If a UK business supplies services related to land situated in an EC state that has implemented the option, then if the customer is registered in that state and receiving the supply for business purposes they account for VAT under the reverse charge. If the customer is not registered or is not receiving the supply for business purposes then the UK business may have to register in that state and charge local VAT if it exceeds the state's registration threshold.

Services involving physical performance

Services involving physical performance include face-to-face education and training, services of entertainers before live audiences, work on moveable tangible property, and services related to exhibitions, conferences and meetings.

The basic rule for services involving physical performance is that they are supplied where performed. So a UK organisation organising a taxable conference in another EC state may be making a supply in that state and so is required to register in that state if the level of income exceeds that state's VAT registration threshold. If a UK organisation organises a conference outside the EC then the place of supply may be outside the EC so no UK or EC VAT is chargeable.

However, as with services related to land, EC states have the option of allowing the reverse charge to apply to services involving physical performance if the customer is registered for VAT and receiving the supply for business purposes.

The UK has implemented this option. If a UK organisation makes a taxable supply of services involving physical performance in an EC state that has also implemented the option, and the customer is locally registered and receiving the supply for business purposes, then the UK supplier does not charge VAT and the customer must account for VAT under the reverse charge. If the UK organisation makes the supply to an unregistered customer or to an organisation receiving the supply for non-business purposes, then no VAT is charged unless that state's registration threshold is exceeded, in which case the UK organisation must register in that state and charge local VAT.

Exhibitions and conferences

For exhibitions and conferences, the place of supply for the sale of tickets by the organiser will be where the event is held. However, if the tickets are supplied together with transport or accommodation the Tour Operator's Margin Scheme may apply (see Chapter 10). Services provided in organising an event will be supplied where they are carried out, which may be different from the event location. A comprehensive package of services related to a stand space (for example, a package of stand space, design, and construction) is likely to be supplied where the exhibition is.

Transport and ancillary services

Transport and ancillary services comprise the supply of passenger or freight transport services. They include transport by air, sea, rail and road. Transport services are supplied in the country in which the transport takes place. If a journey involves several countries it is necessary to apportion the supply between the countries involved. For air and sea journeys, where the journey involves crossing another country's territory without stopping there, the section in that country's territory can be ignored. Note that a supply consisting of a package of transport and accommodation may come under the Tour Operator's Margin Scheme (see Chapter 10).

As with services related to land and services involving physical performance, the UK has extended the reverse charge to cover passenger transport services. So, if a non-UK supplier of passenger transport makes a supply to a UK VAT-registered business receiving the supply for business purposes, then the UK business must account for any VAT under the reverse charge. Note that in the UK many passenger transport services are zero-rated (see Chapter 6).

If a non-UK supplier makes a supply to a non-VAT-registered UK business or to a UK customer using the supply for non-business purposes, the supplier must register for UK VAT and charge VAT if the UK registration threshold is exceeded.

For UK suppliers making supplies of passenger transport in other EC states, the position will depend on whether that state has extended the reverse charge to cover passenger transport. If not, the UK supplier may have to register in that state if its VAT registration threshold is exceeded. Supplies of passenger transport made entirely outside the EC are outside the scope of VAT. See VAT Notices 741 and 744B if you are involved in providing freight transport services.

Schedule 5 services

Schedule 5 to the VAT Act 1994 specifies special treatment for certain intellectual services commonly traded across national borders. The intention is to equalise the treatment of these services across the EC. The affected services are:

1 Transfers and assignments of copyright, patents, licences, trademarks and similar rights. Rights must be capable of being legally enforced and be connected with intellectual property.

2 Advertising services. These include the display of a sponsor's name or product by a sponsored person in return for sponsorship payments and advertising in all forms of media, including press, magazines, TV and radio and placement on advertising hoardings and on the internet.

3 Services of professionals and consultants such as engineers, consultancy bureaux, lawyers, accountants and other similar services, data processing and the provision of information. However, any services that relate to land are supplied where the land is located. The intention is to cover services provided by professionals only but exclude routine administrative or clerical staff. Services include written translation services (though oral translation services are supplied where performed), software development and support.

'Data processing' here is the programmatic analysis of data. The provision of information covers the supply of knowledge of any type and in any form and includes telephone helpdesk services, the provision of online information and the provision of digitised publications which are non-fiction

4   Acceptance of any obligation to refrain from pursuing or exercising, in whole or part, any business activity or any intellectual property rights.

5   Banking, financial and insurance services.

6   The supply of staff. A supply of staff is the placing of personnel under the general control and guidance of another party as if they become employees of that other party. A supply of specific services where the staff involved remain under the supplier's control is not a supply of staff but of the services concerned.

7   The hire of goods. This includes the leasing of all goods which are moveable property but excludes means of transport, land and property or equipment and machinery installed as a fixture. It also excludes supplies which include the services of an operator or technician. Where goods are hired under HP-type agreements where ownership will pass at some point, this is a supply of goods and not of services.

7A Telecommunication services. These include provision of web and email services, the provision of teleconferencing, access to global networks and charges for transmission capacity.

7B Radio and TV broadcasting services, including subscriptions to broadcast services.

7C Electronically supplied services. An electronically supplied service is one that is delivered over the internet or a similar electronic network and is essentially automated, involving minimal human intervention. Examples include web hosting, automated remote support and maintenance, down-loaded software, downloaded images, music, films, text and games, online database access and online information services. However services merely supplied over the internet that require substantial human intervention, such as services of consultants, are not included.

8   The services rendered by one person to another in procuring any of the above services.

The basic rule for Schedule 5 services is:

• **Customer belongs outside the EC**: the place of supply is where the customer belongs. The transaction is therefore outside the scope of VAT. A UK-based VAT-registered supplier charges no VAT. However, UK input VAT attributable to the supply is recoverable if it would have been had the supply been to a customer in the UK.

- **Customer belongs in the EC and receives the supply for business purposes**: the place of supply is where the customer belongs. A UK-based supplier does not charge VAT but attributable UK input VAT is recoverable as if the customer had been in the UK. If the customer is locally registered, they must account for local VAT under the reverse charge. If the customer isn't registered for VAT but receives the supply for taxable business purposes, the value of the supply counts towards the customer's VAT registration threshold.

- **Customer belongs in the EC and receives the supply for non-business purposes**: the place of supply is where the supplier belongs. A UK-based VAT-registered supplier charges UK VAT as if the supply was made to a customer in the UK.

- **Other situations**: if the supplier cannot determine where the customer belongs, or if the supplier cannot determine whether an EC customer will put the services to a business or non-business purpose, the place of supply is where the supplier belongs.

However, there are special rules for items 7: The hire of goods, 7A: Telecommunication services, 7B: Radio and TV broadcasting and 7C: Electronically supplied services. The special rules are known as the 'use and enjoyment' rules and affect supplies by non-EC suppliers that are used and enjoyed in the UK, and supplies by UK suppliers that are used and enjoyed outside the EC. Use and enjoyment occurs where the services are consumed.

For the hire of goods, telecommunication services and radio and TV broadcasting services:

- Such services that would, under the above rules, be treated as supplied in the UK are treated as supplied outside the EC to the extent they are used and enjoyed outside the EC.

- Similarly, such services that would under the above rules be considered supplied outside the EC are considered supplied in the UK to the extent they are used and enjoyed in the UK. This means that a non-EC supplier providing these services to non-business customers consuming them in the UK must register in the UK and charge UK VAT on its supply if such sales exceeds the UK registration threshold.

These 'use and enjoyment' modifications also apply to electronically supplied services provided to business customers. However, the use and enjoyment rules do not apply to electronically supplied services provided to non-business customers. A non-EC supplier making electronically supplied services to non-business EC customers must register for VAT in an EC state and charge that state's VAT to its non-business EC customers. Suppliers can choose which state to register in, and it does not matter where the customer uses and enjoys the services.

Supplies of services after 2010

At the time of writing it seems likely that there will be major changes to the place of supply of service rules from 1 January 2010 onwards. These changes include:

- the basic place of supply rule (where the supplier belongs) will remain for business-to-customer (B2C) supplies, however for business-to-business (B2B) supplies it will become where the customer belongs – affected B2B supplies will be made under reverse charge

- EC sales lists will have to include B2B supplies of services.

10 VAT special schemes

There are many special VAT schemes that apply in particular situations. Some are mandatory and you must apply the scheme if the circumstances require, others are optional and can be applied if you meet the scheme's conditions. Generally, VAT schemes are designed to simplify VAT administration or reduce the burden of VAT for particular types of business or for particular situations. The schemes considered below are:

Mandatory schemes	Optional schemes
• Capital goods scheme • Tour Operators' Margin Scheme • Reverse charge scheme for purchases of mobile phones and computer chips	• Cash accounting scheme • Annual accounting scheme • Margin scheme for second-hand goods, works of art, antiques etc. • The retail schemes • Flat rate scheme for small businesses • Agricultural flat rate scheme • Listed places of worship scheme • Memorials scheme • Galleries and museums scheme

In addition, arrangements and specially devised schemes that result in a tax advantage are subject to special anti-avoidance rules. Under the 'Halifax principles', an arrangement resulting in a tax advantage may be set aside under particular circumstances and the use of certain 'listed' or 'hallmarked' schemes must be reported to HMRC. These issues are considered in the section on VAT mitigation schemes.

Capital goods scheme

Normally if you purchase goods or services that will be used for mixed taxable and exempt activities, VAT is recovered according to the partial exemption calculations for the period in which the expenditure is incurred, with an adjustment in the year-end annual adjustment. VAT recovery is thus determined by the level of taxable use in the year of purchase. However, for certain 'capital items', the capital goods scheme requires you to make adjustments to this VAT recovery in subsequent years if there is any change in the taxable use of the capital item.

For example, if you purchased a new building for £1 million plus VAT of £175,000 and the building was used 80 per cent for taxable activities in the year of acquisition, you would be entitled to recover 80 per cent of the £175,000 VAT. However, if taxable use dropped to 50 per cent in year two, some of this VAT would be repayable under the capital goods scheme to reflect the decreased taxable usage.

The capital goods scheme mainly affects the purchase, construction or acquisition of certain assets that will be used for mixed taxable and exempt activities. However, it can also have consequences for fully taxable activities.

Capital items

The capital goods scheme applies to the purchase, construction, alteration or renovation of certain 'capital items'. See below for how capital items are valued. Capital items are:

- Land and buildings valued at £250,000 or more, net of VAT. The buildings may be purchased (freehold or leasehold) or constructed, and alterations, annexes and extensions are included if they are valued at £250,000 or more and increase total floor area by 10 per cent or more.

- Refurbishments are included from 2 July 1997 if the value of any capital works that are incorporated into the fabric of the building is £250,000 or more. Capital works are works that would be capitalised for accounting purposes – that is works that give rise to or enhance a fixed asset. Generally, works will be incorporated into the fabric of a building if they will be sold with the property and are not portable or easily removed. By concession, you can include the cost of items not incorporated if it is difficult to distinguish them.

- Civil engineering works valued at £250,000 or more where the civil engineering work was first brought into use on or after 2 July 1997. Civil engineering works include roads, bridges, golf courses, running tracks and drainage works.

- A computer or item of computer equipment valued at £50,000 or more. A purchased computer or item of computer equipment is covered by the scheme only if it cost £50,000 or more on its own. This includes any delivery or installation charges unless these are invoiced separately. The scheme does not apply to networks or bulk purchases where the total cost exceeds £50,000 but no individual item exceeds £50,000. It also does not apply to computerised equipment such as telephone exchanges, software and equipment acquired for resale or sold before it is used.

Capital item value

The value of a capital item is the cost that bore VAT, that is, the taxable costs that were standard-rated or reduced rate excluding any VAT paid. If any costs were exempt or zero-rated they are excluded when determining the capital item's value.

If the capital item was also purchased partly for non-business use then the value depends on how you decide to treat the item:

- If you opt to treat it as a mixed business/non-business asset then the value is the VAT-bearing cost of the business component only and excludes the cost of the non-business component.

- If you opt to treat it as a business asset and account for output VAT on any non-business use (the Lennartz scheme, see Chapter 4), then the value of the capital item is the VAT-exclusive cost of the standard-rated and reduced-rate supplies. Any non-business use counts as taxable use for the purposes of the capital goods scheme as the non-business use is a deemed taxable supply.

- If you opt to treat it as a non-business asset then the capital goods scheme does not apply unless there is a deemed self-supply from the business use of the asset, for example, as with a building intended for relevant charitable or residential use (see Chapter 8). In this case the value of the self-supply must exceed £250,000 to bring it within the scheme.

For land and buildings and civil engineering works, professional fees such as architects' and surveyors' fees are included but associated costs such as legal fees and estate agents' costs are excluded. For leases, rent is excluded from the value unless it is payable more than 12 months in advance or is invoiced for a period exceeding 12 months.

The value of a capital item is normally assessed when it is first put to business use. If you do not know the cost of an item at this point but estimate that it will exceed the capital goods scheme limits then you should apply the capital goods scheme, and the scheme will continue to apply even if the actual cost turns out to be less.

Where refurbishment work takes place in phases, it may be possible to treat the phases as separate works if they are carried out under separate contracts or are separate options in a single contract or each phase is completed before work starts on the next.

Adjustment periods

There are:

- 10 adjustment periods for land, buildings and civil engineering works where the interest will last for 10 years or more, for example freeholds or leases lasting 10 years or more

- five adjustment periods for land, buildings and civil engineering works where the interest will last for less than 10 years. If a lease lasts for less than five years then there are still five adjustment periods but a final adjustment occurs in the period when the lease expires – see below

- five adjustment periods for computer equipment.

The first adjustment period runs from the date the capital item is first put to business use by its owner. If the item is initially put to exclusive non-business use then the capital goods scheme is only triggered when business use starts. If a business has a capital item on hand and in business use at registration the first adjustment period runs from the date of registration. The first adjustment period runs to the end of the VAT year. Subsequent adjustment periods normally correspond to complete VAT years, though if the item is disposed of during an adjustment period the subsequent adjustment periods are cancelled and a final adjustment is made in the period of disposal, as explained below.

Adjustment calculations

In the first adjustment period input VAT on the capital item is recovered in accordance with the partial exemption method in place. If the capital item is residual, the recovery percentage for the capital item will be the residual recovery percentage determined by the organisation's partial exemption method. If this recovery percentage does not fairly represent actual use of the capital item, you should agree a special method with HMRC to be applied to the item. Any such agreement should be in writing.

If VAT is accounted for quarterly, input VAT is initially recovered using the recovery percentage for the quarter of acquisition, and then recovery is recalculated in the annual adjustment at the end of the first period.

The recovery percentage applied to the capital item in the first annual adjustment is the baseline against which future capital goods scheme adjustments will be made. No capital goods scheme adjustment is made in the first adjustment period, as this period is used to determine the baseline. In subsequent adjustment periods the capital item's recovery percentage, as calculated in that period's annual adjustment, is used to calculate an adjustment percentage for the capital item as follows:

Adjustment percentage $=$ Baseline percentage $-$ Capital item's recovery percentage for the adjustment period

If the adjustment percentage is positive, VAT will be due to HMRC. If the adjustment percentage is negative, VAT will be recoverable from HMRC. The VAT adjustment is then:

$$\frac{\text{Total input VAT incurred on the capital item}}{\text{Number of adjustment periods}} \quad \text{x} \quad \text{Adjustment percentage}$$

This VAT adjustment is made in the second VAT return of the following tax year, i.e. the VAT return following the return in which the annual adjustment is made.

Example: Basic capital goods scheme adjustment

A business purchases the freehold of a new commercial building for £4 million plus VAT of £700,000. The business treats the building as residual and in the first adjustment period the residual recovery percentage calculated in the annual adjustment is 30%.

This is the building's baseline percentage. The business reclaims 30% x £700,000 = £210,000 of the VAT incurred under the normal partial exemption rules.

In the second adjustment period the residual recovery percentage calculated in the annual adjustment is 20%. This is a drop in taxable use from the baseline so VAT is due to HMRC. The amount due is (£700,000 / 10) x (30% - 20%) = £7,000.

In the third adjustment period the residual recovery percentage calculated in the annual adjustment is 35%. This is an increase in taxable use from the baseline so VAT is due from HMRC. The amount recoverable is (£700,000 / 10) x (35% - 30%) = £3,500

This calculation is repeated for a total of 10 adjustment periods or until the building is disposed of.

Phased payment

In practice payment for many construction, alteration and renovation works will be phased so the costs are incurred over an extended period of time. VAT on invoices

199

incurred up to the end of the first adjustment period is recovered according to the partial exemption method in place. At the end of the first adjustment period the cost of the item is assessed, and if it is determined that the item falls within the capital goods scheme the baseline percentage is calculated as the total VAT recovered to date on the capital item divided by the total VAT incurred to date on the capital item.

Example: Phased payment

A business pays VAT on construction costs for a building as follows:

VAT year	Total VAT incurred	Partial exemption recovery percentage for the year	VAT recovered under normal partial exemption rules
2007–08	£50,000	50%	50% x £50,000 = £25,000
2008–09	£30,000	40%	40% x £30,000 = £12,000
2009–10	£40,000	30%	30% x £40,000 = £12,000
Totals	£120,000		£49,000

The building is first used in 2009–10. The baseline percentage is £49,000 / £120,000 = 40.83%

If input VAT is incurred after the end of the first adjustment period then the VAT incurred is recovered subject to the normal partial exemption method for the period involved. The capital goods scheme calculation is then amended at the end of the following period. There are two ways of doing this:

- the combined adjustment method involves re-calculating the baseline percentage and using the revised baseline percentage in the remaining adjustment periods

- the parallel adjustment method involves carrying out separate calculations for each component for the remaining adjustment periods.

Example: Combined adjustment method

In the above example, assume the business incurs additional input VAT of £20,000 in 2010–11 and the recovery percentage for 2010–11 is 40%.

In 2010–11 the business recovers 40% x £20,000 = £8,000 of this extra VAT under the normal partial exemption rules. The baseline percentage for the period remains 40.83% and the capital goods scheme adjustment is:

(40.83% - 40%) x (£120,000) / 10 = £99.60 due to HMRC

The baseline percentage for 2011–12 and following periods is adjusted to:

(£49,000 + £8,000) / (£120,000 + £20,000) = 40.71%

Note that capital goods scheme adjustments are excluded when calculating revised baseline percentages.

See VAT Notice 706/2 for an example of how the parallel adjustment method works and for sample spreadsheets illustrating how to perform all scheme calculations.

Disposal of a capital item

If a capital item is disposed of after the end of the last adjustment period then there is no capital goods scheme adjustment as the item is fully depreciated for capital goods scheme purposes. If a capital item is disposed of during one of the adjustment periods then, unless the disposal is a part of a transfer of a going concern, at the end of the adjustment period of disposal a final adjustment must be carried out. This has two components:

1. A normal capital goods scheme adjustment is carried out in respect of use during that period. This is calculated as if the item had been in use throughout the period and based on use during the part of the period before disposal.

2. For any remaining adjustment periods use is assumed to be 100 per cent taxable if the disposal was a taxable supply and 100 per cent exempt if the disposal was an exempt supply. However, if the sale is standard-rated, the total amount that may be deducted in respect of the remaining periods is limited to the output VAT charged on the disposal.

Example: Capital goods scheme disposal

A partly exempt business purchased a computer for £60,000 plus VAT of £10,500. The recovery percentage in the first adjustment period was 50%. The business disposes of the computer for £10,000 plus VAT of £1,750 in the third adjustment period, when the recovery percentage is 30%.

The normal capital goods scheme adjustment for the third period is (50% – 30%) x £10,500 / 5 = £420 due to HMRC.

The adjustment for the fourth and fifth periods is 2 x (100% - 50%) x £10,500 / 5 = £2,100 due from HMRC. However, this is limited to the VAT charged on the disposal, i.e.: £1,750.

So the net VAT due from HMRC is £1,750 - £420 = £1,330

If a lease lasts for less than five years then a final adjustment is carried out in respect of the adjustment period of termination, though there is no need to allow for any remaining adjustment periods. If a capital item is lost, stolen or destroyed then no adjustment need be made for remaining complete adjustment periods.

Disposal of capital items used for fully taxable purposes

The final adjustment can have an unexpected consequence for fully taxable businesses. If a new commercial building (standard-rated – see Chapter 8) is purchased and used for fully taxable activities but is disposed of after three years (so the disposal is exempt) but before the expiry of the last capital goods scheme adjustment period, then use during the remaining adjustment periods is deemed to be exempt and a capital goods scheme adjustment must be made. For example, if the building is disposed of at the end of the fifth adjustment period, half the input VAT recovered on the purchase must be repaid.

The seller can get around this by opting to tax the building before it is disposed of. If the purchaser cannot disapply the option, this makes the sale standard-rated and no capital goods scheme adjustment need be made provided the total VAT charged on the sale is more than the final adjustment VAT.

Avoidance schemes

For disposals that are part of a scheme to generate an 'unjustified tax advantage', an anti-avoidance provision called the 'disposal test' may apply. This limits the total VAT that can be recovered on the item (including the initial VAT recovery, capital goods scheme adjustments and final adjustment) to the VAT chargeable on disposal of the item. The disposal test is not intended to apply to bona fide commercial transactions and businesses need only apply the disposal test if there is an 'unjustified tax advantage'. HMRC's position on the disposal test is explained in VAT Notice 706/2 and HMRC state that the disposal test will not be applied to sales of computer equipment, or where items are sold at a loss due to market conditions, depreciation or the need for a quick sale, or where the item was only used for taxable purposes in the final adjustment period.

Disposal is part of a transfer of a going concern

If the capital item is disposed of as part of a transfer of a going concern then no final adjustment is undertaken by the seller. The seller must make a normal adjustment for the period of disposal, then the new owner takes over responsibility for the adjustments for subsequent periods, unless the new owner is also taking over the seller's VAT registration number, in which case the new owner is responsible for the adjustment relating to the period of disposal also. The purchaser of a going concern must check for the presence of capital items in the transfer and obtain full details of any such items.

Other considerations

Adjustments made under the capital goods scheme should be ignored when calculating whether exempt activity is *de minimis* (see Chapter 3). If a capital item is not put to any use for a period of time, the use during that period is deemed to be the same as it was before it went out of use. If a capital item is put to non-business use and it was treated as a business asset at acquisition, then output VAT may be due on the non-business use (see Chapter 4). In this situation the non-business use is a deemed taxable supply so it is treated as taxable use for capital goods scheme purposes.

See VAT Notice 706/2 for full details of the capital goods scheme.

Tour Operators' Margin Scheme

Despite its name, the Tour Operators' Margin Scheme (or TOMS) is not limited to tour operators. It is likely to apply to any organisation that buys in and resells, in its own name, travel or accommodation services ('margin scheme supplies') or packages that include these. The scheme is mandatory – if your supply fits the scheme conditions, you must use TOMS.

The scheme was designed as an EC-wide simplification measure, allowing tour operators to avoid having to register for VAT in every EC state they operate in. However it also applies to supplies that are enjoyed entirely within the UK and supplies that are enjoyed entirely outside the EC.

Overview

Under TOMS, supplies are classified as follows:

- **margin scheme supplies**: these are broadly bought in supplies of accommodation or passenger transport that you re-supply to your customers in your own name and without material alteration. Margin scheme supplies are referred to in the UK legislation as 'designated travel services'

- **in-house supplies**: these are supplies that you make from your own resources or bought in supplies that you make an onward supply of after material alteration, for example a supply of accommodation in your own hotel (own resources) or a leased coach which you use to provide passenger transport using your own driver (bought in subject to material alteration)

- **agency supplies**: these are supplies that you make as agent of a principal. For example if you offer optional insurance cover, this will usually be supplied as agent of the insurance company

- **margin scheme packages**: a package that includes one or more margin scheme supplies together with in-house or agency supplies, for example, a package of in-house passenger transport and bought-in accommodation in an independently run hotel.

Under TOMS, the normal VAT rules are modified for margin scheme supplies:

1. Output VAT is due on the margin (selling price less purchase price) rather than on the selling price. It is the margin that counts towards your taxable turnover and the margin that is used in partial exemption calculations.

2. The output VAT charge is calculated on an annual basis (the 'annual adjustment') using whole year figures. The annual adjustment is also used to calculate a provisional figure for the percentage of TOMS income that is standard-rated during the following year. This percentage is applied to the TOMS income each quarter to calculate the provisional output VAT charge for that quarter. At the end of the year another annual adjustment is carried out with a balancing payment made or refund claimed to adjust the provisional output VAT payments made in the year.

3. Under UK law, the annual adjustment must be carried out in accordance with the rules set out in sections 8–11 of VAT Notice 709/5/04. However, the VAT Notice is incompatible with decisions of the European Court of Justice, and you may be able to rely on these decisions to use an alternative method.

4. The VAT status rules are different. Normally, VAT status is determined by the nature of the supply, for example, a supply of UK hotel accommodation is standard-rated and certain supplies of UK passenger transport are zero-rated. However, under TOMS VAT status is determined by where the supply is 'enjoyed'. 'Enjoyed' means where it is used or consumed by the traveller. If a margin scheme supply is enjoyed in the EC the margin is standard-rated. If it is enjoyed outside the EC the margin is zero-rated. If it is enjoyed partly in the EC and partly outside the EC, it must be apportioned between standard- and zero-rated.

5. You cannot recover any input VAT that is incurred in purchasing margin scheme supplies. However input VAT on in-house costs and the indirect costs of margin scheme supplies is recoverable in the normal way.

6. The 'place of supply' rules are different. The place of supply is where the supplier is established and not, for example, where transport takes place or where accommodation is situated. This allows UK suppliers to avoid registration in other EC states when they make margin scheme supplies in those states, and it allows non-UK suppliers to avoid UK registration when they make margin scheme supplies in the UK.

7. The 'time of supply' rules are different. Under TOMS, the time of supply is the earlier of when the traveller departs or first occupies any accommodation.

TOMS and charities

Charities may have to use TOMS if:

- they supply travel or accommodation as part of a challenge event and the participant must pay a specified amount before departure. Challenge events are covered in detail in Chapter 7. This section deals with the practical aspects of operating TOMS

- they organise training, conferences, sporting, cultural or other events and supply access to the event as a package with travel or sleeping accommodation

- they supply a package holiday or similar. If you just supply your own holiday accommodation then the rules in Chapter 8 apply. However, if you buy in and re-sell holiday accommodation or supply your own holiday accommodation together with transport, travel, excursions and so on for a single price then TOMS is likely to apply.

For an activity to be within the scope of TOMS, it must be a business activity. So if you provide, for example, free or heavily subsidised holidays they may be outside the scope of VAT altogether as a non-business activity – see Chapter 4. Supplies of travel and accommodation as part of an exempt supply of care or education may also be ancillary to the exempt supply and so outside TOMS. See Chapter 5.

VAT Notice 709/5 explains TOMS in detail. If you are or will be making TOMS supplies a thorough reading of the notice is essential, but you must bear in mind that the 2004 version of the notice (the current version at the time of writing) is incompatible with ECJ case law in some areas, as explained below.

Most voluntary organisations offering package travel will have to comply with the Package Travel Regulations (PTR) and, if air flights are provided, the Air Travel Organisers' Licensing (ATOL) Regulations. The PTR cover packages offered for sale in the UK that last longer than 24 hours or include overnight accommodation. The PTR specify the way packages are advertised and marketed, the contractual requirements and the supplier's responsibilities to the customer.

The ATOL Regulations require anyone selling air travel, either on its own or as part of a package, to hold an ATOL licence. However there are exceptions for the authorised agent of an ATOL holder and airline ticketing agents who issue scheduled airline tickets. In practice most voluntary organisations providing flights will either act as agent of an ATOL holder or obtain their own ATOL licence. It is possible to act as agent of an ATOL holder for the supply of flights but as principal for other supplies – this is explained below. See Chapter 14 for PTR and CAA / ATOL web links.

Scope of TOMS

With various exceptions TOMS applies whenever all the following conditions are met:

1. **margin scheme supplies**: you make margin scheme supplies as part of a business activity. The margin scheme supplies can be provided on their own or as part of a package together with other supplies. Margin scheme supplies are supplies of goods or services that you buy in and re-supply without material alteration and are of a type normally provided by tour operators or travel agents such as accommodation or passenger transport

2. **principal or undisclosed agent**: you provide the supply as principal or undisclosed agent. Undisclosed agent means you act as agent of a principal but the identity of the principal is not routinely disclosed to your customer (see Chapter 11 for more on principals and agents)

3. **status of the customer**: the supply is not made to a business for subsequent resale ('wholesale supplies') - though by concession wholesale supplies may be included within TOMS under certain circumstances.

Each of these conditions is explained further below. When you provide in-house or agency supplies as part of a package that includes one or more margin scheme supplies (a 'margin scheme package') the whole package must be dealt with under TOMS unless the margin scheme supplies are incidental or ancillary to the other package supplies. The normal VAT rules apply to the in-house and agency components, however the TOMS annual adjustment calculates the output VAT due on the in-house and agency components for you – you do not have to calculate these separately.

Margin scheme supplies will be ancillary or incidental to other package supplies when:

*   the margin scheme supplies do not constitute for customers an aim in themselves, but a means of better enjoying the in-house supplies, and the margin scheme supplies comprise a 'small proportion' of the package price, or

- when they do not include accommodation or passenger transport and you do not expect your total gross turnover from the margin scheme supplies to be more than 1 per cent of your total gross turnover.

Principal or undisclosed agent

Generally, TOMS only applies if you are supplying a margin scheme supply or margin scheme package as principal or undisclosed agent. 'Undisclosed agent' means you act as agent but the identity of the principal is not revealed to the customer.

You will usually be acting as agent of a principal if both of the following conditions are met:

- Both you and the principal have agreed that you will act as their agent. Normally, an agent will have a contract with the principal that sets out the basis of the agency and grants the agent power to bind the principal in a contract with the customer. An agency contract will normally state this explicitly.

- You are not taking any significant commercial risk in relation to the services you are arranging. If you risk significant financial liability should something go wrong or should take-up be poor then you are likely to be taking a significant commercial risk, even if you take steps to mitigate the risk, for example by insurance cover.

If you are an agent, then you are a disclosed agent if you routinely disclose to the customer the fact that you are acting as agent and provide details of the principal, for example on tickets and in the booking terms and conditions. If no such information is routinely disclosed to customers then you are an undisclosed agent.

If the other scheme conditions are met and a margin scheme supply or margin scheme package is provided as:

- **Principal or undisclosed agent**: It is within TOMS. If you are an undisclosed agent you are treated as if you are the principal, that is, your principal supplies the margin scheme supplies or packages to you and you re-supply them to your customers.

- **Disclosed agent**: It is not in TOMS unless you cannot identify your commission. If you cannot identify your commission the income you receive from the agency supplies and the payments you make to your principal must be included in the TOMS calculations.

A common example of a disclosed agency supply is travel insurance. Travel insurance is frequently offered as an optional extra to a travel package. If all you do is arrange a policy between your customer and the insurance company so the customer is the insured party then you are likely to be considered an agent for the insurance company.

If your commission is readily identifiable, the sale of insurance policies is dealt with outside TOMS. If the commission is not readily identifiable, the sale of insurance is included in TOMS, as explained below.

Margin scheme supplies

A margin scheme supply (also known as a designated travel service) is a supply that meets all of the following conditions:

1. It is of a type ordinarily made by travel agents and tour operators. HMRC regard this as including: accommodation, passenger transport, hire of a means of transport, use of special lounges at airports, trips or excursions and the services of (hired) tour guides. In addition, HMRC consider the following to be margin scheme supplies when provided as part of a package with accommodation, passenger transport etc.: catering, admission tickets and sports facilities.

2. The supply is bought in and supplied for the benefit of a traveller without material alteration or further processing. Material alteration means the nature of the supply has been changed. If a supply has been subject to material alteration then it is an in-house supply (see below).

3. It is supplied from a business establishment in the UK. The place of supply of margin scheme supplies is the business establishment where the supply is organised and put together. For UK-based suppliers, this means margin scheme supplies are subject to the UK rules. However, if, for example, you have a subsidiary or office in France which arranges a margin scheme supply, the place of supply is France and the French VAT rules apply. Here we consider the UK rules.

Under the UK rules, the VAT on margin scheme supplies is calculated on the margin (gross sales value less direct costs). The VAT status of the margin is:

*   **EC sales**: Standard-rated if the supply is enjoyed entirely within the EC.

*   **Non-EC sales**: Zero-rated if the supply is enjoyed entirely outside the EC. HMRC state:

    'Journeys that begin or end outside the EC can be treated as enjoyed outside the EC. Temporary stops for refuelling or comfort breaks can be ignored providing that passengers are not able to break their journey at these times. If a second or subsequent flight is an international flight, it will not be regarded as a separate journey provided the connection is made within 24 hours of the scheduled arrival of the first flight. If the second or subsequent flight is domestic, it will not be regarded as a separate journey provided the connection is made within six hours of the scheduled arrival of the first flight.'

- **Mixed sales**: If the supply includes stops inside and outside the EC (other than as permitted above) it must be apportioned. The part enjoyed inside the EC is standard-rated and the part enjoyed outside the EC is zero-rated. Acceptable apportionment methods include mileage and number of nights spent inside or outside the EC.

The 'time of supply' (tax point) rules are modified for margin scheme supplies. You can treat these as supplied either:

1. on the traveller's departure date or the date any accommodation is occupied if earlier

2. as in 1 but with a tax point also created whenever a part payment exceeds 20 per cent of the total fee or cumulative payments received to date exceed 20 per cent.

It is normally better to use method 1. You do not need permission from HMRC to adopt either method but you cannot change from one method to the other without permission from HMRC.

In-house supplies

In-house supplies are supplies that are provided from the business's own resources or bought-in supplies that have been subject to material alteration or further processing. Examples of supplies provided from the business's own resources include passenger transport in vehicles owned by the business, accommodation in property owned by the business, tour guides and other staff employed by the business. Bought-in supplies will have been subject to material alteration or further processing when the nature of the resultant supply is different from what was purchased. Examples include assets such as vehicles, aircraft and accommodation which the business leases and takes on significant responsibility for.

Where in-house supplies are supplied together with margin scheme supplies in a margin scheme package, the in-house supplies follow the normal VAT rules. However, the methods set out in sections 8–11 of VAT Notice 709/5/04 calculate the output VAT charge on the in-house supplies – you do not charge output VAT in the normal way. This means that if the in-house supply is taxable under the normal VAT rules, all the directly attributable input VAT is recoverable. If the in-house supply is exempt under the normal VAT rules, the directly attributable input VAT is irrecoverable. If the place of supply of the in-house supply is outside the UK, it is outside the scope of UK VAT. Directly attributable UK input VAT is recoverable if the supply would have been taxable had it taken place in the UK. If the place of supply is another EC state you may have to register for VAT in that EC state.

Status of the customer

If you provide a margin scheme supply or margin scheme package as principal or as undisclosed agent (or as disclosed agent but you cannot identify your commission) then:

*   If the supply is to a private individual or organisation using the supply for private or non-business purposes, the supply must be included within TOMS.

*   If the supply is to an organisation for its own consumption in its business activities it must be included in TOMS, though by concession the supply may be dealt with outside TOMS. This concession allows you to issue VAT invoices to business customers. For supplies enjoyed inside the UK permission must be obtained from HMRC. For supplies enjoyed outside the UK you must be able to prove to HMRC that any VAT due in another EC state has been properly accounted for.

*   If the supply is to a business for subsequent resale ('wholesale supplies') the supply must be accounted for outside TOMS, though by concession HMRC may permit the supply to be included within TOMS. You must obtain permission from HMRC, which HMRC will only grant if all wholesale supplies are treated like this.

Annual adjustment

VAT is not applied to margin scheme supplies or margin scheme packages on a supply-by-supply basis. Instead, output VAT is accounted for provisionally during the year, then the provisional output VAT payments are corrected in the annual adjustment using whole-year figures for the values of TOMS sales and TOMS direct costs. The annual adjustment also calculates the provisional output VAT rate for the next year. The annual adjustment must be made in the first VAT return following the end of the VAT year.

The annual adjustment as set out in sections 8 and 9 of VAT Notice 709/5/04 is a five-step process but can be simplified. The full annual adjustment is as follows:

TOMS annual adjustment – full method

1   Calculate the total income from margin scheme supplies and margin scheme packages in the year, as determined by the time of supply rules set out above. Exclude: discounts offered to customers and taken up, forfeited deposits, cancellation charges paid by customers, and agency supplies included in margin scheme packages where the commission is identifiable (e.g. insurance sales).

2   Calculate the costs of the margin scheme and margin packages included in 1 as follows:

(a) The VAT-inclusive purchase prices of margin scheme supplies enjoyed in the EC.

(b) The VAT-inclusive purchase prices of margin scheme supplies enjoyed outside the EC.

(c) The direct costs of in-house supplies that are standard-rated. This means in-house supplies that are standard-rated when supplied by you. Exclude any input VAT but multiply the net cost by the standard rate of VAT.

(d) The direct costs of in-house supplies that are zero-rated. This means in-house supplies that are zero-rated when supplied by you. Exclude any input VAT.

(e) The direct costs of in-house supplies that are exempt. This means in-house supplies that are exempt when supplied by you. Include any irrecoverable input VAT.

(f) The direct costs of in-house supplies that you supply outside the UK. Include any irrecoverable VAT. If VAT has been paid in another EC state, add the VAT paid.

(g) The VAT-inclusive amounts paid by you to your principals in respect of any agency supplies included in step 1 for which the consideration you receive is standard-rated.

(h) The VAT-inclusive amounts paid by you to your principals in respect of the agency supplies included in step 1 for which the consideration you receive is not standard-rated.

3   Calculate the margin (total in 1 above less total in 2 above) and apportion the margin between each of the types 2(a) – 2(h) on the basis of cost.

4   The output VAT due for the year is the VAT fraction ($\frac{7}{47}$ for 17.5% VAT) multiplied by:

- The margin attributed to margin scheme supplies enjoyed in the EC, plus
- The cost plus margin attributed to standard-rated in-house supplies
- The margin attributed to agency supplies.

Deduct any output VAT paid provisionally in the year. The balance is the amount due, or repayable if negative.

5   The provisional percentage for the next year is calculated by totalling the margins attributed to 2(a), 2(c) and 2(g) and the costs at 2(c), then dividing the result by the total in 1 above. This is the provisional figure to be used to calculate the proportion of TOMS income that is standard-rated. The VAT fraction is then applied to the calculated standard-rated TOMS income to determine the output VAT due each quarter.

See sections 8 and 9 of VAT Notice 709/5/04 for full details of the calculations.

The basic example below illustrates the application of TOMS where all TOMS supplies are margin scheme supplies and there are no in-house or agency supplies.

TOMS example: No in-house or agency supplies

An organisation supplies package holidays. At the end of the VAT year total gross margin scheme sales are £80,000. The direct (VAT-inclusive) cost of margin scheme sales is £50,000, split £20,000 for EC holidays and £30,000 for non-EC holidays.

The margin is £80,000 - £50,000 = £30,000.

This is apportioned between EC and non-EC holidays on the basis of cost. The margin apportioned to EC holidays is £30,000 x (£20,000 / £50,000) = £12,000. This is gross of VAT. The VAT due is therefore 7/47 x £12,000 = £1,787.23, assuming the standard rate of VAT is 17.5%.

The margin apportioned to non-EC holidays is £30,000 x (£30,000 / £50,000) = £18,000. This is zero-rated so no VAT is due in respect of the non-EC part.

Total output VAT due for the year under TOMS is £1,787.23. From this deduct any interim payments during the year and enter the difference into box 1 of the VAT return.

The provisional rate for the next year is:

Standard-rated margin / Total sales = £12,000 / £80,000 = 15%

Assume that in quarter 1 of the next VAT year total sales are £25,000.

The standard-rated margin is calculated as 15% x £25,000 = £3,750. The output VAT due in quarter 1 is therefore 7/47 x £3,750 = £558.51.

HMRC state that you must use the simplified calculation (in sections 10 and 11 of VAT Notice 709/5/04) if all component supplies of all your margin scheme supplies and margin scheme packages are liable to VAT at the standard rate. If this is the case then the simplified calculations will produce the same result as the long calculations. However, if this is not the case, for example if you provide holidays outside the EC, the simplified calculation will overstate your VAT liability. If in any doubt you should use the long calculations in sections 8 and 9 of VAT Notice 709/5/04.

Deductible costs

In calculating the costs of margin scheme and in-house supplies only specific costs can be included. These are:

For margin scheme supplies: the cost of goods or services that are bought in and re-supplied without material alteration for the benefit of the traveller. The following will generally *not* meet this definition and therefore be treated as indirect costs: brochures, advertising, inspection trips made to research facilities, office expenses (telephone, IT equipment, office stationery, rent etc.), accountancy, legal and other similar professional services, financial services (including bank and foreign exchange charges), HP, leasing and finance charges for the purchase of assets (including those used in making in-house supplies), market research and commission paid to agents.

Where deductible margin scheme costs are incurred in a foreign currency they must be translated into sterling using one of five permissible methods set out in section TL4 of VAT Notice 709/5/04. You must obtain permission from HMRC to change method. In practice you may find that none of the methods is fully GAAP-compliant and does not match what is in your accounting system. However, HMRC will usually accept the consistent use of figures from the accounting system.

For in-house supplies: the direct costs of in-house supplies that are provided for the benefit of the traveller. If facilities are used to provide in-house supplies within TOMS and also supplies outside TOMS, an apportionment must be made. Typical direct costs of in-house passenger transport include: depreciation on vehicles which you or a member of your VAT group own calculated on the same basis as your audited accounts, rental or leasing of vehicles, crew/drivers' costs, fuel, insurance, repairs and maintenance, garaging and parking, bridge and road tolls, ferry costs and road fund licences. Typical direct costs of in-house accommodation include: depreciation of buildings, fixtures and fittings for which you or a member of your VAT group are liable; and calculated on the same basis as your audited accounts, catering purchases, heating and lighting, rates, building insurance, rental of equipment/furniture, repairs, maintenance and cleaning for which you are liable, and staff costs.

Attributable costs that cannot be deducted are referred to as indirect costs. VAT on indirect costs is deductible subject to the normal VAT rules.

Separate EC and non-EC annual adjustments

The statutory annual adjustment method set out in VAT Notice 709/5/04 assumes that the margins achieved on all your different types of TOMS supply are the same. In particular, the method assumes the margins on EC and non-EC sales are the same.

You are allowed to do separate annual adjustments for EC and non-EC sales. As a general rule, if your margins on EC sales are lower than your margins on non-EC sales then it is beneficial to treat EC sales separately, but if they are higher it is not beneficial. However this is a generalisation, and you should do the calculations for your own circumstances to check. You must obtain the prior permission of HMRC to do separate calculations, and you can only do this from the start of a VAT year. If any supplies are enjoyed partly in and partly outside the EC they must be included in the EC annual adjustment.

Market value based annual adjustments

If you provide in-house supplies as part of a margin scheme package then it is unlikely that the margins on bought in and in-house supplies are the same. The assumption that the margins are the same can be advantageous in some situations and disadvantageous in others. For example, if you provide a UK package of zero-rated in-house transport with bought-in UK accommodation and the in-house margin is higher, your output VAT liability will be higher under a cost-based apportionment that it would on a true split of the margin.

The validity of HMRC's requirement that apportionment is made on a cost-only basis was challenged in two European Court of Justice (ECJ) cases.

In a case involving Madgett & Baldwin (1998, ECJ C94/97) the ECJ decided that a supplier may not be required to calculate the part of a package corresponding to the in-house services by the actual cost method where it is possible to identify that part of the package on the basis of the market value of services similar to those which form part of the package.

In My Travel (2005, ECJ C291/03) the ECJ ruled that:

- Where a reliable market value can be established for the in-house supplies, this should be used to apportion the margin between in-house and margin scheme supplies and, in such a situation, a cost-based apportionment can be used only if the supplier can demonstrate this reflects the actual structure of the package.

- Application of the market value method is not subject to the condition that it must be simpler than the actual cost method or to the condition that it must produce a VAT liability identical or close to that which would result from the cost method.

- The market value method can be used even if a reliable market value can only be established for some of the in-house supplies and a cost-based method must be used for the others.

- A market value method may also be reliable even if the supplier does not provide similar services on a non-package basis.

- However, the market value method must be used consistently, and it is for the national tax authorities and courts to assess whether it is possible to identify the part of the package corresponding to the in-house services on the basis of their market value, and in this context to determine the most appropriate market.

Following Madgett & Baldwin and MyTravel recent cases suggest that HMRC and VAT tribunals are reluctant to accept in-house market valuations based on third-party prices. In a case involving Welsh's Coaches (2007, VAT Tribunal 20193) a coach operator supplied in-house transport and bought-in accommodation as a package. The coach company tried to use the equivalent National Express coach fare to determine the market value of the in-house supply, but this was rejected by the tribunal on the basis that the supplies by the coach company and by National Express were not comparable.

Zero-rating EC travel

TOMS has the unfortunate effect of turning a zero-rated supply of passenger transport into a standard-rated supply when it is bought in and re-supplied without material alteration as part of an EC sale. For example, if you supply a UK package of in-house accommodation together with bought-in coach transport, the margin on the package is standard-rated. If the customer bought the passenger transport directly from the coach company, the travel element would be zero-rated.

Before 1996 EC margin scheme sales were split into supplies of standard-rated accommodation and zero-rated transport, and this problem did not exist. However, this was held to be unlawful by the ECJ and from 1996 all EC margin scheme supplies have had to be standard-rated under TOMS. To mitigate the effects of this change HMRC have suggested three ways around the problem. These are:

1. **The agency option**: Sell the transport element as disclosed agent of the transport provider. This effectively zero-rates the transport element and also zero-rates any commission received by the tour operator. To be effective, the arrangement should be bona fide and the tour operator must not be taking any significant commercial risk. If the tour operator's commission is readily identifiable the agency arrangement is dealt with outside TOMS. If it is not readily identifiable it is included in TOMS. See VAT Information Sheet 04/96 for details of the option and calculations.

2. **The transport company option**: Set up a separate wholly-owned transport subsidiary to buy in the transport from the transport providers, airlines etc. The transport subsidiary must not be in a VAT group with the tour operator. The sales from the transport providers to the transport subsidiary are wholesale supplies and so outside of TOMS. The transport subsidiary then sells the transport to the tour operator at a mark -up calculated to eliminate the margin on the transport, thus effectively zero-rating it. VAT information sheet 01/97 provides full details of the option. Note that at the time of writing (2007) there is an EC proposal to bring all wholesale supplies within TOMS, thus potentially blocking this option.

3. **The airline charter option**: The tour operator must charter a whole aircraft for an entire season. The air flights can then be treated as a zero-rated in-house

supply. This option will be impractical for most voluntary organisations. See VAT Information Sheet 03/96 for details.

Note that these schemes are not necessary for non-EC sales, though it may be simpler to adopt the same structure for all bought-in travel services. If the transport comprises air flights then you must also ensure any ATOL requirements are met.

Reverse-charge scheme for purchases of mobile phones and computer chips

In response to concerns about 'missing trader fraud', a change to the procedures for dealing with qualifying supplies of electronic goods was introduced with effect from 1 June 2007. The qualifying goods are:

*   mobile phones and handsets with a mobile phone function, such as BlackBerrys. Mobile phones supplied with air-time contracts are excluded and mobile phone accessories are excluded if supplied separately. 3G data cards and Wi-Fi cards are also excluded

*   computer chips in a state prior to integration into end-user products.

The reverse charge only applies to purchases of qualifying goods when all of the following conditions are met:

*   the value of qualifying goods on a single invoice exceeds £5,000 (net). If the invoice includes other items these are excluded in calculating whether or not the £5,000 limit is exceeded

*   the supply is between one UK VAT-registered business and another. If the customer is not-VAT registered then the supplier must standard-rate their supply as normal

*   the customer will be using the goods for business purposes. If you are VAT-registered but purchasing qualifying goods for non-business purposes you should provide the supplier with a written statement to this effect.

Where the reverse-charge conditions are met, the supplier does not charge any VAT, but the customer must charge themselves the VAT and pay this over to HMRC as output VAT. This VAT can be treated like other input VAT and recovered subject to the normal recovery rules. The supplier's invoice must include details of the amount of output VAT that the customer must account for. Suppliers must also complete a Reverse Charge sales list detailing all such sales.

The customer should enter the output VAT due in box 1 (output VAT) on the VAT return and any recoverable part of this in box 4 (VAT reclaimed). The invoice value should be entered in box 7 (total purchases) in the normal way, but it is not entered into box 6 (total sales).

If an unregistered customer makes a purchase of qualifying goods and the goods will be used for business purposes, then the net purchase value counts towards the customer's VAT registration threshold. The first £1,000 of purchases in any month is ignored. If the value of qualifying purchases (excluding the first £1,000 in any month) together with the value of taxable supplies exceeds the VAT registration threshold, the customer must register for VAT. However, in many situations, such purchases by voluntary organisations will be exceptional and you may have a case for claiming that, although the registration threshold has been exceeded, outputs in the following 12 months will be below the deregistration threshold, thus exempting you from the need to register (see Chapter 2, section on 'Registering and deregistering').

Qualifying reverse-charge supplies should be excluded from the cash accounting scheme and flat rate schemes, although if the goods qualify for the margin scheme (see below) then the reverse-charge scheme does not apply.

See VAT Information Sheet 06/07 for full details.

Optional schemes

Cash accounting scheme

Normally, output VAT is accounted for under the tax point rules explained in Chapter 12. Output VAT becomes due to HMRC at its tax point and input VAT is recoverable at its tax point. Usually the tax point is the invoice date. All VAT due or recoverable in a VAT period is included in that period's VAT return.

Under the cash accounting scheme, you treat output VAT as due when it is received from your customer and input VAT as recoverable when the associate purchase invoice is paid. This means that output VAT is only included in the VAT return when it is paid by your customer and the input VAT is only included in the VAT return when you pay your supplier, that is on a cash basis.

Example: Cash accounting scheme

Cragson Ltd's VAT quarter ends on 31 March.

For sales	For purchases
It issues a customer invoice for £200 net + VAT of £35.	Cragson receives a supplier's invoice for £100 net + VAT of £17.50.

The invoice is issued on 19 March and payment is received on 15 April.	The tax point of the invoice is 23 March. It pays the invoice on 3 April.
Under the normal VAT rules Cragson records the £35 output VAT as due on 19 March.	Under the normal VAT rules Cragson records the £17.50 input VAT as recoverable on 23 March.
The £35 is included in its VAT return for the quarter ended 31 March and must be paid to HMRC by 30 April.	The £17.50 is reclaimed in its VAT return for the quarter ended 31 March and is netted off VAT paid to HMRC by 30 April.
Under cash accounting it records the £35 as due on 15 April. The £35 is included in its VAT return for the quarter commencing 1 April.	Under cash accounting it records the £17.50 as recoverable on 3 April.
The £35 VAT must be paid to HMRC by 31 July.	The £17.50 is recovered in its VAT return for the quarter ending 30 June. It is netted off VAT paid to HMRC by 31 July.

If you make credit sales this delays you having to pay over the output VAT you charge to your customers. However, if you make credit purchases, it also delays your recovery of the associated input VAT. The scheme provides automatic bad debt relief, as you only have to pay over the output VAT when you have actually received it from the customer.

If your output VAT regularly exceeds your input VAT (so you generally have to make VAT payments to HMRC) then using the cash accounting scheme may improve your cash flow. However, it will not always be advantageous. If your input VAT regularly exceeds your output VAT (so you generally recover VAT from HMRC) then it may make your cash flow worse.

You may only use the cash accounting scheme if you expect the value of your taxable supplies (net of any VAT) in the next 12 months to be less than £1.35 million. When calculating the value of your taxable supplies you should include the net value of any standard-rated, reduced-rate and zero-rated sales but exclude any expected income from the sale of fixed assets. You will also be prohibited from using the scheme if you have been convicted of a VAT offence or penalised for VAT evasion involving dishonesty.

There is no need to apply or inform HMRC that you are starting to use the cash accounting scheme, and you may start using the scheme from registration, though you may only switch to the scheme once registered at the start of a VAT period.

You may leave the scheme voluntarily at the end of a VAT period, but you must stop using the scheme if:

- at the end of a VAT period, your taxable turnover (including any sales of fixed assets) in the last 12 months exceeded £1.6 million unless this was a genuine one-off, or

- you are convicted of a VAT offence or penalised for VAT evasion involving dishonesty, or

- HMRC instruct you to leave the scheme.

The cash accounting scheme does not apply to the following transactions, which should be accounted for under the normal rules:

- goods purchased or sold under lease purchase, hire purchase, conditional sale or credit sale agreements

- goods imported or acquired from another EC state

- supplies where you issue a VAT invoice and payment of that invoice is not due in full within six months of the date it was issued

- supplies of goods or services where you issue a VAT invoice in advance of making the supply or providing the goods.

If you regularly make any of these types of transaction then you will have to consider how practical it is to run two different schemes at the same time.

Where an organisation has a mix of non–business, exempt and taxable activities any business/non-business or partial exemption calculations based on levels of income or expenditure should be based on income received or payments made.

Annual accounting scheme

The annual accounting scheme simplifies the administrative burden of calculating and submitting regular VAT returns. Normally you must submit a VAT return every three months. The annual accounting scheme allows you to submit just one annual VAT return.

You must still pay regular instalments of VAT over to HMRC. You can choose to make three quarterly or nine monthly instalments. These must be paid by direct debit, standing order or other electronic means. At the end of the year you submit a VAT return for the whole year, together with any balancing payment due. You have two months in which to submit the return (compared with one month for the usual quarterly returns). If you have overpaid VAT in the instalments HMRC will refund the difference.

To join the scheme you must:

- expect to make taxable supplies of under £1.35 million in the next 12 months. In calculating the value of your taxable supplies, standard-rated, reduced-rate and zero-rated sales are included net of VAT, but income from the disposal of fixed assets is excluded

- not have stopped using the scheme in the last 12 months

- not be part of a VAT group or divisional registration

- apply to HMRC for permission to join the scheme.

If you register for monthly payments each payment will be calculated as 10 per cent of your previous year's liability. If you register for quarterly payments each payment will be calculated as 25 per cent of your previous year's liability. If you have been registered for 12 months or less, HMRC will estimate your annual liability.

You must inform HMRC if your VAT liability increases by 10 per cent or more since the last time your instalments were calculated.

You can choose to leave the scheme voluntarily by writing to HMRC. You must leave the scheme if your taxable supplies exceeded £1.6 million in a VAT year. You will usually have to revert to submitting regular VAT returns at the start of the next VAT year, though in certain situations HMRC may make you leave the scheme at an earlier date.

If you have a significant level of taxable activity then having to submit quarterly returns is burdensome, but it does help ensure your VAT affairs are kept up to date. If you join the annual accounting scheme you must make sure that you do not leave it all to the last minute to sort out. Even though you have two months after the end of the year in which to submit the annual VAT return, you will have a year's worth of transactions to sort out.

Retail schemes

The retail schemes are for use by businesses that make retail sales to unregistered customers where it is impractical to record the VAT due for every individual item sold. Typically, this will be shops that make large numbers of cash sales and that do not possess sophisticated till systems. The retail schemes are used to calculate the output VAT due by the retailer.

It is important to note that VAT-registered businesses must be provided with proper VAT invoices or VAT receipts (see Chapter 12: *Operational aspects*), so retailers with a significant number of VAT-registered customers must have some way of issuing correct

VAT invoices to customers on demand. This usually means either accounting for VAT on an item-by-item basis or splitting their sales and only using a retail scheme for sales to unregistered customers. However, occasional cash sales to registered businesses are allowed within a retail scheme.

There are five standard schemes. If your sales exceed £100 million then you cannot use one of the standard schemes and must use a bespoke scheme that is agreed individually with HMRC. The standard schemes are:

The point of sale scheme: to use this scheme the systems must be able to distinguish standard-rated, reduced-rate and zero-rated sales separately at the point of sale. This could be, for example, via the till system or by using different tills for each type of sale.

Example: Point of sale retail scheme

		Standard rate	Reduced rate	Zero rate
Gross takings in VAT quarter	a	£1,000.00	£500.00	£500.00
VAT fractions	b	7/47	1/21	0
VAT included in gross takings (a x b)		£148.93	£23.80	£0.00

Total VAT due for the quarter is £148.93 + £23.80 = 108.92.

Apportionment scheme 1: here the proportions of standard-rated, reduced-rate and zero-rated sales are based on the proportions of purchases of scheme goods at each rate. This calculation is performed each VAT period and annually with an annual adjustment. This scheme can only be used if the total turnover from retail sales (excluding VAT) is under £1 million, and cannot be used for supplies of services or of goods which you have made or grown yourself, or of catering.

Example: Apportionment 1 retail scheme

Gross sales in the VAT quarter are £2,000 (a)

	Standard rate	Reduced rate	Zero rate
Gross purchases in VAT quarter	£300.00	£250.00	£50.00

		Standard rate	Reduced rate	Zero rate
Proportion of gross purchases	b	50%	41.67%	8.33%
Apportioned gross takings (a x b)	c	£1,000	£833.40	£166.60
VAT fractions	d	7/47	1/21	0
VAT included in gross takings (c x d)		£148.93	£39.68	£0.00

Total VAT due for the quarter is £148.93 + £39.68 = £188.61. At the year-end the calculation is re-performed with figures for annual sales and purchases.

Apportionment scheme 2: this scheme is available for businesses with a tax-exclusive turnover not exceeding £100 million, but not for supplies of services or of catering. Under this scheme you calculate the Expected Selling Prices (ESPs) of standard- and lower-rated goods you purchase for retail sale on a rolling 12-monthly basis. You then work out the ratio of these to the ESPs of all goods received for retail sale and apply this ratio to your takings. There is no need to do an annual adjustment. When you start to apply apportionment scheme 2 you must include the ESP of opening stock in your first three quarterly calculations.

Example: Apportionment 2 retail scheme

Gross sales in the current quarter are £600 (a)

		Standard rate	Reduced rate	Zero rate
ESP of purchases in last four quarters	b	£1,200.00	£250.00	£1,000
Proportion of total ESP	c	48.98%	10.20%	40.82%
Apportioned gross sales (a x c)	d	£293.88	£61.20	£244.92
VAT fractions	e	7/47	1/21	0
VAT included in gross takings (d x e)		£43.76	£2.91	£0

Total VAT due for the quarter is £43.76 + £2.91 = £46.67.

Direct Calculation scheme 1 is available to businesses with a tax–exclusive turnover not exceeding £1 million, but is not available for supplies of catering. You calculate the Expected Selling Price (ESP) of goods for retail sale at one or more rates of VAT so that you can calculate the proportion of your takings on which VAT is due. As a general rule you must normally calculate the selling price of your 'minority goods'. These are the goods at the rate of VAT which forms the smallest proportion of your retail sales. However, you may mark up your 'majority' goods if this would be a simpler option.

Example: Direct calculation retail scheme 1	
Zero-rated and reduced-rate sales are in the minority.	
Gross sales in VAT quarter	£2,000.00
Less ESP of zero-rated purchases in VAT quarter	(£300.00)
ESP of reduced-rate purchases in VAT quarter	(£50.00)
Standard-rated sales in quarter	£1,650.00
VAT due on standard-rated sales: 7/47 x £1,650	£245.74
VAT due on reduced-rate sales: 1/21 x £50	£2.38
Total VAT due for the quarter	£248.12

Direct Calculation scheme 2 works in the same way as the Direct Calculation scheme 1, but requires you to make an annual stock adjustment. You can use the scheme if your annual tax-exclusive retail turnover does not exceed £100 million.

The apportionment and direct calculation schemes assume that goods bought at one rate of VAT will be sold at the same rate. For supplies of catering this is unlikely to be the case and so the point of sale scheme is the only standard alternative. However, if a catering business has a net turnover under £1 million and can satisfy HMRC that the point of sale scheme is impractical it may use the catering adaptation. You must inform HMRC if you are using the catering adaptation. The catering adaptation works by estimating the proportion of standard-rated sales by analysing your sales for a representative period. The estimation must be redone each tax period, and details of the calculation must be retained.

You can start using a standard scheme without prior approval from HMRC, though HMRC may refuse use of a scheme if the scheme does not produce a fair and reasonable result or you could reasonably be expected to account for VAT in the normal way. You must use a scheme for at least 12 months, unless you become ineligible or HMRC allow an earlier change. You can change schemes at the end of a complete year reckoned from the beginning of the tax period in which you first adopted the scheme.

Flat rate scheme for small businesses

The flat rate scheme is designed to simplify VAT administration for very small businesses. Under the scheme you calculate the VAT due to HMRC as a percentage of your 'flat rate turnover'. The flat rate you use depends on the business sector that you activity belongs in. See VAT Notice 733 for a list of business sectors and the applicable rates.

You still need to calculate output VAT due under the normal rules and issue VAT invoices to VAT-registered customers. However, you do not have to pay HMRC the output VAT charged to VAT-registered customers.

You cannot recover any input VAT charged on purchases. This means you do not have to monitor input VAT charged by your suppliers, though in practice certain transactions such as the purchase of fixed assets are excluded from the scheme, and you will need to monitor input VAT for these.

Your flat rate turnover includes zero-rated sales, the gross value of any reduced-rate and standard-rated sales and exempt income but excludes non-business income such as bank interest, grants and donations.

Example: Flat rate scheme

In a VAT quarter The Learning Association has £1,000 net income from standard-rated management consultancy services. It also has £5,000 exempt income and £100,000 non-business income. Total gross expenditure for the period is £50,000, which includes £100 input VAT attributable to the consultancy services.

The flat rate for management consultancy services is 12.5% (from VAT Notice 733).

Under the flat rate scheme the flat rate turnover is £1,175 + £5,000 = £6,175.

VAT payable to HMRC is 12.5% x £6,175 = £771.87.

The surplus for the period is:	Flat rate scheme	Normal VAT rules
Total income (gross): £1,175 + £5,000 + £100,000	£106,175.00	£106,175.00
Less gross expenditure	(£50,000.00)	(£50,000.00)
Less paid Under the flat rate scheme: to HMRC: 12.5% x £6,175 = £771.87 Under normal VAT rules: £175 - £100	(£771.87)	(£75.00)
Surplus	£55,403.13	£56,100.00

If zero-rated or exempt sales are a significant proportion of income then the flat rate scheme is likely to be disadvantageous.

To join the scheme an organisation must meet all of the following conditions:

- its expected taxable income (net of VAT and excluding any sales of fixed assets) in the next 12 months must be under £150,000

- its expected total business income in the next 12 months must be under £187,500. The expected business income is the expected taxable income plus expected exempt income

- it is not eligible and was not eligible in the previous two years to join a VAT group. Broadly this means that the organisation is not a parent or subsidiary entity and is not under common control with another organisation

- the organisation is not associated with another organisation. This means that it is not controlled by another organisation and is not closely bound to another organisation by financial, economic and organisational links

- the organisation is not using the second-hand goods scheme, Tour Operator's Margin Scheme or capital goods scheme

- the organisation has not used the flat rate scheme in the last 12 months

- the organisation must not have been convicted for an offence involving VAT, accepted a compound penalty offer or been assessed for a penalty for conduct involving dishonesty.

To join the scheme you must apply to HMRC. You can leave the scheme at any time but must notify HMRC. You must leave the scheme if your flat rate turnover exceeds

£225,000 or is expected to exceed £225,000 in the next 30 days, or if you become ineligible under any of the other conditions above.

If your business fits into two or more sectors then you must apply the flat rate applicable to the main activity based on level of turnover. If the balance between activities changes you must continue to apply the same rate until the anniversary of joining the scheme, then apply the new rate. You get a 1 per cent reduction on the flat rate applicable to your business sector in your first year of registration.

If you purchase 'capital expenditure goods' you can reclaim the VAT you have been charged on a single purchase of capital expenditure goods where the amount of the purchase, including VAT, is £2,000 or more. Capital expenditure goods are fixed assets such as computers, vans and furniture. However, if such goods are sold, output VAT must be accounted for on the sale of such goods. If you purchase capital expenditure goods that are covered by the capital goods scheme (e.g. computer equipment costing over £50,000 net of VAT – see the section on the capital goods scheme in this chapter) then you must leave the flat rate scheme.

Before joining the scheme you should assess whether it will be advantageous or not. Though there are some administrative savings these may not be significant, and many voluntary organisations will find that they are financially worse off using the scheme.

See VAT Notice 733 for full details of the scheme.

Agricultural flat rate scheme

The scheme covers the following agricultural activities: crop production, including the growing of ornamental plants and of young plants for sale; stock farming; forestry, comprising the growing, felling and general husbandry of trees in a forest, wood or copse; fisheries, including fresh-water fishing, fish farming, breeding of fish, shell-fish and frogs. The processing of goods is only included if you have grown them yourself, for example the conversion of felled trees into timber products such as fencing material. Where felled timber is processed into more refined products such as furniture this is considered to be outside the scope of the scheme, though it may be possible to split the business into qualifying and non-qualifying parts, as explained below.

The scheme is an alternative to VAT registration. If taxable turnover from non-agricultural activities exceeds the VAT registration threshold then you are ineligible and must account for VAT in the normal way on the agricultural activities. However, it is possible to manage qualifying agricultural activities in one legal entity and non-qualifying activities in another so that the former may be registered under the scheme.

You must apply to join the scheme and HMRC may refuse application if you stand to gain more than £3,000 by joining the scheme. HMRC calculate the gain by comparing the flat rate addition (explained below) to the net input VAT that would be otherwise recoverable.

Under the scheme you charge a 4 per cent flat rate addition on the sale price of qualifying goods or goods and services sold to VAT-registered customers even where these sales would be zero-rated for VAT. The VAT-registered customer can treat this as input VAT and reclaim this in their VAT return subject to the normal recovery rules.

The 4 per cent addition is not VAT and is kept by the flat rate agricultural producer. It does not have to be paid to HMRC and does not have to be reported on a VAT return. The 4 per cent is compensation for being unable to recover input VAT. The flat rate addition should not be charged to customers who cannot recover the addition, such as unregistered customers and other flat rate scheme users. There are special rules for invoicing under the scheme, and the addition must be referred to as Flat Rate Addition or FRA and not as VAT.

The flat rate addition is only added to the sale price of agricultural goods and associated services. If you sell fixed assets or make non-agricultural sales as well no flat rate addition is included.

See VAT Notice 700/46 for full details of the scheme.

Margin scheme for second-hand goods, works of art, antiques etc.

If second-hand goods are donated to a charity then the sale of those goods is zero-rated (see Chapter 6: *Zero and reduced rates*). However, if you pay private individuals and unregistered businesses for second-hand goods as part of a business activity that involves selling those goods, then, unless those goods are inherently zero rated (e.g. books), the sale will be standard-rated, but you may be able to use the margin scheme to reduce the output VAT you must charge to your customers.

VAT is normally due on the full selling price of goods sold. However, where second-hand goods (including works of art, antiques etc.) are purchased from unregistered suppliers (such as members of the public) there is no input VAT paid on the purchase. This means that a person selling second-hand goods may be at a commercial disadvantage compared with a person selling similar new goods where input VAT has been paid. To rectify this discrepancy the margin scheme allows VAT to be calculated only on the margin (selling price less purchase price) providing various conditions are met.

Margin scheme example: Calculating the VAT due

Selling price	£100
Purchase price	£60
Margin	£40
VAT on margin: $\frac{7}{47}$ x £40	£5.95
Net selling price: £100 - £5.96	£94.05

It is the margin that counts towards your taxable turnover and that is entered into box 6 on the VAT return. If the margin is negative, no VAT is due.

It is only the direct purchase cost that is included in the margin calculation. The costs of repairing the goods and of running the business are excluded, but associated input VAT is recoverable to the extent it is attributable to the activity of selling second-hand goods.

The scheme only applies to the following goods:

- **Second-hand goods.** Tangible moveable property that is suitable for further use as it is or after repair. Includes motor vehicles, ponies and horses but excludes certain precious metals and precious stones.

- **Works of art.** See VAT notice 718 for details of what HMRC consider a work of art to be. Generally a work of art must be executed by hand and by the original artist to qualify.

- **Antiques and collectors' items.** For VAT purposes, antiques are goods over 100 years old. Collectors' items are pieces of zoological, botanical, mineralogical, anatomical, historical, archaeological, palaeontological, ethnographic, numismatic or philatelic interest, but exclude unfranked stamps currently valid for postage.

The scheme is optional but will usually be advantageous if you are selling qualifying goods that are not zero-rated to unregistered customers. You can operate the scheme for individual items, classes of qualifying items or all qualifying items and in conjunction with normal VAT procedures for other items you sell. You do not need to apply to use the scheme, obtain permission from HMRC or inform HMRC that you are using the scheme.

To qualify, the goods must have been obtained without VAT being charged (e.g. from a private individual or unregistered business) or obtained under the margin scheme from another margin scheme supplier. There are, however, a few exceptions:

- Where a work of art is purchased from the work's creator or the creator's heirs then it does not matter if the supplier charges VAT. Any input VAT, import VAT or acquisition VAT cannot be recovered and is included in the purchase price for margin scheme calculations.

- Where works of art, antiques and collectors' items are imported from outside the EC, import VAT may be charged. This import VAT is irrecoverable and is included in the purchase price in margin scheme calculations.

You must keep detailed records of all goods purchased and sold under the scheme. Normally this means obtaining a purchase invoice from the supplier (or completing one yourself if the supplier does not provide one), keeping a stock register detailing all qualifying purchases and sales, and providing a sales invoice with the goods that includes the wording 'Input tax deduction has not been and will not be claimed by me in respect of the goods sold on this invoice'. VAT Notice 718 sets out the detailed requirements of what must be included on purchase and sales invoices and what must be recorded in the transaction listing, though some of these requirements are relaxed if you only make occasional sales of qualifying goods.

However, for certain qualifying goods that have a purchase price of £500 or less per item, you may adopt the simplified 'global accounting' procedure. Under global accounting the margin is calculated globally for all qualifying purchases and sales in a VAT period. If this margin is negative, no VAT is due for the period but the margin is carried forward to the next period.

Before adopting global accounting you must carry out a stocktake and add the cost of goods on hand at the start of the first period to your purchases in the first period. Certain goods cannot be included in global accounting. These include motor vehicles, boats, aircraft, horses and ponies.

If an agent acting in their own name handles the purchase or sale of qualifying goods then they will be treated as sold to the agent and resold by the agent (See the section in Chapter 11, 'Agents and principals'.) The deemed sale to the agent and the sale by the agent both qualify for the margin scheme. If the agent acts for the seller then the agent's purchase price is the amount charged to the buyer less any commission charged to the seller. If the agent acts for the buyer then the agent's selling price is the total amount charged to the buyer, including any commission. The agent's purchase price is the amount charged by the owner.

Where qualifying goods are sold at auction and the auctioneer acts in their own name, the auctioneer can choose whether to apply the agent rules for calculating the margin or special auctioneer's rules. Under the auctioneer's rules the auctioneer's purchase price is the hammer price less any commission charged to the seller. The selling price is the hammer price plus any incidental charges made to the buyer such as packing, transport and insurance unless these constitute supplies in their own right. If these are optional extras they will be a separate supply. If the auctioned goods are zero-rated in their own right (for example, books) or are exported then the margin is zero-rated and no VAT is due.

If you acquire qualifying goods as part of a transfer of a going concern (see Chapter 4: *Business and non-business*) then you can only sell them under the margin scheme if the acquired business could have done so.

Listed places of worship scheme

This is a grant scheme to refund VAT incurred on eligible repairs and maintenance to listed places of worship. Approved alterations to listed places of worship that are used for charitable purposes are zero-rated. If the works carried out do not qualify for zero rating then you may be able to recover any VAT incurred under this scheme.

Between 1 April 2001 and 31 March 2004 the scheme only refunded the difference between any standard-rated VAT and the VAT that would have been paid at the reduced rate (5 per cent). Since 1 April 2004 the scheme has refunded all VAT that is not otherwise recoverable. The scheme will continue until 31 March 2011 or until the EC approves the UK's application to grant a permanent reduced rate for eligible works.

The applicant must send a claim that includes original VAT invoices. The minimum value of works that can be included in a claim is £1,000 (net of VAT), though a claim can be made up of several different qualifying pieces of work.

The scheme applies to repairs and maintenance to listed buildings that are used principally as places of worship. To qualify for the scheme:

- The building must be listed and have as its sole or main use being a public place of worship. Where a building includes a significant amount of space used for non-worship purposes, the scheme does not cover repairs to the non-worship areas.

- Being a public place of worship means the building must be used as a place of public worship at least six times a year. Public means attendance is available to anyone, not dependant on invitation, and is publicised. However places of worship used by monasteries, nunneries or other similar establishments and churches owned or vested in certain specific organisations that look after redundant places of worship are exempt from this requirement.

- The worship must be by one or more formally constituted religious organisations.

- Any repair costs must be the responsibility of a local congregation or a recognised denomination or faith group.

The work must be undertaken on the fabric of the building. The following are not eligible: the construction of new buildings or parts of buildings; work to ancillary structures such as gravestones and graveyard monuments, boundary walls, gates, gardens, lychgates or car parks. The following are eligible from 22 March 2006: investigative works leading to eligible works, pipe organ repairs and works to fitted pews, bells and clocks.

Services supplied in connection with the repair works (such as plumbing, heating and electrical) are eligible, but only if they are needed in order for eligible repair works to be undertaken. Such works are not eligible if they are merely carried out at the same time as eligible works. The cost of professional services directly related to eligible repairs such as the costs of architects, structural engineers, surveyors, planning supervisors, archaeologists, H&S advisers, bat inspectors and professional fundraisers are eligible from 22 March 2006.

See www.lpwscheme.org.uk for full details.

Memorials refund scheme

This scheme returns in grant aid any VAT incurred in the construction, renovation and maintenance of memorials on or after 16 March 2005. There is no minimum or maximum limit on the amount reclaimable. The UK has applied to the EC for a permanent reduced rate for works of memorial construction, renovation and main-tenance. The scheme is a temporary measure and will operate until 2011 or until a permanent reduced rate is introduced.

The scheme is restricted to charities and religious groups exempted from registering as charities. The memorial must be a structure. Structures include traditional memorials such as stone crosses, monoliths and statues, as well as plaques fixed to buildings, but exclude any memorial that does not require construction (e.g. a book or portrait), or is intangible (e.g. a theatrical or musical event).

Structures that have a dual purpose are not eligible under the scheme, for example a memorial bench or a playground, though by exception stained glass windows are eligible. Also excluded from the scheme are memorial gardens and trees as these are not considered to be structures capable of construction or renovation. However minor landscaping and planting undertaken in the course of memorial construction will generally be eligible.

All memorials must bear a commemorative inscription or plaque. There is no subject matter restriction beyond a requirement that the memorial commemorates a person or people, an animal or an event.

The memorial must have a minimum 30 hours per week public access, though the access need not be free. If a key must be obtained to access the memorial, the key-holder must be reasonably accessible. If a memorial is constructed in the UK to be erected overseas, any UK VAT incurred on the memorial can be recovered under the scheme.

Claims must be accompanied by original VAT invoices. The invoice must be for works already completed, and must be fully settled prior to submission under the scheme.

See www.memorialgrant.org.uk for full details.

Museums and galleries scheme

Certain museums and galleries that offer free public access can recover any VAT incurred in connection with the free admission of the public that is otherwise irrecoverable. To be eligible an organisation:

- must be a national museum or gallery that has been approved by HM Treasury. VAT Notice 998 contains a list of the approved bodies and the date they are approved from. Other national museums and galleries can request approval (see the address in VAT Notice 998). HMRC state that to be successful an applicant must be a national and not local institution and should normally have the support of the relevant government department such as the Department for Culture, Media and Sport

- must offer free admission to see its principal collections. Where the public is charged to see a special exhibition this will not bar eligibility, however the VAT attributable to the fee-paying exhibitions cannot be recovered under this scheme.

Only VAT incurred on goods or services received after the date of approval can be recovered. The goods and services must be attributable to the collections for which there is free admission. This includes the costs of acquiring and maintaining the exhibitions, the construction, renovation and maintenance of buildings or parts of buildings used to house them, the costs of advertising and promoting the collections, and the provision of free information about the collections including printed literature, websites and lectures. However, any VAT attributable to business activities cannot be recovered under the scheme. Examples include shops and fee-generating educational activities.

VAT-registered organisations make the claim in their VAT return. Organisations that are not registered must make a written claim to HMRC. Where an organisation starts using the scheme, any input VAT already recovered on related fixed assets and stock that is still on hand at the start of the scheme is not repayable by extra-statutory concession.

See VAT Notice 998 for full details.

VAT mitigation schemes

There are many 'schemes' aimed at reducing the effects of the VAT system. Broadly, these may be divided into three types:

1. schemes that are legal and considered acceptable by the tax authorities or courts

2. schemes that are legal but considered unacceptable by the tax authorities or courts

3. schemes that are illegal or involve illegal steps.

This section considers the distinction between the first two. It has long been recognised that businesses cannot be required always to organise their affairs in order to maximise their tax liability, but that there is a certain level of artificiality, in seeking to minimise tax liabilities, beyond which, while legal, it is considered unacceptable to step.

It is an established principle of UK direct tax law that where a preordained series of transactions is entered into for the sole purpose of tax avoidance, transactions in the series can be ignored and the overall effect of the arrangement considered when determining tax liability. For a long time it was not clear if this principle also applies to VAT schemes. However, in the 2006 Halifax PLC case the European Court of Justice (ECJ) ruled that a similar principal does apply to VAT. This is an important decision as it sets boundaries both to what may be considered acceptable VAT mitigation and to when the tax authorities may override the normal operation of VAT law.

It is important to note that schemes within 1 and 2 above are entirely legal. However, the Halifax case establishes that schemes within 2 above can be overridden by the tax authorities and courts. In addition, from 1 August 2004 the use of certain types of scheme must be notified to HMRC. Notifiable schemes may fall within either 1 or 2 above. The second part of this section considers the notification requirements.

The Halifax principles

A fairly common mitigation scheme is the use of a subsidiary company to undertake construction work on behalf of an exempt business. If the exempt business undertook the construction work directly, the VAT incurred on the construction would be irrecoverable. By using a separate company it may be possible to recover some of the VAT on construction, or at least spread the irrecoverable VAT over many years.

Halifax PLC, a 95 per cent exempt banking company, wished to construct four new call centres. It set up a scheme under which the supply of construction services was made to various wholly owned subsidiary companies that would be able to recover the VAT in full. The scheme was designed to allow Halifax use of the call centres while at

233

the same time substantially reducing the irrecoverable VAT burden. However, HMRC refused the claims for input VAT recovery by the subsidiaries. The case went to court and was referred to the ECJ.

HMRC offered two alternative reasons for rejecting the claims. The first was that transactions entered into for the sole reason of gaining a tax advantage and having no commercial purpose cannot be supplies for VAT purposes. There was substantial evidence that the sole or main purpose behind the arrangements was tax avoidance. The second was that a doctrine of abuse of rights must operate to block the tax advantage gained.

The ECJ rejected the first reason and ruled that the subjective intent of a transaction is not relevant when determining its VAT status. So transactions entered into with the sole aim of obtaining a tax advantage are supplies if they meet the normal objective criteria for supplies (see Chapter 4). However, the ECJ ruled that VAT law must be interpreted as precluding any tax advantage to be gained from an 'abusive practice'. For an abusive practice to exist, two conditions must all be met:

1. The practice must result in a 'tax advantage' that is contrary to the purposes of the relevant provisions of the EC 6th Directive and the national legislation transposing it. This means that no transactions conforming with the VAT deduction rules would have enabled the same degree of input VAT recovery.

2. It must be apparent from 'a number of objective factors' that the 'essential aim' of the transactions is to obtain a tax advantage. If the scheme has some other explanation besides obtaining a tax advantage then it will not be abusive, though any purposes that are incidental to a tax avoidance motive do not prevent the scheme from being abusive. In determining the essential aim of the transactions, the national court may take account of the purely artificial nature of the transactions and any links of an economic or personal nature between the parties involved in the scheme.

Where an abusive practice is found to exist it must be 'redefined' so as to establish the situation that would have existed without the scheme. However a finding of abusive practice must not lead to a penalty but rather an obligation to repay any tax advantage gained. The ECJ also emphasised that:

•   businesses need legal certainty when organising their affairs and so any finding of abusive practice must be based on objective and not subjective criteria, and

•   where a business has a choice of two or more commercial alternatives it is open to the business to choose the option that results in the lowest tax liability.

The ECJ ruling leaves as many questions as it answers. The terms 'tax advantage', 'a number of objective factors', 'redefined' and, most importantly, 'essential aim' all need clearer definition. It is also unclear what happens if an abusive practice cannot be redefined or can be redefined in several different ways. We must turn to case law since the Halifax case for interpretations of these terms.

Later abusive practice cases

The 2006 WHA Ltd case illustrates how the Court of Appeal has approached the Halifax tests. In WHA Ltd (2007, EWCA Civ 728), an insurance company arranged contracts for motor breakdown insurance through two wholly owned Gibraltar-based subsidiaries. The effect was to permit recovery by WHA of VAT charged by the garages called out to the breakdowns. If the Gibraltar companies had been omitted, the VAT would have been irrecoverable. The Court of Appeal found that:

- Two of the purposes of VAT legislation are that VAT is borne by the final consumer and that VAT is 'neutral'. Businesses in the supply chain simply collect VAT on behalf of the tax authorities, with the VAT liability passing down to the final consumer, though where an organisation undertakes exempt or non-business activities the organisation is the final consumer in respect of those activities. 'Neutral' means that within each EC state similar goods and services bear similar tax burdens. The court found that the overall effect, recovery of input VAT by an exempt business, was therefore contrary to the purposes of VAT legislation.

- The court accepted the VAT Tribunal's finding of fact that the essential aim of the scheme was to gain a tax advantage. The Tribunal considered the inclusion of two Gibraltar subsidiaries to be entirely artificial and this conclusion was supported by documentary evidence such as minutes of meetings. Though there were some commercial advantages to the scheme, these were collateral benefits to a scheme which was conceived and implemented purely for tax avoidance purposes.

- Various arguments as to why the scheme should not be considered abusive were rejected. One argument was that a finding of abuse would offend against the principle of freedom of establishment – WHA should be free to establish sub-sidiaries in Gibraltar (which is a part of the EU for the freedom of establishment rules but outside the EC for VAT purposes). This was rejected. Though a business is free to establish itself in another member state to take advantage of that state's tax rules, once it is established it cannot then abuse the VAT system.

- WHA argued that there was no satisfactory way in which the scheme could be redefined and the abuse argument must therefore fail. The court rejected this. Once a scheme is found to be abusive it must be redefined, and any difficulty in redefining or the existence of multiple redefinitions cannot be a barrier to a finding of abuse.

The VAT Tribunal case Lime Avenue Sales & Services Ltd. and Benenden School Trust (2007, VAT Tribunal 20140) illustrates the application of the Halifax tests to the exempt education sector. In this case an exempt charitable school had two wholly owned subsidiaries – a separate charitable trust for fundraising and a VAT-registered trading company, LASS. The school wished to construct a new study centre on land it owned. It sold the land to LASS which then arranged the construction, financed by a loan from the trust. The original intention was for LASS to claim the input VAT and sell the new building back to the school for a fee payable in annual instalments.

However it became clear that HMRC would reject LASS's claim as being abusive. The scheme was therefore reorganised. The trust would register for VAT. LASS would then make a standard-rated sale of the completed building to the trust. The trust would then opt to tax the building and lease it to the school for an initial rent of £5,000 plus VAT per annum.

HMRC also rejected the reorganised scheme on two alternate grounds. First, the arrangement was abusive and required the arrangement to be redefined with the construction services being supplied to the school and the trust's acquisition and letting of the building being ignored. Alternatively the lease by the trust to the school was not a business activity as the rent was significantly below market value (following the Yarburgh Trust case – see Chapter 4) so the trust could not recover the VAT on the purchase and could not charge VAT on the rent to the school.

LASS provided arguments to support the schemes. For the first scheme it argued that the LASS's presence in the arrangement was necessary for a variety of reasons including isolating the school from risk, having a more effective and quicker decision-making process and possessing greater expertise. However, this was rejected by the tribunal. There was documentary evidence that such concerns had only appeared later on when it became apparent that the essential aim of LASS's involvement would become an issue. The school had successfully carried out similar construction projects in the past and the school had agreed to underwrite LASS's financial commitments and communicated this to the contractors. The tribunal found the first arrangement to satisfy all the Halifax criteria and was therefore abusive.

For the second arrangement LASS argued that, following rejection of the first scheme, the second scheme was forced on LASS as it was facing insolvency following HMRC's refusal to refund the input VAT. The tribunal rejected the insolvency argument, stating that it could not accept as commercial justification a scheme based on the rejection of an abusive arrangement. The tribunal also noted that the lease by the trust to the school was not a business activity following the Yarburgh Trust case.

In the High Court case Weald Leasing (2008, EWHC 30 Ch) Weald was a special-purpose subsidiary in the Churchill insurance group, set up to purchase assets on behalf of exempt group members. Group members would select and order the assets, with

Weald paying for them using unsecured interest-free loans from the group members. Weald would lease the assets back on 10-year leases. The effect was to spread the irrecoverable VAT cost to group members over 10 years – if the group members had purchased the assets directly they would have suffered the irrecoverable VAT immediately. The lease agreements were not on commercial terms and gave the lessees the right to terminate the lease agreements without penalty. The leasing arrangements were made via an independent company, SUAS (owned by the VAT adviser to the Churchill group), in order to avoid the VAT rules that deem certain supplies between connected persons at under value to be made at market value (see Chapter 11).

It was admitted that the sole purpose of the arrangement was to spread the irrecoverable VAT burden and that the lease agreements between Weald/SUAS and group members were not on commercial terms. HMRC claimed the arrangement fell foul of the Halifax anti-avoidance rules as the essential aim was to obtain a tax advantage and the arrangement was not part of the Churchill group's normal commercial operations. The High Court rejected this. Once it is shown that the essential aim of a scheme is to gain a tax advantage, it must then be shown that this tax advantage is contrary to the purposes of the VAT legislation, not that the scheme is not a part of normal commercial operations. Nothing in the VAT legislation prevents an exempt business from leasing an asset in order to spread the irrecoverable VAT burden, and so the scheme cannot be said to be contrary to the purposes of the VAT legislation.

The court considered that a claim of abusive practice based on the insertion of SUAS into the arrangement (so that a below market rental could be charged) might have succeeded, though that argument was not made by HMRC. If the argument had been made and won, then the whole scheme would not have been set aside. Instead the rentals would have been deemed to be transacted at market value. Redefinitions must go no further than is necessary and must not lead to a penalty.

Conclusions

If you are involved in a scheme that provides or will provide a VAT advantage, it must be evident from the earliest stages of the scheme that:

- any VAT advantage arising from the scheme is not contrary to the purposes of VAT legislation, or

- if it is, that the scheme has other motives besides the VAT advantage.

The other motives must be evident in such documents as minutes of meetings, correspondence with advisers, regulators, connected parties and contractors. If this is not evident, HMRC are likely to claim the scheme is abusive. In such a situation HMRC will probably seek and be entitled to obtain full disclosure of all communications regarding the scheme, including correspondence with advisers, meeting minutes, correspondence between the parties involved and with banks, contractors etc. The time and effort alone in defending a scheme may therefore be substantial.

Notifying listed and hallmark schemes

From 1 August 2004 the use of certain schemes must be disclosed to HMRC. Failure to disclose a notifiable scheme will incur a penalty. There are two types of scheme that must be notified: listed schemes and hallmarked schemes. You do not have to notify use of a scheme if you are not VAT-registered or not liable to be registered (see Chapter 3). Organisations with business income below £600,000 will generally be exempted from all notification requirements, and organisations with business income below £10 million will generally be exempted from the hallmark scheme disclosure requirements. If the organisation is a member of a group the limits apply to the whole group.

It is important to note that, provided each step in a listed or hallmark scheme is legal, use of the scheme is not illegal. However, the Halifax principles, as explained above, may operate to render the scheme ineffective for VAT purposes, and the rules below may require you to notify HMRC of your use of the scheme. Notification of a scheme may also trigger a visit from HMRC to examine the scheme in detail.

Connected persons

Several of the listed schemes involve arrangements between connected persons or organisations. Basically, two organisations are connected if one is the subsidiary of the other or both are subsidiaries of a common parent.

The formal definition is as follows. A person is 'connected' to another if one of them is an undertaking in relation to which the other is a group undertaking as defined by section 259 of the Companies Act 1985 or both of them are connected to the same trust. A person is connected to a trust where he is the settlor of the trust, or a trustee or beneficiary of it; or holds any shares in a company in accordance with the terms of the trust, or is a person on whose behalf such shares are held.

Listed schemes

There are currently (at January 2008) ten listed schemes, as set out below, though new ones may be added in future. The key schemes likely to affect voluntary organisations are schemes 1, 4 and 8. You must notify your involvement in a listed scheme when all the following conditions are met:

- You are registered for VAT or liable to be registered for VAT. See Chapter 3.

- You are a party to a listed scheme. This means you are knowingly involved in a notifiable listed scheme and meet the other notification conditions. Even if there are other parties to the scheme that have notified HMRC, you must also notify HMRC, although you can make a joint notification with the other parties. If you are unwittingly involved in any of the steps of a notifiable scheme, that is, you have no knowledge of either the existence of the scheme or the role you play in it, or you act purely in an advisory capacity, then there is no requirement to notify.

- Your taxable and exempt income exceeds £600,000 in the year immediately prior to the VAT period of the relevant event or £150,000 in the VAT quarter immediately prior to the VAT period of the relevant event for quarterly VAT returns, or £50,000 in the VAT month immediately prior to the VAT period of the relevant event for monthly VAT returns. If you are a member of a Companies Act group the turnover threshold applies to the whole group, including intra-group transactions but excluding any intra-VAT group transactions.

- A relevant event occurs. A relevant event is any of the following:

  (a) You show in a VAT return, in respect of any VAT accounting period starting on or after 1 August 2004, a higher or lower net amount of VAT than would be the case but for the listed scheme. You must notify HMRC within 30 days of the due date of the VAT return.

  (b) You make a claim (such as by submitting a voluntary disclosure), in respect of any VAT accounting period starting on or after 1 August 2004 for which a VAT return has been submitted, for the repayment of output tax over-declared or input tax credit under-claimed that is greater than would be the case but for the listed scheme. You must notify HMRC within 30 days of making the claim.

  (c) The amount of non-deductible VAT you incur, in respect of any VAT accounting period starting on or after 1 August 2005, would have been higher but for the listed scheme. You must notify HMRC within 30 days of the due date for making a return in respect of that accounting period.

- You have not previously notified you involvement in the scheme.

The listed schemes are:

1. **The first grant of a major interest in a building**: where the first grant of a major interest in a building is zero-rated, made to a connected person and the following input tax is attributed to the grant: (a) input tax in respect of a service charge relating to the building; or (b) input tax in connection with any extension, enlargement, repair, maintenance or refurbishment of the building (other than for remedying defects in the original construction).

This scheme will capture a zero-rated first grant of a major interest by a design and build subsidiary if the grant includes any of the supplies described in (a) or (b) above.

2. **Payment handling services**: schemes that aim to reduce the VAT due on the advertised price of retail goods or services by transforming an element of the price into an exempt payment handling service such as credit/debit card or cash handling.

3. **Value shifting**: schemes that aim to transfer value from standard-rated retail supplies into linked zero-rated or exempt supplies where the total consideration due for the retail supply and linked supply is no different, or not significantly different, from what it would be for the retail supply alone.

4. **Leaseback agreements**: schemes that aim to defer or reduce the VAT cost of acquiring goods by a business that cannot recover all of the input tax on those goods were it to directly buy them itself. The scheme includes the following features: (a) a person (the 'relevant person') receives a supply of goods, or the leasing or letting on hire of goods; (b) he uses the goods in his business, but is not entitled to full input tax credit for the VAT on the supply to him; (c) the supply to him is made by a person connected with him; (d) the supplier, or a person connected with him, is entitled to full input tax credit on the purchase of the goods; and (e) the relevant person (or a person connected with him) funds (directly or indirectly) more than 90 per cent of the cost of the goods. For the purposes of this scheme, goods do not include land transactions.

5. **Extended approval periods**: this scheme aims to defer accounting for output tax on retail (including mail order) supplies of goods. The scheme includes the following features: (a) a retail supply of goods where the goods are sent or taken on approval, sale or return, or similar terms; (b) a requirement that the customer pays in full before any approval, return or similar period expires; and (c) for the purposes of accounting for VAT, the supplier treats the goods as supplied on a date after the date on which payment is received in full.

6. **Groups: third party suppliers**: these are schemes that aim to reduce or remove the VAT incurred on bought in taxable services (including outsourced services) by a user that cannot recover all of the input tax charged to it for those services. The scheme description is linked to legislation that took effect from 1 August 2004 and which only applies to businesses that are in VAT groups or intend to join a VAT group where the VAT group concerned has a business turnover exceeding £10 million a year. See VAT Information Sheet 07/04.

7. **Education and training by a non-profit-making body**: this scheme aims to allow a business providing education or training to avoid charging VAT on supplies

to customers by arranging for those supplies to be made through a non-profit-making body. The scheme includes the following features: (a) a non-profit-making body conducts a business whose activities consist wholly or mainly of the supply of VAT-exempt education or vocational training to persons who are not taxable persons; (b) it receives any of the following 'key supplies', for use in that business, from a connected taxable person who is not eligible for the exemption: a capital item (including leasing or letting on hire of a capital item), staff, management services, administration services, or accountancy services; and (c) in any one VAT return accounting period the value of those key supplies comprise 20 per cent or more of the non-profit-making body's costs.

8. **Education and training by a non-eligible body**: this scheme aims to enable eligible bodies (see Chapter 5) that would otherwise make exempt supplies to make taxable supplies and so avoid incurring irrecoverable input tax. This scheme includes the following features: (a) a body that is not an eligible body for the purposes of the exemption is connected to a body that is an eligible body; and (b) the non-eligible body conducts a business whose activities consist wholly or mainly of the taxable supply of education or vocational training. In addition, either:

(a) the non-eligible body benefits or intends to benefit the eligible body by way of gift, dividend or otherwise; or

both (b) the eligible body makes to the non-eligible body, for use in the non-eligible body's business, any supply (including the leasing or letting on hire) of any of the following 'key supplies': a capital item (including the leasing or letting on hire of a capital item), staff, management services, administration services, or accountancy services;

and (c) in any one VAT return accounting period the value of those key supplies comprises 20 per cent or more of the non-eligible body's costs.

9. **Cross-border face-value vouchers**: this scheme aims to avoid paying VAT anywhere in the EU on 'relevant services' originating from UK suppliers and provided to UK residents who use face-value vouchers (such as phone cards) to pay for them. 'Relevant services' are telecommunication services, radio and television broadcasting services and electronically supplied services (such as software, images, music and games supplied over the internet).

10. **Surrender of a relevant lease**: this scheme aims to allow a person to escape, or substantially reduce, the VAT incurred on opted lease rentals while remaining in occupation of the building. This scheme includes the following features: (a) an occupier of a building (or part of a building) agrees with the landlord to the surrender or other early termination of his lease, tenancy or licence to occupy a

building; (b) the building is a capital item within the meaning of the capital goods scheme (whether or not the adjustment period has expired); (c) the occupier, or any person connected with him, is a person who: is a landlord of the building, owns it for the purposes of the capital goods scheme, and has opted to tax it; (d) before the surrender: the occupier paid VAT on the rent of the building (or part of the building), and was unable to recover this VAT in full; and (e) following the surrender the occupier continues to occupy at least 80 per cent of the area previously occupied, and pays no VAT on the rent, or pays less than 50 per cent of the amount of VAT previously paid (comparing similar rental periods).

Hallmarked schemes

You must notify a hallmarked scheme if all the following conditions are met:

- You are registered for VAT or liable to be registered for VAT in the UK.

- Your business turnover exceeds £10 million in the year immediately prior to the VAT return period that includes the relevant event (see below), or the appropriate proportion of £10 million in the VAT return period immediately prior to the VAT return period that includes the relevant event. If you are a member of a group (for Companies Act purposes) the turnover test is applied to the whole group and includes intra-group transactions but excludes any intra-VAT group transactions.

- You are a party to a scheme – as for listed schemes.

- That scheme is not a listed scheme.

- The main purpose, or one of the main purposes, of the scheme is for any person to obtain a tax advantage. The main purpose test is similar to that outlined in the Halifax tests above. A tax advantage happens when, as a result of the scheme:

    (a) any taxable person accounts, or will account, for a lower net amount of VAT than would otherwise be the case in respect of a VAT return for any VAT accounting period starting on or after 1 August 2004

    (b) any taxable person obtains, or will obtain, in respect of any VAT accounting period starting on or after 1 August 2004, a VAT repayment that he would not otherwise obtain, or that is larger than would otherwise be the case, or is earlier than would otherwise be the case

    (c) any taxable person recovers, or will recover, in respect of any VAT accounting period starting on or after 1 August 2004, input tax before the supplier has to account for the corresponding output tax, and the period between the two events is longer than would otherwise be the case

(d) the amount of any taxable person's non-deductible VAT, in respect of any VAT accounting period starting on or after 1 August 2005, is less than would otherwise be the case

(e) in relation to any person who is not a taxable person, the amount of his non-refundable VAT, at any time on or after 1 August 2005, is less than would otherwise be the case.

- A relevant event occurs. A relevant event occurs when one of the following happens:

  (a) You show in a VAT return, in respect of any VAT accounting period starting on or after 1 August 2004 (or 1 August 2005 when the scheme involves only hallmark 8 (face-value vouchers) and no other hallmark), a higher or lower net amount of VAT than would be the case but for the scheme. The scheme must be notified within 30 days of the due date of the return.

  (b) You make a claim (such as by submitting a voluntary disclosure), in respect of any VAT accounting period starting on or after 1 August 2004 for which a VAT return has been submitted (or 1 August 2005 when the scheme involves only hallmark 8 (face-value vouchers) and no other hallmark), for the repayment of output tax over declared or input tax credit under-claimed that is greater than would be the case but for the scheme. The scheme must be notified within 30 days of the claim.

  (c) The amount of non-deductible VAT you incur, in respect of any VAT accounting period starting on or after 1 August 2005, would have been higher but for the scheme. The scheme must be notified within 30 days of the due date for making a return in respect of that accounting period.

- Your scheme contains one or more hallmarks of avoidance. These are set out below.

- You have not already notified HMRC that you are using the scheme or you have not been provided with a scheme number by someone who has registered the scheme with HMRC.

The hallmarks are:

1. **Confidentiality condition agreements**: there is a 'confidentiality condition' hallmark when there is an agreement that prevents or limits a person from giving others details of how a scheme gives rise to a tax advantage. It is standard practice for advisers to include a 'general confidentiality condition' within their terms of engagement, prohibiting the client from passing on advice to third parties. You need not regard a general confidentiality clause as being a confidentiality

condition hallmark if it is simply imposed in relation to all advice, not merely the scheme in question.

2. **Agreements to share a tax advantage**: there is a 'sharing a tax advantage' hallmark when there is an agreement that the tax advantage accruing from the scheme be shared, to any extent, between the person to whom it accrues and the promoter or any other person who is a party to the scheme.

3. **Contingent fee agreements**: there is a 'contingent fee' hallmark when there is an agreement that payment to a promoter of a scheme is partly or wholly contingent on the tax advantage accruing from use of the scheme.

4. **Prepayments between connected parties**: there is a 'prepayment' hallmark when the operation of a scheme involves a prepayment being made for supplies between connected persons. The prepayment may be of any amount and the time between the prepayment and the actual provision of the goods or services may be of any duration.

5. **Funding by loans, share subscriptions or subscriptions in securities**: this hallmark applies when a supply of goods or services made between two connected persons is funded (in whole or in part): by a loan between connected persons; by one person subscribing for shares in another with whom he is connected; or by one person subscribing in securities issued by another with whom he is connected.

6. **Off-shore loops**: this hallmark applies when certain exported services (which allow the exporter to recover related input tax) are used to provide other services to UK persons, and these 'imported' services are not subject to VAT.

7. **Property transactions between connected persons**: this hallmark applies when: (a) a grant, which is not a zero-rated grant, is made of: any interest in, right over or licence to occupy land, or in relation to land in Scotland, any personal right to call for or be granted any such interest or right; (b) the grantor or grantee of the interest or right is a person who cannot recover input tax in full; (c) a work of any construction, alteration, demolition, repair, maintenance or civil engineering has been or is to be carried out on the land; and (d) the grant is made to a person connected with the grantor.

8. **The issue of face-value vouchers**: this hallmark applies when: (a) face-value vouchers are issued for consideration; and (b) either the issuer does not expect at least 75 per cent of the vouchers to be redeemed within three years of them being issued, or whatever the expected redemption rate, the vouchers are issued to a connected person outside of any VAT group to which the issuer belongs.

A 'promoter' is anyone who, in the course of their trade, profession or business of providing taxation services, designs or sells the arrangements entered into.

Notifying schemes

See Chapter 14 for where to notify schemes. Failure to notify to the correct address will be regarded as failure to notify and make you liable to a penalty. When notifying a listed scheme you must provide the following:

- the notification should be prominently headed: 'Disclosure of use of listed scheme – Notification under paragraph 6(2) of Schedule 11A to the VAT Act 1994'.

- your business name and address

- your VAT registration number

- if you are the representative member of a VAT group, notifying as a result of a group member being involved in a notifiable scheme, the name of the member

- the number of the listed scheme being used.

For hallmark schemes you must provide the following:

- the notification should be prominently headed: 'Disclosure of use of hallmarked scheme – Notification under paragraph 6(3) of Schedule 11A to the VAT Act 1994'

- your business name and address

- your VAT registration number

- if you are the representative member of a VAT group, notifying as a result of a group member being involved in a notifiable scheme, the name of the member

- information demonstrating how the scheme works

- a statement as to which hallmark or hallmarks are included in or associated with the scheme

- a statement as to which specific legislation you rely upon for the tax advantage.

See VAT Notice 700/8 for full details.

11 Other topics

This chapter considers various miscellaneous topics: how to determine if you are making a 'single' or 'multiple' supply; the VAT rules for principals and agents; the rules for VAT groups, branches and joint ventures; the special issues relating to supplies of staff and supplies between connected organisations; the transfer of a going concern rules and the VAT planning opportunities that are available to voluntary organisations.

Branches, joint ventures and VAT groups

This section considers the VAT implications of various 'connected party' scenarios:

- **Branches**: many voluntary organisations have a branch structure. In some situations the branches will be considered part of the main entity for VAT purposes and in others as separate entities for VAT purposes. The VAT implications of branches, sections, supporter groups and similar are considered.

- **Joint ventures**: voluntary organisations sometimes enter into joint ventures with other voluntary organisations or with commercial businesses. The VAT implications of various joint venture arrangements are considered.

- **VAT groups**: under certain circumstances a company and its subsidiary companies can be treated as a single entity for VAT purposes by forming a 'VAT group'. The qualifying conditions are explained, and also the advantages and disadvantages of forming a VAT group.

- **Divisional registration**: large companies may be allowed to submit separate VAT returns for their divisions. However, in order to be able to do this the company as a whole must be fully taxable.

Branches

Many voluntary organisations have networks of branches, sections, supporter groups or affiliated organisations. It can sometimes be difficult to determine if these branches should be included with the main organisation or treated as separate entities for VAT purposes. This may affect whether the main entity has to register for VAT or whether the branches must charge VAT on any taxable supplies they make.

If the branches are separately registered legal entities, for example registered as separate companies or as separate registered charities, then there is unlikely to be a problem unless HMRC consider the separation to be artificial. Each legal entity must consider if its own taxable supplies, including any taxable supplies to the main organisation and to other branches, exceed the VAT registration threshold (see Chapter 2 for information about the VAT registration requirements) and, if so, register for VAT. Corporate entities may, under certain circumstances (as explained below) choose to register as a VAT group.

Where branches share registration (such as a company or charity number) with a 'main' body, or the registration status of the branches is uncertain, the situation is less clear cut. The branches may or may not be part of the same entity as the main body for VAT purposes.

A branch will be part of the main entity for VAT purposes if it is closely bound to the main entity by financial, economic and organisational links. This will need to be assessed on a case-by-case basis using the following indicators:

- If the branch has its own constitution and management committee and has substantial control over its affairs, albeit within a framework set by the main body, this suggests that the branch is an independent entity for VAT purposes. Conversely, if the branch has no separate constitution or independent decision-making structure or if all significant decisions are made by employees or trustees of the main body as employees or trustees of the main body, this suggests the branch is part of the main body for VAT purposes.

- If the branch has its own bank accounts, keeps its own financial records, issues its own invoices and makes its own purchases, albeit within a framework or format specified by the main body, this suggests that the branch is an independent entity for VAT purposes. Conversely, if the branch's finances and administration are managed by the main body this suggests the branch is part of the main body for VAT purposes.

- If the branch has its own fixed assets such as premises and equipment and is responsible for maintaining and insuring its assets, that will suggest independence. If the branch shares assets with the main body but a realistic charge is made for the use of the assets this will also suggest independence. If the branch relies entirely on the main body to provide any assets and the main body provides these free or at undervalue this will suggest that the branch is not independent.

- Informal supporter groups such as 'friends of' organisations and fundraising groups are unlikely to be considered part of the same entity for VAT purposes if the groups have discretion as to the extent and timing of any support provided.

The key issue for HMRC is likely to be whether or not business activities have been artificially disaggregated in order to avoid VAT registration. So if branches only undertake non-business or exempt activities and as long as the branches have not been set up solely for the purpose of tax avoidance, for example by hiving off activities with no VAT recovery to improve recovery in the main body, HMRC may be inclined to leave arrangements undisturbed.

Voluntary organisations with separate branches should consider the VAT impact if they decide to change the nature of the relationship between the main organisation and its branches. If the main organisation starts to exert greater control over the branches' affairs or bring administrative functions in house this may affect the branches' VAT status.

Joint ventures

'Joint venture' is a loose term commonly used to describe a variety of situations in which independent venturers co-operate for some common purpose. In order to determine the VAT status of a joint venture it is necessary to identify the legal nature of the arrangement.

Separately registered entity

If the joint venture is a separately registered entity such as a company or registered charity it will be a distinct entity for VAT purposes and must register for VAT if its taxable supplies exceed the VAT registration threshold. Supplies by the venturers to the joint venture may be subject to VAT, as may supplies by the joint venture to the venturers. Transfers of profit from the joint venture to the venturers will be outside the scope of VAT as long as they do not amount to consideration for a supply. If the joint venture was set up purely in order to gain a tax advantage, then its existence may, for VAT purposes, be ignored. See the section on tax mitigation schemes in Chapter 10.

Partnerships

If the joint venture amounts to a partnership then the partnership is a separate entity for VAT purposes that must register for VAT if its taxable supplies exceed the VAT registration threshold. Supplies by the partners to the partnership may be subject to VAT, as may supplies by the partnership to the partners. Transfers of profit from the partnership to the partners will be outside the scope of VAT as long as they do not amount to consideration for a supply.

The determination of whether or not a partnership exists is a complex area of law, and there are differences between the law in England and Wales and the law in Scotland.

A partnership is defined in the Partnership Act 1890 as 'the relation which subsists between persons carrying on a business in common with a view of profit'. There are four main elements to this:

- There must be a relationship based on agreement between the persons involved. The persons can be individuals or corporate bodies such as companies. Usually the agreement is in writing, however there is no requirement that this is so and partnerships can be created purely as a result of the actions of the persons involved.

- The partnership must be formed in order to carry on a business. The definition of 'business' here is not the same as the definition for VAT purposes, though the two are broadly the same. A partnership cannot be created for charitable purposes and it cannot be created merely to hold property – it must do something with that property.

- The business must be carried on in common. The partners must participate together in a business and each partner must be able to bind the others in legal relationships with third parties. If one partner controls the business or controls the other partners then there is no partnership. However, the partners do not have to have equal shares in the business. Suppliers and others who play no part in the business cannot be partners.

- The profit motive must be present. Usually there will be some form of agreement to share profits, though the actual sharing of profits is not essential. An agreement to share profits from a joint venture does not, in itself, create a partnership, though when combined with other factors as above it may suggest that a partnership exists.

Agreements sometimes include clauses that state that the agreement does not create a partnership. However, if a partnership exists as a matter of fact then the clause has no effect.

Where a property developer purports to form a partnership with a property owner in order to redevelop a property then VAT Tribunal cases suggest that the developer must have an interest in the property for a true partnership to exist. If the developer does not hold an interest in the property HMRC will view all payments to the developer as consideration for development services and not as outside the scope partnership distributions.

Similar to an independent branch

If the joint venture is not a separately registered entity and not a partnership it may still qualify as separate from the venturers for VAT purposes if it is not closely bound to any of the venturers by financial, economic or organisational links. The tests are similar to those set out above in the section on branches. If there is an agreement between the venturers as to how profits or surpluses are shared, then any profit shares distributed to venturers in accordance with the agreement, and that do not constitute consideration for some supply, are outside the scope of VAT.

Joint arrangements that are not entities

If the joint venture does not amount to a separate entity for VAT purposes the activities of the joint venture will have to be accounted for by the venturers. This may be by one of the venturers (the 'lead venturer') including all the joint venture's activities with its own or by an apportionment of the activities between the venturers. You will probably have to agree with HMRC how this is done though there are various standard approaches for particular business sectors that suggest what may be considered acceptable by HMRC.

- Where the joint venture involves purchasing goods for resale and the 'lead venturer' purchases and sells the goods, the lead venturer accounts for VAT on the goods in the normal way. Contributions by the other venturers towards the purchase costs and distributions of sales proceeds by the lead venturer are outside the scope of VAT.

- If the goods are purchased by one venturer but sold by another, the following treatment may be possible. The purchasing venturer reclaims the input VAT on the goods. The selling venturer charges output VAT on the goods. Payments to the purchasing venturer are taxable supplies of services, as are payments from the sales proceeds by the selling venturer. HMRC will only allow this procedure if they are satisfied there is no revenue risk involved.

- For joint ventures involving joint ownership of land or buildings it is likely that the joint venture will have to register as a separate VAT entity. HMRC state in VAT Notice 742:

  'Where more than one person owns land or buildings, or receives the benefit of the consideration for the grant of an interest in land or buildings, we treat them as a single person making a single supply for VAT purposes. If the joint owners are making taxable supplies above the registration threshold they will have to register for VAT as a partnership, subject to the normal rules, even if no legal partnership exists. The joint owners may also request voluntary registration where the value of taxable supplies is below the registration threshold.'

- If there is a joint purchase of an asset other than land or buildings (for example, machinery) for use by the joint owners, the purchasing venturer can reclaim the input VAT on the purchase, subject to the normal rules. Payments from the other venturers to the purchasing venturer are regarded as consideration for the right to use the asset and the purchasing venture must account for output VAT on such payments. If the goods are sold output VAT is due from the purchasing venturer, though distributions of the sales proceeds to the other venturers are outside the scope of VAT.

- For a joint supply of services HMRC may accept that each venturer can account for output VAT on their share of the sales proceeds. They will only allow this if this share reflects the level of obligations and resources put in by each venturer and the profit share taken, and if there is no revenue risk.

VAT groups

Under certain circumstances 'bodies corporate' may form a VAT group and be treated as one entity for VAT purposes. Bodies corporate include limited companies (companies limited by guarantee or by share capital), companies established by Royal Charter or Act of Parliament, Industrial and Provident Societies, Friendly Societies and limited liability partnerships, but not charitable trusts or unlimited partnerships.

There are several advantages in forming a VAT group:

- Most supplies between group members can be ignored for VAT purposes. This may result in a saving of VAT and simplify administration. For example, if one group entity makes standard-rated management charges to a group member that is partly exempt, irrecoverable VAT is avoided in the receiving entity.

- The 'representative member' is responsible for submitting VAT returns and dealing with the tax authorities on behalf of all group members. Again, this will often simplify administration, as all the VAT functions and expertise can be focused in one place.

- If any of the entities in the group have non-business or exempt activities, group registration may improve residual VAT recovery (see Chapter 3 for an explanation of residual VAT). For example, if a partially exempt charity is grouped with a fully taxable trading subsidiary, the increased level of taxable activity resulting from the trading subsidiary's inclusion may improve the charity's residual recovery rate. However this will not always be the case, and you should check this for your own situation before deciding to register as a group.

However, there are also disadvantages:

- Each group member is jointly and severally liable for any amounts owed to HMRC. This means that any group entity may become liable for the VAT debts of another and may apply to entities that have left a VAT group in respect of liabilities that arose while it was a member. If there is a charity in the group this may give rise to breach of trust and direct tax problems.

251

- The partial exemption *de minimis* limits (see Chapter 3 for an explanation of these) apply to the whole group. It is therefore less likely that exempt activities will be *de minimis*.

- Other fixed limits also apply to the whole group. So, for example, the limits for the voluntary disclosure of errors (see Chapter 12) apply to the whole group, and it is therefore more likely that you will have to disclose errors to HMRC. You are also less likely to qualify for the cash accounting scheme, annual accounting scheme and other VAT simplifications targeted at small entities.

- If group entities have separate administrations, the quarter (or month) end procedures for getting VAT information to the representative member will need to be efficient. In order to get information to the representative member on time, other group entities may have to set earlier deadlines than would normally apply. This may delay input VAT recovery if purchase invoices are not received or cannot be processed before the deadline.

VAT grouping conditions

For an entity to join a VAT group all of the following conditions must be met:

- The entity must be a body corporate (see above) established in the UK or with a fixed establishment in the UK. A fixed establishment means a permanent place of business with the necessary resources to undertake activities.

- All entities in the group are under common control or one group member controls another. For the common control test the controlling party does not have to be a member of the group, does not have to be a body corporate and does not have to be established in the UK. Control here has the standard section 736 Companies Act 1985 meaning, that is control of 50 per cent or more of the share capital or voting rights or the right to appoint or remove a majority of the directors.

- For certain 'specified bodies', two extra conditions must be met in order to join a VAT group. These rules only affect VAT groups with a business turnover of over £10 million and are designed to prevent partly exempt purchasers of services setting up joint ventures within their VAT group, in order to buy in services without incurring irrecoverable VAT. The joint venture companies are in reality run by and for the benefit of third-party suppliers, who exercise control over them in practice. This scenario is unlikely to apply to most voluntary-sector VAT groups. If you think it may apply, see VAT Notice 700/2 for full details of these anti-avoidance provisions.

Group registration process

Companies seeking to form or join a VAT group must apply to HMRC. When companies form a VAT group any previous VAT registration numbers are cancelled and a new one is provided for the group. All group members must use this. This VAT registration number remains, even when new members join the group or members leave the group. When members leave the group or the group is disbanded, the leaving members are issued with new VAT numbers.

Application to form a VAT group must be made to the normal registration address (see Chapter 14) using form VAT 1 signed by the representative member, form VAT 50 signed by the applicant company and form VAT 51 for each company joining the group. Application is provisionally effective from the date it is received by HMRC, and HMRC have 90 days in which to investigate the application and refuse it. HMRC state that they aim to reply within 15 days to confirm receipt of an application.

HMRC can grant retrospective group registration and will do in certain situations. See VAT Notice 700/2 for details.

If application is refused the group is treated as if it never was. Any returns or VAT treatments that were based on there being a VAT group must be corrected.

HMRC powers

HMRC have the power to refuse an application and also the power to remove members from a VAT group if they consider it 'necessary for the protection of the revenue'. HMRC state that they will not normally use their revenue protection powers when they consider that the revenue loss follows from the normal operation of grouping. To assess this they will normally compare the result to what would happen if the group members were all one company. Where revenue losses go beyond this, HMRC are likely to use their revenue protection powers.

If HMRC have concerns that the revenue loss does go beyond the accepted consequence of VAT grouping, it will ask for relevant information about the administrative savings that grouping brings in the particular circumstances, and an estimate of the revenue impact of grouping. HMRC will normally ask you to comment on the impact of any refusal or removal. For example, you may incur extra costs in having to submit an extra VAT return, or in having to account for VAT on supplies between group members.

See VAT Notice 700/2 for full details of when HMRC will seek to apply these powers.

Intra-group exceptions

For VAT purposes, supplies between group members are usually ignored and supplies to or from outside the group are usually treated as made by or to the representative member. However, there are exceptions:

- In situations where the liability of a supply is determined by the status of the supplier or recipient, it is the status of the entity making or receiving the supply that counts, and not the status of the representative member. For example, where there is a supply of education by a group member, the entity actually making the supply is considered when determining if the supply is made by an eligible body (see Chapter 5 for information about the supply of education and eligible bodies). Where an external supplier makes a supply that is zero-rated when supplied to a charity, such as advertising (see Chapter 6 for information on supplies that are zero-rated when made to a charity), it is the status of the recipient and not the representative member that matters.

- If a group member makes a supply of Schedule 5 reverse-charge services from an overseas branch to a UK branch of another group member, the recipient must account for the supply using the reverse charge. This is commonly known as the 'intra-group reverse charge'. The Schedule 5 reverse-charge services are explained in Chapter 9 and include the supply of advertising, the services of consultants, lawyers, accountants and other professionals, the supply of staff and transfers and assignments of copyright, patents, licences, trademarks and similar. The intra-group reverse charge is subject to various conditions. The supply must not qualify as exempt and it must have been supplied to the supplier for onward supply to the UK member. Generally, a *de minimis* test is applied – if the bought-in supplies form less than 5 per cent of the value of the onward supply, the rule is ignored.

- HMRC may direct that a particular intra-group supply is not ignored for VAT purposes if it considers this 'necessary for the protection of the revenue'. See above for how this phrase is interpreted, and see VAT Notice 700/1 for a detailed explanation of when HMRC will seek to apply this power.

- If a partly exempt group acquires assets from a third party as part of a transfer of a business as a going concern (see below for an explanation of the 'transfer of a going concern' rules), there may be a requirement for the group to account for VAT on the assets. The representative member must treat the transfer as both a supply to and a supply by the representative member at the time the assets are transferred. This will apply to certain standard-rated assets that fall outside the capital goods scheme (see the Chapter 10 section on the capital goods scheme) and were owned by the previous owner for less than three years. See the section below on transfers of a going concern for more details.

Divisional registration

A body corporate may apply for its separate divisions to be registered for VAT separately. See the above section on VAT groups for what constitutes a body corporate. Each division has its own VAT number and submits separate VAT returns, though the entire company still remains a single taxable person. This is done for administrative convenience where it would be difficult for the company as a whole to submit a single VAT return within the required timeframe.

However, the conditions for divisional registration are onerous:

- The company as a whole must be fully taxable. This means that it must have no non-business activities and any exempt activities are *de minimis* (see Chapter 3 for the *de minimis* limits). This will preclude most voluntary organisations.

- The separate divisions must have their own accounting systems, operate from different geographical locations and supply different commodities or carry out different functions.

- HMRC must be satisfied there would be real difficulty in submitting a single VAT return within the required timeframe.

See VAT Notice 700/2 for more on divisional registration.

Supplies between connected parties

This section considers the VAT implications of supplies made between connected parties. Connected parties are broadly entities that are subject to common control or entities together with any entities they control. Control is usually determined according to the standard Companies Act tests and can be via holding the majority of voting rights, holding more than 50 per cent of the share capital or the right to appoint or remove a majority of the directors or trustees.

Supplies considered in this section are:

- **Management charges**: these are charges made by one party for the use of its resources by a connected party. Management charges are commonly encountered in the voluntary sector, for example in the charges made by a charity to its trading subsidiary for use of the charity's resources. Management charges will usually be within the scope of VAT.

- **Grants and transfers of surpluses**: grant payments between charities and transfers of surpluses are also common, for example the transfer of surpluses from a trading subsidiary to its parent charity via gift aid. Though such payments will generally be outside the scope of VAT there are situations in which they will not be.

- **Payments at undervalue**: these are payments for supplies between connected parties where the payment represents less than the market value of the supply. In certain situations, anti-avoidance rules act to deem the supply to be made at market value for VAT purposes

- **Group relief payments**: these are payments by one company to another for the surrender of corporation tax losses. Generally such payments will be outside the scope of VAT, but there are circumstances where they will be subject to VAT.

Management charges

Connected entities often share resources. The owner of the shared resources commonly makes a 'management charge' for the other entities' use of the resources. Management charges typically cover the use of premises, equipment and materials and staff time used in managing or administering the other entities' affairs.

A common example is the management charge made by a charity to its trading subsidiary. Charities may only carry out limited trading when the trading is not in direct fulfilment of the charity's objects ('non-primary-purpose trading'). Non-primary-purpose trading is typically undertaken to generate additional funds for the charity and common trading activities include the sale of manufactured or bought-in goods and the sale of advertising and promotional services. In order to avoid adverse direct tax consequences, many charities set up wholly owned trading subsidiaries to undertake the non-primary, purpose trading. Usually, the charity supports the trading subsidiary, typically providing it with premises and management and administrative services. The charity must charge for these services. If it does not charge for the services or charges at undervalue it will be using charitable resources to support a non-charitable entity and will thereby jeopardise its direct tax charitable tax exemptions.

If management services are provided in return for a supply of goods or services by the other party (effectively a barter arrangement) then this will constitute a supply for VAT purposes. The value of the supply will be determined as the market value of the goods or services supplied in consideration.

If the supplier and recipient of the management services are part of the same VAT group then the management charge is an intra-group charge and therefore, as explained in the section on VAT groups above, ignored for VAT purposes.

Single or multiple supply

If the two entities are not in the same VAT group then, if a single charge is made to cover a variety of different supplies by the charity to the subsidiary, the status of the charge depends on what is being supplied. The 'single/multiple supply tests' (explained in the section 'Single and multiple supplies' below) must be used to determine if there is a single or multiple supply. If there is a single supply, the whole charge follows the VAT status of the predominant element. If there is a multiple supply the VAT status of each of the supplies is determined separately, and the management charge may have to be apportioned between the different types of supply.

If a single management charge is made for vaguely defined management services or similar, the management charge is likely to be standard-rated. If the supplier is not VAT-registered but the management charges (together with any other taxable supplies made by the supplier) exceed the VAT registration threshold (see Chapter 3), then the supplier must register for VAT and start charging VAT on the management charges. Any input VAT that is attributable to the supply of the management services will be recoverable.

Splitting the management charge

One way of avoiding having to standard rate the whole management charge is to split it up into the different types of supply being made. For example, if the management charge covers the use of premises then it may be possible to exempt this component by separating it out and making a separate charge for the use of the premises.

Charges for staff time, such as the management and administrative time involved in running the subsidiary will generally be standard-rated, though see the section below on the supply of staff for situations in which it may be possible to avoid this.

Grants and transfers of surpluses

Grants will generally be outside the scope of VAT (see Chapter 4). Here, a grant is a payment made without any related supply in return. However, where a grant is made to a connected party HMRC are likely to examine the arrangement carefully, and if they consider there is a directly related contra-flow of goods or services, deem the grant to be consideration for the supply of the goods or services.

Transfers of surpluses are also generally outside the scope of VAT. For example, the transfer of surpluses by a trading subsidiary to a parent charity under gift aid will generally be an outside the scope donation. However, the same considerations apply. If the transfer appears to be directly related to a supply, it may be brought within the scope of VAT.

These points are illustrated by the Court of Appeal case Church Schools Foundation Ltd (2001, EWCA Civ 1745). The Church Schools Foundation managed and held the freehold of various properties occupied by its parent company the Church Schools Company. The Company gave a £1 million grant to the Foundation to carry out various improvements to the properties and also agreed to grant various surpluses to the Foundation. HMRC claimed the grants were consideration for the supply of improvements to the properties. The VAT Tribunal decided that there was insufficient linkage between the grants and improvements for a supply to be established. This decision was overturned on appeal to the High Court, which decided that there was sufficient linkage and the grants were subject to VAT. This decision was reversed on appeal to the Court of Appeal which considered there to be insufficient linkage. This was because the Foundation had used funds from other sources for the works, and the grants from the Company were no more consideration for a supply than were the other funds.

The case shows that even the courts find such situations difficult. HMRC must establish a direct link between the grants and any contra-flow of benefits. If they can establish a direct link then the 'grants' may be within the scope of VAT.

Payments between connected parties at undervalue

Anti-avoidance provisions allow HMRC to direct that the value of a supply between connected persons is its market value where:

- The consideration for the supply is monetary and is at undervalue. The supply will be at undervalue if an unconnected person would have to have paid more.

- The recipient cannot recover all the VAT incurred on the supply, usually because the recipient is unregistered or receiving the supply partly or wholly for exempt or non-business activities.

- The supply does not comprise a supply of catering or accommodation by an employer to one or more employees.

Two entities are connected if one controls the other or both are controlled by the same party. Partners in partnerships are connected, as are individuals with their spouses, relatives and relatives of their spouses. Entities are also connected if they are controlled by connected parties.

HMRC state that the provisions are targeted at tax-avoidance schemes and not at supplies made at undervalue for a 'legitimate' reason. Providing that reason can be substantiated, HMRC will not seek to issue a direction.

Group relief payments

Under the corporation tax rules, companies may under certain circumstances surrender corporation tax losses to each other. Sometimes the company receiving the loss makes a compensatory payment to the company providing the loss. This is accepted as being outside the scope of VAT provided that nothing else is provided for the loss surrender and it is not part of a wider arrangement for the supply of goods or services between the parties.

Supplies of staff

The VAT implications of supplying staff between organisations can be complicated. This is an area of developing case law, and there are important concessions by HMRC. When staff employed by one organisation (A) are supplied to another (B), the possible VAT scenarios include the following:

1 There is no supply or the supply is not a business activity	If the staff are provided for no consideration or significantly below cost, or if the supply of staff does not amount to a business activity, it is outside the scope of VAT. See Chapter 4 for how to determine if a supply exists and if an activity is business. If there is no consideration but staff are supplied as part of a broader arrangement there may be non-monetary consideration, bringing the activity within the scope of VAT.
2 The staff are employed under joint contracts of employment	Where staff are employed under joint contracts (where there is more than one employer) there is no supply for VAT purposes when staff are transferred between the employers.
3 A and B are members of the same VAT group	Supplies of staff between members of a VAT group are outside the scope of VAT and no VAT is due on any salary recharge or commission.
4 The supply is between the non-business activities of two non-profit organisations	HMRC accept that the supply of staff between two non-profit-making organisations is a non-business activity when the staff were employed in A's non-business activities and will be employed in B's non-business activities, and any payment for the staff by B to A is on a cost-reimbursement basis.

5	The staff are seconded from A to B	Seconded staff generally retain employment rights in A but temporarily come under the direction and control of B. The 'staff hire concession' allows secondments to escape VAT as long as B discharges A's salary obligations in respect of the seconded staff and the secondment is not carried out with a view to financial gain.
6	The staff cease to be employed by A and become employed by B	Here, VAT is due on any commission or recruitment fee charged by A. Ongoing salary payments by B direct to the employees are not VATable.
7	The staff remain employed by and under the direction and control of A	Here, A is making a supply of the underlying services provided by the staff and not of staff. The VAT treatment follows the nature of the underlying services.
8	The staff remain employed by A but come under the direction and control of B	HMRC's current view is that the whole of the payment from B to A, including any commission and salary costs is VATable. However, you may be able to use the 'staff hire concession' to avoid charging VAT on the salary element, and case law suggests that certain supplies of staff between non-profit organisations in the education, health and welfare sectors may be exempt.
9	The staff remain employed by A but are subject to direction and control by both A and B	This scenario falls into a grey area between scenarios 7 and 8. The VAT situation is unclear and HMRC policy inconsistent. This scenario is especially relevant where regulated staff are supplied and the supplier is legally obliged to retain a significant degree of direction and control over the staff. Examples include supplies of nurses and domiciliary care staff.

Joint contracts of employment

Where staff are employed under joint contracts with two or more employers, transfers between employers are not supplies for VAT purposes and so any charges between the employers for the employees' services are outside the scope of VAT. For staff to be properly employed under a joint contract, the contract of employment must clearly identify the different employers and state that it is a joint contract of employment. Though an attractive option from a VAT perspective, joint contracts can present legal difficulties, for example if the employee needs to be disciplined or dismissed.

Supplies between members of a VAT group

Supplies between members of a VAT group escape VAT (see the section on VAT groups above). Even if two organisations make no VATable supplies, it may be possible for them to form a VAT group in order to avoid having to charge VAT on supplies of staff between the two organisations.

Paymaster services

Where each of a number of associated organisations employs its own staff, but one (the paymaster) organisation pays all salaries, taxes and pension contributions on behalf of the others, then recovery of monies paid out by the paymaster is not subject to VAT as it is a disbursement. If a charge is also made for the paymaster's services, this charge is standard-rated unless the charge is between two members of a VAT group.

The staff hire concession

Following a 1995 court case (the Reed case), HMRC accepted that employment agencies could, under certain circumstances, supply staff as agent so that VAT was only due on the agency's commission and not the salary costs. This was later formalised into the 'staff-hire concession'. HMRC impose various conditions for the staff-hire concession to apply. If these conditions are not met, HMRC's view is that VAT is due on the whole payment made in respect of the agency staff, that is the commission and salary costs. There are three variants to the staff-hire concession:

- **The agency concession**: Here the entity supplying the staff must be an 'employment business' as defined in the Employment Agencies Act 1973, and the staff must be employees of the agency. If the hiring organisation discharges the agency's obligation to pay the staff by paying the staff directly or via a third party then HMRC accept that the salary element can be omitted when calculating the VAT due. Many agencies manage this by setting up a separate payroll company to handle the payments to the staff. HMRC accept that the payroll company can be connected to the agency, though it must be a separate legal entity.

- **The secondment concession**: Where staff are seconded between organisations that are not recognised employment businesses, the salary element can be ignored for VAT purposes where the recipient organisation discharges the seconding organisation's obligation to pay the secondee's salary, either by paying the employee directly or by directly paying a third party. However, the concession does not apply where the secondment is carried out with a view to financial gain.

- **The disabled workers concession**: Where the sponsor of a disabled worker places the worker with a host company under the Sheltered Placement Scheme (or any similar scheme) and the host company is responsible for paying the worker's remuneration directly to the worker or discharges the sponsor's obligations to pay to any third party PAYE, NICs, pension contributions and similar payments relating to the worker, the salary element can be ignored for VAT purposes.

The Conduct of Employment Agencies and Employment Businesses Regulations 2003 came into force on 6 April 2004. Their purpose was to secure the employment rights of agency staff. Under the regulations, agency staff became employees of the agency and self-employed staff are also treated, for the purposes of the regulations, as if they are employees. The effect is to prevent employment agencies from supplying temporary staff as agent. Following the introduction of these regulations HMRC announced a review of the staff-hire concession on the basis that agency treatment was no longer tenable. At the 2008 budget the government announced its intention to remove the agency connection with effect from 1 April 2009. The secondment and disabled workers concessions will, however, remain.

Regulated agencies

Agencies supplying certain types of staff, such as nurses and domiciliary care staff, are required in law to retain a significant degree of control over their staff. For example, under the Nurses Agency Regulations and National Minimum Standards a nursing agency remains responsible for the personal and professional conduct of its nurses while on assignment. The agency must ensure that patients are safeguarded from abuse or neglect. The agency must perform regular CRB, health and registration checks and must maintain insurance to cover itself against negligence or other acts by its nurses.

In such situations it is arguable that there is a supply of the underlying service and not of staff so that the VAT treatment follows that of the underlying service. The supply of services by a health professional registered in one of the statutory registers (such as the register of qualified nurses, midwives and health visitors) is exempt (see Chapter 5). If there was a supply of the underlying service, the agency would be able to exempt the whole of its charge (including its commission) and not just the salary element as provided for in the staff-hire concession.

Advice from HMRC on the VAT status of supplies by regulated agencies is confusing and inconsistent. In the past HMRC accepted that supplies of medical professionals such as doctors and nurses were exempt as supplies of the underlying service. A recent survey of its members by the Recruitment and Employment Confederation (the trade body for employment agencies) found a wide variation in the VAT treatment of supplies of regulated staff and in the advice received by these agencies from HMRC. Most agencies charged VAT on their commission, with others exempting the whole supply or taxing the whole amount.

Following the European Court of Justice (ECJ) decision in the Kingscrest case (see Chapters 5 and 13) HMRC accepted that private (i.e. profit-making) state-regulated welfare agencies were eligible for exemption, and SI 2003/24 exempted such supplies from 31 January 2003. This has sometimes been interpreted as exempting all supplies made by state-regulated welfare agencies, including supplies of staff where the staff are placed under the direction and control of the hiring organisation. However, the matter is not so clear cut and the key issue remains whether or not there is a supply of the underlying service or of staff. Two more recent ECJ decisions suggest that any exemption is more limited.

Supplies between non-profit organisations

In the case *Stichting Kinderopvang Enschede* (2006, C–415/04) a Dutch charity provided childminders to parents. The parents made a weekly payment to the childminder a separate weekly payment to the charity. In effect, the charity was acting as agent (or, in ECJ terms, intermediary) in providing vetted and monitored childminders. The Dutch tax authorities claimed the payments to the charity were fully VATable and the charity that it was making an exempt supply of welfare services. The ECJ ruled that the services provided by a charity as an intermediary were exempt, provided:

- the childminding service itself meets the conditions for exemption

- the parents could not be assured of obtaining a service of the same value without the assistance of an intermediary service (i.e. the parents needed a service that vetted and monitored its childminders)

- the basic purpose of the intermediary services was not to obtain additional income for the service provider by carrying out transactions which are in direct competition with those of commercial enterprises liable for VAT.

In the 2007 ECJ case Horizon College a Dutch college seconded teachers to another college and was reimbursed the staff costs by the other college. The Dutch tax authorities claimed the whole supply was VATable. The court rejected this but also rejected the college's claim that the supply by Horizon to the other college was of exempt education. Instead, it took the view that the supply was closely linked to a supply of education, and therefore exempt providing various conditions were met. The 6th VAT Directive exempts supplies of education and supplies closely linked to supplies of education (see Chapter 5 for more details) when provided by certain bodies such as charities. There are similar provisions for the supplies closely linked to supplies of medical services and of welfare. The court drew clear parallels with the *Stichting Kinderopvang Enschede* case, and the conditions were similarly drawn up:

- the teacher placement must be a means of better enjoying the education deemed to be the principal service

- both organisations must be eligible for exemption under the national rules

- the placement must be of a nature and quality such that, without recourse to such a service, there could be no assurance that the education provided by the host establishment and, consequently, the education from which its students benefit, would have an equivalent value. This will be so if, for example, the host cannot be assured that commercial agencies will be able to be provide staff with the same qualifications or experience or on similarly flexible terms

- the basic purpose of such a placement is not to obtain additional income by carrying out a transaction which is in direct competition with commercial enterprises liable for VAT. The fact that the placement is provided on a cost-reimbursement basis is not in itself sufficient to meet this condition.

Agency supplies

This section considers the VAT status of supplies made as agent of a principal. You will, as a broad rule, be making a supply as agent of a principal when the following conditions are met:

- there is some form of agreement between you and the principal that you will act as their agent in respect of the supplies concerned

- for a supply of goods, you do not own the goods but buy or sell them on behalf the principal and do not alter the nature or value of the goods

- for a supply of services, you do not supply the services from your own resources and do not alter the nature or value of the services.

The main parties involved in an agency arrangement are referred to below as the principal, agent and third party.

Legal background

There is no formal definition of the term 'agent', but broadly an agent is a person who is authorised to act on behalf of another – the 'principal'. In the business world one of the most important authorities is the ability to create legal relations between the principal and third parties. The agent must have authority to carry out the agency transaction, though this authority can arise in several ways:

- **express authority** where the powers and duties of the agent are expressed in some way, typically in a contract between the principal and agent, though it need not be in writing

- **implied authority** where the agent is reasonably entitled to assume they are authorised to act on behalf of the principal even though they do not have express authority. Implied authority usually arises from the words or actions of the principal and may be an extension of express authority to situations not directly covered by the express authority

- **usual authority**: this is a form of implied authority that arises as a result of the relationship between the principal and agent, for example the purchasing authority of a manager. The agent will have implied authority to carry out such acts as are normally undertaken in the agent's position

- **apparent authority** arises where a third party is reasonably entitled to assume that the agent is authorised to act on behalf of the principal even though in fact the agent does not have express or implied authority. In such situations the agent must not have purported to act as principal and the principal must have been responsible for the third party's assumption in some way. The third party must have been acting in good faith in making this assumption.

The liabilities and obligations of the parties depend on the nature of the authority provided and whether the principal is disclosed or undisclosed. Where the existence of a principal is disclosed to the third party the principal is said to be disclosed. This situation is also referred to as a disclosed agency. The disclosed principal may be identified (the third party knows the identity of the principal) or unidentified (the third party does not know the identity of the principal).

- **Undisclosed principal**: where an agent enters into a contract but the principal is undisclosed, the general rule is that the agent will assume personal liability unless the contrary can be gathered from the rest of the contract and the surrounding circumstances. The contract is treated as being between the agent and third party, though the principal may nevertheless assume rights and obligations under the contract. An undisclosed principal may sue and be sued if the agent was acting within the scope of his express, implied or usual authority, though the terms of the contract may, expressly or by implication and within certain limits, exclude the principal's right to sue and liability to be sued.

- **Disclosed principal**: where the principal is disclosed and the agent acted within their express, implied or usual authority the contract is between the principal and third party, and as a general rule the agent drops out of the equation. However, it is possible for both the principal and the agent to be liable to the third party. The agent may also have a duty of care to the third party and be held liable for any fraudulent misrepresentation to the third party. In some situations the fact that the principal is unidentified may mean that a disclosed principal arrangement is treated like an undisclosed principal arrangement.

VAT position

The VAT position broadly follows the legal and depends on whether the principal is disclosed or undisclosed. There are separate rules for supplies of packages that include travel or accommodation (for example, package holidays or overseas challenge events) where the principal is undisclosed. See the section in Chapter 10 on the Tour Operators' Margin Scheme.

It is also sometimes necessary to consider the direction of the transaction:

- **Selling agent:** the agent will be a selling agent if the supply goes from the principal to the third party, for example if it sells its principal's goods or services to a third party.

- **Buying agent:** the agent will be a buying agent if the supply goes from the third party to the principal, for example if it buys goods or services from a third party on behalf of the principal.

Disclosed principal

Here, the agent discloses the fact that it is acting as agent of a principal to the third party. Normally the identity of the principal will also be revealed to the third party, though this will not necessarily be so. Typical disclosed principal situations in the voluntary sector include:

- Selling goods such as second-hand items, craft items and works of art on behalf of their owners. If the owners and customers are mostly unregistered it is usually better to sell the items as agent rather than take ownership in order to avoid having to charge VAT on the full selling price – VAT is just due on the commission. Note that the seller may also be able to use the margin scheme for second-hand goods (see the section in Chapter 10), and if the goods are themselves zero-rated (for example books, children's clothing and some food items – see Chapter 6) it will usually be better to take ownership in order to avoid a standard-rated commission. Also note that the sale of goods donated to a charity is generally zero-rated (see Chapter 6).

- Selling insurance as agent of an insurance company. Here the agent must act to bring the insurer and the third party together, and the eventual contract for the insurance must be between the insurance company and the third party.

For VAT purposes the transaction is normally regarded as comprising two separate supplies:

- A supply directly between the principal and the third party. In a selling agent situation the supply will be from the principal to the third party and in a buying agent situation the supply will be from the third party to the principal. The VAT status of this supply is determined according to the normal VAT rules as explained in the rest of this book.

- A supply of agency services by the agent to the principal. The VAT status of the supply of agency services does not automatically follow that of the underlying supply between the principal and the third party, though it may do so in some situations. See the section on supplies of agency services, below.

If the supply between the principal and the third party is taxable and if both the principal and the third party are registered for VAT, then:

- in a selling agent situation: the principal must normally issue a VAT invoice addressed to the third party if the third party is to be able to recover the input VAT

- in a buying agent situation: the third party must normally issue a VAT invoice addressed to the principal if the principal is to be able to recover the input VAT.

Undisclosed principal

The principal is undisclosed if the agent does not disclose the fact that it is an agent to the third party. As the principal is undisclosed any payments will normally be made via the agent and any invoices will be to or from the agent rather than directly between the principal and the third party. For VAT purposes there are two possible treatments:

- **Domestic treatment**: the underlying supplies are treated as being made to the agent with a separate supply of the same goods or services by the agent. There is a third supply of agency services by the agent to the principal. The domestic treatment can only be used for supplies that take place entirely within the UK. If the commissionaire treatment (see below) is not adopted the domestic treatment is mandatory for a supply of goods but is optional for a supply of services.

- **Commissionaire treatment**: there is a supply to the agent then a different supply by the agent. The difference takes into account any commission due from the principal. The commissionaire treatment must be used for supplies that involve other EC states or states outside the EC, and may also be used for supplies of goods or services that take place entirely within the UK.

The commissionaire treatment was introduced to avoid the need for UK agents to charge VAT to non-EC principals and to circumvent some of the problems caused by variations in agency law between different counties. However it can be used for supplies that take place entirely within the UK.

Domestic treatment

Under the domestic treatment there are effectively three supplies:

1. In a selling agent situation, a deemed supply from the principal to the agent and another deemed supply from the agent to the third party. The two supplies are for the same value, and the VAT status of each is determined according to the normal VAT rules. The agent may not recover any input VAT before having paid any associated output VAT.

2. In a buying agent situation, a deemed supply from the third party to the agent and another deemed supply from the agent to the principal. The two supplies are for the same value and the VAT status of each is determined according to the normal VAT rules. The agent may not recover any input VAT before having paid any associated output VAT.

3. A separate supply of agency services from the agent to the principal. The supply of agency services does not automatically follow that of the supply between the principal and third party, though it may do so in some situations. See the section on supplies of agency services, below.

In 1 and 2 above, the two supplies will normally have the same VAT status, though it is possible for them to be different, for instance when the VAT treatment of the supply depends on the status of the customer or supplier. An example is where an undisclosed agent provides zero-rated advertising services to a charity (see Chapter 6 for information on the zero-rating of advertising when provided to a charity). The supply by the principal to the agent cannot be zero-rated if the principal does not possess an eligibility declaration. The supply by the agent to the charity may be zero-rated if the eligibility declaration requirements are met.

Any taxable supplies under 1 or 2 above made to the agent count towards the agent's VAT registration threshold (see Chapter 3 for information on the registration requirements). As the agent must pay any output VAT on the deemed supplies before recovering the associated input VAT, the arrangements are usually set up so these are recovered in the same VAT return so there is no net VAT effect on the agent.

Where agents act as selling agents for goods and the principal is VAT-registered, the use of a self-billing arrangement is common. The principal will not necessarily know the value of goods sold by the agent and so may have difficulties in generating bills themselves. Under the self-billing arrangements the customer (the agent) makes out VAT invoices for a VAT-registered supplier (the principal) and sends a copy to the supplier with the payment. A self-billing arrangement must be approved in advance by HMRC.

Example: Domestic treatment

Agency Ltd sells standard-rated goods on 10% commission. It holds the goods as consignment stock and pays the principal the selling price less commission when the goods are sold. In VAT quarter 1 total sales were £2,000 + VAT of £350. Agency Ltd uses self-billing to pay the principal.

At the end of quarter 1 Agency Ltd self-bills the principal for £2,000 + VAT of £350 in respect of the goods sold and creates a separate agency services invoice to the principal for £200 + VAT of £35.

In quarter 1 Agency Ltd includes the following in its VAT return:

Box 1 (output VAT): £350 on sales to customers + £35 for agency services	£385
Box 4 (input VAT): £350 billed by the principal	£350
Box 5 (net VAT due)	£35
Box 6 (total value of sales): £2,000 billed to customers + £200 for agency services	£2,200
Box 7 (total value of purchases): £2,000 billed by the principal	£2,000

Commissionaire treatment

Under the commissionaire treatment the commission is incorporated into the value of the supply between the agent and the principal. There is no separate supply of agency services to the principal and the agent's commission is treated as a mark–up on the cost of the supply to the agent by the principal (in selling agent situations) or third party (in buying agent situations).

Example: Commissionaire treatment

In the above example, Agency Ltd adopts the commissionaire treatment.

At the end of quarter 1 Agency Ltd self-bills the principal for £1,800 + VAT of £315 in respect of the goods sold less commission. In the VAT return for quarter 1 Agency Ltd includes:

Box 1 (output VAT): £350 on sales to customers	£350
Box 4 (input VAT): £315 billed by the principal	£315
Box 5 (net VAT due)	£35
Box 6 (total value of sales): £2,000 billed to customers	£2,000
Box 7 (total value of purchases): £1,800 billed by the principal	£1,800

Where the agency arrangement involves a principal or third party in another EC state or outside the EC, see VAT Notice 700 section 24 for further information and examples.

Supplies of agency services

If you are agent to a disclosed principal then you make a supply of agency services to your principal. If you are agent to an undisclosed principal and do not adopt the commissionaire treatment, you also make a separate supply of agency services to your principal.

A supply of agency services is by default standard-rated. Key exceptions include:

- Many services that comprise the making of arrangements for zero-rated passenger transport are also zero-rated (note that if you supply passenger transport as principal or undisclosed agent you may have to use the Tour Operators' Margin Scheme: see the section in Chapter 10). Zero rating covers disclosed agency services that comprise the making of arrangements connected with scheduled flights, journeys from a place within to a place outside the UK and vice versa and most UK transport in vehicles with a carrying capacity of not less than ten people. See Chapter 6 for information on zero-rated passenger transport services and VAT Notice 744A for information on when disclosed agency services are zero-rated.

- Many intermediary services connected to insurance products are exempt. An intermediary service is provided when someone brings together someone seeking and someone providing insurance. See VAT Notice 701/36 for more details.

- Many intermediary services connected to financial products are exempt. Qualifying products include loans, securities, credit facilities and HP instalment finance. An intermediary service is provided when someone brings together someone seeking and someone supplying certain financial services. See VAT Notice 701/49 for more details.

Disbursements

Certain costs incurred by a supplier may be treated as incurred on behalf of the customer. Such costs are referred to as disbursements. In effect, the supplier is acting as agent for the customer in incurring the cost. A payment may be treated as a disbursement when all of the following conditions are met:

1. The customer actually received and used the goods or services provided by the third party. This condition usually prevents the supplier's own travelling and subsistence expenses, telephone bills, postage, and other costs being treated as disbursements for VAT purposes.

2. The customer was liable for the payment.

3. The customer authorised the supplier to make the payment on its behalf.

4. The customer knew that the goods or services would be provided by a third party.

5. The supplier's payment is separately itemised on an invoice to the customer.

6. The supplier recovers only the exact amount paid to the third party.

7. The goods or services are clearly additional to the supplies made by the supplier to the customer on its own account.

There are two possible ways of dealing with disbursements:

1. **Disbursement treatment**: The supplier does not recover any VAT incurred on the disbursement but passes it on gross to the customer. The disbursement is excluded when calculating any VAT charged to the customer. If the third party supplying the disbursement goods or services makes out its invoice for the disbursement to the customer and the supplier passes the invoice on to the customer, the customer can recover the input VAT subject to the normal recovery rules. However, if the customer does not possess a valid VAT invoice for the disbursement the input VAT cannot normally be recovered.

2. **Expense treatment**: The supplier recovers the VAT on the disbursement and charges it as an expense to the customer. The expense is included when calculating any VAT charged to the customer. The supplier must be entitled to recover VAT on the disbursement. This will be so if, for example, the supplier is acting as undisclosed agent and any VAT invoice for the disbursement is made out to the supplier.

Example: Disbursement

Consultant Ltd supplies advice to Customer Ltd. Consultant Ltd raises an invoice for standard-rated fees of £1,000, expenses of £50 and qualifying disbursements of £100 + VAT of £17.50. The two possible treatments are:

Disbursement treatment (£)		Expense treatment (£)	
Fee	1,000.00	Fee	1,000.00
Expenses (£50)	50.00	Expenses (£100 + £50)	150.00
Subtotal	1,050.00	VAT at 17.5% (1,150 x 17.5%)	201.25
VAT at 17.5% (£1,050 x 17.5%)	183.75	Total due	1,351.25
Disbursements	117.50		
Total due	1,351.25		

The disbursement treatment will only be advantageous where the disbursement carries no VAT and the customer is not registered, or the customer is incurring the expense for non-business, exempt or residual purposes.

Single and multiple supplies

Where a supply comprises a package of separately identifiable components ('elements') with different individual VAT statuses you will need to decide if the package comprises a single supply with a single VAT status or if it comprises a multiple supply each element of which may have a different VAT status. Common examples in the voluntary sector include: a supply of exempt tuition that includes zero-rated printed matter, the provision of standard-rated catering at an exempt conference, an exempt entrance charge to an exhibition which includes a zero-rated catalogue and the supply of a standard-rated DVD with a zero-rated book.

There are three possible VAT scenarios:

- **Single supply**: one element of the package is predominant. All the other elements follow the VAT status of the predominant element.

- **Multiple supply**: no one element is predominant. The consideration for the package must be apportioned between the different types of supply involved (standard–rated, zero–rated, exempt etc.).

• **A special rule or concession applies**: in some situations special rules or concessions operate to turn what would otherwise be a single supply into a multiple supply or vice versa. The special rules and concessions are considered in the section below.

Outline of the single/multiple supply tests

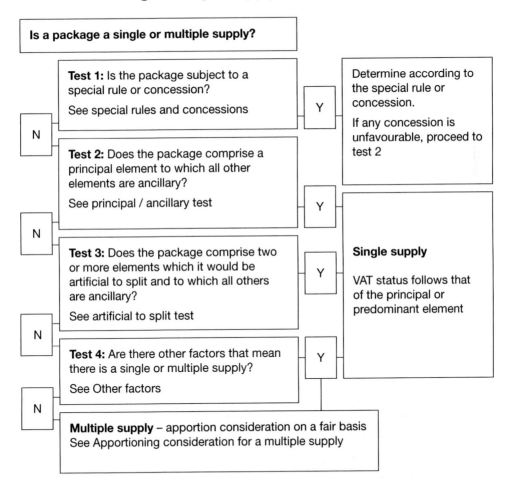

Single price

Usually the problem only arises where a package is supplied for a single price. Where the elements of a package can be purchased separately in arm's-length transactions the individual purchase prices of each element will generally be their value for VAT purposes. Any discount for purchase as a package must be apportioned between the elements on some reasonable basis.

However, the existence of separate prices is not the determining factor, and it is possible for a package that comprises two or more elements each charged for separately to be a single supply. This may apply if the elements must be purchased together or if the price split is artificial. A common example is a magazine supplied as part of a package where the magazine has a cover price but is either not sold separately or the level of separate sales is very small. If the cover price is used as a basis for apportioning the package price, this is likely to be viewed with suspicion by HMRC.

The 'principal/ancillary test'

In the 1999 case Card Protection Plan, the European Court of Justice (ECJ) established a set of rules for determining whether a single or multiple supply exists:

1. You must consider all the circumstances in which the transaction takes place and determine what it is that is being supplied to a typical customer.

2. Every supply of a service must normally be regarded as distinct and independent; however, a supply which comprises a single service from an economic point of view should not be artificially split so as to distort the functioning of the VAT system.

3. There is a single supply where one or more elements are to be regarded as constituting a principal service, while the other elements are to be regarded as ancillary services.

4. A service must be regarded as ancillary to a principal service if it does not constitute for customers an aim in itself but a means of better enjoying the principal service.

5. The fact that a single price is charged is not decisive, though it may indicate that there is a single supply.

6. If a package comprises a multiple supply, the simplest possible method should be used to apportion the consideration between the different types of supply.

The key test is the fourth. This is referred to as the 'principal/ancillary test'. It asks what the main aim of a typical customer is in purchasing the package. If the typical customer has one main aim and all the other elements of the package merely enable the customer to achieve that aim, then the one main aim is the principal supply and all the others are ancillary to it. To take an extreme example, when a typical customer purchases a new TV, the main aim is to purchase a new TV and not a cardboard box, instruction booklet or statutory warranty. However crucial these are, they are ancillary to the supply of the TV.

The 'artificial to split test'

The 'principal/ancillary test' deals with the situation where there is a single principal supply, with all other elements being ancillary to this. It does not deal with situations where there are several 'principal' supplies with different VAT statuses, that is, elements that a typical customer regards as being aims in themselves. Examples are:

- Food supplied in a restaurant: the food, its preparation and the service are all aims in themselves and none are ancillary to the other. Nevertheless the ECJ held in the case of *Faaborg-Gelting Linien* (1996, C–231/94) that the supply of food in a restaurant is a single supply of catering services. This is so even though it is possible that for an expensive meal the vast majority of the cost is in the food.

- The House of Lords in Benyon & Partners (2004, UKHL 53) held that the administration of drugs such as vaccines by a doctor is a single exempt supply of medical services. This is so even though neither the drugs nor the administration are ancillary to each other.

In the case *Levob Verzekeringen BV* (see Chapter 13: *VAT cases*) the ECJ formulated the 'artificial to split test' to deal with such situations. The artificial to split test says that where two or more elements are not capable of practical use as intended without each other, they constitute a single supply.

In the *Levob* case the court was considering whether the supply and customisation of a software package by a US company to Levob comprised a single supply or two distinct supplies. The software and its customisation had been treated as two separate supplies for separate prices by the US supplier. However, Levob could not use the software without customisation and the customisation was not minor. The court decided that this meant there was a single supply for a single price.

This still leaves the question of how the status of the single supply is determined. In the *Levob* case the court suggested that it may be possible to determine the 'predominant' element on the basis of cost, the extent of the work involved or the time spent on the different elements.

In the House of Lords case College of Estate Management (2005, UKHL 62) the college provided a distance learning course, the major part of the students' time being spent on studying supplied printed materials. The supply of printed matter is in itself zero-rated (see Chapter 6), however the course was nevertheless held to be an exempt supply of education because this was the main purpose of the course from the student's perspective. Though the printed study material was not ancillary to the education, the education was nevertheless the predominant element.

Other cases (such as *Faaborg-Gelting Linien* above) suggest that two or more elements that are artificial to split may constitute a new supply with its own character when combined.

These cases suggest three ways of identifying the VAT status of the supply when the artificial to split test is met:

- the resultant supply is different in character to its constituent elements and has its own VAT status

- it is not sensible to describe one or more elements as ancillary to another but one element can nevertheless be identified as the key one from the point of view of a typical customer

- there is no key element but one element predominates in terms of cost, time, effort or some other factor

Other factors

Court cases have repeatedly emphasised that it may be neither possible nor desirable to establish an exhaustive series of tests that can be applied in every situation to determine whether there is a single or multiple supply. Each situation has to be assessed on its own facts and there may be other factors that lead to the conclusion that there is a single or multiple supply.

No clear tests beyond the principal/ancillary and artificial to split tests have emerged from the case law to date, though it is possible that other tests may arise in future. The tests should not be applied mechanically, and it is important to consider all the facts and circumstances and to apply common sense.

Apportioning consideration for a multiple supply

Where a multiple supply is provided for a single price (or multiple prices but the split is artificial) the price must be apportioned between the different types of supply. The price only needs to be split between standard-rated, reduced rate, zero-rated and exempt supplies and it is not always necessary to go to the level of splitting out into the individual supplies.

See Chapter 5 for specific considerations relating to the apportionment of member-ship subscriptions charged by non-profit organisations.

Apportionments are usually based on the costs or market values of the different supplies, though they may be based on other methods as well. HMRC can only challenge an apportionment on the basis that it produces a result that is unfair.

In theory the value of a supply is everything which constitutes the consideration for the service, that is, what is received for it. This implies that a market value-based apportionment should be used wherever possible. This interpretation is supported by the ECJ cases of Madgett & Baldwin and MyTravel (see the section on the Tour Operators' Margin Scheme for more about these cases). However, in practice it is often difficult to determine the market value of a supply, for example if the supply is not otherwise available. Generally, HMRC and the courts will only accept a market value-based method where the same goods or services are supplied separately by the same organisation.

A cost-based apportionment has the potential disadvantage of assuming that the mark-up on all the different supplies is the same, though it may be possible to correct for this where there is some evidence to support the use of different mark-ups.

Where the costs of some of the supplies can be determined but the costs of others cannot, it is sometimes accepted by HMRC that the value of the other supplies can be calculated by applying a mark-up to the determinable costs and then subtracting this from the total price. The difficulty often lies in determining the mark-up or mark-ups to be used. Options include using known mark-ups on similar supplies, using sector norms for mark-ups and using the organisation's overall profit level on related activities.

Special rules and concessions

There are many special rules and concessions that apply in various situations or that have been agreed between HMRC and particular business sectors. Some of these of relevance to voluntary organisations are:

*   **Subscriptions to non-profit organisations**: where a subscription to a non-profit-making organisation would be, under the above rules, treated as a single supply, the organisation may by concession treat it as a multiple supply and apportion the subscription between the supplies involved. If it is clear that the cost of the subscription exceeds the value of all the supplies, the excess may be treated as an outside the scope donation. See Chapter 5 for more details.

*   **Qualifying fundraising events**: any activity that is part of a qualifying fundraising event (see Chapter 7) is exempt. This means that you do not need to determine if packages provided at such events are single or multiple supplies. However, if an exempt supply also qualifies for zero rating, you can choose to zero rate the supply. If you are VAT-registered this will generally be beneficial as it will allow you to recover the attributable VAT. So if any packages within the event include a zero-rated element you will be able to zero rate the package if it is a single zero-rated supply or the zero-rated part if it is a multiple supply, the other components being exempt.

*   **Affinity credit cards**: there is a special concession whereby payments under affinity credit card arrangements between a bank and a charity or its trading subsidiary can be treated as a part standard-rated and part outside the scope. See Chapter 7 for details.

- **Packaging**: where packaging is normal and necessary for the goods it is ancillary to the supply of the goods and follows the VAT treatment of the goods. This is so even if the packaging forms a major part of the overall cost, as long as it is necessary to contain, protect and promote the goods. However, if the packaging is more than is normal or necessary, for example if the packaging is designed to have a use of its own and could be sold separately, there may be a multiple supply.

If there is a multiple supply of zero-rated goods (such as food) with standard-rated packaging then, by concession, it can be treated as a single zero-rated supply provided the packaging is not charged for separately, it costs no more than 20 per cent of the total cost of the supply and it costs no more than £1 excluding VAT.

See also the package tests and package test for charities in Chapter 6 for concessions that apply to multiple supplies of zero-rated and standard-rated printed matter.

If a deposit is charged for the safe return of a container, the deposit is outside the scope of VAT.

- **Delivery charges**: delivery charges include charges for postage, courier delivery and any special packing that is necessary for delivery. If goods are delivered with no separate charge for delivery or if delivery is part of the contract for the purchase of the goods, then the delivery is ancillary to the supply of the goods and there is a single supply that follows the VAT status of the goods. Delivery will typically be part of the contract where goods are supplied by mail order or via the web and you remain responsible for the goods until they are received by the customer. This applies even if the invoice shows a separate charge for delivery. If delivery is an optional extra the delivery charge is standard-rated unless the delivery is to a place outside the UK, when it is generally zero-rated. For the detailed rules on deliveries outside the UK, see VAT Notice 744B.

Where a supplier provides a service of posting mail, for example where a printer prints material and also sends it out to a specified distribution list, the postage charges may be treated as a disbursement made by the supplier on behalf of the customer provided the disbursement conditions are met (see the section on disbursements in this chapter); the customer specifies the mailing list or has access to the mailing list before distribution; the supplier's responsibilities for the mail cease when it is accepted by the postal company; and the supplier passes on any discounts obtained from the postal company. The postal company must be licensed by Postcomm. Note that this concession is only likely to be beneficial where items are posted by Royal Mail.

- **Promotional items in magazines**: by concession, promotional items supplied with magazines can treat them as zero -rated if the following conditions are met:

1. a separate charge is not made for the item

2. issues with promotional items are sold at the same price as those without, and

3. the cost of all promotional items included in any individual issue does not exceed £1 (excluding VAT) and 20 per cent of the total of the combined supply (excluding VAT).

The transfer of a going concern

Where a business is sold or transferred, a special set of rules may apply to simplify the VAT situation. These are known as the 'transfer of a going concern rules' – commonly abbreviated to TOGC. When the TOGC conditions are met, the transfer of a business is neither a supply of goods nor a supply of services and so is outside the scope of VAT. This avoids the need to value and charge VAT separately on the individual assets.

Even though the transfer is outside the scope, VAT on costs that are attributable to the transfer may be recoverable. Such costs are usually attributed to the activity transferred, and so are recoverable to the extent VAT incurred on the activity is recoverable.

The TOGC rules apply where a business is transferred to a different person or entity. It can be the entire business or a part that is capable of separate operation, for example a building with tenants. However, it must be the assets of the business that are transferred rather than shares – with a transfer of shares the assets still remain in the same legal entity.

To qualify as a TOGC, all of the following must apply:

*   The effect of the transfer must be to put the new owner in possession of a business which can be operated as such. If only part of the business is being transferred, that part must be able to operate alone. It does not matter whether it will, in fact, be operated separately from any other businesses the new owner carries on.

*   The business, or part business, must be a going concern at the time of the transfer. It can still be a going concern even though it is unprofitable, or is trading under the control of a liquidator or administrative receiver, or a trustee in bankruptcy, or an administrator appointed under the Insolvency Act 1986.

*   The assets transferred must be intended for use by the new owner in carrying on the same kind of business. This is a strict condition. However if the same kind of business is carried on for a short period then it is restructured this is generally acceptable.

- There must not be a series of immediately consecutive transfers of the business. Where A sells its assets to B who immediately sells those assets on to C, because B has not carried on the business the TOGC provisions do not apply to any of the transactions.

- Where the seller is registered for VAT, the buyer must be registered or at the date of the transfer be required to be registered for VAT because all of the conditions for compulsory registration are met, or be accepted for voluntary registration. However, there can be a TOGC where the seller is not registered for VAT, for example if the seller is trading below the registration limit or making wholly exempt supplies.

- There must be no significant break in the normal trading pattern before or immediately after the transfer. A short period of closure that does not significantly disrupt the existing trading pattern, for example for redecoration, will not prevent the business from being transferred as a going concern.

If the business being transferred includes a new building or a building on which the option to tax has been exercised (see Chapter 8), then special anti-avoidance rules apply to exclude the building, unless the buyer has also opted to tax the building.

Transfers into a partly exempt VAT group

Where assets are transferred under the TOGC rules into a partly exempt VAT group (for information on VAT groups, see the section above) special rules apply. The group must account for output VAT on certain of the assets transferred. This output VAT can then be recovered in accordance with the group's partial exemption method, treating the affected assets as if they had been purchased in the normal way. If all the assets transferred will be used entirely for taxable activities this rule will have no net effect. These rules do not apply to the following assets:

- any assets which were assets of the previous owner more than three years before the date of the transfer

- goodwill such as unidentifiable goodwill, use of a trademark or trading name and the sole right to trade in a particular area

- any assets which are zero-rated or exempt (for example zero-rated or exempt freehold or leasehold interests in land)

- items which fall within the capital goods scheme. See the capital goods scheme section in Chapter 10 for details of the scheme.

If the affected assets were acquired below market value, then the output VAT charge must be calculated on the open market value. Where the transferor is unconnected, the price paid will normally be assumed to be the open market value. If separate prices were not specified for affected assets, the consideration must be apportioned.

HMRC may be prepared to accept that no output VAT is due in respect of the following:

- assets on which the previous owner's input VAT recovery was blocked (for example, cars)

- assets purchased in a year in which the transferor's partial exemption recovery rate was lower than the transferee's recovery rate in the year of transfer.

See VAT Notice 700/9 for full details of the transfer of a going concern rules.

Planning for VAT in charities and voluntary organisations

Charities are often complex organisations with many different activities. Their VAT situation may, therefore, be complex. Various aspects are examined in detail in the rest of this book. There are, however, some important points which should be borne in mind at the time when considering an organisation's VAT position:

- An organisation will not necessarily be worse off or better off if it has to register for VAT.

- It is important to look at the overall picture, not at particular activities in isolation.

- Consider who your customers are and what their VAT position is. They may be able to reclaim all the VAT you charge, or it may effectively increase your prices.

- A lot of the input VAT you have paid on your purchases should be recoverable if your affairs are to be arranged tax efficiently.

- Organisations which are mainly service providers (where their main costs are wages) are likely to have little input VAT to recover but, if they register for VAT, will have to charge VAT on their labour.

- Registration for VAT is not optional! It is a matter of fact and law as to whether an organisation or person should register for VAT or not and there are severe penalties for non-registration.

- VAT should not be considered in isolation – you need to think about direct tax, business rates, gift aid, and other legal requirements as well.

It is therefore important that organisations obtain proper advice before committing themselves to a course of action. It is always important to see VAT as one of the considerations you should take into account when deciding how to plan your activities. Direct tax, the law and the organisation's objects and strategic direction all have to be taken into consideration.

Including VAT in planning new activities

You must take great care in planning activities to ensure that your organisation does not unexpectedly find itself liable for VAT, penalties and interest. Also look at all aspects of the planned activity, as VAT will certainly not be the only consideration. Other taxes, laws and the management structure will also impact on any decisions about how activities should be organised.

There are many ways, however, in which an organisation can improve its VAT position. Some of the strategies available generally are described below. Not all of these will be suitable in all situations; in some cases the strategy requires substantial change in your management or activities. It is not possible to cover every situation which will arise, but it should be a useful guide to some common situations.

Typical VAT problems in charities

The main problem for most charities is that they suffer VAT on purchases that they cannot recover. Beyond the many reliefs covered in Chapters 6 and 8, they will be looking for ways to recover this VAT. For this, charities need to be registered for VAT and need to see how they can then maximise their VAT recovery. Usually this will involve increasing the level of taxable activity.

It is important to consider the VAT status of your customers:

- If the people to whom you make charges for goods and services are able to recover VAT on purchases, then it is a lot easier to consider strategies that increase your VATable activity. You will be better off because you can charge the same price and recover VAT on your purchases, thus lowering your costs.

- If your customers are not registered for VAT, then it will be more difficult to simply add the VAT on top of the price you normally charge. You may have to keep your charge the same and treat this as the VAT-inclusive amount. Once the VAT is taken off the income, the net amount of income you receive may be lower. Of course, this will not be the case if the activity is zero-rated. This is the best situation from the point of view of VAT planning, as you do not have to charge VAT on the outputs, but you can recover the related input VAT.

Some common situations for charities are:

- A charity may not have any VATable activities and therefore cannot register for VAT.

- A charity is about to embark on a significant expansion which will involve capital purchases and building works. It wishes to avoid or recover as much VAT as possible.

- A VAT-registered charity has a very low recovery rate and wishes to increase the amount of input VAT it recovers.

- A charity has to set up a trading subsidiary because it is starting activities which fall outside its main charitable objects. Staff costs and other costs will have to be recharged to the trading company.

- A charity does not want to lose income by having to account for VAT on income earned.

- A charity wants to avoid the administrative burden of VAT and considers that it would have little VAT to recover.

Charities will therefore be looking at strategies which:

- Increase the amount of taxable supplies overall in order to achieve registration or increase the overall rate of recovery.

- Make a particular activity taxable, rather than non-business or exempt, so that all input VAT relating to that activity may be recovered.

- Manage activities in such a way to avoid breaching the *de minimis* limit for partial exemption, where the charity is generally below the limit.

- Enable the charity to purchase goods without paying VAT – most of these are covered in Chapter 6.

- Explore organisational structures which are more beneficial for VAT.

- Avoid VAT registration where there is a likelihood of low recovery.

- Plan fundraising events to maximise VAT.

In planning for VAT, you should generally arrange your affairs properly before the transactions take place. It will be very difficult to claim that the correct VAT treatment should be applied afterwards. Sometimes it is possible to backdate a claim for overpaid or under-recovered VAT, but this will be subject to the three-year limit for claims.

It also important that you can demonstrate that there were good commercial reasons or organisational reasons for the action that you have taken. Changing the structure of the organisation or creating separate entities purely for the avoidance of tax may be challenged. See the comments on VAT mitigation schemes in Chapter 10.

12 Operational aspects

This chapter covers the practical aspects of VAT including: the VAT invoice rules, how to determine the time of supply, how to complete the VAT return, advice on dealing with HMRC, the 'blocking rules' on motor vehicles and business entertaining, and how to set up the tax codes in Sage 50 to deal with exempt and non-business activities.

Time of supply

The 'time of supply' rules determine when a supply takes place and hence the VAT return in which the VAT is to be recorded. The time of supply is also known as the tax point.

The basic tax point is, for a supply of goods, the date the customer takes possession of the goods, and for services, the service being completed. However, if the supplier issues an invoice within 14 days after the basic tax point, the tax point is the invoice date unless the supplier opts to make it the basic tax point.

If the supplier, before the basic tax point, issues a VAT invoice or receives payment, this creates an actual tax point. If the supplier both issues a VAT invoice and receives payment before the basic tax point, the actual tax point is the earlier of the two.

The tax point of the supply is the actual tax point if the supplier raises an invoice for full payment or receives full payment before the basic tax point. If the supplier issues an invoice for part payment or receives part payment before the basic tax point, then there will be two tax points: one at the actual tax point and one for the balance due later. If several interim invoices are issued then there will be multiple tax points.

Example: Time of supply

On 25 April Mr Smith signs a contract to supply consultancy services for £500 + VAT. He starts the work on 2 May and issues an interim invoice for £200 + VAT on 31 May, and receives payment on 8 June. He completes the work on

20 June and issues a final invoice for £300 + VAT on 30 June. Final payment is received on 15 July.

The basic tax point is when the work is completed: 20 June. However, the final invoice is issued within 14 days after the basic tax point, so the tax point is the date the final invoice is issued.

The interim invoice on 31 May creates an actual tax point for part of the supply. So there are two tax points: one on 31 May for £200 + VAT and one on 30 June for £300 + VAT.

There are many exceptions to these basic rules. Some exceptions are:

Where a deposit is taken, this creates an actual tax point if the deposit is part payment towards the total due. If the deposit is normally returned complete then no actual tax point is created, even if the deposit is forfeited.

Under the cash accounting scheme (see Chapter 10: *Other topics*) output VAT is recognised when payment is received from the customer. If a cheque bounces then an adjustment can be made for any VAT recognised. Credit and debit card payments are recognised when the payment is made by the customer. Input VAT is recognised when payment is made to the supplier. Where an invoice is paid in instalments, each payment creates a tax point.

Where a retention is held (for example, under a construction contract) the tax point for the retention element is delayed until the retention is invoiced or paid.

For a continuous supply (such as renting of property) a tax point is created whenever an invoice is issued or payment made, though if the supplier issues an annual invoice in advance showing the payments due in the year the tax points are whenever the payments are due or paid. If there is a continuous supply of taxable services between connected parties then, under certain circumstances, a tax point is created every year if no invoice has actually been issued in the year. See VAT Information Sheet 14/03.

For a supply of freehold land, the basic tax point is completion. If a deposit is paid at exchange then a tax point is created if it is payable to the vendor or to a solicitor acting as the vendor's agent. However, if the deposit is paid to a stakeholder who holds the payment on behalf of both parties pending satisfactory performance of the contract, this does not create a tax point until payment is released to the vendor. If the total consideration cannot be determined at completion (for example, when the vendor is entitled to a further payment if the purchaser obtains planning permission) then the tax point for any further payment is the earlier of invoice or receipt of the further payment.

If goods are supplied to a customer in another EC state, then, if the customer is not VAT-registered, the tax point is determined under the basic rules above. If the customer is VAT-registered, the tax point is the earlier of the date of issue of a VAT invoice and the 15th of the month following the month of removal from the UK.

If goods are supplied on sale or return or on approval then the basic tax point is the date the goods are adopted by the customer, or 12 months after they are given to the customer if this is earlier. The basic tax point is modified if there is an actual tax point.

If goods are supplied under an agreement where the supplier retains title to the goods until some specified event and the price is determined at the specified event, then the basic tax point is the date the event occurs.

Under the Tour Operators' Margin Scheme (see Chapter 10), the tax point of a margin scheme supply is the earlier of the traveller's departure or first occupation of accommodation by the traveller.

See VAT Notice 700 for further information on the 'time of supply' rules.

VAT invoices

Generally, a VAT-registered organisation must issue VAT invoices for all taxable supplies made to other VAT-registered organisations, including organisations registered for VAT in other EC states. There is no requirement to issue a VAT invoice for exempt supplies and zero-rated supplies to a customer in the UK. However, a VAT invoice must be issued for zero-rated supplies to a person in another EC state.

A VAT invoice must, as a minimum, contain the following:

- a unique identifying number (invoice number or reference). From 1 October 2007 this must be a sequential number based on one or more series which uniquely identify the invoice

- the supplier's name and address and VAT registration number. If the customer is in another EC state, the supplier's VAT registration number must be prefixed 'GB'

- the time of supply (tax point) and, if different, the date the invoice is issued

- the customer's name and address. If the customer is registered in another EC state, their VAT registration number and country prefix must also be shown

- a description of the goods or services supplied. For each description the following details must be provided: if the goods or services are countable, the quantity and unit price; the amount payable excluding VAT; and the rate of VAT applicable. Amounts may be expressed in any currency

- the total payable (for all description lines) excluding VAT, in any currency

- details of any cash discount

- the total VAT chargeable in sterling. The VAT on a whole invoice may be rounded down to the nearest whole penny. VAT on individual lines in the invoice may be either rounded down to the nearest 0.1p or rounded to the nearest 1p or 0.5p.

Example: VAT invoice

Invoice   Supplier Name

To: Customer Name   Supplier Address

Customer Address   VAT registration number: 123 4567 89

Invoice number: 123456

Tax point: 12 August 2007   Invoice date: 15 August 2007

Quantity	Description	Unit price £	Net £	VAT Rate
10	Widgets	10.00	100.00	17.5%
1	The Book of Widgets	25.00	25.00	0.00%
	Delivery		15.00	17.5%
	Net		140.00	
	VAT		20.12	
	Total due		160.12	

A VAT invoice must be issued within 30 days of a tax point arising, unless the tax point arose as a result of an invoice being issued. However, the 30-day limit can be extended if you are awaiting invoices from your own sub-contractors or you are newly registered but have not been notified of your VAT registration number.

287

VAT invoices must not be issued for supplies made under the second-hand goods scheme and supplies made under the Tour Operator's Margin Scheme. There are special rules for invoices issued under the agricultural flat rate scheme (see Chapter 10). For intra-EC supplies which are reverse-charge supplies, exempt supplies or zero-rated supplies of goods (dispatches) the invoice must describe the VAT nature of the supply.

Retailers' invoices

There are simplified rules for invoices issued by retailers. A retailer does not have to provide a VAT invoice unless the customer requests it.

If the customer requests a VAT invoice and the total payable is less than £250, the retailer can provide a simplified invoice containing the following: the retailer's name, address and registration number; the time of supply; a description of the supply; the total payable including VAT; for each rate of VAT chargeable, the gross payable including VAT and the rate of VAT.

If the customer agrees, a retailer can issue a VAT invoice modified to show for each description the VAT-inclusive value of the supply rather than the VAT-exclusive value, provided the invoice also provides an analysis of the total invoice net, VAT and gross due between the different rates of VAT.

Credit and debit notes

If you issue a VAT invoice which is incorrect in some way, you cannot simply scrap it and issue a corrected invoice. You must either issue a credit or debit note to correct the original invoice or issue a credit note to completely reverse the original invoice and then issue a new invoice.

Credit and debit notes should use the rates of VAT applicable at the original time of supply. A credit or debit note should be headed 'credit note' or 'debit note' as appropriate and include, as a minimum, the following:

* an identifying number and date of issue

* the reason for issue – for example, 'returned goods'

* the number and date of the original VAT invoice. If this is not possible or practical, the supplier must be able to show HMRC that they have accounted for VAT on the original supply

* the name, address and registration number of the supplier

* the name and address of the customer

* descriptions of the supplies being credited or debited, and for each description the quantity and unit price, the total amount excluding VAT and the rate of VAT

- totals for the net amount and VAT. If credit notes are issued without VAT adjustment, they should state 'This is not a credit note for VAT'.

For further details, see VAT Notice 700.

Bad debts

If a customer fails to pay then you cannot deal with this by issuing a credit note. Instead, you must claim bad debt relief through your VAT return. You can claim for any output VAT that you have paid to HMRC but not received from the customer.

Before you can claim:

- the goods or services must have been provided to the customer

- the debt must be over six months old (but not more than three years old)

- the debt must have been written off in your accounts.

You cannot reclaim VAT on a debt that has been sold, factored or assigned. If the supply is partly paid, you can claim for the unpaid part. If goods are sold with reservation of title until the goods are paid for (a *Romalpa* clause) then this does not prevent bad debt relief being claimed.

Note that if you are using the cash accounting scheme (see Chapter 10) you only account for output VAT when the customer pays. If the customer fails to pay then no output VAT will have been accounted for. If, under the cash accounting scheme, the customer pays by cheque but the cheque bounces after you have paid the output VAT to HMRC, you may adjust for this in your next VAT return.

Discounts

Unconditional discounts such as bulk discounts and customer status discounts that are granted at the time of the supply have the effect of reducing the customer's liability and hence may also reduce any VAT chargeable.

If a discount is conditional on some future event, for example a retrospective discount if the customer's total purchases exceed a certain level, then invoices raised before the condition is met should ignore the discount. Any credit note or retrospective discount provided when the condition is met should include an adjustment to the VAT already charged.

If a prompt payment discount is offered, the price charged is taken to be the lower discounted price, whether or not the prompt payment offer is taken up.

Example: Prompt payment discount

Jones Ltd issues a standard-rated invoice for £250 + VAT.

There is a 2% discount for payment within 14 days.

Net invoice amount	£250.00
VAT: £250 x 98% x 17½%	£42.87
Gross invoice amount	£292.87

Input VAT evidence

In order to be able to deduct input VAT, an organisation must hold appropriate evidence that the input VAT has been validly incurred. Normally this means possessing a valid VAT invoice from the supplier. Note that only UK VAT can be recovered in a UK VAT return. See Chapter 9: *International aspects of VAT* for details of how to recover VAT incurred in other EC states.

Pro-forma invoices, reminders and statements are not valid VAT invoices, even if they contain all the information required on a VAT invoice. Valid VAT debit and credit notes can be used to support VAT adjustments. If a VAT invoice omits minor details then in practice HMRC will usually accept it. However, key information such as the supplier's details and VAT registration number, amount of VAT charged and tax point must always be present.

A VAT invoice is not needed if the total invoice value (including VAT) is £25 or less and is for: telephone calls from public or private telephones; purchases through coin-operated machines; car-park charges (on-street parking meters are not subject to VAT) or a single or return toll charge. Note that toll charges on some bridges, roads and tunnels operated by public authorities are outside the scope of VAT and so no VAT will have been included in the toll charge.

Missing VAT invoices

Where VAT invoices are not present, HMRC officers have discretion in what they can accept as appropriate evidence to support recovery of input VAT. HMRC officers must exercise their discretion and consider whether suitable alternative evidence exists. They should look for evidence that the transaction did actually occur as described, on normal commercial terms, for business purposes and between validly UK-registered businesses.

Even if a supply takes place and the VAT invoice contains all the information required it will not be valid if it has been issued fraudulently, for example using a false company name and address or false VAT registration number. If you can demonstrate that you carried out normal commercial checks on the supplier and acted in good faith then HMRC may use their discretion to allow input VAT recovery. HMRC expect more stringent supplier checks where the goods are ones that are subject to widespread fraud and abuse such as alcohol, road fuel, computers and telephones. You can check if a VAT registration number is valid, and is valid for a given address, by ringing HMRC (see Chapter 14 for contact details).

If you do not possess a valid VAT invoice and are unable to obtain one, then, provided you meet these evidence requirements, you may deduct the input VAT subject to review by HMRC at your next VAT inspection. If an HMRC officer simply rejects input VAT recovery on the basis of absence of a valid VAT invoice and without having fairly and reasonably considered all the circumstances, their assessment can be challenged in the VAT Tribunal.

If you have been defrauded by a supplier sending you a VAT invoice which you have paid but the associated goods and services are not supplied, then the input VAT is not recoverable as no supply has taken place. If you have already recovered the input VAT when it becomes clear that you have been defrauded, then you must correct this in the next VAT return.

Unpaid supplier invoices

If you receive supplies and claim input VAT on those supplies but have not paid for them by six months after the payment became due, then you must repay the input VAT to HMRC in your next VAT return. The payment is regarded as being due on the later of date of the supply or the date when the consideration for the supply became due, normally the invoice date. If you have part paid then you need only repay the unpaid proportion.

If you are in dispute with the supplier and the supplier agrees to extend the due date, the six-month period runs from the revised due date.

If you later pay the supplier then you can reclaim any input VAT that was repaid.

Invoices made out to third parties

If a VAT invoice is made out to another person then the input VAT may not be deductible. If the invoice is made out to another person by mistake then the supplier should be asked to correct this. No VAT should be deducted until the corrected invoice is received.

If a third party pays for supplies made to another person the third party can-not normally deduct the input VAT. However, HMRC will usually accept that input VAT on an invoice made out to a third party is deductible in the following circumstances:

- the invoice is made out to an employee, and

- is for road fuel, subsistence expenses (meals, hotel accommodation etc.) or allowable removal expenses, and

- is incurred by the employee in carrying out the organisation's business activities, and

- the organisation either pays the supplier directly or refunds the employee.

Input VAT may also be deductible in other circumstances where it is clear that the supply is in substance to the organisation claiming deduction and the person the invoice is made out to has not recovered the input VAT.

The VAT return

Completing the VAT return

The standard VAT return (form VAT 100) has nine numeric boxes for completion:

Box 1: VAT due in this period on sales and other outputs

Include: all UK output VAT charged in the period, UK VAT charged on distance sales of goods to unregistered customers in other EC states and UK VAT charged on supplies of services where the place of supply is the UK, VAT due on the sale of assets, VAT on fuel scale charges, VAT on non-business use of business assets, estimates and annual adjustments under the Tour Operators' Margin Scheme.

Exclude: foreign (non-UK) VAT charged, assessments raised by HMRC.

Deduct: VAT on credit notes issued to customers.

Box 2: VAT due in this period on acquisitions from other EC member states

Include: acquisition VAT on goods acquired from suppliers in other EC states.

Exclude: VAT on supplies of services, VAT on reverse-charge supplies.

Box 3: Total VAT due

This is the sum of boxes 1 and 2.

Box 4: VAT reclaimed in this period on purchases and other inputs (including acquisitions from the EC)

Include: recoverable input VAT, acquisition VAT and import VAT for the period, bad debt relief claimed in the period.

Exclude: foreign (non–UK) input VAT, irrecoverable VAT such as VAT that is attributable to non-business or exempt activities (unless *de minimis*), input VAT on supplies where proper VAT documentation is not held, blocked input VAT such as VAT on business entertaining and cars which are available for private use, input VAT on goods and services purchased under the second-hand goods margin scheme or on margin scheme supplies under the Tour Operator's Margin Scheme.

Deduct: VAT on credit notes issued by suppliers to the extent the associated input VAT was recovered.

Box 5: Net VAT to be paid to Customs or reclaimed by you

This is the difference between boxes 3 and 4.

Box 6: Total value of sales and all other outputs excluding any VAT

Include: the net value of all taxable supplies, exempt supplies, EC sales included in box 8, the net value of reverse charge purchases, the net margin on margin scheme supplies under the Tour Operators' Margin Scheme.

Exclude: non-business income such as grants, donations, insurance claims and bank interest.

Box 7: Total value of purchases and all other inputs excluding any VAT

Include: purchases attributable to taxable and exempt activities (net of any input VAT), outside the scope supplies with the right of recovery, reverse charge purchases.

Exclude: purchases attributable to non-business activities, irrecoverable VAT, taxes (PAYE and national insurance, business rates, IPT), wages and salaries, MOT certificates, motor vehicle licence duty, purchases of margin scheme supplies under the Tour Operators' Margin Scheme.

Box 8: Total value of all supplies of goods and related costs, excluding any VAT, to other EC member states

Include: the net value of sales of goods to VAT-registered businesses in other EC states, directly related charges such as freight and insurance, distance sales to customers in other EC states above the respective states' distance-selling thresholds, despatches of own goods to a branch in another EC state for business purposes.

Exclude: sales of goods to unregistered customers in other EC states below the respective states' distance-selling thresholds, sales of services to customers in other EC states.

Box 9: Total value of all acquisitions of goods and related costs, excluding any VAT, from other EC member states

Include: the value of goods purchased from suppliers in other EC states, directly related charges such as freight and insurance.

Exclude: supplies of services received from suppliers in other EC states. Goods received from suppliers outside the EC.

Record keeping

For VAT purposes you must keep detailed accounting records to support the VAT return for a minimum of six years and in a readily accessible manner. In some situations (for example if you opt to tax a building) you may need to keep records for considerably longer. The documents that must be kept are:

- The accounting records, including, where relevant, statutory accounts, cash books, nominal ledgers, sales and purchase ledgers, day books and petty cash records.

- Transaction records such as till rolls, bank statements and paying-in slips.

- Sales documentation including copy sales invoices, credit and debit notes, orders, delivery notes, packing notes and related correspondence.

- Purchases documentation, including original purchase invoices, credit and debit notes, orders, delivery notes and related correspondence.

- Documentation relating to imports, exports, acquisitions and disposals (see Chapter 9: *International aspects of VAT*).

- A listing of transactions to the VAT account, copy VAT returns with supporting documentation and computations.

- VAT-related correspondence with HMRC, HMRC written agreements, copy zero-rating certificates and similar.

If you have opted to tax any property you should keep the associated documents at least until the option has expired (see Chapter 8: *Property*).

If you are partially exempt or have a mix of business and non-business activities then your records must cover your exempt and non-business activities as well. If keeping records for six years presents storage problems or will cause undue expense then you may apply to HMRC for agreement to reduce the length of time some of the records must be kept for.

Paper records may be transferred to microfilm or scanned and stored electronically with prior agreement from HMRC. It is acceptable to store accounting records in electronic form (for example as backups of the accounts system), provided they are readily accessible and convertible into a legible form.

Submission of VAT returns

If you submit paper VAT returns, the return and cheque for any amount due to HMRC must be sent in to arrive by the due date shown on the VAT return. The due date is normally the last day of the month following the end of the VAT period. You can send a return by first class post, allowing one clear day for delivery, and be deemed to have submitted your return on time, even if it does arrive late. However, if posting a return close to the deadline it is recommended that you obtain a certificate of posting in case the return is delayed in the postal system.

Where payment is sent electronically via BACS, CHAPS or giro credit, the deadline for submission of the return and payment is extended by seven days (unless you are using the annual accounting scheme or paying on account). However, this is the date by which HMRC must have received cleared funds, so you should check how long the payment will take to clear. If the seventh day falls on a weekend or bank holiday HMRC expect it to have cleared in their account by the last normal weekday before.

You can also complete and submit VAT returns online via the HMRC website. You must first obtain a Government Gateway Account. This provides you with a login and password to access and submit your VAT returns. You must pay any VAT due electronically, and the seven-day extension applies. You can also pay by direct debit, in which case HMRC will take the payment from your account three days after the due date of the return after allowing for the extra seven days allowed for electronic payment.

Late returns and payments

If the VAT return or payment are late, then this is referred to as a 'default'. If no return is sent in, then HMRC will estimate the VAT due. If a payment bounces, HMRC will not re-present it so you should make sure you have sufficient cleared funds in the relevant account. If you do not have the funds or can make only a part payment, you should contact HMRC and explain the situation.

The first time you default, HMRC will send you a Surcharge Liability Notice. This warns you that if you default again within 12 months of the date of the notice, you become liable for a default surcharge. If you default again within this period, then you will have to pay the default surcharge and you will receive a Surcharge Liability Notice Extension, extending the defaulting period by a further 12 months.

The default surcharge is calculated as a percentage of the VAT that is outstanding, so if no VAT was actually outstanding, the default surcharge is zero. The percentage increases each time you are late. The first time a surcharge is payable, it is 2 per cent. The surcharge is 5 per cent the second time it is payable, then it increases by 5 per cent each time you are late. There is a minimum of £30 and a maximum rate of 15 per cent. If the surcharge at the 2 per cent or 5 per cent rates is less than £400, HMRC will waive the penalty, though you will be issued with a Surcharge Liability Notice Extension, and the rate for the next default will go up. Small businesses (turnover below £150,000) will also be let off their very first default and just issued with a warning instead.

Reasonable excuse

You may be able to avoid liability for a surcharge if you had a reasonable excuse for not paying on time. An excuse is reasonable if a conscientious person, having due regard for the law and exercising reasonable foresight and due diligence, would have been unable to avoid the default. However, you must also have dealt with the problem as quickly as the conscientious person would have done.

HMRC have provided some guidance on what they consider might be reasonable excuses. They include computer breakdown, theft or destruction of key records, sudden illness or loss of key personnel and an unexpected cash crisis. However, the key test is that a reasonable person would have been unable to avoid the default. Illness or loss of key personnel is less likely to be considered reasonable in larger organisations. Planned holiday will never be a reasonable excuse. Lack of funds is not in itself a reasonable excuse, though if the lack was genuinely unexpected and caused by fraud, act of God or sudden non-payment by a normally reliable customer or funder, then it may have a reasonable cause.

A reasonable person will be expected to have contacted HMRC and informed them of any problem as soon as possible. If you know that you are going to be in default, you should contact HMRC and explain the problem. If you are having problems with accounting, such as a computer breakdown, or if the person who normally prepares the return is unavailable, you can request permission to submit an estimated return. If you do not have enough funds to pay then you should contact HMRC and try to arrange a payment schedule.

If you cannot pay then HMRC have an extensive range of powers to recover the debt, including the power to enter your premises and seize your goods without the need for a court order.

Errors and mistakes

If, after you have submitted a VAT return, you discover it contained errors, you must follow set procedures to correct the return. Errors can arise in many ways, for example:

- the accounting system produces incorrect figures

- data is entered incorrectly into the accounting system

- you misunderstood the VAT status of one or more transactions

- court cases have since established that a treatment you applied was incorrect.

There is no need to correct errors that are more than three years old. Generally, you cannot reclaim overpaid VAT and do not have to pay underpaid VAT if it relates to a VAT period that ended more than three years after you discovered the error. However, you must deal with an error when you discover it. If you do not you may be judged to have acted dishonestly, which may give rise to an assessment going back up to 20 years and for which there are severe penalties.

You should keep a record of the error, the date it was discovered, the date it was dealt with and details of how it was dealt with. If the net value of over- or under-declared VAT on previous returns is £2,000 or less you can include an adjustment in your next VAT return. If the net value is greater than £2,000 you must make a 'voluntary disclosure' of the error. In the 2008 budget it was announced that the threshold for voluntary disclosure will, from 1 July 2008, rise to the greater of £10,000 and 1 per cent of turnover, subject to a limit of £50,000. The turnover figure is the figure entered into box 6 of the VAT return for the VAT return period in which the disclosure is made – this includes exempt income but excludes non-business income. Note that, despite its name, the making of a voluntary disclosure is mandatory. You can use form 652 to make the disclosure (available for download from the HMRC website) or you can just write to your local VAT Business Advice Centre detailing the error. HMRC will then contact you and let you know how much you should pay or how much you can recover, including any interest due.

Unjust enrichment

If, by making a VAT refund, a claimant would be put in a better position than they would have been without the error, HMRC may claim unjust enrichment and deny or reduce the claim. The burden of proof is on HMRC, and HMRC must be able to show that someone other than the claimant bore the VAT burden. For example, if a supplier mistakenly assumed that a supply was standard-rated when it was zero-rated, the supplier will have overcharged its customers. It may not be clear that the burden of the overcharge fell on the customers if the supplier had to reduce its margins in order to remain competitive. If the claimant undertakes to repay any overcharged

VAT to affected customers then HMRC will generally consent to repayment, subject to a written agreement.

The three-year cap

The three-year capping rules act to limit your ability to make retrospective claims for overpayments made to HMRC. The capping rules work both ways, preventing you from reclaiming and preventing HMRC from assessing unless the underpayment was fraudulent. The rules from the taxpayers' perspective are:

- you cannot claim input tax more than three years after the due date of the return for the period in which the VAT was chargeable

- you cannot claim overpaid output VAT more than three years after the end of the VAT period in which the output VAT was accounted for

- if you overpaid VAT as a result of an erroneous voluntary disclosure, or as a result of an assessment based on an erroneous voluntary disclosure, the time limit is three years after the end of the VAT period in which the disclosure was made

- if you have overpaid output VAT as a result of an assessment (other than an assessment based on an erroneous voluntary disclosure), the time limit is three years after the end of the VAT period in which the assessment was made

- for any other payment made to HMRC that was not due, the time limit is three years after the payment was made.

The three-year cap does not apply in various situations including:

- Where a late VAT invoice is received from a supplier that relates to a supply made more than three years before as a result of an error by the supplier or the supplier's backdated registration for VAT. By concession, HMRC will treat the three-year time limit as running from the date the invoice was received. However, this does not apply if you received the invoice in time but forgot to claim or mislaid the invoice or did not receive a proper VAT invoice. In the latter situation HMRC consider that you should have asked HMRC to allow the use of other evidence to recover the VAT.

- Penalties paid but which are shown not to be due.

- Returns made following compulsory backdated registration.

- Claims under the DIY house-builder scheme (see Chapter 8).

See VAT Notice 706 for HMRC's policy on situations where a VAT period is capped but the related annual adjustment period is not.

The three-year capping legislation was introduced in 1997. Before 1997 there was no cap on claims for input VAT. However, the legislation was introduced with no transitional provisions, and in a 2002 case brought by Marks and Spencer, the European Court of Justice held this to be unlawful. In a recent House of Lords case (Fleming/ Condé Nast, 2008, UKHL 2) the Lords decided that there was no effective cap on input VAT claims arising prior to 1 May 1997. HMRC announced in Revenue & Customs Brief 07/08 that they would accept that claims can be made for output VAT arising in accounting periods ending before 4 December 1996 and input VAT in respect of which the entitlement to deduct arose in accounting periods ending before 1 May 1997. In the 2008 budget it was announced that a proper transition period would be introduced and the deadline for claims set at 31 March 2009.

Protective claims

As a result of the three-year cap, it is sometimes necessary to submit a protective claim to ensure a claim period is not timed out while litigation is in progress.

HMRC policy is to hold the claim on file and reconsider in light of any judgment that subsequently supports the validity of the claim. In the event that the judgment does go in the taxpayer's favour, the date on which the protective claim was originally submitted will be treated as the effective date for the purposes of applying the three-year cap.

However, HMRC state that a claim will only be accepted and kept on file if the claimant is either prepared to defend the basis of the claim at the VAT Tribunal or the matter is subject to ongoing litigation by another trader.

Dealing with HMRC

It is always better to enquire whether a particular activity is going to be taxable or not if there is any doubt at all. There are many activities undertaken by voluntary organisations which fall into 'grey areas'.

For general queries concerning charities phone the Charities helpline, and for other general queries phone the National Advisory Service (see Chapter 14 for phone numbers and addresses).

However, you should not rely on telephone advice for significant issues or if significant amounts are involved. In such situations you should get HMRC's advice in writing by making a written enquiry. Written enquiries concerning charities should be sent to HMRC charities office in Bootle, and there are also specialist offices for international supplies, the option to tax, registration and deregistration. All other written enquiries should be sent to the National Advice Service in Southend. The National Advice Service will pass your query on to the relevant office if it cannot deal with it itself.

When obtaining advice it is important that you disclose all potentially relevant information. If you fail to do this, HMRC may disregard their advice and assess you for any underpayment of VAT. If you have relied on written advice provided by HMRC that was based upon full disclosure of the facts then, if that advice turns out to be incorrect, HMRC will generally not raise a backdated assessment.

There are two points you should bear in mind when seeking advice from HMRC:

- Initial written enquiries, especially when dealt with by the National Advisory Service, will often produce nothing more than a straightforward regurgitation of the relevant parts of the appropriate VAT Notice. If you had already looked at those and were addressing a specific issue you may need to reply to their first letter and ask again for them to confirm your interpretation.

- In situations where there is uncertainty as to the facts or the law, there is a tendency among HMRC staff to choose the interpretation which maximises tax revenue to HMRC. This means that HMRC cannot necessarily be relied upon to provide impartial advice. However, this is not invariably the case and, especially where charities are concerned, some HMRC staff can be very supportive and even, on occasion, stretch the rules in your favour.

HMRC assessments

If HMRC discover mistakes in your VAT returns or if you fail to submit a VAT return, they may raise an assessment for the VAT due. If necessary, HMRC will estimate the amount due. Once an assessment has been issued it cannot be overturned simply because it is numerically incorrect. It can be overturned only if it is wrong in law or was made vindictively or capriciously, or is completely lacking in judgement or wholly unreasonable. It will therefore generally be to your advantage if you can agree with HMRC that you will perform any calculations involved and have them checked and confirmed by HMRC.

HMRC must issue an assessment for a VAT period within two years after the end of the period or within one year of the evidence coming to light. However, HMRC assessments are also limited by the three-year cap (see above) unless the assessment arises from fraud or dishonesty.

Appealing against HMRC decisions

If you disagree with a decision made by HMRC, you can ask them to reconsider it. HMRC are under no obligation to reconsider decisions but will generally do so if you can make a case for why the decision is flawed. The review will be undertaken by staff that were not involved in the original decision, and HMRC state that they aim to complete the review within 45 days.

If you ask HMRC to reconsider a decision, it is important that you do not lose your right of appeal to the VAT Tribunal. You can appeal to the VAT Tribunal simultaneously (see below) or ask HMRC to extend the deadline for appeal to the VAT Tribunal. HMRC have the power to extend the time limit for appeal to the VAT Tribunal while the reconsideration is carried out. If the reconsideration upholds the decision, you have 21 days from the date of the decision within which to appeal. If a new decision is made you have 30 days within which to appeal to the Tribunal.

The VAT Tribunal

You can appeal against most HMRC decisions to the VAT Tribunal. At the time of writing (2007), the tribunal system is about to be overhauled so you should check the latest position – see below and see Chapter 14 for website details.

You must generally appeal to the VAT Tribunal within 30 days of the HMRC decision, though HMRC can extend this deadline. You can also apply to the Tribunal for an extension of the deadline. If you ask HMRC to reconsider a decision you must be careful that you do not lose any right of appeal to the VAT Tribunal. You can ask HMRC to extend the deadline, but it may be safest to lodge an appeal with the VAT Tribunal and at the same time ask HMRC to reconsider. The fact that you have lodged an appeal with the VAT Tribunal may cause HMRC to look at the decision more carefully, and you may be able to make a claim in the Tribunal for the costs of negotiating with HMRC.

To make an appeal to the VAT Tribunal, you complete a notice of appeal form (Trib 1), which can be downloaded from the Tribunals website (see Chapter 14). This should be sent together with the disputed decision to your local Tribunal centre. Details of the Tribunal centres and the areas they cover are provided on the finance and tax tribunals website, together with detailed advice on the processes involved.

There are no fees for Tribunal hearings, though you will have to cover your own costs. Legal aid is only available in very limited circumstances. You can ask for an award of costs, but if you lose your case HMRC can also ask for their costs. HMRC policy is only to ask for costs in substantial and complex cases where large sums are involved, unless the appeal involves an important general point of law requiring clarification. HMRC will also ask for costs if they consider the Tribunal process is being abused, the case is frivolous or vexatious or the appellant has acted dishonestly or the case involves a tax avoidance scheme.

The costs you can claim are the costs of legal advice and representation, witness costs, and travel and subsistence. You cannot usually claim for your or your staff's time and opportunity costs such as loss of business. Where an award of costs is made it will often not reflect the full costs but be based on what is considered to be proportionate for the case.

Though you can represent yourself, it is usually a good idea to obtain professional representation, especially in complex or unusual cases. The Tribunal system is designed to provide access to the law without the need for expensive professional advice. Nonetheless it is a fact that Tribunal cases do sometimes fail because the case was poorly presented or argued or the correct procedures were not observed. Lawyers, accountants and tax professionals commonly represent claimants at tax tribunals and the websites of many of the main professional bodies have search facilities for specialists in your local area. See Chapter 14: *Further information* for website details.

The higher courts

Tribunal decisions can be appealed on a point of law to the High Court (or in Scotland the Court of Session). However, the Tribunal's findings on the facts of a case are usually final. Note that the VAT status of an activity is usually considered a point of law. In addition to being able to decide on a point of law, the higher courts can also challenge the means by which a decision was reached and set aside decisions they consider to be unreasonable, even if legally correct.

It may be possible to appeal higher court decisions upwards in the chain to the House of Lords. Tribunals and courts can also refer questions to the European Court of Justice, though referrals to the European Court of Justice can only be made by the Tribunal or court and not by the contending parties.

Review of the tribunals system and appeals procedures

The Tribunals, Courts and Enforcement Act received Royal Assent in July 2007. Under the Act all tribunals (tax and non-tax) will be unified into a single structure. The stated intention is to implement the tax appeal system from April 2009. There will be a tax chamber which hears all tax-related cases, and there will be a two-level structure, with most cases going initially to a local first-tier tribunal but appealable to an upper tier which will replace the High Court. Important cases may go straight to the upper tier. It is not yet clear if the VAT Tribunal's current power to award costs will be retained, the Government's stated intention being to remove this.

HMRC are also consulting on their review procedures in view of the changes to the tribunal system. The intention is to introduce a unified review system to apply across all taxes. It is possible that a case may have to have gone through HMRC's review process before it may be appealed to a tribunal.

Blocked input VAT

There are two key areas where input VAT recovery is blocked by special rules: motor vehicles and business entertaining. Each of these areas is considered below.

Business entertaining

Business entertainment means the provision, in the course of a business activity, of free entertainment to people who are not employees. Entertainment includes food, drink, accommodation and entrance to events. If entertainment is incidentally supplied to employees then the associated input VAT is also blocked, for example a restaurant meal for customers at which staff are present.

Input VAT is not blocked if it relates to:

- subsistence expenses paid to employees while travelling for business purposes

- staff entertainment such as annual parties, team-building exercises and outings, though if attendance at the event is restricted to the directors or partners of a business the input VAT may be blocked

- entertainment provided by clubs and associations which is available to all eligible members without specific charge. This is considered to be part of the benefits received in return for payment of the appropriate membership subscription

- free drinks given to customers paying for meals at a restaurant or similar establishment

- entertainment provided by local authorities at civic functions

- entertainment of a non-personal nature provided freely by a store, or similar establishment, to members of the general public to attract custom or to advertise a trader's premises. This includes hiring circus performers, musicians, or other entertainers but does not apply to promotional events where customers attend by invitation only

- reciprocal hospitality arrangements between sporting clubs. HMRC guidance states that it is common practice for sporting clubs to provide free hospitality to visiting teams on the understanding that similar facilities will be provided by the visiting team when they are hosts of the return fixture. The guidance states that in these circumstances input tax may be deducted by the team providing the entertainment.

Motor cars

Where cars are purchased and the car will be available for private use then recovery of the associated input VAT is blocked. Input VAT recovery is also blocked on certain payments for car fuel.

Purchasing or leasing cars

Where an organisation buys cars for use by its employees, recovery of input VAT on the purchase of the car is completely blocked if the car is intended to be available for private use. The test is not whether the car is actually put to private use, but whether it is available for private use. To avoid being available for private use there must be physical or legal barriers that prevent it, the barriers must be enforced and they must be effective. Though it is possible to make a car unavailable for private use, the many tribunal and court cases on this subject demonstrate that this is far from easy.

Even if the car is unavailable for private use, input VAT recovery may be restricted by the normal VAT rules if there is any use for exempt or non-business activities.

Input VAT is also blocked on optional accessories bought at the same time as the car, though if bought afterwards the input VAT is not automatically blocked. However, even when input VAT on purchase costs is blocked, input VAT on maintenance costs is recoverable subject to the normal recovery rules.

If a car on which input VAT was blocked is sold, no output VAT should be charged on the sale. If no input VAT was charged when purchasing the car, for example, if it was bought second-hand from an unregistered person, then the car can be sold under the second-hand margin scheme (see Chapter 10).

If an organisation leases a car for 10 days or less then VAT on the leasing cost is not blocked. If the lease is for a longer period and the car is available for private use then 50 per cent of the VAT is blocked. Charges for maintenance and excess mileage by the leasing company may avoid the 50 per cent block if they are identified separately on the invoice.

Where VAT on a leased car is blocked and the car is partly used for non-business or exempt activities then the VAT should be attributed in the following order:

- first, apportion the VAT between business and non-business use

- 50 per cent of the VAT attributable to business use is then blocked

- apportion the unblocked VAT between exempt and taxable use.

Private use of company cars

If input VAT was blocked on the purchase or lease of a company car then the organisation does not have to charge itself output VAT on the private usage. However, if input VAT on the purchase or lease of a car was not blocked and the car is actually put to private use, there is a taxable supply by the organisation to the private user.

Even if the organisation makes no actual charge to the private user, it must account for output VAT on the supply. HMRC state that the output VAT should either be based on the organisation's costs incurred in making the vehicle available for private use (e.g. depreciation, repairs and running costs) or be based on one of the HMRC agreements with the motor trade set out in VAT Notice 700/57. However, if private use of the car forms part of a salary sacrifice arrangement with an employee then HMRC accept that no output VAT need be accounted for.

Fuel payments

If an employer pays for fuel used by its employees then there may be VAT complications. The car may be owned by the organisation or by the employee and the employer may pay for fuel directly, for example by providing staff with company credit cards or company fuel cards, or it may refund employees for the fuel they purchase personally.

If the employer refunds the employee then, irrespective of the way in which the employee is refunded, the employee must obtain a VAT invoice for the fuel and give this to the employer in order for the employer to be able to deduct any input VAT. HMRC accept that in practice fuel invoices are unlikely to match the amounts claimed but suggest that employers instruct employees who make fuel claims to obtain VAT invoices for all fuel purchases. The total amount on the invoices must equal or exceed the amount claimed and, in HMRC's view, the invoices should predate the claim.

Possible fuel payment scenarios are:

Scenario	Treatment
The employer buys the fuel or refunds the employee on production of VAT invoices. There is no private use of the fuel.	VAT on the fuel may be treated as input VAT and recovered subject to the normal rules.
The employee buys the fuel and gives VAT invoices to the employer. The employer keeps mileage records that separate private use from use for the employer's purposes. The employer refunds the employee on the basis of a mileage allowance.	The employer may treat a part of the mileage allowance as input VAT and recover this subject to the normal rules. See Advisory Fuel Rates below.

The employer buys the fuel and there is private use. The employer keeps mileage records that separate private use from use for the employer's purposes. The employer charges the employee for private use.	As long as the charge reflects or exceeds actual cost or is based on the Advisory Fuel Rates (see below) the employer can treat the VAT on the fuel as input VAT and recover subject to the normal rules. The charge to the employee is a standard-rated taxable supply. Note that if the employer charges the employee below cost or below the Advisory Fuel Rates then the next point applies to the difference.
The employer buys the fuel or refunds the employee on production of VAT invoices. There is private use but the employer does not charge the employee for this. The employer keeps mileage records that separate private use from use for the employer's purposes.	The input VAT can be apportioned between private use and use for the employer's purposes. The former is not recovered. The latter may be recovered subject to the normal rules.
The employer buys the fuel or refunds the employee on production of VAT invoices. There is private use. The employer does not keep mileage records separating private use from use for the employer's purposes.	The employer may use the Fuel Scale Charge (see below) to determine the value of the supply to the employee. The employer can treat the VAT on the fuel as input VAT and recover subject to the normal rules.
The employer buys the fuel or refunds the employee with or without production of VAT invoices. There is private use. The employer does not claim any input VAT on the fuel.	There is no need to keep mileage records or to use the Fuel Scale Charge.

Advisory Fuel Rates

HMRC publish advisory fuel rates which can be used to calculate the fuel component of a mileage allowance. The rates are based on engine size and fuel type (petrol, diesel or LPG) and change regularly. You should check the HMRC website for the latest rates.

> **Example: Advisory fuel rates**
>
> Medical Assistance Charity pays an employee a mileage allowance for 250 miles business travel in the employee's car which has a 1400cc petrol engine. The advisory fuel rate for a 1400cc petrol engine at the date of the claim is 10p per mile.
>
> The deemed fuel component of the allowance is 10p x 250 = £25
>
> This includes VAT, so the associated input VAT is 7/47 x £25 = £3.72
>
> Medical Assistance Charity may treat this as input VAT and recover subject to the normal rules as long as the employee provides one or more VAT invoices to cover the fuel (totalling at least £25 including VAT).

Fuel scale charge

For normal commercial businesses the fuel scale charge can be used to determine the VAT-inclusive value of the deemed supply that is made when fuel is put to private use. The organisation can recover all the VAT charged on the fuel as input VAT. However, the organisation must charge itself the fuel scale charge as output VAT. This avoids the need to keep mileage records, though if private use is small it is likely to be more expensive than exact apportionment.

Since 1 May 2007 the fuel scale charge has been based on the car's CO_2 rating. Before 1 May 2007 it was based on the car's engine capacity and type of fuel. For new cars the CO_2 rating is shown on the registration certificate issued by the DVLA. Alternatively, you can search by make and model at: carfueldata.direct.gov.uk. For very old cars that do not have an official CO_2 rating, the scale charge is based on the engine's capacity. See VAT Notice 700/64 for up-to-date details of scale charge rates.

HMRC provide three tables of scale charges – one for use with monthly VAT returns, one for use with quarterly VAT returns and one for use with annual VAT returns. If an employee starts or stops using a car in a return period or changes car you can apportion the scale charge.

If the organisation has a mix of non-business, exempt and taxable activities then the situation is more complicated. If the car is only used for private and taxable activities then all input VAT on the fuel is recoverable. If the car is used for a mix of private, non-business, exempt and taxable activities then there are two options.

If the fuel can be split between private and organisational use, then VAT on the fuel for private use can be recovered and VAT on the organisational use is treated as residual and put into the business/non-business and partial exemption calculations.

However, the fuel scale charge will generally be used when the split between private and organisational use is not known. In such a situation all the VAT on the fuel is put into business/non-business and partial exemption calculations but the scale charge is reduced accordingly. This calculation must be repeated in the annual adjustment.

Example: Fuel scale charge

The Lost Animal Charity pays all fuel for an employee's company car which has a CO_2 rating of 150g/km. The car is used privately by the employee and for the non-business, exempt and taxable activities of the charity. However, no records are kept of how use is split. For the quarter ended 30 September 2007 the fuel scale charge for a 150g/km car is £207. The charity's residual business recovery rate is 75% (business activity/total activity) and its residual taxable recovery rate is 63% (taxable activity/business activity).

The Lost Animal Charity must charge itself output VAT of $\frac{7}{47}$ x £207 x 75% x 63% = £14.56. This is included in box 1 on the VAT return.

The value of the supply is £207 x 75% - £14.56 = £140.69. This is included in box 6 on the VAT return. The charity can recover 75% x 63% = 47.25% of the VAT charged on the fuel. These calculations must be repeated with annual amounts in the annual adjustment.

Using Sage 50 Accounts to manage VAT

Many small voluntary organisations use Sage 50 Accounts (previously called Sage Line 50) to manage their finances. Sage 50 Accounts is primarily designed for commercial businesses, however it can be adapted to the needs of voluntary organisations that have a mix of non-business, exempt and taxable activities.

Sage 50 Accounts manages VAT by using 'T-codes'. There are 100 T-codes available (T0 – T99). Every transaction is assigned a T-code, and the T-code determines the transaction's VAT treatment. By default, Sage is set up with the following T-code structure:

Code	Description	Rate	In use
T0	Zero-rated transactions	0%	Y
T1	Standard-rated transactions	17½%	Y

T2	Exempt transactions	0%	Y
T4	Sales to VAT-registered EC customers	0%	Y
T5	Reduced-rate transactions	5%	Y
T7	Zero-rated purchases from EC suppliers	0%	Y
T8	Standard-rated purchases from EC suppliers	17½%	Y
T9	Non-VATable transactions	0%	N

The 'Rate' determines how Sage calculates the associated VAT and the 'In Use' flag determines whether or not associated transactions are included in the VAT return. For example, if you make a purchase and code it to T1, Sage will, by default, add 17½ per cent VAT to the net purchase price you enter and post this VAT to the Purchase Tax Control Account in the Nominal Ledger. If you make a sale and code it to T1, Sage will add 17½ per cent VAT to the net sale price you enter and post this VAT to the Sales Tax Control Account in the Nominal Ledger.

When you activate Sage's VAT routine, it will analyse the postings to the Purchase and Sales Tax Control accounts and compile the VAT return. It will ignore transactions coded to T9 (In use = 'N'), but include transactions coded to the other T codes where In Use = 'Y'. The net value of transactions coded to T4 is included in box 8 on the VAT return, and codes T7 and T8 are used to calculate any acquisition VAT due (box 2) and complete box 9.

In preparing the VAT return Sage assumes that all input VAT posted to the purchase tax control account is recoverable. If you have non-business or exempt activities this is unlikely to be the case. You will need to know the input VAT attributable to exempt and non-business activities and also, if you are using a 'standard' income-based non-business method or partial exemption method (see Chapter 3: *Recovering VAT*), the income (excluding VAT) attributable to non-business and exempt activities.

Sage's default T-code structure will not necessarily provide you with this information. However, the T-codes can be adapted to do so. The following is an example of a T-code structure that could be used to provide this information for an organisation with a mix of taxable, exempt and non-business activities and that uses standard income-based methods to apportion residual VAT. It assumes there are no EC supplies or purchases.

Example: T-code structure

Code Type	Code	Description	Rate	In use
Income codes	T0	Zero-rated income	0%	Y
	T1	Standard-rated income	17½ %	Y
	T2	Exempt income	0%	Y
	T3	Non-business income	0%	Y
Expenditure codes	T4	Standard-rated purchases directly attributable to taxable activities	17½ %	Y
	T5	Standard-rated purchases directly attributable to exempt activities	17½ %	Y
	T6	Standard-rated purchases directly attributable to non-business activities	17½ %	Y
	T7	Standard-rated overheads	17½ %	Y
	T8	Reduced-rate overheads	5%	Y
Other	T9	Non-VATable transactions	0%	N

Codes T0 – T3 are used to identify the different types of income.

Only income coded to T1 will generate any output VAT. The net income coded to T0, T1 and T2 is entered into box 6 on the VAT return. As the level of non-business income is required for the business/non-business split, it is coded to T3 rather than T9. As T3 is in use, this ensures that the level of non-business income is recorded in the Sage VAT reports.

Codes T4 – T8 are used to identify the different types of VAT-bearing expenditure.

VAT on purchases that relate directly to taxable activities is recoverable. By coding standard-rated purchases that relate directly to taxable activities to a separate code (T4), the related recoverable VAT can be easily identified. If the organisation has exempt activities a separate code is created for standard-rated purchases directly attributable to exempt activities (T5). The VAT posted to T5 will feed into the *de minimis* computation.

Standard-rated purchases directly attributable to non-business activities are coded to T6. The VAT posted to T6 will not normally be recoverable. Non-business activities are likely to include grant-funded activities.

For overheads and other types of expense that include VAT but which cannot be directly attributed to a particular type of activity there are two codes: T7 for standard-rated costs and T8 for reduced-rate costs such as fuel and power. If any reduced-rate costs are directly attributable to a particular type of activity you may need to create a separate T-code for these.

Code T9 is used for transactions that do not have any VAT. Examples include salaries, PAYE , National Insurance payments and business rates.

The following example shows how this T-code structure can be used to complete the VAT return.

Example: Sage 50 Accounts T-codes with mixed taxable, exempt and non-business activities

The Advice for All Charity has a mix of taxable, exempt and non-business activities. It uses the above T-code structure and has 'standard' income-based non-business and partial exemption methods. The Sage VAT printout for a VAT quarter is:

T code	Output VAT £	Net income £	VAT on purchases £	Net purchases £
T0: zero rate income	0.00	1,000.00		
T1: std rate income	350.00	2,000.00		
T2: exempt income	0.00	5,000.00		
T3: non-business income	0.00	10,000.00		
T4: standard-rated purchases for taxable activities			87.50	500.00
T5: standard-rated purchases for exempt activities			131.25	750.00

T6: standard-rated purchases for non-business activities			175.00	1,000.00
T7: standard-rated overheads			262.50	1,500.00
T8: reduced-rate overheads			15.00	300.00
T: Totals	350.00	18,000.00	671.25	4,050.00

Recoverable input VAT is calculated as follows. First calculate the 'standard method' recovery ratios:

a	Business income/total income	(T0+T1+T2) / T	£8,000/£18,000	44.44%
b	Exempt income/business income	T2 / (T0+T1+T2)	£5,000/£8,000	62.50%
	This can be rounded down to the nearest whole per cent			62%

Next, use these percentages to attribute residual VAT between taxable, exempt and non-business activities:

c	Total residual VAT is	T7 + T8	£262.50 + £15.00	£277.50
d	Attributed to business activities	c x a	£277.50 x 44.44%	£123.32
e	Attributed to exempt activities:	d x b	£123.32 x 62%	£76.46
f	Attributed to taxable activities	d - e	£123.32 - £76.46	£46.86

Next attribute all purchase VAT between taxable, exempt and non-business activities:

Attribute input VAT	Total	Taxable	Exempt	Non-business
T4: taxable purchases	87.50	87.50		
T5: exempt purchases	131.25		131.25	
T6: non-business purchases	175.00			175.00
T7 & T8: residual purchases	277.50	46.86	76.46	154.18
Totals	671.25	134.36	207.71	329.18

Next, apply the *de minimis* test:

1. Is exempt input VAT less than £625? YES (£207.71 < £625)

2. Is exempt input VAT less than taxable input VAT: NO (£207.71 > £134.36)

So the *de minimis* test is not met and exempt input VAT is irrecoverable.

Recoverable input VAT is thus the amount attributed to taxable activities, i.e. £134.36

The following amounts are entered into the VAT return:

Box 1: Output VAT	T1	£350.00
Box 2: Acquisition VAT		£0.00
Box 3: Total VAT due	Box 1 + Box 2	£350.00
Box 4: Input VAT	As calculated above	£134.36
Box 5: Net VAT due	Box 3 – Box 4	£215.64
Box 6: Sales	T0+T1+T2	£8,000.00
Box 7: Purchases	T4+T5+ a x (T7+T8)	£2,050.00
Box 8: EC sales of goods		£0.00
Box 9: EC acquisitions		£0.00

Note that boxes 6 and 7 should exclude income and purchases attributable to non-business activities. For residual purchases this has been estimated using the business/total income ratio.

13 VAT cases

These are just some of the VAT cases that have particular relevance to voluntary organisations. The bare facts and decision have been outlined to give an overview.

VAT cases may only have gone to the VAT Tribunal; some will go further through the courts and may get as far as the House of Lords. The tribunal or courts may also refer questions to the European Court of Justice. Older court cases use the *Simon's Tax Cases* (STC) reference. Newer court cases use the neutral citation number with the following abbreviations:

EWHC: England and Wales High Court

EWCA: England and Wales Court of Appeal

CSIH: Court of Session, Inner House

UKHL: House of Lords

EUECJ: European Court of Justice

APPLE AND PEAR DEVELOPMENT COUNCIL

[1988] EUECJ R–102/86

Area: meaning of 'supply', Chapter 4

The Council was a statutory body formed to promote apples and pears. Commercial growers were required to register with the council and pay an annual levy based on the area under cultivation. The UK tax authorities claimed the levy was consideration for the supply of promotional services by the Council. The court rejected this. It found no direct link between the levy and the promotional activities as:

- the Council's activities benefited the industry as a whole and individual growers only benefited indirectly

- there was no relationship between the benefit derived by an individual grower and the levy paid. The levy was always due, irrespective of the level of benefit derived by an individual grower.

Therefore the levy was outside the scope of VAT.

BELL CONCORD EDUCATIONAL TRUST

[1989] STC 264

Area: the education exemption, meaning of 'not-for-profit', Chapter 5

The Bell Concord Educational Trust ran the Concord College as its only activity, which was within its charitable objects of the advancement of education. It budgeted for a profit every year and so Customs challenged the 'not-for-profit' basis of its activities. A successful challenge would have meant that the college was no longer able to exempt its fees. On appeal it was held that the constitution of the organisation should be looked at to discover the purposes for which it was established, and if there was a prohibition on distributing profits then this would mean that the organisation operated 'otherwise than for a profit'.

BOURNEMOUTH SYMPHONY ORCHESTRA

[2006] EWCA Civ 1281

Area: the cultural exemption, meaning of 'financial interest', Chapter 5

This is a development of the Zoological Society of London case (see below). To exempt a supply of cultural services, the supplying organisation must be 'managed and administered on a voluntary basis by persons who have no direct or indirect financial interest in its activities'. The case concerned the interpretation of the phrase 'direct or indirect financial interest'. The managing director and musical director were paid employees but also voting members of the board. The musical director's participation was essentially voluntary as an elected employee representative, but the managing director's was not; it was part of his duties as managing director and one in which he took an active part in practice. The court decided by a majority that the orchestra failed to meet the conditions for exemption – though the managing director did not have a financial interest in that he was paid a market-rate salary and could not profit if the orchestra did well, his remunerated participation in management at the highest level precluded management on a voluntary basis.

BOWTHORPE COMMUNITY TRUST (TRUSTEES OF)

[1995] VAT Tribunal 12978

Area: meaning of 'supply', Chapter 4

315

The Trust provided training and work experience for disabled people in woodwork, pottery and other crafts. The local authority provided some funding and referred applicants for training. The Trust had tried to make the connection and argue that they made a supply to the local authority and therefore should be entitled to treat it as a business supply. The tribunal found against it and held that the Trust supplied training to the trainees, not to the local authority. The Trust was therefore barred from recovering VAT incurred on refurbishment of the workshop premises.

BRITISH FIELD SPORTS SOCIETY

[1998] STC 315

Area: meaning of 'supply', Chapter 4

Subscription to the Society entitled members to various benefits such as insurance and publications. The Society had agreed an apportionment on the basis that the insurance element was exempt, the publications element was zero-rated and the balance standard-rated. It claimed back input tax on the basis of those apportionments. Customs & Excise sought to challenge the recovery of input tax, on the ground that the lobbying undertaken by the Society was not a business activity. The court of appeal found in favour of the Society, recognising that the members joined the Society because of its lobbying activities. The fact that non-members benefited from the lobbying was a necessary consequence.

CARD PROTECTION PLAN

[1999] EUECJ C-349/96

Area: single and multiple supplies, Chapter 11

Card Protection Plan Ltd offered credit card holders a package of services for a single fee to cover any loss resulting from the loss of their credit card. Customs claimed this was a standard-rated supply and the case went all the way to the House of Lords, which referred several questions to the ECJ. The key question asked was: what are the proper tests to be used in determining whether a transaction comprises a single or multiple supply? The ECJ replied as follows:

- Where a transaction comprises a bundle of features and acts, regard must first be had to all the circumstances in which that transaction takes place.

- Every supply of a service must normally be regarded as distinct and independent.

- A supply which comprises a single service from an economic point of view should not be artificially split, so as not to distort the functioning of the VAT system.

- The essential features of the transaction must be ascertained in order to determine whether the taxable person is supplying the customer, being a typical consumer, with several distinct principal services or with a single service.

- There is a single supply where one or more elements are to be regarded as constituting the principal service, while one or more elements are to be regarded as ancillary services which share the tax treatment of the principal service.

- A service must be regarded as ancillary to a principal service if it does not constitute for customers an aim in itself, but a means of better enjoying the principal service supplied.

- The fact that a single price is charged is not decisive. If the service provided to customers consists of several elements for a single price, the single price may suggest that there is a single service. However, if circumstances indicate that the customers intended to purchase two or more distinct services then it is necessary to identify the parts of the single price which relate to the separate supplies. The simplest possible method of calculation or assessment should be used for this.

CHURCH OF ENGLAND CHILDREN'S SOCIETY

[2005] EWHC 1692 (Ch)

Area: attribution of input VAT, Chapter 3

The Society sought to recover input VAT attributable to its committed givers' scheme, including the costs of professional fundraisers and of producing a free newsletter targeted at committed givers. HMRC argued that the input VAT was attributable to the non-business donations from the committed givers. However, the court decided that, where the income raised is unrestricted and used to fund general activities, the input VAT is residual. It also decided that the free newsletter constituted the disposal of a business asset and hence a deemed zero-rated supply, so input VAT attributable to the newsletter was wholly recoverable.

COÖPERATIEVE AARDAPPELENBEWAARPLAATS

[1981] EUECJ R-154/80

Area: meaning of 'supply', Chapter 4

This case established that, for a supply to exist, there must be a direct link between the goods or services supplied and any consideration received, and that the consideration must be capable of being valued. A Dutch agricultural co-operative ran a warehouse in which members stored potatoes. The co-operative normally charged members for their use of the warehouse, however for two years it waived all charges and did not account for any output VAT as no consideration was paid for the supply of storage facilities. The Dutch authorities decided that VAT was nevertheless due, the consideration paid by members being the reduction in the value of their shares in the co-operative.

The law at that time stated that a provision of services was taxable when the service was provided against payment, and the basis of assessment for such a service was everything which made up the consideration for the service. The court decided that this required there to be a direct link between the supply and the consideration, and the consideration must be capable of being expressed in monetary terms. This was clearly not the case here. The reduction in value of the shares as a result of the waiver of rent was unquantifiable and any loss in value could not be regarded as payment for the provision of services.

DONALDSON'S COLLEGE

[2005] VAT Tribunal 19258

Area: meaning of 'business activity', Chapter 4

The college provided education for deaf children, with pupils being taken from all over Scotland. 60 per cent of costs were met by a grant from the Scottish Executive, 35 per cent by fees charged to the child's local authority, and the remainder from donations. The college sought to zero rate construction costs on the grounds of relevant charitable purpose. HMRC argued that there was a business supply to the local authorities. The tribunal found that there was no supply to the local authorities and hence the college's core activity was non-business. This was because the college's predominant concern was providing a service which is required to be provided by the state, that the split of costs between the Scottish Executive and local authorities was decided by the Scottish Executive and the supply received by the local authorities bore no relation to its cost.

FRIENDS OF THE IRONBRIDGE GORGE MUSEUM

[1991] VAT Tribunal 5639

Area: meaning of 'supply', Chapter 4

This was a separately established charity raising funds for the main charity: the Museum. A subscription to the Friends entitled a member to reduced entrance fees and discounts on goods in the Museum shop, however the monetary value of the benefits was very small in comparison with the amount of the subscription. Because the benefits were provided by a third party, it was held that there no benefits provided in return for the subscription and that the subscriptions were therefore outside the scope of VAT.

GLASTONBURY ABBEY

[1996] VAT Tribunal 14579

Area: cultural exemption, meaning of 'managed and administered on a voluntary basis', Chapter 5

This case concerned the definition of 'managed and administered on a voluntary basis' in the exemption applying to cultural services. UK legislation had omitted the word 'essentially' when implementing this part of the 6th EC Directive, and this did make a difference, the Tribunal held. Given that it had only 11 paid staff, 14 trustees and 101 volunteers, the Tribunal held that it was essentially managed and administered on a voluntary basis and therefore could treat admission fees to the museum as exempt. In addition, the paid staff had no financial interest in the profits from the enterprise, as they were only paid their salary.

HALIFAX PLC

[2005] EUECJ C-255/02

Area: VAT avoidance schemes, Chapter 10

Halifax, a partly exempt business, sought to recover VAT on the construction of four call centres by setting up a complex scheme involving associated companies. HMRC blocked VAT recovery on the basis that artificial tax avoidance schemes do not constitute economic activities. The VAT Tribunal referred various questions to the ECJ, which ruled that avoidance schemes can constitute economic activities but that abusive schemes can be blocked by the national courts and treated as if they did not exist. To be abusive, a scheme must result in the accrual of a tax advantage the grant of which would be contrary to the purpose of EC legislation. It must also be apparent from a number of objective factors that the essential aim of the transactions concerned is to obtain a tax advantage.

HELP THE AGED

[1997] EWHC Admin 195

Area: zero-rating reliefs, Chapter 6

This case was concerned with the supply of minibuses to charities and whether these could be zero-rated. Help the Aged bought vehicles and adapted them for disabled access, selling the finished item to other charities. The case focused on two questions: whether the adaptations made the vehicles 'relevant goods' and whether the recipient charities qualified as eligible bodies. It was held that the adaptations were to last for a substantial time, and that even though it was possible to put seats back into the vehicle, it was not necessary for adaptations to be irreversible for the item to come under the 'relevant goods' definition. Secondly, the recipient charities did 'care' for the individuals, using the vehicles in the normal sense of the word, and there was no justification to limit the meaning of the word 'care' to health or nursing care.

HILLINGDON LEGAL RESOURCE CENTRE

[1991] VAT Tribunal 5210

Area: meaning of 'supply', Chapter 4

The charity provided legal advice to citizens of Hillingdon. It was funded by fees to the Legal Aid Board (taxable) and grants from the local authority and London Boroughs Grants Unit. It was claiming all input VAT back, but this was disallowed on the ground that there was no service provided to the funding authorities, since the services provided were provided free of charge to the users.

HORIZON COLLEGE

[2007] EUECJ C-434/05

Area: supply of staff, Chapter 11

This case concerned the status of intermediary supplies of teaching staff. Horizon College, a Dutch educational institution, made teachers available to other educational institutions. The host institutions assumed responsibility for the teachers and paid Horizon College a fee to cover its costs, which included the teachers' salaries. Horizon College did not charge VAT, and this was challenged by the Dutch tax authorities. The case was referred to the ECJ which decided that Horizon College was not making a supply of education to the host institutions, but it could be making a supply closely related to education (and thus exempt) if:

- both supplying institution and host institution are eligible bodies (as defined in Article 13A(1)(i) of the 6th EC Directive), and

- the placement is of a nature and quality such that, without recourse to such a service, there could be no assurance that the education provided by the host establishment and, consequently, the education from which its students benefit, would have an equivalent value, and

- the basic purpose of such a placement is not to obtain additional income by carrying out a transaction which is in direct competition with commercial enterprises liable for VAT.

JUBILEE HALL RECREATION CENTRE

[1999] STC 381

Area: meaning of 'village hall' for the relevant charitable purpose tests, Chapter 8

A sports centre in Covent Garden was established to provide recreation in the area of Greater London in the interest of social welfare for the benefit of the local community. In fact, the people who used the centre were people who worked in the area as well as residents and the centre was operated on a commercial basis. The Centre wished to claim zero rating for refurbishment work to the premises, which were in a listed building, on the ground that it was used as a village hall or similar in providing social or recreational facilities for a local community and therefore qualified for relevant charitable use. It did not win the right to have the works zero-rated.

KINGSCREST ASSOCIATES & MONTECELLO LTD

[2005] EUECJ C-498/03

Area: welfare exemption, Chapter 5

Article 13A(1)(g) and (h) of the 6th EC Directive limits the exemption for welfare services to public bodies and organisations recognised as charitable by the member state concerned. In this case the ECJ decided that although UK law does not consider private profit-making entities to be charitable, the word 'charitable' has its own independent meaning in community law, and this meaning does not preclude private profit-making entities.

The ECJ left it to the national courts to decide whether private profit-making entities should be considered charitable for the purposes of Article 13A(1)(g) and (h). As a result of this case the UK decided that private welfare institutions and agencies do qualify for exemption when they are state-regulated. Certain private welfare institutions and agencies, including domiciliary care agencies, independent fostering agencies, voluntary adoption agencies and nursing agencies, are state-regulated and therefore their supplies of regulated welfare are now exempt.

LEVOB VERZEKERINGEN BV & OV BANK

[2005] EUECJ C-41/04

Area: single and multiple supplies, Chapter 11

Levob was a Dutch insurance company that purchased customised software from a US supplier. Levob sought to treat the supply of the software and its customisation as separate supplies and arranged to make separate payment for the two. The ECJ decided that this split was artificial as the software was of no use to Levob without customisation. There was thus a single supply. The court decided that the single supply was of customisation services, as that component was the most important. The customisation services were the services of professional programmers and hence subject to the reverse charge.

This case led to the 'Levob test': where two or more elements or acts supplied by a taxable person to a customer, being a typical customer, are so closely linked that they form objectively, from an economic point of view, a whole transaction which it would be artificial to split, all these elements or acts constitute a single supply for the purposes of the application of VAT.

MELLERSTAIN TRUST (TRUSTEES OF)

[1989] VAT Tribunal 4256

Area: meaning of 'capital asset' for determination of taxable turnover, Chapter 3

The Tribunal held that paintings sold from a historic house open to the public were capital assets which had been used to make taxable supplies, and as such did not render the Trust liable to register for VAT.

NORTH OF ENGLAND ZOOLOGICAL SOCIETY

[1999] STC 1027

Area: educational exemption, Chapter 5

The North of England Zoological Society, which operates Chester Zoo, argued that its admission fees should be exempt as an educational supply. It lost in the High Court, as it was ruled that the meaning of 'education' in the VAT legislation was its narrower meaning, in the sense of a course, a class or lesson of instruction, as opposed to education in its broader sense.

NATIONAL SOCIETY FOR THE PREVENTION OF CRUELTY TO CHILDREN

[1992] VAT Tribunal 9325

Area: VAT status of investment income, Chapter 4

The NSPCC claimed that the activities of investing funds and receiving investment income were part of the business activities of the charity. The Tribunal held that the mere investment of money did not in itself amount to a business activity. It further noted that the primary purpose of the charity was the charitable objects. This was in contradiction to the statement in the VAT leaflet for charities at the time, which was subsequently changed. Thus, investment income in charities should be deemed a non-business activity.

PLANTIFLOR

[2002] UKHL 33

Area: single and multiple supplies, delivery charges, disbursements, Chapter 11

Plantiflor sold plants, bulbs, seeds and other garden products via mail order catalogues. In January 1994 it restructured its arrangements for the delivery of goods ordered by its customers. It entered into a separate contract with Parcelforce under which goods would be delivered to its customers at an agreed flat-rate price. On its order forms customers were asked to indicate whether they wished for Plantiflor to arrange delivery of goods to them by Parcelforce. The postal charge was made known to the customers, who had the option of collecting the goods themselves if they preferred. Plantiflor claimed that in these circumstances it was not liable to account for VAT on the postal charges, as they were in fact disbursements.

By a majority decision the House of Lords decided that Plantiflor did not act as agent for Parcelforce as Parcelforce made the deliveries under contract to Plantiflor and not the customer. The Lords also decided that this was a single supply of delivered goods and not a multiple supply, as this is what the typical customer was expecting, so the status of the delivery charges followed that of the goods – in this case standard-rated.

ST DUNSTAN'S EDUCATIONAL FOUNDATION

[1999] STC 381

Area: meaning of 'relevant charitable purpose', Chapter 8

A school with fee-paying pupils was run on land owned by a separate Foundation. The Foundation made the land available to the school free of charge and built a sports hall over an existing swimming pool with Lottery funding. The Foundation planned to allow the school free use, and local authority-nominated users were to be allowed to use the facilities for a fee. This was not allowed as non-business use, but the Tribunal did consider that the sports centre was to be used as 'a village hall or similarly in providing social or recreational facilities for a local community'.

ST PAUL'S COMMUNITY PROJECT LTD

[2004] EWHC 2490 (Ch)

Area: meaning of 'business activity', Chapter 4

The project included a nursery which charged fees of £85 – £95 per week. The cost of a place was £130 per week, the balance being covered by grants. The court decided that the nursery was a non-business activity. Contributing factors were that the nursery was provided for social reasons, the fees were set so as just to cover costs and to be as affordable as possible to parents, and the fees were lower than commercial alternatives despite there being higher staff/child ratios and better-qualified staff.

TOLSMA

[1994] EUECJ C-16/93

Area: meaning of 'supply', Chapter 4

Mr Tolsma played a barrel organ on the public highway in the Netherlands and solicited donations from passers-by. The Dutch tax authorities claimed that the donations were consideration for the supply of musical entertainment and assessed Mr Tolsma for VAT. The court decided that, on the basis of the existing case law (see *Coöperatieve Aardappelenbewaarplaats*, above), for a supply to exist, there must be a legal relationship between the supplier and recipient under which there is reciprocal performance, so that the payment received by the supplier reflects the value of the supply made. Here, this was not the case. There was no legal agreement, passers-by merely making voluntary donations. There was no link between the value of the supply and the donations, each passer-by giving what they thought appropriate and many presumably giving nothing at all despite benefiting from the musical performance.

TRON THEATRE LTD

[1994] STC 177

Area: meaning of 'consideration', Chapter 4

Tron Theatre raised sponsorship from supporters. The Theatre claimed that part of the amount received should be a donation, as the value of the sponsorship was well in excess of the real value of the benefits given in return, such as priority booking. The Theatre lost – it was held that the full amount of sponsorship was the price sponsors were prepared to pay, so the full amount was the consideration and therefore fully taxable.

WATFORD AND DISTRICT OLD PEOPLE'S HOUSING ASSOCIATION LTD

[1998] VAT Tribunal 15660

Area: meaning of 'care' for the purposes of the welfare exemption, Chapter 5

This case concerned the definition of 'care'. Customs had interpreted it narrowly, meaning personal services such as bathing, dressing, etc. In this case, the Tribunal agreed that domestic help services such as cleaning, cooking and shopping could constitute care when supplied to 'people for whom there is either current or imminent substantial risk to the health and welfare of the person and who are unable to provide even basic self care or who have major difficulty in safely carrying out some key daily living tasks'.

WELLCOME TRUST

[1996] EUECJ C-155/94

Area: VAT status of investment income, Chapter 4

The Wellcome Trust held a substantial portfolio of investments which was actively managed, though the trustees were required to avoid engaging in trade when exercising their investment powers. In 1992 the trust sold 288 million shares in Wellcome PLC. The sale costs were considerable and the trust sought to recover the VAT on the basis that the sale was an economic activity similar to the activities of professional dealers, or that had the sale been spread out over a period of time it would have been accepted as a business activity. The court decided that because the trust was prohibited from engaging in trading in investments, the trust was managing its investment portfolio in the same way as a private investor. Neither the scale of the sale nor the appointment of professional advisers could turn the sale into an economic activity, and arguments about fiscal neutrality are only relevant to economic activities. The court also considered the issue of predominant concern to be irrelevant to determining the nature of the activity in this case.

WOLVERHAMPTON CITIZENS ADVICE BUREAU

[2000] VAT Tribunal 16411

Area: meaning of 'business activity', Chapter 4

Wolverhampton Citizens Advice Bureau had a service level agreement with the local authority for the provision of advice to local people. Customs won a case that argued that the CAB provided free advice which was a non-business activity, for which it received funding. Crucial to the decision was the fact that the supply was to the individual users, not to the Council, and therefore the Council's financial support amounted to a grant.

YARBURGH CHILDREN'S TRUST

[2002] STC 207

Area: meaning of 'business activity', Chapter 4

The Trust constructed premises for a charitable playgroup which were let to the playgroup at a nominal rent. The playgroup had a significant level of parental involvement in its management and set charges to parents and childcarers so as just to cover costs. The Trust sought to zero rate construction costs on the ground of relevant charitable purpose. HMRC claimed that the use by the playgroup was a business activity. The High Court decided that as the let by the Trust to the playgroup was substantially below cost, it was not a business supply. It also decided that the activity of the playgroup was not business, as its predominant concern was charitable. Charges were set just to cover costs and the playgroup lacked the elements of commerciality necessary to render it a business activity.

YOGA FOR HEALTH

[1984] STC 630

Area: scope of the welfare exemption, Chapter 5

This case looked at the application of the 6th EC Directive and in particular Article 13A(1)(g) relating to welfare services. The charity provided therapeutic services to clients, most of whom suffered from ill health, who paid fees and made donations to support the work of the charity. Customs argued that it was a taxable service. The charity won its appeal against the Tribunal decision. The word 'welfare' connoted general physical and mental wellbeing and was not confined to material benefits. The language of Article 13A went beyond mere material benefit and standard of living. Neither was para (g) restricted to services providing for the relief of poverty to the exclusion of services providing health care.

ZOOLOGICAL SOCIETY OF LONDON

[2002] EUECJ C-267/00

Area: cultural exemption, meaning of 'managed and administered on an essentially voluntary basis', Chapter 5

To be eligible for the cultural exemption, an organisation must, under Article 13A(2a) of the 6th EC Directive, be 'managed and administered on an essentially voluntary basis.' Prior to this case, UK Customs interpreted this as meaning that any organisation that employed staff to manage its activities did not qualify for exemption. The Zoological Society of London was a charity, overseen by a board of voluntary trustees but managed and administered on a day-to-day basis by paid staff. It claimed a refund of VAT on the basis of qualifying for the cultural exemption, and the case went to the High Court which referred the matter to the ECJ.

The ECJ decided that Article 13A(2a) refers only to the trustees and to other persons who do in fact take the decisions of last resort concerning policy and carry out the higher supervisory tasks.

14 Further information

This chapter provides HMRC contact details and explains how to locate information on the HMRC website. It also provides details of other useful websites and other sources of information about VAT.

Please note that all website addresses and links are correct at January 2008 but are liable to change. For up-to-date links, go to the Sayer Vincent website: www.sayer vincent.co.uk

Sayer Vincent website

Website: www.sayervincent.co.uk

Specifically for charities and not-for-profit organisations, the Sayer Vincent website has a section on VAT, where latest news and developments are covered as well as detailed guidance on aspects of VAT relevant to charities. It also has sections on other areas of finance, management, governance and fundraising for charities. Details of update seminars and training are also available.

Other publications by Sayer Vincent:

A Practical Guide to Charity Accounting
Kate Sayer (ed.) (Directory of Social Change, 2003)
ISBN 978 1 903991 21 3

A Practical Guide to Financial Management for Charities and Voluntary Organisations
Kate Sayer (3rd edition, Directory of Social Change, 2007)
ISBN 978 1 903991 72 5

Contacting HM Revenue & Customs

Website   www.hmrc.gov.uk – see below for a guide to the information on the HMRC website.

Registration for VAT   You can register for VAT online. Follow the VAT Online Services link from the HMRC website homepage. Alternatively:

For all general VAT registration and deregistration applications and any notification of changes in details, send application forms and any supporting documents to:

Wolverhampton HM Revenue & Customs
Deansgate
62–70 Tettenhall Road
Wolverhampton
WV1 4TZ
Tel 0845 039 0129

For all VAT 68 applications (request to retain VAT registration number of previous owner of the business), VAT Group applications, Flat Rate Scheme applications, Annual Accounting requests, VAT 66s (Certificate of Status) and Agricultural Flat Rate Scheme applications, send all relevant forms and supporting documents, including VAT 1 (where appropriate) to:

Grimsby HM Revenue & Customs
Imperial House
77 Victoria Street
Grimsby
DN31 1DB
Tel 0845 039 0279

Local VAT offices   Your local VAT office will deal with most queries once you are registered for VAT or if you have a query about whether you should be registered. You can find the telephone number of your local VAT office by looking in the telephone directory under 'HM Revenue & Customs' or by contacting the National Advisory Service on 0845 010 9000.

Call your local office to check whether you come within their geographical area or not. They are called 'HM Revenue & Customs VAT Business Advice Centres'.

Helplines   National Advisory Service: 0845 010 9000 (+44 2920 501 261 from outside the UK), open 8am to 8pm, Monday to Friday. For general questions related to VAT.

Charities helpline:	08453 02 02 03, open from 8.30am to 6pm, Monday to Friday. For topics specifically related to charities (also deals with direct tax and gift aid queries).

Checking the validity of a UK VAT registration number: 01737 734 then 516, 577, 612 or 761.

Written enquiries	For more complex queries or to get a formal decision from HMRC on a matter, you should make a written enquiry. You should quote your VAT registration number (if registered) in all correspondence, as this will be used to log the enquiry. If you are not VAT-registered, your organisation's name and postcode are used instead. If seeking a formal decision it is important that you include all matters relevant to the decision, otherwise HMRC may later overturn a decision on the basis that they were not fully informed. If you are in doubt as to whether a matter is relevant or not, it is safest to include it in your written enquiry.

All written enquiries from charities are dealt with at a specialist office. They should be sent to:

HMRC Charities
St John's House
Merton Road
Bootle
Merseyside L69 9BB

Written enquiries relating to imports, exports and customs duties should be sent to:

HM Revenue & Customs
International Trade Written Enquiries Team
Crownhill Court
Tailyour Road
Plymouth PL6 5BZ

All other written enquiries, other than registration or deregistration enquiries, should be sent to:

HMRC National Advice Service
Written Enquiries Section
Southend on Sea
Alexander House
Victoria Avenue
Southend
Essex SS99 1BD

If your enquiry needs to be dealt with by one of the many HMRC specialist offices, Southend will pass your enquiry on.

Notifications Option to tax notifications should be sent to:

Option to Tax National Unit
HM Revenue & Customs
Portcullis House
21 India Street
Glasgow
G2 4PZ
Tel: 0141 555 3548/3599 Fax: 0141 555 3367

Notification of listed and hallmarked VAT schemes can be made by post or e-mail. By post to:

VAT Avoidance Disclosures Unit
Anti-Avoidance Group (Intelligence)
HM Revenue & Customs
1st Floor
22 Kingsway
London
WC2B 6NR
By e-mail to: vat.avoidance.disclosures.bst@hmrc.gsi.gov.uk.

HMRC website

Website: www.hmrc.gov.uk

This is an extensive website, with sections on VAT and new developments. It can be difficult to find what you want and, though the site possesses a search facility, this does not prioritise search results very well. Sometimes external search engines such as Google and Yahoo! are better at locating what you want. Many of the sections below can be accessed from the library at www.hmrc.gov.uk/library.

The website is useful for:

- **Forms**: from the home page click the quick link for 'Forms'.

- **Charity-specific tax information**: much of the charity-specific tax guidance can be accessed via www.hmrc.gov.uk/charities

- **Basic VAT Guides**: from the library at www.hmrc.gov.uk/library, click on 'Guides and Business Briefs' then follow the link for 'Basic Guides'.

- **VAT Notices**: HM Revenue & Customs produce an extensive range of VAT Notices covering most aspects of VAT in detail. However, you should note that the notices mostly explain HMRC's interpretation of the law, and there are some areas where HMRC's views are contentious. It can also take time for notices to be updated following a change in law or HMRC policy. Key notices of relevance to charities are detailed below. To get to the VAT Notices, follow the 'Leaflets and Booklets' link from the library at www.hmrc.gov.uk/library

- **Customs and Revenue Briefs**: these announce changes in HMRC policy, often following changes in legislation or court cases. From the library at www.hmrc.gov.uk/library, follow the link for Guides and Business Briefs. Before 2007 the Revenue & Customs Briefs were referred to as 'Business Briefs'.

- **VAT Information Sheets**: from the library at www.hmrc.gov.uk/library, follow the link for 'Public Notices and Information Sheets'.

- **HMRC Internal Guidance**: you can access much of the HMRC internal guidance on VAT, written for the use of HMRC staff. However, key parts are often blanked out. From the library at www.hmrc.gov.uk/library, follow the link for 'Internal Guidance' then click on the link 'V series – VAT guidance'.

- **VAT News**: Budget changes, press releases, recent changes to VAT legislation and new developments. From the library at www.hmrc.gov.uk/library, follow the link for 'What's New'.

Other websites

ec.europa.eu	EC VAT legislation and information on VAT regulations in other EC member states (see below).
www.lpwscheme.org.uk	Full details of the listed places of worship scheme.
www.memorialgrant.org.uk	Full details of the memorial grants scheme.
www.bailii.org	Extensive case law database including many VAT Tribunal, High Court, Appeal Court, House of Lords and ECJ decisions. The database becomes patchier the further back in time you go.
www.opsi.gov.uk	Original UK VAT legislation including the VAT Acts, Finance Acts and statutory instruments. Note that earlier legislation is not updated for amendments made by later legislation.

www.legislation.gov.uk	Ministry of Justice statute law database. Contains updated primary legislation: however, at the time of writing (January 2008), much of the VAT legislation is not fully updated.
www.taxaid.org.uk	Targeted at individuals who are experiencing tax problems, but much of the advice will also be relevant to voluntary organisations experiencing tax problems.
www.justice.gov.uk/guidance/courts-and-tribunals/tribunals/tax-and-chancery-upper-tribunal/index.htm	Information about the VAT tribunals, forms for starting the appeal process and selected decisions.
www.tax.org.uk	Chartered Institute of Taxation website. Tax news, articles and provides a search facility for local members specialising in VAT.
www.ctrg.org.uk	Charity Tax Group website. The Charity Tax Group (CTG) was formerly known as the Charities' Tax Reform Group (CTRG) and has over 400 members of all sizes representing all types of charitable activity. CTG was set up in 1982 to make representations to Government on charity taxation, and it has since become the leading voice for the sector on this issue.
www.cfdg.org.uk	Charity Finance Directors' Group website. Regular updates on the website about changes in law, regulation and rules affecting charities. CFDG also organises seminars and members' meetings which may contain useful and relevant material.
www.financehub.org.uk	An online resource for charities and voluntary organisations providing a wide range of advice on issues connected to funding and finance.
www.icaew.co.uk	Institute of Chartered Accountants in England and Wales. The tax faculty provides tax news and updates. The website also has a search facility enabling you to locate VAT specialists in your area.
www.lawsociety.org.uk	Website of the Law Society. Includes a search facility enabling you to locate tax specialist lawyers in your area.
carfueldata.direct.gov.uk	Provides a search facility to establish a car's CO_2 rating.

www.caa.co.uk	The Civil Aviation Authority website. Provides details of the ATOL rules covering the sale of air travel.
www.bis.gov.uk	Provides details of the Package Travel Regulations (PTR).
www.acre.org.uk	ACRE stands for 'Action with Communities in Rural England'. Produces a range of guides for village halls, including information sheets on VAT and village halls.

VAT in other EC states

The following websites contain information about the VAT rules in other EC states. Some of these contain information in English.

EC state & websites

Austria
www.bmf.gv.at

Belgium
minfin.fgov.be

Bulgaria
www.nap.bg, www.minfin.bg

Cyprus
www.mof.gov.cy/ce

Czech Republic
www.mfcr.cz, cds.mfcr.cz

Denmark
www.skat.dk

Estonia
www.emta.ee

Finland
www.vero.fi, www.finlex.fi

France
www.impots.gouv.fr

Germany
www.bundesfinanzministerium.de

Greece
www.gsis.gov.gr

Hungary
www.apeh.hu

Ireland
www.revenue.ie

Italy
www.finanze.it

Latvia
www.vid.gov.lv

Lithuania
www.vmi.lt

Luxembourg
saturn.etat.lu/etva/index.do

Malta
www.vat.gov.mt

Netherlands
www.belastingdienst.nl

Poland
www.mf.gov.pl

EC state & Websites

Portugal
www.dgci.min-financas.pt

Slovenia
www.durs.gov.si

Romania
www.mfinante.ro

Spain
www.aeat.es

Slovakia
www.finance.gov.sk

Sweden
www.skatteverket.se

Checking VAT numbers

EC VIES system: ec.europa.eu/taxation_customs/taxation/vat/traders/
vat_number/index_en.htm

Follow the 'database' link from the above web page. The VIES system only allows you to check the validity of a VAT number – not its association with a particular business.

HMRC   Phone the National Advice Service on 0845 010 9000 (+44 2920 501 261 from outside UK) to verify a UK or EC VAT number and the details of the business it is linked to.

Modulus 97 check   You can check the integrity of a UK VAT number as follows.

List the first seven digits of the VAT number vertically and multiply the first by 8, the second by 7 etc., then add the results.	VAT number 123 4567 82 $1 \times 8 = 8$ $2 \times 7 = 14$
Subtract 97 from the sum as many times as is required to get a negative number.	$3 \times 6 = 18$ $4 \times 5 = 20$
Multiply the negative number by -1.	$5 \times 4 = 20$ $6 \times 3 = 18$ $7 \times 2 = 14$
The resulting number should be the same as the last two digits of the VAT number.	Total 112 $112 - 97 = 15$
See the example on the right.	$15 - 97 = -82$ the number is therefore numerically valid

VAT Notices relevant to charities

Key notices of relevance to charities and other voluntary organisations are:

700	The VAT Guide
700/12	Filling in your VAT return
701/1	Charities
701/2	Welfare
701/5	Clubs and Associations
701/6	Charity-funded equipment for medical, veterinary etc. uses
701/7	VAT reliefs for disabled people
701/10	Zero rating of books etc.
701/28	Lotteries
701/30	Education and vocational training
701/31	Health institutions
701/33	Trade unions, professional bodies and learned societies
701/34	Competitions in sport and physical recreation
701/35	Youth clubs
701/41	Sponsorship
701/45	Sport and physical education
701/47	Culture
701/57	Health professionals
701/58	Charity advertising
701/59	Motor vehicles for disabled people
706	Partial exemption
706/2	Capital Goods Scheme
708	Buildings and construction
709/5	Tour Operators' Margin Scheme
741	Place of supply of services
742	Land and property

742A	Opting to tax land and buildings
742/1	Letting of facilities for sport and physical recreation
CWL4	Fundraising events
998	VAT refund scheme for national museums and galleries

Books and reference texts

Tolley's Value Added Tax: updated twice every year. Aimed at practising accountants and tax professionals, this is a technical reference guide which covers all the main areas, referenced to the legislation and VAT notices. Published by LexisNexis: www.lexisnexis.co.uk

Tottel's Value Added Tax: updated annually. Easier to read general guide, aimed mainly at commercial businesses. Many practical points and suggestions, with detailed discussion of key cases. Published by Tottel Publishing: www.tottelpublishing.com

Tolley's Orange Tax Handbook: up-to-date VAT legislation. Also available on CD-ROM and online. The online version is updated weekly. Published by LexisNexis: www.lexisnexis.co.uk

The Voluntary Sector Legal Handbook by Sandy Adirondack and James Sinclair Taylor. This covers employment law, constitutional issues and many other areas. Use to check the fundraising regulations, the law and regulations relating to lotteries. Published by the Directory of Social Change: www.dsc.org.uk

15 Glossary

Terms highlighted in **bold** are also included in the Glossary.

Term	Meaning	See chapter
Acquisition	**Goods** brought into the **UK** from another **EC** state.	9
Acquisition VAT	VAT due on certain **acquisitions** from other **EC** states. Instead of the supplier charging **output VAT**, the customer must account for acquisition VAT as if the goods had been purchased from a UK supplier. The acquisition VAT must be paid over to **HM Revenue & Customs** like output VAT. Acquisition VAT can be treated like **input VAT** and is potentially **recoverable**.	9
Activity	A set of actions through which resources are mobilised to produce specific outputs. If an activity involves making **business supplies** then the activity is within the scope of VAT and VAT may have to be charged on the supplies.	4
Actual tax point	An actual tax point is created for a **supply** if, before the **basic tax point** a **VAT invoice** is issued or payment is received for the supply. The actual tax point is the earlier of the invoice being issued and payment being received.	12
Agent	An agent is a legal person that is authorised to act on behalf of a **principal**. An agent can be **disclosed** or **undisclosed**.	11
Annual adjustment	Organisations with a mix of **exempt, taxable** or **non-business** activities must usually perform a periodic calculation of input VAT **attributable** to taxable activities and re-perform this calculation on an annual basis in the annual adjustment.	3

Term	Meaning	See chapter
Attributable	Purchases and their associated **VAT** are attributable to a **supply** or activity if they have a direct and immediate link with the supply or activity. Generally the attributable costs of an activity are, for VAT purposes, its **direct costs**, and a portion of the **residual costs** of the organisation.	3
Barter transaction	A **supply** (say, from A to B) where **consideration** is paid in the form of another supply (from B to A). For VAT purposes there are two supplies (A to B and B to A) with the consideration for each being offset.	7
Basic tax point	The basic tax point is: for a **supply of goods**, when the customer takes possession of the goods, and for a **supply of services**, when the service is complete. See Chapter 12 for various exceptions to this.	12
Business (activity)	Certain **activities** are deemed to be business activities (see **Deemed business activities**). Otherwise for an activity to be business there must be a **supply** for **consideration** and the intrinsic nature of the activity must be **economic**.	4
Business tests	Court cases in the 1970s and 1980s established various tests to be used in determining whether or not an activity is a **business activity**. These tests have now largely been superseded in the courts by the **economic activity** tests. The old business tests are:	4

1. Is the activity a serious undertaking, earnestly pursued?

2. Is the activity an occupation or function, which is actively pursued with reasonable or recognisable continuity?

3. Does the activity have a certain measure of substance in terms of the quarterly or annual value of taxable supplies made?

4. Is the activity conducted in a regular manner and on sound and recognised business principles?

5. Is the activity predominantly concerned with the making of taxable supplies for a consideration?

6. Are the taxable supplies that are being made of a kind which, subject to differences of detail, are commonly made by those who seek to profit from them?

Term	Meaning	See chapter
	The fifth test, the test of predominant concern, was generally considered to be the most important test.	
Capital goods scheme	Special VAT scheme applicable to the purchase, construction, alteration or renovation of **capital items** that are put to mixed **taxable** and **exempt** use.	10
Capital item	Land, buildings or civil engineering works valued at £250,000 or more, or an item of computer equipment valued at £50,000 or more.	10
Charity	An organisation registered with one of the UK charity regulators or recognised as charitable by **HMRC**. HMRC may also accept that non-UK organisations are charitable for the purposes of VAT legislation.	6
Consideration	Everything received in return for making a **supply**. Includes **barter transactions**, part exchange, granting of rights and acceptance of constraints or limitations. Consideration must be capable of being expressed in money and there must be a direct link between the supply and the consideration. An indirect link or a possible link is not enough.	
De minimis	If quarterly **input VAT attributable** to **exempt activities** is less than £1,875 and is less than quarterly input VAT attributable to **taxable activities**, then the exempt activity is *de minimis* and all attributable activity is **recoverable**. The quarterly calculations must be repeated with annual figures in the **annual adjustment**.	
Deductible	**Input VAT** is said to be deductible if it can be recovered, or netted off against any **output VAT** due, in the VAT return. Input VAT is only deductible if it is **attributable** to a **taxable activity**, is attributable to an **exempt supply** and *de minimis*, or allowable under some other legislative provision.	3

Term	Meaning	See chapter
Deemed business activity	Certain supplies are deemed to be undertaken in the course or furtherance of a **business activity**:	4
	• the provision by a club, association or organisation, for a subscription or other consideration, of the facilities or advantages available to its members (though there are some concessions for charities)	
	• the admission, for a consideration, of persons to any premises	
	• where a person accepts any office in the course or furtherance of a trade, profession or vocation, services supplied as holder of that office are treated as being made in the course or furtherance of that trade, profession or vocation	
	• anything done in connection with the termination or intended termination of a business is treated as being done in the course or furtherance of that business	
	• the disposal of a business (as a going concern or of its assets and liabilities) is a supply made in the course or furtherance of the business.	
Deemed non-supplies	Certain **activities** never give rise to a **supply** for VAT purposes. They include:	4
	• transactions within a legal entity (for example between two branches in the UK)	
	• certain business gifts and samples	
	• the **transfer of a going concern**, subject to various conditions.	
Deemed supplies	Certain **activities** are deemed to be **supplies** even if there is no **consideration**:	4
	• the permanent transfer or disposal of business assets	
	• the temporary use of **business** assets for non-business purposes	
	• retention of business assets on deregistration	

340

Term	Meaning	See chapter
	• certain **self-supplies**	
	• non-business use of services supplied to a business.	
Despatch	**Goods** sent to a destination in another **EC** state.	9
Direct costs, directly attributable	(Of an activity). The costs that are incurred by the **activity** and for no other purpose.	3
Disclosed agent	An **agent** that routinely discloses the identity of its **principal** to the third party.	11
Economic activity/ economic content	The EC 6th directive defines an economic **activity** as: All activities of producers, traders and persons supplying services including mining and agricultural activities and activities of professions. Included is the exploitation of tangible and intangible property for the purposes of obtaining income on a continuing basis.	4
	Case law suggests that for an activity to be economic there must be some element of commerciality. If the activity includes factors that lack commercial logic this may indicate that the activity is not economic. The whole activity must be considered and the factors suggesting the presence or absence of economic content compared.	
European Community (EC)	The VAT territory of the European Community, comprising (at January 2008): Austria, Belgium, Bulgaria, Cyprus, Czech Republic, Denmark, Estonia, Finland, France, Germany, Greece, Hungary, Ireland, Italy, Latvia, Lithuania, Luxembourg, Malta, Netherlands, Poland, Portugal, Romania, Slovakia, Spain, Sweden and the UK, but excluding various territories within these states.	
Exempt supply	Certain **business activities** do not carry any VAT because they are specifically exempted by VAT legislation. Examples include certain health, welfare, educational, cultural and sporting supplies.	5
Export	**Goods** supplied to an organisation or individual outside the EC. The goods may either be sent by the supplier to a destination outside the EC (direct exports) or collected by the customer (indirect exports).	9

Term	Meaning	See chapter
Goods (supply of)	Goods are tangible moveable objects. A supply of goods is the transfer of both title to and possession of the goods.	4
HM Revenue & Customs (HMRC)	The **UK** Government body responsible for the administration and collection of UK VAT.	14
Import	**Goods** brought into the **UK** from outside the **EC.**	9
Import VAT	VAT due on certain **goods imported** from countries outside the **EC.** Import VAT is normally payable at the point of importation along with any Customs duties that may be due.	9
Input VAT	VAT incurred on purchases that are **attributable** to **business** activities.	3
Lennartz mechanism	Where an asset is purchased, acquired or constructed and the asset will be put to mixed **business** and **non-business** use, the asset may be assigned as a business asset. This allows full recovery of any VAT attributable to the **taxable** and non-business use of the asset. **Output VAT** is due on any non-business use of the asset. This is known as the Lennartz mechanism.	4
Margin scheme supply	Supplies ordinarily made by tour operators or travel agents that are bought in and re-supplied as **principal** or **undisclosed agent** without material alteration or further processing. For example, supplies of accommodation and passenger transport.	10
Non-business activity	An **activity** which is not **business**. Activities funded entirely by grants or donations are typically non-business. The activity of generating income from financial investments (e.g. bank interest) is normally, in the hands of a charity, considered to be non-business.	4
Output VAT	The VAT you charge on sales and which you have to collect from customers. You then pay this over to **HMRC** after deducting **input VAT** you have paid out on purchases.	1

Term	Meaning	See chapter
Outside the scope (of VAT)	Activities which are not covered by the VAT regime. An activity may be outside the scope for various reasons: • it is specifically excluded, for example salaries and other taxes • it is not a **supply** for VAT purposes • it is a supply but the **place of supply** is outside the **UK**. If the supply is another **EC** state then it may be within the scope of that state's VAT regime but it will be outside the scope of the UK's VAT regime. If the place of supply is outside the EC then the supply will be outside the scope of EC VAT altogether • it is a supply but the supply is undertaken for **non-business** purposes.	4
Place of supply	The **place** where a **supply** takes place. The place of supply normally determines which country's VAT rules (if any) apply to the supply. If both the customer and supplier are in the **UK** the place of supply will normally be the UK. If either the customer or supplier is outside the UK then the place of supply may be outside the UK.	9
Principal	You are principal when you **supply** your own **goods** or **services** to a third party.	10
Reduced rate	Certain **taxable supplies** carry VAT at a reduced rate of 5%, such as fuel and power.	6
Relevant charitable purpose	Use by a **charity** in either or both of the following ways: • otherwise than in the course or furtherance of **business** • as a **village hall** or similarly in providing social or recreational facilities for a local community.	8
Relevant residential purpose	Use as one or more of the following: a home or other institution providing residential accommodation for children; a home or other institution providing residential accommodation with personal care for persons in need of personal care by reason of old age, disablement, past	8

343

Term	Meaning	See chapter
	or present dependence on alcohol or drugs or past or present mental disorder; a hospice; residential accommodation for students or school pupils; residential accommodation for members of any of the armed forces; a monastery, nunnery or similar establishment; or an institution which is the sole or main residence of at least 90% of its residents.	
	But excludes use as a hospital or similar institution, prison or similar institution or hotel, inn or similar establishment.	
Removal	**Goods** supplied to an organisation or individual in another **EC** state.	9
Residual expenses / costs	Costs that cannot be **directly attributed** to one type of activity: **non-business**, **exempt** or **taxable**. Typically residual expenses include the overheads and central function costs of an organisation.	3
Residual VAT	VAT incurred on **residual expenses**	3
Self-supply	Where an organisation must charge itself output VAT. Self-supplies can arise in a variety of ways, including: • using business assets for non-business or private purposes – see Chapter 4 • constructing a building from your own resources – see Chapter 8 • using motor vehicles for private purposes – see Chapter 12.	
Services (supply of)	Any **supply** which does not constitute a supply of **goods.**	4
Single/multiple supply tests (CPP tests)	The single/multiple supply tests arising from the Card Protection Plan and Levob cases: • Every supply of a service must normally be regarded as distinct and independent. • A supply which comprises a single service from an economic point of view should not be artificially split, so as to distort the functioning of the VAT system.	11

Term	Meaning	See chapter
	• The essential features of the transaction must be ascertained in order to determine whether the taxable person is supplying a typical consumer with several distinct principal services or with a single service.	
	• There is a single supply where one or more elements are to be regarded as constituting the principal service, with the remainder regarded as ancillary services which share the tax treatment of the principal service.	
	• A service is ancillary to a principal service if it does not constitute for customers an aim in itself, but a means of better enjoying the principal service supplied.	
	• Where two or more elements supplied by a taxable person to a typical customer are so closely linked that they form objectively, from an economic point of view, a whole transaction, which it would be artificial to split, all those elements or acts constitute a single supply.	
Standard-rated	VAT must be charged by VAT-registered businesses at 17½% (currently).	1
State-regulated private welfare institution or agency	An establishment that provides welfare services and is registered with, and/or regulated by, one of the following regulatory bodies: Commission for Social Care Inspection, Scottish Commission for the Regulation of Care, Care Standards Inspectorate for Wales, Northern Ireland Health and Personal Social Services Regulation and Improvement Authority, Office for Standards in Education (OFSTED) or any other similar regulatory body. State-regulated private welfare agencies include domiciliary care agencies, independent fostering agencies, voluntary adoption agencies and nursing agencies. Following the ECJ Kingscrest judgment (see Chapter 13: *VAT cases*) HMRC has accepted that supplies of welfare by state-regulated private welfare institutions or agencies are exempt.	5

345

Term	Meaning	See chapter
Supply	Certain **activities** are always deemed to be a supply (see **deemed supplies**) and certain activities are never supplies (see **deemed non-supplies**).	4
	Otherwise there is a supply when something is done in return for **consideration**. This includes the sale or hire of **goods**, the provision of **services**, **barter arrangements** and agreements to refrain from actions.	
	For the supply to be made in return for the consideration, there must be a direct link between the supply and consideration. If the supply would be received whether or not consideration is paid or vice versa, there is no supply.	
Tax point	The tax point of a supply is the **basic tax point** unless there is an earlier **actual tax point**, in which it is the actual tax point, or a **VAT invoice** is issued for the supply within two weeks of the basic tax point, in which case it is the invoice date. This rule is modified for certain types of supply.	12
Taxable supply	All **business supplies** which are not **exempt** are taxable. The UK currently applies three different rates of VAT to taxable activities, the **zero rate** (0%) and **reduced rate** (5%) to certain specified goods and services and the **standard rate** (17½%) to all others.	6
Tour Operators' Margin Scheme (TOMS)	Special scheme that applies to **margin scheme supplies** or packages that include margin scheme supplies.	10
Transfer of a going concern	Where the assets of a **business** are transferred as a going concern and the purchaser intends carrying on the business, then special VAT rules apply to the assets transferred.	11
Undisclosed agent	An **agent** that does not routinely disclose the identity of the **principal** to third parties.	11
United Kingdom (UK)	The VAT territory of the UK. For VAT purposes this includes England, Wales, Scotland, Northern Ireland and the Isle of Man but excludes the Channel Islands and Gibraltar.	9

Term	Meaning	See chapter
VAT fraction	The proportion of the gross amount (net + VAT) that is VAT. For VAT at 17½% the VAT fraction is $\frac{7}{47}$. For example, if the VAT-inclusive price is £100, the VAT included in this price is $\frac{7}{47}$ x £100 = £14.89. The VAT is always rounded down to the penny. For VAT at 5%, the VAT fraction is $\frac{1}{21}$.	1
VAT invoice	An invoice containing specific information such as the VAT registration number of the supplier and the VAT charged.	12
VAT law	VAT is an **EC**-wide tax that is implemented nationally and the subject of numerous EC Directives. Each EC state must implement these Directives into its national legislation. In the **UK** the principal legislation is in the Value Added Tax Act 1994.	12
VAT return	A periodic return which must be made to **HMRC**. Normally VAT returns must be submitted every three months, though returns can also be submitted monthly or annually under certain circumstances.	12
Village hall	A building which is used to provide social and recreational activities for a local community. There must be a high degree of community and voluntary involvement in the running of the building, a desire to promote the use of the facilities by members of the community, a great emphasis on the needs of and benefits to the local community, and any charges should not be set commercially.	8
Within the scope of VAT	An activity is within the scope of VAT if it is covered by **VAT law**.	4
Zero-rated	Certain **business activities** are **taxable**, but carry VAT at zero rate. Examples include the sale of books and leaflets, and the sale of donated goods by a **charity**.	6

Index